STreeT TALK

Da Official Guide to Hip-Hop & Urban Slanguage

WARNING

THIS BOOK CONTAINS SLANGUAGE THAT MIGHT
NOT BE SUITABLE FOR LAMES

STREET TALK

Da Official Guide to Hip-Hop & Urban Slanguage

by
Randy "Mo Betta" Kearse

Published by Barricade Books Inc.
185 Bridge Plaza North
Suite 308-A
Fort Lee, NJ 07024

www.barricadebooks.com

Library of Congress Cataloging-in-Publication Data
A copy of this title's Library of Congress Cataloging-in-Publication Data
is available on request from the Library of Congress.

ISBN 1-56980-320-X

First Printing
Printed in Canada

Publisher's Note: The book you have in your hands is the book that was produced
by the author. We made very few changes, choosing to allow the style, somewhat
rough around the edges, to speak for the subject matter. This was a massive effort
by the author, who decided to use his time while incarcerated to turn his life
around and produce a book that is both an entertaining and valuable resource.

Table of Contents

To my big lil Brother….
Jamal "Goobie" Kerase
I have madd love 4 you
for holdin' me down!

Preface

This book is meant to serve as the main reference guide for the Hip-Hop and Urban slang language.

By collecting and combining all the various elements which influence, contribute to, and at times dictate the pulse of Hip-Hop and Urban "street" culture; *prison, the illegal drug trade, the criminal persona, male and female bravado, creative ways to boast about one's sexual exploits or conquests, and expressions that capture and reflect one's experiences, thoughts, and emotions,* this book more than serves its purpose of interpreting the Hip-Hop and Urban slang vernacular.

STREET TALK is the most authentic Hip-Hop and Urban slang language guide and dictionary found anywhere. In this book you will find the words, metaphors, and terms most commonly spoken amongst those who are a part of the Hip-Hop and Urban community. Excluding those words, metaphors, and terms which blatantly disrespect women, race, sexual preference, ethnicity, or religion.

At the same time, this book is neither watered down nor softened up. The slang found in this book is some of the same slang many of todays biggest rappers like to use in their music. This book doesn't create the slang, it only interprets it.

The contextual examples provided with all entries will assist you further in completely understanding when and how to use Hip-Hop and Urban slang. Knowing the words, metaphors and terms is cool, but knowing when to use them is even cooler.

In no time **STREET TALK** will have you talking Hip-Hop and Urban slang fluently and with ease. Keep this book close and you will never be confused about Hip-Hop and Urban slang again.

Acknowledgements

Putting this book together took a long time, a lot of effort and a lot of patience—not only my part—but on the part of several very special individuals. From the initial idea and concept all the way to the completion of *STREET TALK*, there's no way I could have done this by myself. These people, my peoplez, have shown me continuous love and madd crazy support. When people were "hatin," they said, "shake the haters." When I expressed doubt they said, "make it happen." And on many occasions they reminded me, "if anybody can do the dam thing it's you." To these people, my peoplez, I say **THANK YOU**. Thank you for supporting me and another one of my many, from a long list of good, bad, and crazy ideas... Ma Dukes aka **Beverly "Superwoman" Kearse** (you're the best momz a son could have), my main man fifty grand from the muthaland Heavy aka Bear aka **Anthony Smith** (real people do real things and you definitely the realist), **Tina Laire Miller** (you believed in me when very few people did your friendship and support have brought me a long way now watch me do what I do like I'm doin' it for TV), A.D. aka **Ahmed Dickerson** (after all these years still friends love is love), **Marguerite Spence** (I know I don't deserve a friend like you but you never let that stop you from being my friend), Joc Black aka **Joseph Reddick** author of *Street Team* and *Squeeze Play* two of the grittiest urban "street" novels to hit since Donald Goines (you showed a fella madd love kid and wherever I go I'm tellin' em I'm illstreetz affiliated and they can cop that fire at illstreetz.com), another thorough urban novelist **J.M. Benjamin** aka Mustafa aka Squirm destine to make a powerful impact on the street literary game. Your opening teaser *Charge It To The Game* a short story for Nikki Turner's anthology *STREET CHRONICLES* and your soon to be realeased headbanger *Down In The Dirty* proves your pen-game is guaranteed to put Jersey on the map. (yo son, you opened doors for da kid, ya name still heavy, real recognized and respect real), my comrade and friend Stan aka **Aloysius Wayne**

Stanley Hall from Mt. Vernon by the way of Barbados W.I. (your friendship and genuine generosity is something I will never ever forget you played a very big part in this), my heaven sent friend **Sharon Chisholm** from Savannah GA (heaven sends angels down to earth and we call them friends you are my angel), Doc **aka Geoffrey Richstone, MD** (you are a scholar and a gentleman I am forever humbled by your generosity), Hollywood John aka **John A. Igein** author of *Code 49: House Arrest* (your continuous encouragement, input, and insight to the publishing game helped me take Street Talk to the next level), **Harvey Ziskis** author of *License to Steal* a hot book on the corruption inside the gaming industry; a true story of murder, political corruption and some more ish (you the one who put me on to this publishing company and never tired of my endless questions), **Dan Wright** my former literary agent from Ann Wright Representatives (Dan you believed in this work from its infancy maybe we can do somrthing in the future), **Carole** from APS company (your help was instrumental and greatly appreciated maybe we can do something in the future), and to the dude who brought everything together **Rey Dixon-Stewart** aka Reyflex (you demonstrated madd patience while working with me on this even when I <u>Know</u> I was frustrating to say the least you put you're your work in son) THANK YOU ALL!!

Introduction

The language we use and how we choose to communicate are important qualities to our lives. Being able to communicate clearly and unmistakably often helps to highlight the character of the person speaking or expressing himself. Along with words and verbal expressions, hand gestures, facial expressions, and body language are other forms of communication that help us to understand what is being communicated to us.

This book is about the unique words, metaphors and terms which make up the Hip-Hop and Urban slang language. In Hip-Hop and Urban "street" culture, changes in the slang vernacular happen at blinding speeds. New words and terms are created instantaneously, while other words and terms become obsolete just as quickly. Old words become popular again or change their definitions altogether. Part of understanding Hip-Hop and Urban "street" culture is understanding how amorphous and ever changing the slang language is.

More than twenty plus years ago when Hip-Hop first stepped on the scene, there were only a few slang words and terms making their rounds in the Urban "street" culture. But today, with Hip-Hop and Urban "street" culture being at the forefront of what is driving popular youth culture here in the United States and abroad, there are thousands upon thousands of slang words, metaphors and terms banding together to form this incomparable dialect. For example a common phrase like "know what I mean?" is transformed into **"na'mean?"**

Many times a word, metaphor, or term can have more than one meaning, so to better help you comprehend this unique style of communication I have made this guide as organized and simple to read as possible.

The use of slang has always been frowned down upon by standard English intellectuals and by the "proper English" elite. However, with Hip-Hop and Urban "street" culture's strangle-hold on popular youth culture and the mainstream masses, slang language has risen far beyond being just a passing fancy and has incorporated itself into the standard English vocabulary as well as into mainstream commercialism. The affects have been **bananas**.

And while a great deal of the words, metaphors and terminology originates from the grittier sides of society, these contributions do not define the totality of the slang language. Different slang from different cities and different experiences have the greatest impact on Hip-Hop and Urban slang language more than any other influence. Hip-Hop music is the main vehicle in which Hip-Hop and Urban slang is able to be exposed to the mainstream audience. Rappers expose and create the slang verbiage for a language and culture that feeds on creativity, uniqueness, and originality.

Since slang is the primary focus of this guide and dictionary all words, metaphors, and terms appearing in bold are slang unless otherwise stated. All entries are listed alphabetically. This was simple when dealing with single words, but alphabetizing metaphors or terms can get quite complicated. Most lexicons and language guides usually use the first significant word in a phrase to alphabetize, but to make it easy for you, this book lists metaphors and terms in their broadest and most frequently used form. You will also find cross-references and variations when applicable to an entry. Contextual examples are also provided for most entries. While it is not possible to give etymological references for each entry, this book provides them when possible.

Each entry in this book makes a reference to a specific origin or geographical area from which a word, metaphor, or term originates or was most frequently used before being officially inducted into the Hip-Hop and Urban slang language. On page xv you will find a complete list of the origins and geographical areas that contribute to most of the slang used in the Hip-Hop and Urban "street" culture.

Each entry is followed by its functioning label; n. (noun), adj. (adjective), v. (verb), interj. (interjection), or phrase, followed by its origin, and whether the entry is old school, new school, or both. (example below)

[someone who's] **burnin'** adj. (sexual sl.) old & new school
1. one who is infected with a sexually transmitted disease. See also: [someone who's] **on fire**
ex: "Word is, shortie might be burnin'."

[someone who's] **tore up from the floor up** adj. (e. coast sl.) new school
1. unattractive; out of shape; haggard and unkempt; ugly. See also: [someone who's] **beat up from the feet up**
ex: "She looked good in H.S., now she tore up from the floor up."

As Hip-Hop and Urban "street" culture continues to evolve, there's a sure bet that Hip-Hop and Urban slang language will continue to intertwine itself into mainstream English. When one day everyone young and old will know **fa s heezy** means "for sure", **a ride or die chick** is a female who will be there for her boyfriend even if it means putting herself in harms way, or when you are **pushin' somethin' phat** it means you own or drive a new or expensive automobile.

Origin & Geographical Areas of
Hip-Hop & Urban Slanguage

Criminal slang   (criminal sl.)

Prison slang   (prison sl.)

Drug slang   (drug sl.)

East Coast slang   (e. coast sl.)

West Coast slang   (w. coast sl.)

Southern slang   (southern sl.)

General slang   (general sl.)

Old School / New School

Sexual Slang is the words, metaphors, and terms that are used to express male/female interpersonal interactions within the Hip-Hop and Urban community.

General Slang for the purpose of this book, is the slang that is hard to identify the origins of, but is frequently used throughout the Hip-Hop and Urban community.

Old School slang is the slang used in the early years of Hip-Hop up to and ending in, 1995. *New School* slang is the slang used after 1996 and up to the present.

Note: This book in no way suggests or implies that one geographical area from which slang comes, slang is better than the rest. Each area contributes equally to the totality of the Hip-Hop and Urban slang language.

Hip-Hop & Urban Slanguage
Words, Metaphors, and Terms

From

a to z

a

[a female who has] **a ass of life** adj. (sexual sl.) new school
1. an extremely large butt. (var. [a female whose] **ass** [is] **on blast**)
ex: "You should see her cousin, shortie got a ass of life." "Ya girl definitely got the ass of life."

[someone who's] **a beast** adj. (e. coast sl.) new school
1. the very best at what he/she does; one who excels pass his/her peers [usually used as a praise or boast]. (var. [someone who's] **a beast at** [something]) See also: [someone who's] **like that**
ex: "I'm a beast son." "Watch shortie, she's a beast."

a blind squirrel gonna find a nut once in awhile phrase (southern sl.) new school
1. a sarcastic way to tell someone he/she was lucky.

a body n. (criminal sl.) old & new school
1. a murder charge.
ex: "They said I had something to do with a body."

[a firearm with] **a body** [on it] phrase (criminal sl.) old & new school
1. a firearm that was used in a homicide.
ex: "Why you ain't tell me the fifth had a body?"

a bold face lie adj. (general sl.) old & new school
1. an extremely bad lie. 2. a lie told in the face of truth. (var. [to tell] **a bold face lie**, [someone who's] **a bold face liar**)
ex: "She's tellin' a bold face lie." "I can't believe you, you a bold face liar."

a buck fifty n. (prison sl.) old & new school
1. a long slash across one's face caused by being cut/slashed with a razor blade [injury often requires stitches to close wound]. (var. [to] **give** [someone] **a buck fifty, a telephone wire**) See also: [to] **rip** [someone], [to] **bust** [someone] **down**
ex: "They gave ya man a buck fifty when he went to the Island."

a bullet n. (prison sl.) old & new school
1. a one year prison sentence.
ex: "I'm thinkin' about takin' a bullet."

a bump n. (drug sl.) old & new school
1. a very small piece of crack cocaine.
ex: "A crackhead will wash five cars for just a bump."

a case n. (criminal sl.) old & new school
1. any criminal charge that will require a court appearance and possibly result in jail time.
ex: "Shortie got a case for cashin' bad checks."

[someone who's] **a cold coward** adj. (e. coast sl.) old & new school
1. extremely cowardly.
ex: "That cat was a cold coward in H.S."

[a subject that's] **a dead issue** phrase (general sl.) old & new school
1. no longer open for discussion or debate, final.
ex: "We shouldn't be talkin' cause this is a dead issue." "I already told you that was a dead issue."

[a female who's] **a dime** adj. (general sl.) old & new school
1. extremely good looking. (var. [a female who's] **a dime piece**)
ex: "My new shortie is a dime." "I met a dime piece on the way over here."

[things that come/are] **a dime a dozen** phrase (general sl.) old school
1. things that are plentiful.
ex: "Clowns like that come a dime a dozen."

a dopefiend n. (e. coast sl.) old & new school
1. a covert name for a headlock, strangle-hold, or choke-hold [usually applied in the commission of a mugging]. See also: [to] **yolk** [someone], [to] **fiend** [someone] **out**
ex: "He put dude in a dopefiend and took his sneakers."

[someone who's] **a dopefiend** n. (drug sl.) old & new school
1. someone who is addicted to hard narcotics [usually heroin].
ex: "I know you ain't goin' out with that dopefiend."

a drive-by phrase (w. coast sl.) old & new school
1. the act of shooting from a moving automobile while it rides by its intended targets.
ex: "Drive-bys didn't start in Cali, they started in Chicago during prohibition."

[when there's] **a drought** phrase (drug sl.) old & new school
1. there's a shortage of drugs on the wholesale level which makes drugs harder to get on the retail level.
ex: "After 9/11 there was a drought all over N.Y."

a duck adj. (e. coast sl.) old school
1. one who is not cool or hip. 2. one who is easily suckered, fooled, or manipulated. See also: **lame**
ex: "I haven't seen that duck in years." "You was a duck back in the days."

a fade n. (general sl.) old & new school
1. a haircut that is cut real low around the sides and back and blended in with the hair on top.

a fair one phrase (e. coast sl.) old & new school
1. a fair fight between only two people. (var. **a one-on-one**) See also: [to] **shoot a fair one**
ex: "Make sure I get a fair one." "All I want is a fair one."

a fake ass wanna be adj. (general sl.) old & new school
1. someone who is trying extremely hard to act and talk tough but you know that he/she is not tough [usually used to dismiss or disrespect]. See also: [a] **wanna be**
ex: "You ain't nothin' but a fake ass wanna be."

a fiend shot phrase (prison sl.) new school
1. the intended or unintended exposure of a woman's private parts one can get a discreet view of [whether live, in a picture, or on television]. (var. [a female who's] **givin'** [up] **a fiend shot**)
ex: "Between Foxy and Kim I don't know who gives a better fiend shot."

a four-four n. (criminal sl.) old & new school
1. a forty-four (44) magnum handgun.
ex: "She couldn't even lift the four-four."

a fresh cut n. (general sl.) old & new school
1. a haircut not five days old [usually a term used by males]. 2. a new haircut.
ex: "You know I keep a fresh cut."

a frozen wrist phrase (e. coast sl.) new school
1. a wrist that is draped in a diamond [encrusted] watch, bracelet, or bangle. See also: [to] **freeze** [someone's] **wrist**
ex: "You not ballin' without a frozen wrist."

a gang of [something] adj. (general sl.) new schoool
1. a large quantity of something. (var. **a rack of** [something])
*ex: "We brought back a gang of that sh**."*

[a female with] **a ghetto booty** adj. (general sl.) new school
1. a term used praisingly when describing a female's very large butt. (var. [a female with] **a/the big ol' ghetto booty**)
ex: "Now that's what you call one of those ghetto booties."

[someone who has] **a good look** adj. (e. coast sl.) new school
1. an outstanding or impressive look that exudes an air of confidence and authority. 2. a hip, trendy or fashionable appearance.
ex: "Losing that weight was a good look for you."

[something that's] **a good look** adj. (e. coast sl.) new school
1. an extremely good idea. 2. something that enhances the appearance of something greatly.
ex: "Those twenty-twos on the Benz is a good look."

a gutless gat n. (criminal sl.) new school
1. an empty firearm. (var. **a gat that's gutless**)
ex: "I can't believe ya man walkin' around with a gutless gat."

a hater adj. (general sl.) new school
1. one who refuses to recognize, give praise to, or give respect to someone who has earned it or deserves it. 2. one who negatively critiques people because he/she is jealous or envious. (var. [to] **hate on** [someone]) See also: [to] **player hate**
ex: "Don't be a hater ya whole life." "Haters always say that."

a hit [of something] n. (general sl.) old & new school
1. a small dosage of something [usually an illegal drug].
ex: "All I want is a hit." "Save me a hit of that."

a hog n. (w. coast sl.) old school
1. the one who gives the orders; the boss.

a holster n. (prison sl.) new school

1. the person whose main function is to stash or carry weapons for others.
ex: "He's no threat, he just a holster."

a hookup phrase (general sl.) old & new school
1. an inside line or connection to or on something. 2. a favor. 3. preferential treatment.
ex: "I got us a hookup." "Look here, I need a hookup."
"When we get there, we got a hookup."

a hot minute phrase (general sl.) old & new school
1. a real short period of time; not long. See also: **with the quickness**
ex: "I said this not gonna take nothin' but a hot minute."

[someone who's] a hound adj. (general sl.) old & new school
1. annoying; a pest.
ex: "He startin' to be a hound."

a hundred miles an hour phrase (general sl.) old & new school
1. a term used to emphasize how fast someone was doing something [append term to action being described]. (var. **a thousand miles an hour**)
ex: "She was lyin' a hundred miles a hour." '"She was runnin' her mouth a thousand miles an hour."

ain't that some bullsh**?! phrase (southern sl.) new school
1. a matter of fact way to express one's discontent, dissatisfaction, annoyance, disbelief, frustration, surprise or shock in response to a unpleasant surprise or unfair treatment. (var. [now] **ain't this some bullsh**?!**)
ex: "Aint't that some bullsh**, we was here before them and we still waiting to get in."

a lil light somethin' phrase (general sl.) old & new school
1. of no big deal or importance. 2. not worth getting upset over. 3. a modest way to accept praise.

ex: "Let that go dun, that's a lil light somethin'." "It wasn't that hard, just a lil light somethin'."

a lil somethin' somethin' phrase (sexual sl.) new school
1. a hip way to refer to sex. See also: [to] **break** [someone] **off a lil somethin' somethin'**
ex: "You think a fella can get a lil somethin' somethin' tonight?"

[a female who's] **a live wire** adj. (e. coast sl.) old school
1. extremely hip and cool [often with a flirtatious side].
ex: "Shortie a lil live wire."

a loose doo-doo [handshake] adj. (e. coast sl.) new school
1. a less than enthusiastic handshake; a limp or weak handshake [usually given as a sign of indifference or disrespect]. (var. [to] **hit** [someone] **with the/a loose doo-doo**)
ex: "He still don't get the hint after I gave'em a loose doo-doo."

a low low n. (w. coast sl.) old & new school
1. an automobile that sits and rides extremely low to the ground [often late model cars].

a mouth can say anything phrase (southern sl.) new school
1. a term used to dismiss someone's attempt to convince you that he/she is sincere or being truthful.(var. **a mouth will say anything**) See also: **your mouth ain't no prayer book/bible**

[someone who's] **a nut** adj. (general sl.) old & new school
1. outrageously funny; zany. (var. [someone who's] **a fool/straight stupid**)
ex: "Did you ever meet his aunt, she's a nut."

a pair of wheels beats a dressed pair of heels [any day] phrase (southern sl.) new school
1. a sarcastic or witty way to tell someone that riding in a car no matter the condition is better than having to walk where one has to go.

a pound n. (general sl.) old & new school
1. a handshake or hand-slapping between two people to express respect, friendship, agreement, congratulations, or compliments [usually when meeting, greeting, or departing company]. (var. [to] **give** [someone] **a pound**)
ex: "Can I get a pound?" "He wouldn't even give dukes a pound." "He gave everybody a pound expect dukes."

a pound n. (general sl.) old & new school
1. five dollars.

[a female who's] a quarter piece adj. (southern sl.) new school
1. extremely attractive and has a nice body.
ex: "You wouldn't even know how to handle that quarter piece."

[someone who's] a rider adj. (w. coast sl.) old & new school
1. brave; fearless; loyal; ready and willing to do whatever it takes [even if it puts oneself in harms way].
ex: "I like shortie cause she's a rider." "You know I'm a rider kid."

a run phrase (drug sl.) old & new school
l. the period of time one was able to get away with dealing drugs before he/she was caught [and usually sent to prison].

a shot of life phrase (sexual sl.) old & new school
1. an orgasm. 2. sex.
ex: "When's the last time you had a shot of life?"

a solid n. (general sl.) old & new school
1. a favor. (var. [to] **do** [someone] **a solid**)
ex: "I need a solid from you."

[someone who's] a tick tick boom adj. (e. coast sl.) new school
1. someone who is likely to explode at any given moment.
ex: " You didn't tell her she was messin' with a tick tick boom?"

a trap off phrase (e. coast sl.) new school
1. a situation designed to get one in trouble if one acts or proceeds without caution.
ex: "I'm not goin' in there, that's a trap off." "I knew this was gonna be a trap off."

[a male who's] **a viking** adj. (prison sl.) old & new school
1. a male who has extremely poor hygiene habits as well as keeps a dirty house, apartment, or living quarters.
ex: "Don't let 'em fool you, he's a straight viking."

[a female who's] **a winner** adj. (general sl.) new school
1. extremely good looking [also appears to be smart].
ex: "Looks like you got yaself a winner there youngin'."

abc rappers adj. (general sl.) new school
1. rappers whose raps are very simplistic, lack creativity, or any real rhyming skill.
ex: "Ya man was hot in 97-98, but now he just like the rest of these abc rappers."

[to be] **about** [something] adj. (general sl.) old & new school
1. serious; determined; dedicated. 2. guaranteed to get job done.
(var. [to be] **about** [one's] **business**)
ex: "The only thing I'm about is gettin' this paper." "I'm about this shortie."

[to be] **about** [one's] **money** phrase (general sl.) old & new school
1. serious, focused, and dedicated to whatever means one uses to make money. (var. [to be] **about gettin'** [one's] **money**)
ex: "I'm just about this money, that other stuff is nonsense to me."

[an] **Ac** (pron. ack) n. (general sl.) old & new school
1. an Acura Legend automobile.
ex: "Dawg had the gold Ac in 96."

[to] **act brand new** phrase (e. coast sl.) old & new school

1. to exhibit a new or different attitude toward people after one has become successful, acquired, or accomplished something others have not [usually acting snobbish, obnoxious, or like one is better than others]. (var. [to] **get brand new on** [someone]) See also: [to] **highside**
ex: "You don't hafta act brand new cause you bought a car."

[to] **act funny-style** v. (e. coast sl.) new school
1. to exhibit behavioral mood swings or agitation for no apparent reason making it difficult to be understood. See also: [someone who's] **funny-style**
ex: "They all be actin' funny-style if you ask me."

[to] **act hard** v. (general sl.) old school
1. to act tough. 2. to exhibit "thuggish" behavior. See also: [to] **play/act the role**
ex: "He just tryin' to act hard." "Why you always actin' like you hard?"

[to] **act high post** v. (e. coast sl.) old school
1. to exhibit a new or different attitude toward people after one has become successful, acquired, or accomplished something others have not [usually acting snobbish, obnoxious, or like one is better than others].
ex: "She always comin' in here actin' like she's high post."

act like a rash and break-out phrase (general sl.) old school
1. a witty or sarcastic way to tell someone to leave, get away from you, or leave you alone [usually when one is annoying you].

act like I [said it/did it] **then** phrase (general sl.) new school
1. a term used after one has tired of trying to explain he/she did not say or do what he/she is being accused of saying or doing [signaling one is not afraid of a physical confrontation over the issue].

[to] **act like** [one] **is on his/her period** phrase (general sl.) old
& new school
1. to exhibit rude, obnoxious, moody, or unpleasant behavior. (var.
[to] **act like** [one] **has got his/her period**)
*ex: "I asked'er one question and she all actin' like she on her
period or somethin'."*

[to] **act/talk like** [one] **is on killer/gangsta status** phrase (e. coast
sl.) new school
1. a way to describe one's attempt to act or talk like
he/she is a hardcore "street" character. (var. [to] **walk around like**
[one] **is on killer/gangsta status**)
ex: "Ya man was out there actin' like he was on killer status yo."

act like you know phrase (general sl.) new school
1. a matter of fact way to demand someone give you the respect,
recognition, or praise that you deserve and earned. (var. [better]
act like you know)
ex: "You need to act like you know before you get hurt up in here."

[to] **act shady** adj. (e. coast sl.) old & new school
1. to demonstrate unscrupulous or untrustworthy behavior. (var.
[someone who's] **shady**)
ex: "Them catz started actin' too shady for me."

[to] **act stink** v. (general sl.) old & new school
1. to exhibit rude, obnoxious, moody, or unpleasant behavior. (var.
[to] **act stank** [with someone])
ex: "They be actin' too stink for me."

[to] **act the fool** phrase (general sl.) old & new school
1. to exhibit loud, rowdy, or disruptive behavior. 2. to cause
an unpleasant scene. 3. to act zany, silly, or humorous. See also:
[to] **clown**, [to] **trip**
ex: "You shoulda seen her act the fool in here."

[to] **act up** v. (general sl.) old & new school

1. to exhibit loud, rowdy, or disruptive behavior. 2. to cause an unpleasant scene. (var. [to] **act out**)
ex: "Tell ya friends please don't act up in here."

act up and get smacked up phrase (general sl.) new school
1. a playful or sarcastic way to warn someone not to get loud, rowdy, or disruptive [also used as a threat or challenge to someone who is about to cause an unpleasant scene].

act ya age [and] **not ya shoe size** phrase (general sl.) old school
1. a playful or sarcastic way to reprimand someone for acting silly or immature. 2. a way to say "grow up".

[someone who's] **actin' funny v.** (general sl.) old & new school
1. displaying strange, unfriendly, moody, or suspicious behavior towards a friend or love one [usually in an attempt to hide a secret or attitude].
ex: "I'm not the one who's actin' funny."

[a male who's] **actin' like a** [lil] **bit****** adj. (general sl.) old & new school
1. a male who is whining, pouting, or acting babyish when he cannot get his way or when things don't go his way.
*ex: "He in his room actin' like a bit**."*

[someone who's] **actin' like he/she is hurtin' somethin'** phrase (general sl.) old & new school
1. a way to describe someone who is acting like he/she is tough, dangerous, one to be feared [usually because he/she talks tough and threateningly]. (var. [someone who's] **actin' like he/she is gonna hurt somethin'**)
ex: "Don't come in here like you hurtin' somethin'."

[the] **actual factual** phrase (e. coast sl.) new school
1. the truth; the facts; the untold version of a story. See also: **the real**

ex: "Just hit me with the actual factual."

[to] add yeast [to a story] v. (e. coast sl.) new school
1. to embellish a story in an attempt to make it sound or appear worse than it really is. 2. to exaggerate.
ex: "She added a lil yeast to make it seem like it wasn't her fault."

aggie adj. (general sl.) old & new school
1. aggravated; annoyed; upset. (var. **a.g.**)
ex: "I been aggie like that all weekend."

agua [agua] phrase (criminal sl.) old & new school
1. a verbal warning shouted to alert people that the police are coming or that there is police activity in the area. See also: **mahondo, man down, five-o**

[when things are] aiight phrase (e. coast sl.) new school
1. things are "all right", "cool", "o.k.", "agreeable" "satisfactory", or "mediocre" [sometimes used mockingly].
ex: "It's aiight with me, if it's aiight with you." "Are you aiight with this?" "Things turned out aiight."

ain't a whole lot to that phrase (e. coast sl.) new school
1. a playful, sarcastic, or boastful way to respond to someone's compliment or praise. 2. a matter of fact way to express that one stands by his/her claim or confidence.
ex: "Ain't a whole lot to that dawg, she comin' home with me."

[you] ain't but ninety pounds soakin' wet [with bricks in both ya pockets] phrase (general sl.) old & new school
1. a playful or sarcastic way to dismiss someone's challenge or mock their threat. See also: [you] **too light to fight** [and] **too thin to win**

[you] ain't done nothin' wrong phrase (e. coast sl.) new school

1. a way to reassure someone who's unsure of whether he/she took the right course of action. 2. a way to say, "you did the right thing".
ex: "She ain't done nothin' wrong."

ain't even the word phrase (e. coast sl.) new school
1. a term used to agree with someone's assertion, description, or view of someone or something [append term to description being used].
ex: "Stupid ain't even the word." "Homeboy, desperate ain't even the word to describe her."

[it/this] **ain't gone be nothin' nice** phrase (e. coast sl.) new school
1. a term used to emphasize one's warning of an unpleasant outcome.
ex: "Next time we see each other it ain't gone be nothin' nice." "Stand back, this ain't gone be nothin' nice."

[you] **ain't gone bust a grape** phrase (general sl.) old & new school
1. a way to dismiss someone as being not as tough as he/she thinks or wants people to believe he/she is. 2. a playful or sarcastic response to someone's threats or claims of bravado. (var. [you] **ain't/wouldn't bust a grape with combat boots on**, [you] **ain't gone kill nothin'** [let nothin' die], [you] **ain't gone do nothin' but run ya mouth**)

[you] **ain't got a pot to piss in** phrase (general sl.) old & new school
1. a strong condemnation of someone who possesses nothing of value [usually used when a person becomes unappreciative or tries to project an image of one who is financially secure]. (var. [you] **ain't got a pot to piss in** [or] **a window to throw it out** [or a cup to catch it in])

[you] **ain't got it in you** phrase (e. coast sl.) new school

1. a term used to call someone's courage or toughness into question [usually used challengingly, as a dare, or to prod]. (var. [you] **ain't cut/built like that**)
ex: "I know you ain't got it in you."

[I] **ain't got nothin' but love for you** phrase (e. coast sl.) old school
1. a way to tease or mock someone you have told no to and that person is expressing his/her anger or disappointment.
ex: "Say what you want, I ain't got nothin' but love for you."

[you] **ain't got nothin' comin'** phrase (general sl.) old school
1. a sarcastic way to dismiss someone's request for something [usually after that person has angered or offended you].
ex: "You of all people know you ain't got nothin' comin'."

[you] **ain't hafta go there** phrase (general sl.) new school
1. a term used to respond to someone who said something that was purposely meant to hurt your feelings [usually used in an attempt to make that person feel guilty].
ex: "I thought me and you was cool, you ain't hafta go there."

[you] **ain't hear me though** (pron. doe) phrase (southern sl.) new school
1. an enthusiastic way to affirm or reaffirm one's claim or boast [usually used mockingly when one has proven his/her claim is true or correct].

[you] **ain't hurtin' nothin'** phrase (general sl.) old & new school
1. a way to tell someone that he/she is not as tough as he/she thinks or want others to believe he/she is. 2. a playful or sarcastic response to someone's tough talk or empty threats. (var. [you] **ain't hurtin' nothin' but my ears**, [you] **ain't movin' no mountains**, [you] **ain't gonna hurt nothin'**)
ex: "You know I know, you ain't hurtin' nothin'."

ain't no biggie phrase (general sl.) old school
1. a matter of fact way to say something is "no big deal", "of no
real importance", or "nothing to get upset about/over" [also used to
mask one's anger]. (var. **ain't no big thing, ain't nothin'**)
ex: "Ain't no biggie, I can always get another one."

ain't no bolts in my neck phrase (general sl.) old & new school
1. a witty way to tell someone "I'm not stupid/dumb" when you
realize he/she is trying to con, manipulate, or convince you of
something ridiculous. (var. **my head don't screw off/come off
and on**)
ex: "You hafta try harder than that, ain't no bolts in my neck."

ain't no doubt! phrase (e. coast sl.) new school
1. an enthusiastic way to affirm or reaffirm one's thought, position,
or claim leaving no room for doubt or question.
ex: "Ain't no doubt, you know I'mma be there."

ain't no fear in my heart phrase (general sl.) old school
1. a term used to profess one's fearlessness or bravery [usually
when called into question or when answering a dare].
ex: "I'll go in there boy, ain't no fear in my heart."

ain't no fun if I don't get none/some phrase (general sl.)
old school
1. a playful or sarcastic way to tell someone you want to be,
deserve to be, have to be a part of the plan even if you have to
force your way in.

ain't no fun when the rabbit got/gots the gun phrase (southern
sl.) new school
1. a witty way to tease, taunt, or mock someone when you have
gained an advantage over him/her [usually after that person
previously held an advantage over you].

ain't no future in frontin' phrase (general sl.) old & new school

1. a way to tell someone to stop lying, stop pretending or stop acting like he/she is better than everyone else. See also: **stop frontin'!**
ex: "Just tell'er the truth, ain't no future in frontin'."

ain't no mystery to my history phrase (e. coast sl.) old school
1. a boisterous way to claim to be the best at something.
2. a way to respond to someone who is questioning your character, reputation, or abilities.
ex: "I been doin' this since H.S. ain't no mystery to my history."

ain't no shame to/in my game phrase (e. coast sl.) old & new school
1. a matter of fact way to admit having no pride, shame, or principals when someone accuses one of being unscrupulous, petty, or having no morals.

ain't no sharks in the water phrase (prison sl.) new school
1. something you tell someone who needs to or doesn't like to bathe. (var. **waters free**)

ain't no thang [but a chicken wing] phrase (general sl.) old school
1. a way to dismiss something as being unimportant or not a problem. 2. a humorous way to down play how you feel when someone may have offended you. (var. **ain't no thang**)

[you] **ain't nobody** phrase (general sl.) old & new school
1. a term used to dismiss one's importance and/or one's use of tough talk and threats.
ex: "Who you think you talkin' to, you ain't nobody."

ain't nothin' phrase (southern sl.) new school
1. a nonchalant way to respond to someone's inquiry about your welfare; "I'm all right" "I'm fine" "things are okay".
ex: "Ain't nothin', what's up with you?"

ain't nothin' between us but air (inhale) **now half of that is gone** phrase (southern sl.) new school
1. a playful or sarcastic way to respond to someone who is hurling verbal threats of confronting you physically. 2. a way to let someone know you are not afraid to fight him/her.

ain't nothin' goin' on but the rent phrase (general sl.) old school
1. a term females use to make it clear to males that, there can be no intimacy between them if the male doesn't have money/isn't making a certain amount of money, or isn't willing to take care of her financially.

ain't nothin' in the world like a big butt girl phrase (general sl.) old school
1. a term of admiration men use to give praise to females with big butts.

[someone who] **ain't right** adj. (criminal sl.) new school
1. one who is or suspected of being an police informant or a prosecution witness. (var. [someone who's] **not right**)
ex: "You know ya man ain't right, right?"

[you] **ain't runnin' nothin' but ya mouth** phrase (c. coast sl.) new school
1. a stern way to respond to someone's claim that he/she is "runnin' things" or the one who is in control.

[you] **aint sayin'/said nothin'** [but a thing] phrase (general sl.) old & new school
1. a sarcastic way to respond to another's challenge or dare [usually used to convey one's bravery or confidence in one's self]. (var. [you] **aint sayin'/said nothin'** [my brotha])
ex: "You ain't sayin' nothin' we can play right now."

[someone who] **ain't sh**** phrase (general sl.) old & new school
1. someone who exhibits an extreme sense of selfishness and pettiness. 2. untrustworthy; unscrupulous.

ex: " I knew he wasn't sh** when you first introduced me to' em."

ain't that a bit**! phrase (general sl.) old & new school
1. a response to something shocking, surprising, or unbelievable.
See also: **what part of the game is this?**
ex: "Ain't that a bit**, I thought I could trust you."

ain't that the truth phrase (general sl.) new school
1. a way to express being in agreement or being able to relate to another's assessment or feeling. See also: **you know that's right**
ex: "Ain't that the truth, I been ready to leave."

[I] ain't tryin' to hear that [punk/sucker] **sh**** phrase (e. coast sl.) old & new school
1. a sarcastic way to dismiss someone's feeble attempt to explain or off an excuse.
ex: "I think you should leave cause I ain't tryin' to hear that punk sh** you talkin'."

[someone who] ain't with [something] phrase (general sl.) old & new school
1. one who doesn't partake in a specific behavior.
ex: "I already told you I ain't with that." "I'm tellin' you right now, I ain't with this."

[to] air [someone] **out** v. (criminal sl.) new school
1. to shoot someone [usually more than once and/or fatally].
(var. [someone who's been] **aired out**)
ex: "Tell ya man to chill, before them catz air his ass out."

[to] air the block out phrase (criminal sl.) new school
1. to shoot indiscriminately into a crowd of people causing them to frantically run for cover. See also: [to] **lick shots**, [to] **bust** [one's] **gun**

[to be] **all about** [oneself] adj. (general sl.) old & new school
1. selfish; self centered; only concerned about one's own interests.
ex: "Don't count him, he's all about him." "You have to be all about you sometimes."

[to be] **all about** [something] phrase (general sl.) old & new school
1. serious about; dedicated to; focused on.
ex: "I don't know about you, but I'm all about gettin' this paper."

[to receive] **all day** [in prison] phrase (prison sl.) new school
1. a life sentence without the possibility of parole. (var. [to receive] **all of it**)
ex: "They lookin' at all day if they blow trial." "He's facin' all of it this time."

all day every-day phrase (general sl.) old & new school
1. constantly; consistently; all the time. See also: **24/7**
ex: "I'm here all day every-day."

all downs a bet phrase (general sl.) old & new school
1. a term used to notify bettors in an illegal dice game that the only bets that will be honored are the ones that are placed in front of the bettor [usually on the floor or table].

[when things are] **all gravy** phrase (southern sl.) new school
1. things are "all right", "cool", "agreeable", "fine", or "satisfactory [sometimes used un-sincerely]. (var. [when things are] **all good, all to the good**)
ex: "It's all gravy partna, just call me back later."

[when] **all hell breaks loose** phrase (general sl.) old & new school
1. when there's a sudden burst of chaos, mayhem, or uncontrollable disruption.
ex: "Next thing I know, all hell breaks loose." "All hell about to break loose in here."

all I find all I keep? phrase (general sl.) old school
1. a term meant to put someone on the spot with a request to search his/her possessions or person to confirm he/she is telling the truth about not having what he/she denies having.

all I wanna see is assholes and elbows phrase (criminal sl.) new school
1. a term arm robbers use to get their intended victims to lay on the ground while announcing the robbery.

[to be] **all in** [someone's] **business** phrase (general sl.) old & new school
1. to interfere with the affairs of someone [usually when that person doesn't want one to]. 2. the act of being nosy. (var. [to be] **all in** [someone's] **mix**)
ex: "Every time I turn around, you all in my business."

[to be] **all in** [someone's] **mouth** phrase (general sl.) old & new school
1. to rudely stare at someone while that person is talking to someone else. 2. the act of trying to eavesdrop. (var. [to be] **all in** [someone's] **mouth** /piece / face / throat)
ex: "Daaaam, why you all in my mouth?"

[to be] **all in** [someone's] **sh**** v. (general sl.) old & new school
1. the act of rummaging through someone else's property.
ex: "I walk through the door, and shortie all in my sh**."

[to be] **all in the Kool Aid and don't know the flavor** phrase (general sl.) old school
1. to interrupt or attempt to add to a conversation only to learn one does not know what the conversation is about or misunderstood what was being discussed.
ex: "Shut up, you all in the koolaid and don't even know what the flavor is."

all jokes aside phrase (general sl.) old & new school

1. something you say to get someone to take what you are saying serious. (var. **on the up & up**) See also: **on the real, word up, word is bond**
ex: "I was with her last night all jokes aside kid."

[something that's] **all love** phrase (general sl.) new school
1. "fine", "agreeable", satisfactory", "all right".
ex: "Its all love dawg, we can try again tomorrow." "Its all love in here."

[something that's] **all of it** adj. (e. coast sl.) new school
1. outstanding; unique; the best of its kind.
ex: "The new 745 is all of it."

[someone who's] **all of it** adj. (e. coast sl.) new school
1. extremely good looking. 2. the best at what he/she does; one who performs outstandingly.
ex: "Shortie all of it, for real."

[something that's] **all that** adj. (e. coast sl.) old & new school
1. outstanding; unique; the best of its kind. (var. [something that's] **all that and then some, all that and a bag of chips** [with some dip])
ex: "The X-men was all that."

[someone who's] **all that** adj. (e. coast sl.) old & new school
1. extremely good looking. 2. the best at what he/she does; one whose performance excels his/her peers. (var. [someone who's] **all that and some**)
ex: "My new shortie is all that son."

[to be] **all up in** [someone's] **face** phrase (general sl.) old & new school
1. to be extremely close to someone while talking [usually while being flirtatious or confrontational]. (var. [to be] **all in** [someone's] **face**)
ex: "I come back, and she all up in my manz face."

all you is, is mouth phrase (general sl.) old & new school
1. a term used to dismiss someone's tough talk and empty threats.
ex: "You been sayin' that for years, all you is, is mouth dawg."

alotta adj. (general sl.) old & new school
1. a lot of; a large amount. See also: **madd**
ex: "Alotta y'all shouldn't even be here."

[to] **amp on** [someone] v. (e. coast sl.) new school
1. to yell, scream, or shout at someone; to express one's anger or
dissatisfaction loudly. See also: [to] **scream on** [someone]
ex: "Ma Dukes amped on me when I came in late."

[to] **amp** [someone] **up** v. (e. coast sl.) new school
1. to give someone a false sense of courage or confidence [making
that person believe he/she can do the impossible]. 2. to incite or
hype someone up.
ex: "They amped ya manz up to steal a car."

[to] **amp** [something] **up** v. (e. coast sl.) new school
1. to embellish a story to make it sound worse that it really is/was
[in hopes that it will inflame the passions or emotions of others]. 2.
to lie; to exaggerate.
ex: "That's not what happened, he just amped up the whole story."

amped adj. (e. coast sl.) new school
1. excited; hyped up; pumped up. (var. **amped up**)
*ex: "That old Wu-Tang sh** will have you amped."*

...and all that good sh** phrase (general sl.) new school
1. a term used to put finality to one's statement, claim, boast, or
threat in a way that says "I mean/meant that" or "I have nothing
else to say/talk about".
*ex: "I hope this letter finds you well and all that good sh**." "I
tore shortie back out and all that good sh**."*

...and the whole nine phrase (general sl.) old & new school
1. a term used to sum up, emphasize, or put finality to one's statement, claim, boast, or threat in a way that says "I mean/meant that".
ex: "I left'em alone and the whole nine."

and you know that's right phrase (southern sl.) new school
1. an enthusiastic way to agree with someone. 2. a way to say "I can relate to/agree with [you on] that".
ex: "And you know that's right, no money no honey."

an'nim phrase (general sl.) old & new school
1. a way to say "and them."
ex: " Have you seen Moe an'nim?"

ante up phrase (criminal sl.) new school
1. a command given during the commission of a robbery to get one to hand over his/her valuables. See also: **get naked**
ex: "Ante up fool, I ain't got all day."

anybody workin'? phrase (drug sl.) old & new school
1. a term used to inquire if someone is selling drugs in a high traffic drug area. (var. **anybody holdin'?, anything goin' on?/happenin'?**)

anything beats a blank phrase (general sl.) old & new school
1. a term used to say "something is better than nothing" [usually used to express appreciation or gratitude]. (var. **beggars can't be choosy**)
ex: "Look here, anything beats a blank right about now."

anyway! interj. (general sl.) new school
1. a rude, sarcastic, or obnoxious way to dismiss someone's offhanded or crude remark [often cutting the person off while he/she is talking]. 2. a term used to express disinterest in hearing what someone wants to or is saying.

ex: "Anyway!, ain't nobody come to see you play."

ardeen (pron. r dean) adj. (e. coast sl.) old & new school
1. an extremely long period of time.
ex: "I haven't spoken to or seen my cousin Ka-born in ardeen."

armor n. (criminal sl.) new school
1. a bulletproof vest.
ex: "You can't get up in here with that armor on."

around the way phrase (general sl.) old & new school
1. one's neighborhood or community. (var. **around** [one's] **way**)
ex: "Last time you been around the way?" "She's from around the way."

[an] **around the way girl** phrase (general sl.) old & new school
1. a female with a hip "down to earth" personality and attitude from one's neighborhood [who also follows the latest hip-hip and urban "street" fashions, styles, and trends].

[to] **argue** [someone] **down** v. (general sl) old & new school
1. to have a drawn out debate/argument with someone in an attempt to get one's point across, to avoid admitting being wrong, or to avoid telling someone he/she is right. (var. [to] **argue** [someone] **to death**)
ex: "He tried to argue me down about how much this cost."

...**as a bit****! Interj. (general sl.) old & new school
1. a term used as an exclamation point to emphasize a description, assessment or observation. (var...**as a mug/muhf**ka**)
ex: "It's cold as a bit** out there."

ash n. (drug sl.) new school
1. hashish.

ashy feets n. (southern sl.) new school
1. females that males only want to be with or be seen at night with when they're on the way to a sexual encounter. See also: [a] **hoochie momma**, [a] **hood rat**
ex: "We on our way to the mo-mo with a couple of ashy feets we met at the club."

ask about me phrase (general sl.) old & new school
1. a boisterous way to make a claim to having a undenible and fearsome reputation. (var. **you better ask about me**)

ask me do I give a dam! phrase (general sl.) old & new school
1. a matter of fact way to express "not caring" or "caring-less" about a piece of information that has just been divulged to you. (var. **ask me do I give a f**k/sh****)

[someone who's] **ass** adj. (e. coast sl.) old & new school
1. cowardly. 2. not tough. See also: [someone who's] **butt**
ex: "Say what you want, ya manz ass."

ass n. (sexual sl.) old & new school
1. a way to refer to sex.
ex: "You only call when you want some ass."

[to] **ass bet** [someone] v. (e. coast sl.) old & new school
1. to bet or wager without having the money to cover the bet or wager if one loses [usually the person one is betting thinks one can cover].

ass, cash, or grass nobody rides for free phrase (general sl.) old school
1. a witty way to inform someone that he/she must pay in order to ride in one's automobile. (var. **ass, gas, or grass nobody rides for free**)

ass out n. (e. coast sl.) old & new school
1. in real bad trouble. (var. [someone who's] **assed out**)

ex: "He gonna be ass out when she finds out."

ass out adj. (e. coast sl.) old & new school
1. without money; destitute. (var. [someone who's] **assed out**)
ex: "Dawg I been ass out all week."

ass out phrase (e. coast sl.) new school
1. too late to take advantage of an opportunity or situation.
ex: "If they not here by 10:00, they ass out cause I'm leavin'."

[to] **assassinate** [someone's] **character** v. (e. coast sl.) new school
1. the act of spreading lies, rumors, or innuendo in an
attempt to destroy or discredit one's reputation or chances for
success. See also: [to] **put a bone out on** [someone]
*ex: "Your right hand man is the one tryin' to assassinate your
character."*

[an] **asshole full** adj. (criminal sl.) old & new school
1. an extremely long prison sentence.
ex: "Them dudes lookin' at an asshole full down in Virginia."

[an] **asshole full of** [something] adj. (general sl.) old & new school
1. a large amount or quantity. (var. [a] **rack/gang of** [something])
*ex: "We brought a asshole full of that sh** back with us."*

[to be] **audi** v. (e. coast sl.) old school
1. to leave; depart. 2. a term used as a verbal notification of one's
intention to leave. (var. [to be] **audi 5000**) See also: [to] **jet**
*ex: "As soon as I saw her pops, I was audi." "I'm about to be audi
5000 in ten minutes."*

ayo! (pron. a-yo) interj. (e. coast sl.) old & new school
1. an enthusiastic way to get someone's attention. 2. a term used to
express shock, displeasure, discontent, or a serious and stern tone.
*ex: "Ayo, I already told you before hand." "Ayo!, where y'all
headed son?"*

b

B n. (e. coast sl.) old & new school
1. a term of endearment among friends; friend. 2. a way to address someone whose name you do not know or do not want to use in front of others. (var. **G**) See also: **dawg**
ex: "What up B?" "Ayo B, let me holler at you for a minute."

[a] **B-boy** n. (e. coast sl.) old school
1. a young male who is a part of the Hip-Hop culture.
ex: "B-boys were the first Hip-Hop kids."

[a] **B-Boy stance/stand** adj. (e. coast sl.) old school
1. a tough or defiant pose [favored among individuals in the Hip-Hop community].

babooski (pron. bah boo ski) n. (southern sl.) new school
1. an affectionate pet-name a male uses for his girlfriend.
ex: "Shortie you know you my babooski."

baby baaaay-bay! interj. (e. coast sl.) new school
1. an enthusiastic yell, shout, or expression of jubilation in celebration of or congratulations for.
ex: "This party about to get crackin' baby baaay-bay."

baby boy n. (southern sl.) new school
1. a term of endearment among friends; friend. 2. a way to address someone whose name you do not know or do not want to use in front of others. (var. **baby pa/bubba**)
ex: "Look here baby boy, I don't see that happenin'."

[a female's] **baby daddy** n. (southern sl.) new school
1. the father of her child/children. 2. a term some females use to trivialize the relationship they have with the father of their child/children.
ex: "You need to call ya baby daddy." "He ain't nothin' but my baby daddy."

baby daddy privileges phrase (e. coast sl.) new school
1. the privilege a male has of being able to have sex with the mother of his child/children even if they are not in a relationship or she is in an intimate relationship with another male.
ex: "Let me know now if he still has baby daddy privileges."

baby doll n. (general sl.) old school
1. an affectionate term males use to address females. (var. **baby/baby girl**)
ex: "You lookin' real good baby doll."

baby momma drama phrase (southern sl.) new school
1. the problems and unpleasant situations that females cause for the father of their child when the relationship between them turns sour [usually causing additional problems for the female the father is now involved with].
ex: "I think you a nice guy and everything, but I can't take all this baby momma drama."

baby needs a new pair of shoes phrase (general sl.) old school
1. a witty way to express a wish for luck as one tosses the dice in any game that requires dice tossing. (var. **baby needs a new car/new coat/her rent paid**)

[a] **baby nine** n. (criminal sl.) old & new school
1. a small nine millimeter handgun. (var. [a] **baby 380**)
ex: "You can easily stash the baby nine right here."

[to] **baby-sit** [something] v. (general sl.) old & new school

1. to take longer than one should before passing something to another [usually something edible, drinkable or smokeable].
ex: " How long you plan to baby-sit that homie?"

babylon n. (criminal sl.) old school
1. law enforcement agents or agencies; the police; correctional officers. 2. anyplace where one feels himself oppressed [jail, home, society].
ex: "Here comes babylon."

[a female who has] **back** adj. (southern sl.) new school
1. a big butt; a butt that is worthy of praise and admiration. (var. [a female who has] **more buns than the army got/has guns**) See also: [a female who's] **thick**
ex: "Shortie momz got madd back kid."

[to] **back** [someone] **down** v. (criminal sl.) old & new school
1. to brandish a weapon threateningly in self defense or to intimidate during a confrontation [usually making others cower]. See also: [to] **click on** [someone]
ex: "I had to back down her ex-boyfriend and some of his boys."

[to be] **back in affect** phrase (general sl.) old school
1. the state of making a return.
ex: "In a couple of months I'mma be back in affect."

back in the days/day phrase (general sl.) old & new school
1. in the past; a long time ago; years ago.
ex: "Back in the days you was the man homie."

[to] **back stab** [someone] v. (general sl.) old & new school
1. to betray a friend or family member for one's own personal gain [usually because one is jealous or envious]. (var. [someone who's a] **back stabber**, [to] **stab** [someone] **in the back**)
ex: "Ya manz be the first one to back stab you when you go to jail."

back that thang up phrase (southern sl.) new school
1. a term males use to express admiration and praise for a female's butt or body.
ex: "While you at it, let me see you back that thang up." "Can you back that thang up for a minute?"

back up off me and smell the coffee phrase (general sl.) old school
1. a playful or sarcastic way to tell someone to move back or away from you [usually after one has said or done something ridiculous or offensive]. 2. a term used to dismiss someone. (var. **back up off me**)
ex: "Come on man, back up off me and smell the coffee."

[someone who's] **background coachin'** v. (e. coast sl.) new school
1. instigating; voicing one's opinion when it's not wanted; giving unwanted advice. See also: [someone who's] **coachin' from the sidelines**
*ex: "Here comes ya momz with that background coachin' sh** again."*

[a female's] **backyard** n. (w. coast sl.) old school
1. a female's butt.
ex: "Would you look at the backyard on shortie."

[someone who's] **bad business** adj. (general sl.) old & new school
1. one who's actions, character, and behavior brew trouble. 2. one who is unreliable.
ex: "If I was you I'd be careful, that cat's bad business."

[something that's] **bad business** adj. (general sl.) old & new school
1. any act that is mean, spiteful, wrong, or garners a negative reaction.
ex: "You hafta cut that out, that's bad business."

[something that's] **badd** adj. (general s1.) old & new school
1. outstanding; unique; the best of its kind. See also: [something that's] **dope**
ex: "That's a badd jacket you got."

[a female who's] **badd** adj. (general sl.) old & new school
1. extremely good looking [usually with a nice body].
(var. [a female who's] **badd as I don't know what**)
ex: "You have to admit, his new shortie is badd."

[someone who's] **badd** adj. (general sl.) old & new school
1. tough. 2. bold and daring.
ex: "Ya man thinks he's badd." "You ain't that badd."

badd mamma jamma phrase (general sl.) old & new school
1. a covert way to say "bad mother f**ker" when describing or referring to.
ex: "Can you fix this badd mamma jamma?" "I like this badd mamma jamma."

[a female's] **badunkadunk** (pron. ba dunka dunk) adj. (sexual s1.) new school
1. an extremely large butt; a butt worthy of praise and admiration.
(var. [a female who has a] **badunka**)
ex: "The shortie I met earlier got the badunkadunk."

[to] **bag** [a female] v. (general sl.) old & new school
1. the act of acquiring a female's personal information such as an address, telephone number, e-mail address, or pager number [usually on the pretense of getting to know her better].
ex: "I'm tryin' to bag shortie over there."

[to] **bag** [someone] v. (criminal sl.) old & new school
1. to rob someone; to take one's possessions using violence or the threat of violence. See also: [to] **house** [someone]
ex: "Some kids tried to bag me comin' out the club."

[to] **bag up** v. (drug sl.) old & new school
1. to package drugs in small amounts for sale on the street or retail market.
ex: "I need your help to bag this up."

[to get] **bagged** v. (criminal sl.) old & new school
1. arrested; caught. See also: [to get] **knocked**
ex: "They got bagged by the Feds." "She got us bagged."

bail n. (e. coast sl.) old & new school
1. help or assistance [usually to get out of trouble or out of a tense situation]. (var. [to] **give** [someone] **bail**, [to] **bail** [someone] **out**)
ex: "Ya man needs some bail again."

[to] **bail** v. (w. coast sl.) old & new school
1. to run away from to avoid capture [usually from the police]. 2. to leave in a hurry.
ex: "Everybody just bailed at the same time."

[a] **ball** n. (general sl.) old school
1. one hundred dollars; numerations of a hundred.
ex: "You already owe about two balls."

[to] **ball** v. (w. coast sl.) new school
1. to make and spend large amounts of money freely and carelessly.
ex: "Catz was ballin' out of control all star weekend."

[to] **ball out** v. (general sl.) new school
1. the act of freely spending large amounts of money.
ex: "We goin' down to the ATL and ball out for the weekend."

ball 'til you fall phrase (southern sl.) new school
1. a term used to encourage someone to make and spend large amounts of money [also used as a declaration]. (var. **I'mma ball 'til I fall**)

[to] **ball** [a female] **up** v. (sexual sl.) new school
1. a male term for having sex. (var. [to] **have** [a female] **balled up**)
ex: "I used to have shortie balled up like this."

Ballamore n. (e. coast sl.) new school
Baltimore MD.

[a] **ballaholic** adj. (southern sl.) new school
1. one who makes and spends large amounts of money freely and
frequently [usually to show off or impress others].
ex: "That whole click is ballaholics."

[a] **baller** (pron. balla) adj. (w. coast sl.) new school
1. one who makes and spends large amounts of money freely and
carelessly [money usually earned through illegal or shady means].
ex: "Oh, now you think you a baller?" "He showed up with a
bunch of his lil baller friends."

[to] **baller block** phrase (w. coast sl.) new school
1. the act of purposely trying to get in the way of someone who is
trying to achieve a specific goal [trying to make money, meet a
female, or trying to excel] because one is jealous and envious. See
also: [to] **player hate** [someone]
ex: "I couldn't do nothin' last night, them catz was out there baller
blockin' again."

[a] **baller** [who's] **on a budget** phrase (general sl.) new school
1. a humorous way to describe a male who is trying to project an
image of being able to spend large amounts of money but who has
a limited access to money.
ex: "That fool was a baller on a budget."

balloons n. (prison sl.) old & new school
1. drug laden rubber balloons used to smuggle drugs into prison by
visitors on visitation day [the receiving prisoner either swallows or
stuffs the balloon into his/her rectum as a way to smuggle them

from the visiting room into the prison]. (var. **loonies**) See also:
papers

[someone who's a] **bamma** adj. (e. coast sl.) old & new school
1. not cool or hip; nerdy. 2. one who dresses ridiculously or
without coordination. (var. [someone who's] **bammafied/country/
countrified/** [a] **bamma ass** [person]/ [a] **country bamma**)
ex: "They got bammas right in Brooklyn kid."

[something that's] **bananas** adj. (e. coast sl.) new school
1. outstanding; unique; the best of its kind. 2. extremely funny. See
also: [something that's] **sick**
ex: "Meth's flow is bananas son."

[to] **bang** v. (w. coast sl.) old & new school
1. to be a member of a gang that is actively involved in gang
related activities [usually having violent feuds and confrontations
with rival gangs]. (var. [to] **gang bang**, [someone who's a]
banger/gang banger)
ex: "Its crazy to see catz in N.Y. tryin' to bang."

[to] **bang** [a female's] **back out** v. (sexual sl.) new school
1. the act of having sex [term usually used by males as a boast
about his stamina and skills during sex].
ex: "I took shortie home and banged'er back out for two hours."

[to] **bang** [someone] **out** v. (e. coast sl.) new school
1. to beat someone up. (var. [to] **bang** [someone] **up,** [to] **get
banged out/up**)
ex: "I was about to bang this cat out for real."

[to] **bang them thangs/things** v. (criminal sl.) new school
1. a covert way to refer to the shooting of one's gun [usually used
as bravado]. (var. [to] **bang them hammers**)
ex: "I don't bang them thangs no more."

[a] **banger** n. (prison sl.) new school
1. a homemade knife or sharp weapon. See also: [a] **shank**
ex: "The C.O. found two bangers this big."

[a] **banger** n. (criminal sl.) old & new school
1. a handgun.
ex: "The banger misfired."

[something that's] **bangin'** adj. (e. coast sl.) old & new school
1. outstanding; unique; the best of its kind. See also:
[something that's] **off the meat rack**
ex: "Shortie had the bangin' outfit on."

[a female with a] **bangin'** [body/ass] adj. (sexual sl.) old & new
school
1. a body or butt worthy of praise and admiration. (var. [a female
who's body/ass is] **bangin'**)
*ex: "Her body is overrated, I'mma tell you who has a bangin'
body."*

bank n. (general sl.) old school
1. money.
ex: "That's all the bank I had left."

[to] **bank** [someone] v. (w. coast sl.) old school
1. to attack someone [often taking the person by surprise].
ex: "This fool don't even know he about to get banked."

[to] **bank on** [someone/something] v. (general sl.) old & new
school
1. to depend on; to have one's hopes on something or someone.
ex: "You don't know how much I was bankin' on you."

bap n. (southern sl.) old school
1. poor quality marijuana.
ex: "Where'd you get this bap from?"

[to] **bar** [someone] v. (general sl.) old & new school
1. to prohibit.
ex: "They barred from comin' around here."

barbwire n. (general sl.) new school
1. braces for teeth.
ex: "Even with the barbwire shortie was cute as hell."

[to] **bark on** [someone] v. (e. coast sl.) new school
1. to yell, scream, or shout loudly at someone when expressing one's anger.
ex: "Shortie barked on me for no reason."

barnyard pimp n. (southern sl.) new school
1. a witty way to refer to chicken; fried chicken.
ex: "Smell like ya momz cookin' that barnyard pimp." "Let's pick up a bucket of that barnyard pimp."

base n. (drug sl.) old school
1. a smokable form of cocaine. (var. **free base**) See also: **crillz, crack, jums**
ex: "They snuck some base inside of her weed."

[a] **basehead** n. (drug sl.) old school
1. one who smokes and is addicted to the smokable form of cocaine. (var. [a] **crackhead**)
ex: "I know you don't think you bringin' that basehead in my house."

[to] **bass on** [someone] v. (e. coast sl.) old school
1. to use a loud voice when reprimanding someone or when expressing anger. See also: [to] **scream on** [someone]
ex: "I don't appreciate you bassin' on me like that."

[the] **bat cave** n. (e. coast sl.) old & new school
1. the neighborhood house or apartment that everyone likes to get together or hangout in. 2. one's private or special room or one's secret dwellings.
ex: "Just tell everybody to meet up at the bat cave."

[the] **Bay area** n. (w. coast sl.) old & new school
1. San Francisco, CA. (var. [the] **Yay area**)

be a man, use ya hand phrase (general sl.) old & new school
1. a witty response to someone asking for toilet paper.

be all you can be phrase (general sl.) new school
1. a term used to encourage someone to do the best he/she can or to exert maximum effort [usually during competition]. See also: **handle ya business**
ex: "Go out there and be all you can be dun."

be like that [sometimes] phrase (general sl.) old school
1. a modest or nonchalant way to say, "that's how things are/go sometimes", "tough luck", or "things happen". (var. **be's like that** [sometimes])
ex: "It just be like that sometimes, what can you do about it?"

[to] **be out** v. (e. coast sl.) old & new school
1. to leave; depart from. See also: [to] **jet**, [to] **slide**
ex: "We about to be out son." "When y'all tryin' to be out?"

be there or be square phrase (general sl.) old school
1. a witty way to taunt someone about meeting you at a prearranged time and place [usually to settle a challenge].

beads n. (general sl.) old school
1. little hard curled up hairs located at the nape of the neck. (var. **buckshots, beady beads**)

[to] **beam in** [on someone] v. (general sl.) old & new school
1. to eavesdrop and/or watch someone very closely in an attempt to be nosy. See also: [to] **clock** [someone]
ex: "Them two old ladies sittin' over there tryin' to beam in on what we talking about."

[a] **beam me up** phrase (drug sl.) old school
1. a person who smokes and is addicted to the smokable form of cocaine. (var. [a] **beam me up Scotty**)

beam me up phrase (drug sl.) old school
1. a term people who smoke crack cocaine use when begging someone to give them some drugs to get high from.
ex: "Come on man, I haven't had nothin' all day, beam me up."

[a] **bean** n. (general sl.) old school
1. one hundred dollars; numerations of a hundred.
ex: "He's the one who loaned me the two beans to get this."

[the] **beast** n. (criminal sl.) old & new school
1. any law enforcement agent or personnel; the police. See also: **jake, po-po**
ex: "Beast pulled us over twice today."

[to] **beast out** v. (e. coast sl.) new school
1. to explode in anger when upset, angered, wronged, or disrespected [usually causing an unpleasant scene]. (var. [to] **beast out on** [someone])
ex: "I had to calm shortie down cause she definitely was about to beast out in here." "I hope you don't beast out on me."

[someone who's] **beastly lookin'** adj. (e. coast sl.) new school
1. extremely ugly; unattractive. See also: **mugly**
ex: "Tell me, where'd you get them beastly lookin' broads from?"

beat n. (drug sl.) old & new school
1. fake drugs.

ex: "People don't even know you can go to jail for sellin' beat to the police."

[to] **beat** [someone] v. (general sl.) old & new school
1. to sucker, fool, or trick someone out of his/her possessions. (var.
[to] **beat** [someone] **out of** [something])
ex: "He let shortie beat'em for the chain." "Why does it feel like I just got beat?"

[someone who's] **beat** adj. (e. coast sl.) new school
1. in a need to talk [usually about nothing meaningful].
ex: "Yo, do I look beat to you?" "I'm not beat dawg."

[someone who's a] **beat freak** adj. (e. coast sl.) new school
1. a term used to describe someone who loses constantly and miserably yet keeps coming back for more. 2. one who seems to like being mentally or emotionally abused. See also: [someone who's a] **pain freak**
ex: "I see right now, you just a plain ol' beat freak."

beat me there, don't meet me there phrase (general sl.) new school
1. a matter of fact way to tell someone to arrive at a prearranged destination before you do or there will be consequences to pay.

[to] **beat** [one's] **meat** v. (sexual sl.) old & new school
1. a term for male masturbation. (var. [to] **choke** [one's] **chicken**, [to] **strangle** [one's] **snake**)

[to] **beat** [someone] **over the head** [with/about/over something] phrase (e. coast sl.) new school
1. the act of repeatedly telling someone the same thing over and over again [usually in an attempt to persuade, convince, explain, or make one feel guilty]. (var. [to] **beat** [someone] **in the head** [with/about/over something])
ex: "Yeah, she beat me over the head about what happened." "Please don't beat me over the head with this."

[to] **beat** [someone] **over the head with that bullsh**** phrase
(general sl.) new school
1. to repeatedly try to convince someone with the same lie,
story or excuse. (var. [to] **beat** [someone] **over/in the head with
that** [same ol'] **b-b-b-bullsh****)

beat street phrase (w. coast sl.) old & new school
1. a stern way to tell someone to leave or get away from you [used
dismissively].
ex: "Beat street chump, before I get really mad."

[to] **beat the blood outta** [someone] v. (e. coast sl.) old
& new school
1. a term used to describe an extremely bad beating physically or
during some sort of competition [often used to taunt one's
opponent]. (var. [to] **beat the sh** outta** [someone])
ex: "C.O.'s beat the blood outta dukes on the Island."

[to] **beat the brakes off** [someone] v. (southern sl.) new school
1. to beat someone badly [usually during a physical confrontation].
2. to win overwhelmingly.
ex: "I was about to beat the brakes off this lame."

[to] **beat** [someone] **to the curb** v. (w. coast sl.) new school
1. to administer an extremely bad physical beating. See also: [to]
stomp a mudhole in [someone's] **ass**
ex: "She didn't wait, she just beat his ex-girl to the curb."

[someone who's] **beat up** adj. (general sl.) old & new school
1. one who is unattractive due to their haggard and unkempt
appearance. (var. [someone who's] **all beat** [the f**k] **up**)
ex: "Only kinds of girls he likes is them beat up ones."

[someone who's] **beat up from the feet up** phrase (e. coast sl.)
new school

1. one who is unattractive due to being haggard, unkempt, or being physically out of shape. See also: [someone who's] **tore up from the floor up**
ex: "In H.S. she had it goin' on, seen'er the other day... shortie was beat up from the feet up."

[to] **beat up the coochie** phrase (sexual sl.) new school
1. a male term used to describe uninhibited sex with a female (var. [to] **beat it up**) See also: [to] **smash** [a female]
ex: "I'm about to take shortie home and beat up the coochie for a couple hours."

[to] **beat** [someone] **with a sucker stick** phrase (e. coast sl.) new school
1. to con, deceive, or manipulate someone using a convincingly good lie, story, or scam [often leaving that person embarrassed or dismayed]. (var. [to] **get beat with a sucker stick**)
ex: "Feel like I been beat with a sucker stick."

beat ya feet phrase (e. coast sl.) new school
1. a witty way to tell someone to leave you alone, get away from you, or to stop bothering you [used as a dismissal].
ex: "Come on homes, beat ya feet talkin' that nonsense."

[I'mma/I'll] **beat you like you stole somethin'** phrase (general sl.) old & new school
1. a playful or sarcastic way to threaten someone with a beating [often used to prod someone into a challenge or as a way to dismiss someone's challenge]. (var. [I'mma/ I'll] **beat you like a runaway slave/'til I break my hands/ 'til my hands come off**)

[a] **beatdown** adj. (general sl.) old & new school
1. a very bad beating. 2. to lose miserably. (var. [the] **beatdown of life**, [to] **beat** [someone] **down**)
ex: "Boy, you might get beatdown for that."

[one's] **beatgame** phrase (e. coast sl.) new school

1. one's unique ability to lie, deceive, or convince someone in order to sucker, trick, or manipulate that person out of his/her possessions. (var. [to] **put** [one's] **beatgame down** [on someone])
See also: **game**
ex: *"You mean to tell me, you fell for shorties beatgame?"*

beats n. (criminal sl.) new school
1. police who walk a beat; foot patrolmen.

bee-otch n. (w. coast sl.) old & new school
1. a covert way to call someone a bit** or use the word bit** in general. 2. a term used as an exclamation point to emphasize one's boast, claim or threat.
ex: *"I'm rich bee-otch!" " You can't stop this bee-otch."*

beef n. (general sl.) old & new school
1. ongoing problems or conflicts between two or more people [often causing bad and bitter feelings or animosity between those having the problems or conflicts].

beef and broccoli n. (drug sl.) new school
1. chocolate tye and hydro brands of marijuana mixed and rolled together in rolling paper or in a blunt.
ex: *"My manz an'nim bringin' the beef and broccoli with them."*

[the] **beef and broccoli** [Tims] n. (e. coast sl.) new school
1. the brown leather and green gortex style of Timberland Boot.
ex: *"Those beef and broccolis look good on small feet."*

[someone who's] **beefin'** v. (general sl.) old & new school
1. being argumentative; nagging.
ex: *"Why ya momz always be beefin'?" "You be beefin' too much for me."*

[someone who's] **beefin' for rap** phrase (e. coast sl.) old & new school

1. one who is saying trivial, meaningless, or things that make no sense in an attempt to start or become part of a conversation when its obvious no one is interested in what that person has to say.
ex: "Don't pay him any mind, he's just beefin' for rap." "Sounds like you beefin' for rap to me."

[someone who's] **been down** phrase (prison sl.) old & new school
1. has already spent several years in prison on a long prison sentence.
ex: "Them catz been down a while." "How long ya cousin an'nim been down?"

been there done that phrase (w. coast sl.) new school
1. a term used to signify one has already experienced, indulged, or attempted something without wanting to do it again.
ex: "Fake players, been there done that."

beenies. n. (e. coast sl.) new school
1. little exotic cigarettes.

beggars can't be choosy phrase (general sl.) old & new school
1. a playful or sarcastic way to tell someone to "stop complaining" when you give him/her less than the amount or not exactly what he/she asked you for [usually on a "take it or leave it basis"].

[a] **beggin' Billy** n. (general sl.) old school
1. a name used to refer to someone who is always asking or looking to borrow something. See also: **if ya nose ain't snotty you beggin' somebody**
ex: "Ahhh hell, here comes beggin' Billy."

[you] **believe everything you hear, you'll eat everything you see** phrase (general sl.) old school
1. a term used to advise against listening to and believing lies, rumors, or innuendo. (var. [you] **believe that you'll believe anything**)

believe that! (pron. bleed dat!) interj. (e. coast sl.) new school
1. an enthusiastic way to express one's claim or boast is unquestionable and never doubted [also used to signal that one is willing to stand by that claim or boast].
ex: "Shortie didn't even want me to go home last night son, believe that!"

believe that sh** if you want to phrase (general sl.) new school
1. a term used to cast doubt on a statement, claim, or explanation being touted as truthful.
ex: "Y'all can believe that sh** if y'all want to, but I know better."

believe you me... phrase (general sl.) old & new school
1. a term used as a prelude to expressing one's seriousness about a thought he/she professing or trying to get across.

benjamins n. (e. coast sl.) new school
1. one hundred dollar bills; money. (var. **benjies**)
ex: "Shortie just out to get them benjamins."

bent adj. (e. coast sl.) new school
1. drunk; intoxicated. See also: **leanin', pissy**
ex: "We got bent at my manz birthday party."

bent adj. (e. coast sl.) new school
1. to be confused or mistaken about. (var. [to] **have** [someone] **bent**)
ex: "Dukes got me bent if he thinks he can talk to my girl like that."

bent adj. (e. coast sl.) new school
1. angry; mad; upset. (var. **bent** [the f**k] **out of shape**)
ex: "She left here kinda bent about what you said."

bent up adj. (e. coast sl.) old & new school
1. hurt very badly [usually as a result of being in a car accident]. 2. to be aggressively restrained.
ex: "Dukes an'nim got bent up racing back from VA." "Police got ya man bent up around the corner."

[a] **benzi** n. (general sl.) old school
1. a portable car radio that slides in and out of a box installed in one's automobile. (var. [a] **benzi box**)
ex: "I got the benzi so the crackheads can't steal my sh**."

[a] **Benzito** n. (e. coast sl.) new school
1. a Mercedes Benz automobile. (var. [a] **Benzo**)

bet it up phrase (southern sl.) new school
1. an enthusiastic way to accept one's challenge, dare, or wager [also used to express one's willingness to wager]. (var. **bet it up then**)
ex: "Stop all that yappin' and bet it up." "What you wanna do, we can bet it up if you want."

[you] **better ask somebody** phrase (e. coast sl.) new school
1. a playful or sarcastic way to dismiss someone's attempt to question your character, abilities, capabilities, dignity, bravery, dedication, or seriousness [used as a way to exude pride and confidence]. (var. [you] **better ask somebody about me**)
ex: "Yeah that might be true, but you better ask somebody kid!"

[you] **better duck what I got for you** phrase (southern sl.) new school
1. a playful or sarcastic warning to someone who is hurling empty threats or challenges at you [also used as a threat to the possibility of a physical confrontation].

[you] **better recognize!** phrase (general sl.) new school
1. a playful or sarcastic way to demand someone give you the respect, recognition, or praise you deserve and have rightfully earned [usually used when someone is attempting to question or express doubt about your abilities, accomplishment, or claim]. (var. **recognize!, recognize it!**) See also: **recognize or get penalized**
ex: "You better recognize boy, if it wasn't for me you wouldn't be here."

[one's] **B.I.** n. (general sl.) old school
1. one's personal business. (var. [one's] **B.I. business / biz**)
ex: "Mind your own B.I." "You need to get you some B.I. business."

[a] **bid** n. (prison sl.) old & new school
1. a period of time spent in prison; a prison sentence. (var. [to] **do a bid**, [someone who's] **biddin'**)
ex: "This my first real bid." "I'm about to go do a bid next month." "Shortie up north biddin'."

big baaay-bay! interj. (e. coast sl.) new school
1. an enthusiastic way to express one's jubilation when arriving somewhere and trying to bring attention to oneself.
ex: "I'm here now big baaaay-bay."

[a] **big body** n. (southern sl.) new school
1. the Mercedes Benz 600. (var. [the] **big body Benz**)
ex: "Women love ridin' in the big body."

big body/bottom girls phrase (general sl.) old school
1. females with extremely big butts.
ex: "I love my big body girls."

big boy moves phrase (general sl.) new school
1. to do the things that only successful, wealthy, or people with power can do or can afford to do.

ex: "Ya peoples out there makin' big boy moves now."

[the] **big boys** adj. (general sl.) old & new school
1. the successful, wealthy, or people with the power.
ex: "You up there with the big boys now."

big dawg n. (southern sl.) new school
1. a term of endearment, respect, or admiration among friends/peers. 2. the person in charge/with the authority.
ex: "Where you on ya way to big dawg?" "Talk to him he's the big dawg."

[a] **big eighth** n. (drug sl.) old & new school
1. 125 grams (4 ounces) of cocaine. (var. [a] **bigs**)
ex: "The Feds will give you 20 years for a big eighth."

big faces n. (e. coast sl.) new school
1. the new big faced hundred dollar bill [that went into circulation in 1995]. (var. **big head benjamins/benjies**) See also: [a] **face card**
ex: "I paid about three big faces for these tickets."

big [say the person's name] **from the group home** phrase (e. coast sl.) old school
1. an enthusiastic way to great, praise, congratulate, or acknowledge someone or someone's achievement.
ex: "Yoooo, big Shake from the group home."

big homie n. (w. coast sl.) new school
1. a term of endearment among friends; friend. 2. a way to address someone whose name you do not know or do not want to use in front of others. (var. [the] **big homie**, [one's] **big homie**)
ex: "I got the big homie on the phone."

[one's] **big homie** n. (w. coast sl.) old & new school
1. a way to refer to an older male friend.
ex: "I'm talkin' about my big homie Jerry from Camden."

[you] **big ol' pimp you** phrase (southern sl.) new school
1. a complimentary or congratulatory praise given among friends or love ones.
ex: "Happy birthday, big ol' pimp you."

[to be] **big on** [someone] v. (e. coast sl.) new school
1. to like; to be infatuated. 2. to have feelings for. See also: [to] **dig** [someone]
ex: "I been big on you for a while."

[to be] **big on** [something] v. (e. coast sl.) new school
1. to like, admire, or envy. See also: [to] **dig** [something]
ex: "I'm big on that East Coast sh** right now."

big pimpin' phrase (southern sl.) new school
1. a hip term males use to describe attending an event for the main purpose of socializing with and impressing females [while spending large amounts of money at the event].
ex: "It's big pimpin' goin' down when we get there kid."

[to] **big** [someone] **up** v. (e. coast sl.) old & new school
1. to verbally acknowledge someone [usually in the way of a praise]. 2. to talk good or positive about someone. (var. [to] **big up** [someone]) See also: [to] **shout** [someone] **out**

[a] **big Willie** adj. (e. coast sl.) old school
1. a male who makes and spends large amounts of money freely [money often obtained illegally].
ex: "You don't see too many big willies in Brooklyn like back in the days."

[you/we] **bigger than that** phrase (e. coast sl.) new school
1. a term used to coach someone about not letting a situation upset or get the best of him/her [in a way that the person's character suffers or is lessened]. 2. a term used to emphasize friendship or bond with a friend when a situation threatens that friendship or bond.

ex: "Don't do that son, you bigger than that."
"We bigger than that dawg, no girl is gonna come between us."

Billy bad ass n. (southern sl.) new school
1. a term used mockingly to refer to or address someone who is trying to act tough or boasting about how tough he/she is. (var. **tough Tony**)
ex: "Let me see you do it Billy bad ass." You just talkin' Billy bad ass."

bimmie adj. (e. coast sl.) new school
1. scared; afraid; nervous. See also **p-noid**
ex: "I was kinda bimmie about that all night."

[the] **bing** n. (prison sl.) old & new school
1. the punitive/segregated section of a prison where one is held in solitary confinement. (var. [the] **box/hole/ SHU** [special housing unit])
ex: "One time I did 11 months in the bing for nothin'."

[a] **bing monster** n. (prison sl.) old & new school
1. an inmate who spends a lot of time in solitary confinement for disciplinary reasons.

[a] **bird** n. (drug sl.) old & new school
1. a kilo of cocaine.
ex: "They drove down to Miami to cop a couple birds."

[a] **bird** n. (general sl.) new school
1. a female [usually a silly or immature one].
ex: "Help me get rid of this bird."

[a] **biscuit** n. (criminal sl.) old & new school
1. a handgun. See also: [a] **gat**, [a] **hammer**

[a] **bit** ** **ass** [person] adj. (e. coast sl.) old & new school
1. a derogatory way to describe someone who is cowardly

or moody.
ex: *"Get your bit** ass out my car." "Tell ya bit** ass cousin I said no."*

[someone with a] **bit** ass attitude** adj. (e. coast sl.) new school
1. a term used to describe someone's attitude and moody disposition.
ex: *"Don't nobody care about your bit** ass attitude."*

[to] **bit**-out** v. (general sl.) old & new school
1. to allow one's cowardice to stop him/her from doing something [usually waiting until the last moment to back out]. (var. [to] **bit**-out** [on someone])
ex: *"You know he bit**ed-out again."*

[to] **bit** slap** [someone] v. (general sl.) old & new school
1. to slap someone with the back of one's hand [usually used as a threat]. (var. [to] **back-hand** [someone]) See also: [to] **pimp slap** [someone]
ex: *"Don't make me bit** slap ya ass." "I wanted to bit** slap his ass."*

[to] **bit** up** v. (general sl.) old & new school
1. to cower in fear.
ex: *"Shut up cause you bit**ed up." "I don't bit** up for nobody."*

[a male who has] **bit**** [ass] **ways** adj. (e. coast sl.) new school
1. a term used to describe a male's attitude and moody disposition, behavior, or general ways. (var. [a male who has] **lil bit** ways**)
ex: *"That's one of his bit** ways."*

[to] **bite** v. (general sl.) old & new school
1. to copy; imitate. 2. the attempt to do the same as. (var. [to] **bite off** [someone/something])
ex: *"A lot of rappers bite Biggie sh**."*

[to] **bite** [someone's] **head off** v. (general sl.) old & new school
1. to verbally snap at someone when angry or annoyed.
ex: "This fool tried to bite my head off."

[dam] **bite my head off next time** phrase (general sl.) old & new school
1. a sarcastic way to respond to someone's angry response to your comment or question.

[to] **bite** [someone's] **sh**** v. (general sl.) old school
1. to imitate someone's words or actions.
ex: "I get to school and everybody bitin' my sh** now." "Why you bitin' my sh**?"

[to] **bite** [one's] **tongue** v. (general sl.) old school
1. to hold back one's thoughts or feelings to avoid a confrontation or to spare another's feelings.
ex: "You hafta learn how to bite your tongue sometimes."

[someone who's a] **biter** adj. (general sl.) old & new school
1. one who copies or imitate others.
ex: "I could name you about three biters off the top of my head who try to sound like Pac."

[a] **bittie** n. (e. coast sl.) old school
1. a female.
ex: "How about callin' them bitties we met earlier."

black n. (e. coast sl.) old & new school
1. a term of endearment among friends; friend. 2. a name used to address someone whose name you do not know or do not want to use in front of others. (var. **blizzack**)
ex: "What up black?"

[a] **black** n. (prison sl.) new school
1. a Black and Mild cigar.

ex: "The store man got blacks, one for two stamps."

black blood n. (prison sl.) new school
1. coffee. (var. **mud, donkey piss**)

[the] **black top** n. (general sl.) new school
1. a tar surfaced basketball court.
ex: "Are they still ballin' on the black top at Tillary Street?"

blades n. (general sl.) new school
1. 20 inch chrome rims for car tires.

[to] **blank** [on someone] v. (general sl.) new school
1. to hurl profanity or offensive language when expressing anger.
(var. [to] **blank out** [on someone], [to] **black out** [on someone])
ex: "You tell'em I don't want him blankin' on me."

[to] **blast** [someone] v. (criminal sl.) old & new school
1. to shoot someone. (var. [to] **blast at** [someone])
ex: "Them the same catz that tried to blast ya man."

[to] **blast off on** [someone] v. (southern sl.) new school
1. to strike or attack someone first [usually taking that person by surprise]. See also: [to] **snuff** [someone]
ex: "I was so mad, I just wanted to blast off on his ass."

blasted adj. (general sl.) old & new school
1. drunk; intoxicated.
ex: "Shortie was at the party blasted."

[to] **blaze** v. (drug sl.) new school
1. to light and then smoke a marijuana cigarette or blunt [can also be used for cigarettes and cigars].
ex: "I caught them out back gettin' ready to blaze this."

[to] **blaze** [a female] v. (sexual sl.) new school
1. to have sex with a female.

ex: "I blazed shortie when we was in H.S." "I still blaze'er every once in a while."

[to] **blaze** [someone] v. (criminal sl.) new school
1. to shoot someone [possibly fatally]. (var. [to] **blaze at** [someone])
ex: "I heard ya man got blazed over some dumb sh**."

[something that's] **blazin'** adj. (e. coast sl.) new school
1. outstanding; unique; the best of its kind. (var. [something that's] **blazin' hot**)
ex: "The new 745 is blazin'."

[a female who's] **blazin'** adj. (e. coast sl.) new school
1. extremely gook looking [usually with a nice body].
ex: "I met this blazin' ass chick at my job."

[when it's] **blazin'** adj. (e. coast sl.) new school
1. the temperature is extremely hot. (var. [when it's] **blazin'** [outside/inside])
ex: "Open the window, it's blazin' in here."

[a CD or song that is] **blazin' up the chart** phrase (general sl.) new school
1. a term used to refer a CD's or song's success being charted on a music tracking chart.
ex: "50 cent's CD is still blazin' up the charts."

[when its] **bleedin'** [outside] adj. (e. coast sl.) old & new school
1. extremely cold.
ex: "All I'mma say is, its bleedin' out there."

[to] **bless** [someone] v. (e. coast sl.) new school
1. to give someone something substantial or of a great quantity. (var. [to] **bless** [someone] **with** [something])
ex: "When I was locked up, my man Heavy was blessin' me on the regular with them money orders."

[to] **bless** [someone] v. (prison sl.) new school
1. to cut or slash someone with a razor blade [usually across the face requiring stitches to close wound]. See also: **a buck fifty**
ex: "Catz was about to bless ya man for them sneakers."

[to] **bless** [someone] v. (sexual sl.) new school
1. a covert way to refer to oral sex.
ex: "I might bless shortie on her birthday."

blewcups n. (drug sl.) old school
1. fake pieces of crack cocaine. See also: **dummies**
ex: "Somebody sold'em a blewcup and he came back mad."

[a] **blicky** n. (prison sl.) new school
1. a homemade knife or sharp weapon. See also: [a] **shank**
ex: "The C.O. found about three blickies behind his locker."

blickies n. (prison sl.) new school
1. years [used in reference to the years on a prison sentence].
ex: "They each facin' twenty blickies."

[someone who's] **blind** adj. (general sl.) old & new school
1. not aware, unsuspecting. (var. [someone who's] **blinded**)
ex: "Shortie got ya manz blind kid."

bling bling n. (southern sl.) new school
1. expensive diamond jewelry; diamonds.
ex: "Everybody had the bling bling on this weekend."

bling bling adj. (e. coast sl.) new school
1. glitzy.
ex: "It was one of those bling bling type of parties."

blitz phrase (e. coast sl.) old school
1. a term used to prod or incite someone into a physical confrontation.
ex: "All you hafta do is blitz and its on."

[to] **blitz on** [someone] v. (e. coast sl.) old school
1. to strike or attack someone first [usually in the midst of an
argument or confrontation]. 2. to spew profanity at someone when
upset or angered.
ex: "She just blitzed on dude for no reason."

blitzed adj. (general sl.) old school
1. drunk; intoxicated.
ex: "His pops came home blitzed from work."

[one's] **block** n. (general sl.) old & new school
1. the street one lives upon.
ex: "You can't come around my block talkin' like that."

[one's] **block** n. (drug sl.) old & new school
1. the street one claims to be his/her exclusively prohibiting
anyone else from selling drug upon.
*ex: "They had this block for years." "Police shut down his block
months ago."*

[when the] **block is hot** phrase (drug sl.) old & new school
1. when there is police activity on a specific street, street corner, or
area preventing people from selling their drugs openly. (var. [when
it's] **hot on the block**)
*ex: "I went through Carver St. and that block is hot." "After Slick
got shot the block was hot for days."*

[a] **Blood** n. (w. coast sl.) old & new school
1. a member of a street gang known as the "Bloods" who
 wear the color red for identity and whose main rivalry is a street
gang known as the "Crips".
ex: "It's hard to believe they have Bloods in N.Y."

blood is thicker than mud phrase (general sl.) old school
1. a term used to emphasize that the bond between family is strong
or overrules that of friendships.

ex: "When it comes down to it, blood is thicker than mud, so you shouldn't be upset."

[something that's] **blood raw** adj. (e. coast sl.) old school
1. outstanding; unique; the best of its kind. See also: [something that's] **raw**
ex: "I'm about to put the blood raw system in my sh**."

blood was everywhere phrase (southern sl.) new school
1. a graphic way to describe and emphasize one's lost, win, or beating. (var. **there was blood everywhere**)
ex: "Did she win, man blood was everywhere."

[someone who's] **Bloodin' and Cripin'** v. (e. coast sl.) new school
1. one who is a active member of the Blood or Crip street gang.
ex: "I heard ya homie Bloodin' and Cripin' now." "Boy I better not find out you Bloodin' and Cripin' now."

[to] **blow** v. (general sl.) old & new school
1. to achieve financial wealth [and sometimes success and fame].
(var. [to] **blow up/blow up like nitro**)
ex: "Trust me son, we about to blow." "I heard ya man blew up."

[to] **blow** v. (general sl.) old & new school
1. to miss out on an opportunity or chance. 2. to let a good mate or potential mate get away from you.
ex: "You about to blow this one shortie."

blow n. (drug sl.) old & new school
1. powder cocaine.
ex: "I heard he's hooked on blow now."

[to] **blow** v. (general sl.) old & new school
1. to leave. See also: [to] **jet**, [to] **slide**
ex: "I been ready to blow."

[to] **blow** [someone] v. (prison sl.) new school

1. to cut or slash someone with a razor blade [usually across the face requiring stitches to close wound]. See also: [to] **rip** [someone]
ex: "Ya man keep runnin' his mouth, somebody gonna blow'em." "Shortie got blow'd at the skatin' ring last night."

[to] **blow an el/blunt** v. (drug sl.) old & new school
1. to smoke a cigar that has been emptied of its tobacco and refilled with marijuana. See also: [to] **take one to the head**
ex: "They blew two els on the way here."

[to] **blow crazy** phrase (general sl.) new school
1. to become extremely wealthy in a short period of time; to get rich. (var. [to] **blow up crazy**)
ex: "They blew up crazy off their first single."

[to] **blow crazy blunts/weed/trees** v. (drug sl.) old & new school
1. to smoke a large amount of marijuana during a small period of time.
ex: "They was blowin' crazy trees on the way down here."

[to] **blow haze** v. (drug sl.) new school
1. to smoke a brand of marijuana named "purple haze".
ex: "All they do is blow haze after they get home from work."

[a] **blow job** v. (sexual sl.) old & new school
1. oral sex received by a male. (var. [to] **blow** [a male])

[a] **blow-out** n. (general sl.) old school
1. a short afro style of haircut.
ex: "Man don't nobody wear blow-outs anymore."

[to] **blow** [someone] **out** v. (general sl.) old school
1. to out perform; do better than one's competitors.
ex: "I'm about to go out there and blow this hoochie momma out." "You think you can blow me out like that?"

[to] **blow** [someone] **out the water** phrase (e. coast sl.) new school
1. to out perform; do better than one's competitors.
ex: "I can blow you out the water anytime I want to."

[to] **blow sh** outta proportion** phrase (general sl.) old & new
school
1. to make more of a situation than it really is; to overreact to
something minor or trival.
ex: "You the one always blowin' sh** outta proportion."

[to] **blow smoke** v. (general sl.) new school
1. to talk tough or hurl threats that one is not capable to
back up or see through.
ex: "Don't pay her no mind, she's always blowin' smoke."

[to] **blow** [one's] **spot up** phrase (e. coast sl.) new school
1. the act of revealing one's secret in an attempt to ruin his/her
reputation or relationships with others. (var. [to] **blow** [someone]
up, [to] **blow the spot up,** [to] **blow up the spot,** [to] **blow**
[someone's] **spot)**
ex: "Shortie tried to blow my spot up."

[to] **blow trial** v. (criminal sl.) old & new school
1. to be found guilty by a jury after one's trial.
ex: "They lookin' at fifty years if they blow trial."

blow up n. (drug sl.) old school
1. a secret ingredient added to powder cocaine when
manufacturing crack cocaine that swells the cocaine in a way that
makes the finished product weigh more than it normally would
without this ingredient.

[to] **blow** [someone] **up** v. phrase (prison sl.) new school
1. to cut or slash someone with a razor blade [usually across the
face requiring stitches to close wound]. See also: [to] **chop**
[someone]

ex: "I'm the one who stopped' em from blowin you up."

[to] **blow up** [someone's] **2way/pager/e-mail/voice mail** v.
(general sl.) new school
1. to repeatedly page, call, e-mail, or leave messages on someone's
answering machine [usually when one thinks that his/her attempts
to contact that person are being purposely ignored].
ex: "Shortie been blowin' up my 2way for three days."

blow'd adj. (drug sl.) new school
1. high from smoking marijuana. (var. [to] **get blow'd**)
*ex: "They was blow'd before they got here." "We was gettin'
blow'd the whole way up."*

[a] **blower** n. (prison sl.) new school
1. a telephone. See also: [a] **horn**

[something that] **blows** [something] **out the water** phrase
(e. coast sl.) new school
1. a term used to describe an object that is better than what it is
being compared to [usually in performance or appearance].
ex: "The Lexus truck blows all that stuff out the water."

blue diamonds n. (southern sl.) new school
1. viagra.
*ex: "Ask your grandpops for a couple of them blue diamonds for
me."*

[one's] **bluff game** n. (e. coast sl.) new school
1. one's unique ability to mislead or deceive.
ex: "Come on dawg, all that is is ya bluff game."

[a] **blunt** n. (drug sl.) old & new school
1. a cigar that has been emptied of its original tobacco and refilled
and re-rolled with marijuana.
ex: "Kid, you lettin' the blunt go out."

[someone who's] **blunted** adj. (drug sl.) old & new school
1. one who is "high" from smoking a cigar filled with
marijuana [or several of them]. (var. [to] **get blunted**)
*ex: "You know I got blunted for my birthday." "Look like y'all
already blunted to me."*

[a male's] **B.M.** n. (e. coast sl.) new school
1. a male's "baby momz", "baby mother".
ex: "What you think ya B.M. would say about that?"

B-More n. (e. coast sl.) old & new school
1. Baltimore, MD
ex: "You definitely hafta watch them B-More catz."

[to] **boat** v. (general sl.) old school
1. to leave; depart. (var. [to] **boat out/up**)
ex: "We was just about ready to boat."

boat n. (drug sl.) old & new school
1. an illegal narcotic that uses embalming fluid as its main
ingredient. (var. **love boat**) See also: **sherm**
ex: "Them catz from DC love that boat."

[a female with a] **bodacious** (pron. boe dey shus) **butt** adj.
(general sl.) old school
1. an extremely large butt; very big [can also be used in reference to
breasts].
*ex: "Now if you want to talk about bodacious butts then I
have to mention Jewels from 191."*

[someone who's] **bodied up** phrase (criminal sl.) old & new
school
1. one who is known to have, suspected of having, or accused of
having some connection to more than one murder. (var. [someone
who has] **a body**)
ex: "Them catz was bodied up from here to Ohio."

[to] **body** [someone] v. (criminal sl.) old & new school
1. to intentionally cause another's death. (var. [to] **put**
[someone] **in a body bag**, [to] **body somethin'**)
ex: "They went and bodied the dude for no reason."

[a female whose] **body is bangin'** adj. (general sl.) new school
1. a female who has an extremely nice body; a body worthy of
praise. (var. [a female who has a] **bangin' body**)
*ex: "After all these years, shortie body is still bangin'." "Tell me
shortie body ain't bangin'."*

boe-boes n. (general sl.) old school
1. cheap sneakers.
*ex: "His momz sent him to school sportin' some boe-boes the first
day of school."*

[to] **bogart** [someone] v. (e. coast sl.) old school
1. to bully someone. See also: [to] **house** [someone]
ex: "You always tryin' to bogart somebody."

[something that's] **bogus** adj. (general sl.) old & new school
1. fake; imitation. 2. untrue; a lie. 3. not cool or hip. See also:
whack
*ex: "Where she think she goin' with the bogus Manolo
Tims on?" "That was some bogus sh** you told me." "All them
catz down there are bogus."*

[a male who's] **bolo** adj. (prison sl.) old school
1. has a body-building physique. See also: [a male who's] **cock
diesel**
ex: "Ya man bolo, but he soft."

bolos n. (drug sl.) new school
1. large pieces of crack cocaine [usually sold for $5, $10, or $20].
*ex: "Go check my man over there, he got the bolos for
ya ass."*

bolos n. (criminal sl.) new school
1. bullets. See also: **hot ones**
ex: "I almost got hit with a couple bolos comin' through here last night."

[a] **bomb** n. (drug sl.) old school
1. a large amount of drugs [usually cocaine].
ex: "Shortie got knocked with a bomb comin' off Amtrak in DC."

[to] **bomb** [someone] v. (general sl.) old & new school
1. to verbally set someone straight [sometimes loudly] when that person has offended or disrespected you.
ex: "Shortie bombed me for not showin' up last night."

[to] **bomb** [a train/bus] v. (general sl.) old school
1. to spray paint graffiti on a train or bus.
ex: "Very rarely do see a cat bombin' a train anymore."

bomb bay n. (drug sl.) old school
1. marijuana.

[to] **bone** [female] v. (sexual sl.) old & new school
1. a male term for having sex. (var. [to] **bone** [a female] **out**)
ex: "They got caught in there bonin'."

[a] **bone crusher** n. (prison sl.) new school
1. an exceptionally large, sharp and lethal homemade knife/weapon.
ex: "They have bone crushers buried out in the yard."

[to] **bone out** v. (w. coast sl.) old & new school
1. to leave in a hurry.
ex: "They came in the front door, we boned out the back."

[the] **bone yard** n. (w. coast sl.) old & new school

1. the name for the place the extra dominoes are set aside when there are only two people playing.
ex: "Be quite and get in the bone yard."

[a] **boner** n. (sexual sl.) old school
1. an erection.

bones n. (general sl.) old & new school
1. cigarettes.

bones n. (w. coast sl.) old & new school
1. dominoes.

[someone who's] **bonin'** phrase (sexual sl.) old & new school
1. one who is sexually active.
ex: "I don't think she's bonin' yet."

[the person one is] **bonin'** v. (sexual sl.) old & new school
1. the person one is having sex with and/or involved with in an intimate relationship.
ex: "Of all people, that's who you bonin'?" "I was bonin' his wife for years."

[a] **bonus** adj. (sexual sl.) new school
1. oral sex along with regular sex on the first date or first sexual encounter.
ex: "Shortie gave me the bonus last night."

[one's] **boo** n. (general sl.) new school
1. one's boyfriend or girlfriend. 2. a term or endearment among females [and sometimes between a male and female] who are friends.
ex: "Call me later boo." "What you want to do this weekend boo?"

[a] **boo-fire** n. (drug sl.) old school
1. a cigarette laced with crack cocaine.

ex: "You smoke boo-fire you a crackhead without the stem."

[one's] **boo game** phrase (southern sl.) new school
1. one's ability to scare and intimidate others through tough talk, threats or by talking loud [often works until one is challenged]. (var. [the] **boo game**, [to] **put** [one's] **boo game down**)
ex: "Ya man got a hellava boo game."

[to] **boogie** v. (general sl.) old school
1. to leave; depart from. (var. [to] **boogie out of** [somewhere])
ex: "I'm sorry but its time for me to boogie."

[to] **book** v. (general sl.) old school
1. to leave [usually in a hurry].
ex: "I could have booked three hours ago, but I didn't."

boom n. (drug sl.) new school
1. marijuana.

[to] **boom bash** [someone] v. (prison sl.) old school
1. the act of a group administering a very bad physical beating to one individual. See also: [a] **universal beatdown**
ex: "As soon as he came outside we boom bashed'em."

[a female with a] **boomin' body** adj. (sexual sl.) old school
1. a female with large breasts and a large butt.
ex: " I don't know what she's eatin' but she got the boomin body."

[to] **boost** [something] v. (criminal sl.) old & new school
1. to steal something from a store [usually clothing].
ex: "They got caught boostin' in Macy's."

[to] **boost** [someone] **up** v. (e. coast sl.) old & new school
1. to give someone a false sense of courage, pride, or confidence [usually to prod or manipulate that person].
ex: "Stop tryin' to boost me up son."

[a] **booster** n. (criminal sl.) old & new school
1. one who steals from stores [often taking orders of what to steal in advance].
ex: "The most notorious boosters came from Nostrand avenue in Brooklyn."

booster cables phrase (general sl.) old & new school
1. the actual thing one says to give someone a false sense or courage, pride, or confidence [usually to prod that person into doing something].
ex: "Go 'head and give ya man some booster cables." "Look hear dawg I don't need no booster cables for this."

[a] **boostin' charge** n. (criminal sl.) old & new school
1. a criminal charge one gets as a result of being caught and arrested for stealing out of a store.
ex: "I think this like shortie third boostin' charge."

[one's] **boostin' game** n. (e. coast sl.) old & new school
1. one's unique ability to steal merchandise from out of stores [usually clothing].
ex: "Tanya's boostin' game was on blast back in days."

boots n. (sexual sl.) old school
1. a covert way to refer to sex [usually used by males]. See also: [to] **knock** [a female's] **boots**
ex: "How was the boots?" "Did you get the boots yet?"

booties n. (e. coast sl.) old school
1. females.
ex: "What time them booties comin' over tonight?"

[something that's] **booty** adj. (general sl.) old school
1. not cool, hip, trendy or fashionable. 2. poor in quality and performance. (var. [something that's] **straight up booty**)
ex: "His show was booty dawg."

[someone who's] **booty** adj. (e. coast sl.) old school
1. cowardly.
ex: "For real, you and ya manz Annim are booty."

[a] **booty bandit** n. (prison sl.) old & new school
1. a male who preys on other males in prison for sex [often using violence or manipulation to coerce another male into a sexual relationship].
ex: "Everybody know ya man was a booty bandit up north."

[a] **booty call** n. (sexual sl.) old & new school
1. a phone call made or received with the hopes that the conversation will lead to a sexual encounter in the very immediate future.
ex: "Last time you made a booty call?" "I'm overdue for a booty call."

[a] **booty club** n. (southern sl.) new school
1. a male or female strip club. (var. [a] **booty bar**)
ex: "You better not tell'er we goin' to the booty club if you want to go."

booty cutters n. (southern sl.) new school
1. shorts that reveal too much of a person's butt. See also: **daisy dukes**
ex: "She came to the picnic with these booty cutters on... you had to see it to believe it."

boo-yow! interj. (e. coast sl.) new school
1. an enthusiastic expression or shout of pleasure, confidence, or jubilation.
ex: "Boo-yow, two front-row tickets for the game later."

bop n. (e. coast sl.) old school
1. a term of endearment among friends; friend. 2. a way to address someone whose name you do not know or do not want to use in front of others.

ex: "I got you bop, don't worry about that."

[the] **bopsee twins** n. (general sl.) old school
1. a term used to refer to two people who are always around each other.
ex: "Who invited the bopsee twins?"

boss n. (southern sl.) old school
1. a term of endearment among friends; friend. 2. a way to address someone whose name you do not know or do not want to use in front of others. (var. **bossman)**
ex: "I'm really sure boss." "Nah, we don't serve that here bossman."

[one's] **bossman** n. (southern sl.) new school
1. the person one is employed by or takes orders from.
ex: "Here comes ya bossman now."

bounce phrase (e. coast sl.) new school
1. a playful or sarcastic way to tell someone to leave or get away from you [usually used as a dismissal].
ex: "I think its time for you to bounce son."

[to] **bounce** v. (e. coast sl.) new school
1. to leave; depart from. See also: [to] **slide**
ex: "I'm ready to bounce when you are." "Y'all could have been bounced."

[to] **bounce** [on someone] v. (e. coast sl.) new school
1. to abandon or leave another behind.
ex: "He bounced on us years ago."

[to] **bounce** [something] **off** [someone] v. (general sl.) new school
1. to share an idea or thought with someone for the purpose of getting feedback from that person. (var. [to] **throw** [something] **at** [someone])
ex: "Let me bounce this off you for a minute."

[females that are] **boushi** (pron. boo gee) adj. (general sl.) old & new school
1. females who think they are more sophisticated and intelligent than everyone else. 2. females who have an extremely overrated sense of their own self worth.
ex: "One thing I can't stand is them boushi actin' broads from uptown."

[someone who's] **'bout his/her work** phrase (e. coast sl.) new school
1. one who is very serious, dedicated, and committed to completing a goal, succeeding or doing the best he/she can [even if it means putting one's own self into harms way]. (var. [someone who's] **'bout his/her business**)
ex: "One thing I can say is, you always 'bout ya work."

[someone who's] **'bout it** phrase (southern sl.) new school
1. one who is willing to go all the way with something [even if it means putting one's own self into harms way]. 2. one who is fearless, bold and daring, and not afraid to take chances. (var. [someone who's] **'bout it -'bout it**)
ex: "Brooklyn chicks always been 'bout it."

[a] **'bow** n. (southern sl.) new school
1. an elbow. (var [to] **throw** [them] **'bows**)
ex: "He hit 'em with a 'bow and got tossed out the game."

[to] **bow down** v. (w. coast sl.) old school
1. to quit or submit [usually used to taunt one's opponent].
ex: "I'mma make you bow down before this is over."

[a] **box** n. (general sl.) old school
1. a large portable radio.

[a] **box** n. (prison sl.) old & new school
1. a single edged razor blade. See also: [an] **ox**

ex: "Life taught me how to carry a box in my mouth."

[a female's] **box** n. (sexual sl.) new school
1. a covert word for vagina. See also: [to] **stab the box**
ex: "I been tryin' to get the box for a year now."

boy n. (drug sl.) old & new school
1. heroin. (var. **dope**)

[one's] **boys** n. (general sl.) old & new school
1. one's male friends [also used as a term of endearment among friends].
ex: "Next time don't bring ya boys." "Don't talk about my boys like that."

[the] **boys in blue** phrase (e. coast sl.) old school
1. the New York City Police.
ex: "Half the boys in blue are fat and outta shape."

[a] **bozack** n. (sexual sl.) old school
1. a covert way to refer to a penis.
ex: "I caught her peekin' at my bozack."

braggin' rights phrase (general sl.) new school
1. the right to boast or brag after winning [usually touted as the prize].
ex: "We can play for the braggin' rights." "He won the braggin' rights."

brains n. (sexual sl.) new school
1. a male term for oral sex.
ex: "The brains was off the meter."

branches n. (drug sl.) new school
1. the little sticks found in marijuana.

bread n. (general sl.) old & new school

1. money.
ex: "Did she say anything about the bread you owe her?"

[to] **break** [someone] v. (general sl.) old & new school
1. to win all of someone's money while gambling against him/her.
2. the act of making someone spend all of or a large amount of money on you.
ex: "I'm about to break these lames."

[to] **break bad** [on someone] v. (general sl.) old & new school
1. to display a sudden surge of toughness [verbally and through body language] in an attempt to standup for oneself.
ex: "I don't know what he did, but homes just got up and broke bad on ya man, like what!?"

[to] **break bread** [with someone] v. (e. coast sl.) old & new school
1. to formally or informally dine with someone [usually as a setting to socialize or discuss a specific subject].
ex: "We need to go out sometime and break bread." "I only break bread with the fam."

[to] **break camp** v. (e. coast sl.) old school
1. to leave; depart from. (var. [to] **break north/ boogie**)
ex: "Let me know when you ready to break camp."

break dancing n. (e. coast sl.) old school
1. a dance consisting of freestyle moves and spins using one's hands, feet, and leg coordination. (var. **free styling**)

[to] **break day** phrase (general sl.) old & new school
1. to stay up or out until the morning of the next day.
ex: "We used to break day sittin' out on the benches in the projects all the time."

[to] **break** [something] **down in baby terms/words** phrase (general sl.) new school
1. to make something really simple for someone to understand.

ex: "She a lil slow, so break it down in baby terms."

[to] **break** [someone's] **ends** phrase (e. coast sl.) new school
1. to make someone spend a fair amount of money on you. (var.
[to] **break** [one's] **ends on** [someone])
ex: "Only way I'mma break these ends on you, if you tryin' to be my girl."

[to] **break fly** v. (e. coast sl.) old school
1. to say something sarcastic or witty in response to someone's often modest comment, criticism, or opinion.
ex: "Why shortie try to break fly on you like that?"

[to] **break fool** [on someone] v. (e. coast sl.) old & new school
1. to explode in anger when offended or disrespected [often causing an unpleasant scene].
ex: "Next time she come through here I'mma break fool on her ass."

[to] **break** [one's] **neck** v. (general sl.) old & new school
1. to almost injure one's self while trying to be nosy, faster than everyone else, or trying not to miss out on an opportunity.
ex: "Ya aunt almost broke her neck tryin' to see who was in the car." "He was about to break his neck lookin' for a pen to get your number."

[to] **break** [someone] **off** v. (general sl.) new school
1. to give someone something. 2. to beat someone at something [used mockingly or as a taunt]. (var. [to] **break** [someone] **off proper/proper like/somethin' proper/somethin' proper like**)
ex: "I need you to break me off 'til I get paid." "I'mma break ya ass off when we play."

[to] **break** [someone] **off a lil somethin' somethin'** phrase (sexual sl.) old & new school
1. to give someone sexual satisfaction. (var. [to] **break** [someone] **off a lil taste/whiff/piece/bit**)

ex: "If you didn't talk so much, I'd break you off a lil somethin'."

[to] **break** [someone] **off like the Feds** phrase (e. coast sl.) new school
1. to give someone a large quantity of something; the act of being extremely generous.
ex: "I broke my manz off like the Feds."

[to] **break on** [someone] v. (general sl.) old & new school
1. to hurl profanity and tough talk at someone who has upset, disrespected, or offended you; to express one's self angrily.
ex: "I had to break on my girl's pops."

[to] **break out** v. (general sl.) old & new school
1. to leave; depart from.
ex: "We tryin' to break out around six in the morning."

[to] **break** [someone] **outta** [something] v. (general sl.) old & new school
1. to force someone to change a bad habit or a habit that bothers you.
ex: "I'mma break you outta all that lyin'."

[to] **break wind** v. (general sl.) old school
1. to flatulate (fart). (var. [to] **pass gas**)
ex: "I know you didn't break wind in my new car?"

[I'll] **break ya/that ass up** phrase (general sl.) old & new school
1. a way to threaten someone with a beating. (var. [to get one's] **ass broken up**, [to get] **broken up/the f**k up/broke up**)
ex: "You know I'll break that ass up." "I heard they both got their asses broken up."

breastasis n. (sexual sl.) new school
1. a covert way to refer to breasts (titties).

[to] **breeze** v. (general sl.) old & new school

1. to leave; depart. (var. [to] **breeze** [up] **outta** [somewhere]).
ex: "We about to breeze now." "I breezed up outta there when I seen y'all leave."

[a] **brick** n. (drug sl.) old & new school
1. a kilogram of cocaine. See also: [a] **key**
ex: "A brick run about 22.5 now."

[when its] **brick** [outside] adj. (e. coast sl.) new school
1. extremely cold.
ex: "I just came from out there, it's brick son no lie."

[a] **brick** n. (general sl.) old school
1. a large wad of money [folded in a way that resembles a real brick when carried in one's front pocket]. See also: [a] **knot**
ex: "Let me hold one them bricks you got in ya pockets."

Brick City n. (e. coast sl.) old & new school
1. Newark, N.J.
ex: "You always hear Redman reppin' Brick City."

[to] **bring heat** [to someone] v. (general sl.) old & new school
1. to bring someone unwanted attention [usually when one is trying to be discreet or doing something wrong].
ex: "You know every time you come in here, you bring heat."

bring it phrase (general sl.) old & new school
1. a term used to respond to a threat or challenge [usually used conrontationally]. (var. **bring it don't sing it**)
ex: "Whenever you ready just bring it."

[to] **bring it to** [someone] v. (general sl.) old & new school
1. to approach someone in a confrontational way. 2. to physically assault someone.
ex: "I was about bring it to ya man."

bring the noise phrase (e. coast sl.) old & new school

1. a term used to issue or respond to a threat or challenge [usually used to taunt one's opponent]. (var. **bring the pain**)
ex: "When you ready, just bring the noise."

[to] **bring the noise to** [someone] v. (e. coast sl.) old & new school
1. to approach someone in a confrontational way either in competition or hostilely. 2. to physically assault someone. (var. [to] **bring the pain/ruckus/drama to** [someone])
ex: "We brought the noise to these clowns on the West side."

[to] **bring** [one's prison sentence] **to the door** v. (prison sl.) new school
1. to do one's whole prison sentence without receiving any time off for good behavior, work release, or halfway house benefits or parole.
ex: "If I have to bring this to the door, so be it."

Britishes n. (e. coast sl.) old school
1. British Walker brand shoes.
ex: "You don't know about these two tone Britishes."

[one's] **broad** n. (general sl.) new school
1. a male's girlfriend or female lover.
ex: "Tell ya broad to bring her friends."

[a] **broad** n. (general sl.) new school
1. a female.
ex: "I been broke up with that broad." "I can't stand them broads."

[to] **broadcast** [someone's] **business** v. (e. coast sl.) new school
1. to reveal one's private affairs or secrets. (var. [to] **put** [one's] **business out in the streets**)
ex: "Why you always have to broadcast our business?"

[to] **broady** [something] v. (e. coast sl.) old & new school

1. to take something by force or intimidation. 2. to bully someone.
ex: "They tried to broady the basketball court from us, she told them to get lost."

broccoli n. (drug sl.) new school
1. marijuana.

broccoli n. (e. coast sl.) new school
1. money. (var. **green**)

[someone who's] **broke as a joke** phrase (w. coast sl.)
old & new school
1. without money; destitute. (var. [someone who's] **broke**)
ex: "Man I already told you, I'm broke as a joke."

brokedown adj. (southern sl.) old school
1. to have an appearance that is old looking, shabby, haggard and unkempt, or roughly aged.
ex: "Still tryin' to holler at them brokedown lookin' broads I see."

[a] **brokedown superfly** phrase (southern sl.) new school
1. a male who attempts to present a self image of being hip, cool, and a lady's man but falls ridiculously short because his appearance is shabby, haggard and unkempt.
ex: "Why all the brokedown superflys always tryin' to holler at me?"

[I] **broke'em down like grandpa's old shotgun** phrase (southern sl.) old school
1. a witty way to boast about making one's opponent quit or submit.

[I'm] **broker than a broke d**k dog** phrase (e. coast sl.) old & new school
1. a term used to emphasize being without money or destitute. (var. [I'm] **so broke I can't pay attention**)

brolic adj. (e. coast sl.) new school
1. tough. 2. bold and daring. (var. [someone who's] **actin' brolic**)
ex: "Ya manz an'nim came through tryin' to get brolic with my peoples an'nim, whassup with that?"

Brooklawn n. (e. coast sl.) new school
1. Brooklyn, N.Y.

[we] **brothers from different mothers** phrase (e. coast sl.) new school
1. a term of endearment among close friends 2. a way to emphasize the bond and friendship two males share who aren't blood relatives.

browny points phrase (general sl.) old & new school
1. an imaginary point system that allots points to people who go out of their way to receive favorable treatment and/or recognition from someone who has authority, power, or in a position to help.
ex: "She comes in early to get browny points with the boss."

[to] **bubble** v. (drug sl.) old school
1. to sell or deal illegal drugs. 2. to open up a place of business as a front for selling illegal drugs. (var. [to] **bubble a spot**)
ex: "Ya cousin asked me to bubble for him." "We about to bubble this spot in N.C."

bubble gum rap phrase (e. coast sl.) new school
1. rap lyrics that are very simplistic, lack creativity and the edginess of real Hip-Hop and rap music.
ex: "Man, ain't nobody wanna hear them bubble gum raps you kickin'."

bubble guts n. (general sl.) new school
1. an upset and bubbly stomach causing diarrhea.
ex: "She left early with the bubble guts."

[somewhere where it is] **bubblin'** adj. (drug sl.) old school
1. a location where there is a high volume of illegal drug traffic and sales.
ex: "In three months this spot gonna be bubblin'."

[something that's] **bubblin'** adj. (general sl.) old school
1. outstanding; unique; the best of its kind.
ex: "Them joints are bubblin' shortie."

bubbly n. (general sl.) old & new school
1. champagne. (var. **bub**)

bubonic (pron. boo bon nic) n. (w. coast sl.) old & new school
1. a brand of strong marijuana.

[to] **buck** v. (general sl.) new school
1. to rebel against; the refusal to follow orders or rules. 2. to make a stand against. (var. [to] **buck** [something])
ex: "Y'all can do it if y'all want, I'm buckin'." "If you buck you gonna lose out."

[to] **buck at** [someone] v. (criminal sl.) old & new school
1. to shoot at someone. (var. [to] **buck/lick/bust shots at** [someone])
ex: "They started buckin' at me for no reason."

[to] **buck** [one's] **number** v. (general sl.) old & new school
1. to make the number you want to make when you toss the dice in any game that requires the use of dice.
ex: "When I buck this number, that's gonna be the end of the game."

[to] **buck on** [someone] v. (general sl.) new school
1. to show rebellious and disrespectful behavior towards someone who cares about you and is trying to help you. 2. to stand up to someone.
ex: "I can't believe that little snot tried to buck on me."

[to] **buck up on** [something] phrase (e. coast sl.) new school
1. to discover something by surprise or by chance. 2. to get lucky.
ex: *"Came home early and bucked up on a cat leavin' my crib."*

bucked v. (criminal sl.) old & new school
1. to be shot; wounded by gunfire. (var. [to] **buck** [someone])
ex: *"I'm not about to get bucked because of you."*

[a] **bucket** n. (w. coast sl.) old & new school
1. an old car.
ex: *"What kinda bucket you ridin' in?"*

Bucktown n. (e. coast sl.) new school
1. Brooklyn, N.Y.

[someone who's] **buckwild** adj. (e. coast sl.) new school
1. a person who is out of control, rebellious, and exhibits
extremely bad behavior; to demonstrate destructive behavior.
ex: *"That whole lil click is buckwild." "Why you so buckwild?"*

bud n. (drug sl.) old & new school
1. marijuana.

[to] **buff** [a male's] **helmet** v. (sexual sl.) old & new school
1. to give a male oral sex.

[to] **bug** v. (general sl.) old & new school
1. to act strange or bizzare. 2. to be confused or unable to
comprehend something for a short period of time; shocked. 3. to
say or do somethingt that is outrageous, zany or humorous. (var.
[someone who's] **bugged/bugged out/ buggin'/buggin' out**)
ex: *"He just looks bugged to me." "You gonna bug when you hear
this."*

[a] **buggie eye** [Benz] n. (e. coast sl.) new school
1. the E-class Mercedes Benz. (var. [a] **bug eye** [Benz])
ex: *"I'm not really feelin' the new buggie eye."*

[to] **build** [with someone] v. (e. coast sl.) old & new school
1. to talk to or with someone; to converse. See also: [to] **kick it**
[with someone], [to] **politic**

[a female who's] **built** adj. (general sl.) old & new school
1. has a very big butt and large breasts.
ex: "Shortie used to be built back in the days."

[someone who's] **built like that** adj. (e. coast sl.) new school
1. one whose abilities or capabilities exceeds his/her peers. 2. one
who has many resources at his/her disposal. 3. one who is steadfast
and unwavering under pressure. (var. [someone who's] **cut like
that**)
*ex: "You and I know you not built like that." "You better check my
record, I'm built like that."*

bulletproof love phrase (e. coast sl.) new school
1. the protection a non-gang member receives from a gang because
he/she is friends with a high ranking member of that gang
[even if the non-gang member has a problem with a lower ranking
member of the same gang].
*ex: "Whenever you come around here, you got bulletproof love
homie."*

bulletproofed up phrase (criminal sl.) new school
1. the wearing of a bulletproof vest.
*ex: "Back in the late eighties, everybody was walkin' around bullet
proofed up."*

[a] **bullpen** n. (criminal sl.) old & new school
1. a jail cell or holding pen where prisoners are held in awaiting a
court appearance or waiting to return or be transferred to a jail
facility.

[a] **bullpen sandwich** n. (prison sl.) old & news school
1. a bologna and cheese sandwich on extremely dry bread [usually
served to prisoners while held in a bullpen].

ex: "Yo, his momz came out servin' the bullpen sandwiches son, I was like, nah I'm aiight."

bullpen therapy phrase (prison sl.) old & new school
1. the long monotonous wait in a jail cell or holding pen one experiences while waiting to appear in court or to be transferred to a jail facility [often enduring such conditions as sleeping on the floor or wood/steel bench, overcrowding, and eating bullpen sandwiches].

bullsh** ain't nothin'! interj. (southern sl.) new school
1. a matter of fact way to say, "I'm serious", "I mean/meant that", "this is for real/serious", "I'm not jokin' around", or "I'm not playing around" [usually used to emphasize one's seriousness]. (var. **bullsh** ain't nothin' but chewed up grass**)
ex: "Bullsh** ain't nothin' let him don't be there when I get home."

[someone who's] **bullsh**in'** adj. (general sl.) old & new school
1. procrastinating; stalling. 2. not serious. (var. [someone who's] **playin' games**)
ex: "Let's go, these catz bullsh**in'."

[to] **bum rush** [someone/someplace] v. (general sl.) old & new school
1. to use the force and momentum of a crowd to overwhelm someone in an attempt to push past or into a point of entry. (var. [to] **put the bum rush on** [someone])
ex: "Soon as a couple more people come, we gonna bum rush this party."

[to] **bump** [something] v. (southern sl.) old & new school
1. to sell something.
ex: "How much you tryin' to bump these for?"

[to] **bump and grind** phrase (sexual sl.) new school
1. to have sex.

ex: "I'm tellin' you right now, ain't no bumpin' and grindin' goin' on in here."

[to] **bump heads** [with someone] v. (general sl.) old & new school
1. to unexpectedly see someone you know somewhere. 2. to have an unpleasant confrontation with someone. (var. [to] **bump** [with someone])
ex: "This is the second time we've bumped heads, are you following me?" "I don't want to bump heads with you."

[to] **bump into** [someone] v. (general sl.) old & new school
1. to unexpectedly see someone you know somewhere. (var. [to] **run into** [someone])
ex: "Of all the people I hafta bump into you here."

bump that! interj. (general sl.) new school
1. a covert way to say, "f**k that!" when expressing one's discontent or willingness to stand by his/her position. (var. **bump that sh**!**)
ex: "Man bump that, I don't hafta listen to this."

bump that phrase (general sl.) new school
1. a way to tell someone to turn up the volume when one hears a song he/she likes. (var. **pump that**)
ex: "Bump that shortie, I haven't heard that in a while."

[something that's] **bumpin'** adj. (general sl.) new school
1. outstanding; unique; the best of its kind. See also: [something that's] **dope**, [something that's] **phat**
ex: "Jay Z new sneakers are bumpin'."

[a] **bundle** n. (drug sl.) old & new school
1. ten individual packets of heroin banded together and sold as a single item.
ex: "Somebody said they caught ya man with ten bundles."

[to] **bungee jump** v. (general sl.) new school

1. to take unnecessary and dangerous chances without weighing the consequences or risks; to proceed without thinking. (var. [to] **bungee jump without the cord**) See also: [to] **jump out there**
ex: *"This fool was about to bungee jump man."*

[to] **burglarize** [someone's] **conversation** v. (e. coast sl.) new school
1. to eavesdrop [usually repeating what one overhears to others]. See also: [to] **ear hustle**
ex: *"She got that from burglarizin' my conversation."*

[to] **burn** v. (drug sl.) new school
1. the act of smoking marijuana.
ex: *"Y'all can't burn in here." "We just burned before y'all got here."*

[to] **burn** [someone] v. (sexual sl.) old & new school
1. to give someone a sexually transmitted disease. (var. [to be] **burnt** [by someone]) See also: [a male who has the] **sick d**k**
ex: *"Did you tell shortie she burned you?" "I can't believe my boyfriend burned me."*

[a female who can] **burn** v. (southern sl.) old school
1. a female who knows how to cook extremely well. (var. [a female who knows how to] **burn**, [a female who can] **cook her ass off**, [a female who can] **tear sh** up in the kitchen**)
ex: *" I'mma tell who can burn, shortie moms, word!"*

[to] **burn** [someone] v. (general sl.) old & new school
1. to trick or manipulate someone out of something.
ex: *"Shortie almost burned me for the watch."*

[a] **burn-out** n. (e. coast sl.) new school
1. a cloned cellular phone one uses until it is no longer usable [because it's been deactivated].
ex: *"I know where you can get a burn-out for three hundred dollars."*

burn the road up phrase (southern sl.) old & new school
1. a playful or sarcastic way to tell someone to leave or to get away from you [usually used as a dismissal]. 2. a way to inform someone of your intentions to leave.
ex: "Its time for you to burn the road up son."

[a] **burner** n. (criminal sl.) old & new school
1. a firearm. See also: [a] **flamer**
ex: "You can't bring the burner in here."

[someone who's] **burnin'** adj. (sexual sl.) old & new school
1. one who has a sexually transmitted disease.
ex: "Watch out cause I heard he's burnin'."

burnt out [on something] adj. (general sl.) new school
1. tired of. (var. **burnt out off** [something])
ex: "I'm burnt out on commercial rappers."

[someone who's] **burnt out** adj. (general sl.) new school
1. a term used to describe someone who acts strange or does things that question his/her intellect.
ex: "Ya man burnt out, he tried to jump out the cab while it was moving."

[to] **bust** [someone] v. (general sl.) old & new school
1. to catch someone [usually doing something wrong].
ex: "I knew I was gonna bust you sooner or later."

[to] **bust a cap** v. (criminal sl.) old & new school
1. the act of firing a gun. (var. [to] **bust caps at** [someone])
ex: "It sounded like somebody busted a cap out there."

[I'll] **bust a cap in ya ass** phrase (general sl.) old & new school
1. a playful or sarcastic way to threaten someone with shooting him/her.
ex: "You keep it up, I'mma bust a cap in ya ass."

[to] **bust a move** phrase (general sl.) old & new school
1. to demonstrate one's ability or inability to dance.
ex: "Let's go out there and bust a move."

[to] **bust a move** phrase (general sl.) old & new school
1. to do something [usually something sneaky or deceitful].
ex: "I caught her tryin' to bust a move." "Watch me go over there and bust a move."

[to] **bust a nut** v. (sexual sl.) old & new school
1. to experience an orgasm [usually a male term].
ex: "All you wanna do is bust a nut and then leave."

[to] **bust a u-ee** v. (general sl.) old & new school
1. to make a U-turn. (var. [to] **bust a left/right**)
ex: "We might be able to bust a u-ee up there."

[to] **bust** [one's] **ass** v. (general sl.) old & new school
1. to work extremely hard. 2. to fall down hard.
ex: "I go out here and bust my ass and this is the thanks I get?" "He almost busted his ass."

[to] **bust** [someone's] **ass** v. (general sl.) old & new school
1. to beat someone up badly during a physical confrontation. (var.
[to] **bust** [someone's] **sh****)
ex: "Somebody gonna bust ya ass over that same dumb sh**."

[to] **bust** [one's] **bubble** v. (general sl.) old & new school
1. to put a damper on one's excitement, good mood, positive thought, plans, or enthusiasm.
ex: "I hope this doesn't bust ya bubble, but you can't go with us."

[a] **bustdown** n. (w. coast sl.) new school
1. an extremely promiscuous female. 2. a female easy to have sex with.
ex: "Can't believe dude feel in love with the bustdown."

[to] **bust** [someone] **down** v. (prison sl.) new school
1. to cut or slash someone with a razor blade [usually across the face requiring stitches to close wound].
ex: "Moe busted'em down for runnin' his mouth too much." "I think she got bust down comin' out the club."

[to] **bust** [something] **down** v. (general sl.) old school
1. to explain something in simple terms. (var. [to] **bust** [something] **down for** [someone])
ex: "Do you need me to bust this down for you?"

[to] **bust** [someone] **down** v. (general sl.) old & new school
1. to give someone something. (var. [to] **bust** [something] **down**)
ex: "You think you can bust me down 'til Friday?" "I can't keep bustin' you down like this."

[to] **bust** [one's] **gun** v. (criminal sl.) old & new school
1. the act of shooting one's gun. (var. [to] **bust** [one's] **gat**)
ex: "I hope I never have to bust my gun."

[to] **bust** [someone] **in the head** phrase (criminal sl.) new school
1. to testify against a friend or family member in a court of law and as a result of that testimony that person faces or goes to prison; to inform on someone. (var. [to] **hit** [someone] **in the head**)
ex: "I couldn't believe he'd bust me in the head."

[to] **bust** [someone] **in the head** phrase (general sl.) old & new school
1. to hit someone over the head with an object.
ex: "You not gonna be satisfied 'til I bust you in head, keep playin'."

bust it phrase (general sl.) old & new school
1. a term used to gain someone's attention. 2. a way to say, "listen", "listen to this", or "listen up". (var. **bust this**)
ex: "Bust it, I have something I want to tell you."

[to] **bust off** v. (general sl.) new school
1. to flatulate (fart).
ex: *"You can't tell me somebody didn't just bust off in here."*

[to] **bust off** v. (sexual sl.) new school
1. to have an orgasm.
ex: *"Me and shortie bust off at the same time." "As soon as she bust'd off she fell asleep."*

[to] **bust off** v. (criminal sl.) old & new school
1. the act of firing a gun.
ex: *"At first I thought they were bustin' off at me." "Who busted off first?"*

[to] **bust on** [someone] v. (criminal sl.) new school
1. to inform on a friend or family member to law enforcement; the act of testifying against a friend or family member in a court of law.
ex: *"He's the one that bust on his whole crew."*

[to] **bust** [something] **out** v. (general sl.) old & new school
1. the act of completing an objective. 2. to finish something.
ex: *"Is it cool for me to bust this out?" "Let me bust this out for you so we can leave."*

[to] **bust** [a female] **out** v. (sexual sl.) old school
1. to have sex with a female.
ex: *"All you wanna do is bust me out anyway."*

[to] **bust** [someone] **out** v. (southern sl.) new school
1. to reveal someone's secret.
ex: *"He bust me out in front the whole family." "Don't make me bust you out in here."*

[to] **bust** [someone's] **sh**** v. (e. coast sl.) old & new school
1. to beat someone up badly.

*ex: "I was about to bust her sh** for lyin' on me." "Don't have
me bust ya sh** over some nonsense."*

[to] **bust** [one's] **sh** wide open** phrase (e. coast sl.) new school
1. the act of assaulting someone causing that person a bloody head
injury. (var. [to] **bust** [one's] **sh** to the white meat**) See also:
[to] **split** [someone's] **sh****

[to] **bust slob** v. (sexual sl.) old school
1. to tongue kiss someone (French kissing).
ex: "Did she let you bust some slob?"

[to] **bust slugs** v. (criminal sl.) old & new school
1. the act of firing a gun. (var. [to] **bust slugs at** [someone])
ex: "You could hear them bustin' slugs two blocks away."

[to] **bust** [someone's] **snotbox** v. (e. coast sl.) old & new school
1. the act of punching someone in the nose and making it bleed.
(var. [to] **bust** [someone's] **sh****)
ex: "She cold bust'd ya man's snot box."

bust the scenario phrase (e. coast sl.) old school
1. a term used as a opening to an explanation or declaration. 2. a
way to say, "listen", "listen to this", "hear me out". (var. **bust the
move/science**) See also: **peep the move**
ex: "Bust the scenario we don't hafta talk like this to each other."

[someone who's] **busted** adj. (general sl.) old & new school
1. unattractive; ugly. 2. without money; destitute.
ex: "I don't want to meet any of his busted ass homeboys."

[something that's] **busted** adj. (general sl.) old & new school
1. old and worn looking.
ex: "Check out those busted shoes he got on."

[to be] **busted** v. (criminal sl.) old & new school

1. arrested. 2. caught [usually doing something wrong].
ex: "We almost got busted last time."

[a] **buster** (pron. busta) adj. (w. coast sl.) old & new school
1. one who is easily tricked, suckered, or manipulated. 2. one who is not hip, cool, or trendy; a nerd. See also: [a] **herb**
ex: "You need to tell that buster to stop callin' here like he don't have no sense."

[someone who's] **busy doin' nothin'** phrase (general sl.) old & new school
1. a way to mock someone who is supposed to be or is pretending to be busy but really isn't busy at all.
ex: "Yeah he's busy ... busy doin' nothin'."

butt n. (sexual sl.) old & new school
1. a way to refer to sex. (var. **the butt**)
ex: "You just want some butt." "The butt was so-so."

[someone who's] **butt** adj. (e. coast sl.) old & new school
1. cowardly; afraid. See also: [someone who's] **ass**
ex: "Stop actin' like you butt."

[someone who's] **butt ass** adj. (e. coast sl.) old & new school
1. a way to emphasize being without money or destitute.
ex: "I'd like to help you, but right now I'm butt ass." "You knew you was butt ass before you got here."

[to be] **butt ass naked** adj. (general sl.) old & new school
1. completely naked/ unclothed. (var. **butt ball, butt ball naked, butter ball, butter ball naked**)
ex: "Opened the door, and homeboy was butt ass naked."

[something that's] **butter** (pron. butta) adj. (general sl.) old & new school
1. outstanding; unique; the best of its kind. 2. hip and fashionable.
ex: "That was butter the way you put that together."

butter (pron. butta) n. (drug sl.) old school
1. off white colored crack cocaine.

[a] **butter honey** adj. (general sl.) new school
1. a female with real soft skin.

[something that's] **butter soft** adj. (general sl.) old & new school
1. anything really soft to the touch.

[a] **buzz** adj. (drug sl.) old & new school
1. a slight high from smoking marijuana and/or consuming alchohol. See also: **lifted, stemo, zooted**
ex: "I feel a lil buzz, that's it."

by hook or crook phrase (general sl.) old & new school
1. a way to affirm or reaffirm the determination and commitment one has to getting something no matter what it takes/what the obstacles are.

B. Y. O. D. phrase (e. coast sl.) new school
1. abbreviation for "Bring Your Own Dough".
ex: "We goin' B.Y.O.D. tonight."

C

c-cipher n. (e. coast sl.) old school
1. a covert name for "police" or any law enforcement personnel.
ex: "I seen'em talkin' to the c-cipher."

cabbage n. (general sl.) old & new school
1. money. 2. a person's head.
ex: "I need to earn a lil extra cabbage." "The ball almost hit'em in his cabbage."

cables n. (e. coast sl.) old school
1. big gaudy rope chains [usually favored by rappers and drug dealers].
ex: "Run DMC had catz rockin' the cables back in the days."

[a] **Cadilac** n. (prison sl.) new school
1. a Newport cigarette.
ex: "You only smoke Cadilacs when you have money."

'caine n. (drug sl.) old & new school
1. any form of cocaine.
ex: "The 'caine had shortie messed up for a while."

cake n. (general sl.) old & new school
1. money.

cake n. (drug sl.) old & new school
1. kilogram quantities of cocaine. (var. **pies**)

cake mix n. (drug sl.) old & new school
1. baking soda; the main ingredient added to powder cocaine then mixed and cooked to produce crack cocaine.

[a] **cakeaholic** n. (e. coast sl.) new school
1. one who is addicted to making money [often by any means possible].
ex: "He's good peoplez, but he's a cakeaholic."

[someone who's] **caked up** adj. (general sl.) old & new school
1. someone who's rich or earns a large amount of money;
financially successful.
ex: *"Them catz been caked up from way back."*

[to] **call** [something] v. (general sl.) old & new school
1. to predict or make an accurate assumption.
ex: *"I don't know how to call this."*

[to] **call good money** phrase (e. coast sl.) new school
1. to predict or assess something accurately.
ex: *"You called good money, she came back twice."*

call me what you want, just don't call me collect phrase
(southern sl.) new school
1. a way to respond to someone who is calling you "scared"
because you refuse to do something that you know will lead to
trouble [possibly leading to going to jail].

[to] **call** [someone] **out** v. (general sl.) old & new school
1. to verbally challenge someone.
ex: *"You got the nerve to call me out?" "I know you not gonna
let'er get away with callin' you out like that."*

[to] **call** [someone] **out his/her name** v. (e. coast sl.) new school
1. to replace someone's name with a profanity or disrespectful slur
when addressing or referring to that person.
ex: *"Don't you ever call me out my name again." "I didn't call
you out your name."*

[to] **call the shots** phrase (general sl.) old & new school
1. to give the orders or be in charge; to be the chief decision maker.
See also: [someone's who's a] **shot caller**
ex: *"Which one of y'all callin' the shots in here?"*

[something that] **came out love** phrase (e. coast sl.) new school

l. anything that has an exceptional good ending; an extremely satisfactory conclusion. (var. [something that] **came back love**)
ex: "We tried it again and this time it came back love." "Its not gonna come back love all the time."

[one's] **camp** n. (general sl.) old & new school
l. one's friends or the group of people one is associated with. See also: [one's] **peops**
ex: "Bring ya whole camp with you."

cancel Christmas phrase (general sl.) old & new school
l. a way to mock someone when the end of something is inevitable. 2. a way to tell someone not to make plans.
ex: "You can cancel Christmas now, all I need is one more point."

can I eat? phrase (e. coast sl.) new school
l. a way to ask someone who is successful or has the means to help you for help [usually financially]. (var. **can I eat with you?**) See also: [to] **eat off** [someone]
ex: "Can I eat with you kid?" "When can me and my peoples eat?"

can I get that? phrase (general sl.) new school
l. a way to request something that is owed to you or promised to you. 2. a way to request or demand recognition, respect, or praise for accomplishing something or proving oneself. See also: **let me get that**
ex: "I don't have all day my man, can I get that?"

[you] **can learn a lot from a dummy** phrase (general sl.) old school
l. a witty way to tease someone you observe making a mistake or bad decision. 2. a term used to warn someone not to listen, seek guidance, or advice from a particular individual.
ex: "Take notes dawg, you can learn a lot from a dummy."

[I] can show you better than I can tell you phrase (southern sl.) new school
1. a matter of fact way to assure someone you can back up your claims, boasts, or threats [often used in a confrontational manner].

[someone who] can talk his/her ass off phrase (general sl.) old & new school
1. a person who can talk for long periods of time [often dominating the conversation]. See also: [to] **talk** [someone's] **ear off**
ex: *"Maaan, that chick can talk her ass off."*

[you] can talk 'til ya mouth catch on fire phrase (southern sl.) new school
1. a way to tell someone he/she can talk as long as he/she wants and you still won't believe, be convinced, feel differently, or be any less suspicious. (var. **[you] can talk 'til ya tongue fall out, [you] can talk ya ass off**)

cancer sticks n. (general sl.) old & new school
1. cigarettes.
ex: *"You can't smoke them cancer sticks in here."*

candy n. (drug sl.) old school
1. powder cocaine. (var. **'caine, nose candy**)

candy paint n. (southern sl.) new school
1. bright translucent paint on an automobile.
ex: *"Once I put the candy paint on this muthaf**ka that's all she wrote."*

can't beat that with a baseball bat phrase (general sl.) old school
1. a way to assure someone that he/she is getting a fair deal, the best deal, or won't find a better deal anywhere [also used when agreeing to a deal one feels is fair]. (var. **can't beat that with a stickball bat**)

[you] can't catch me if I was standin' still phrase (general sl.) new school
1. a way to mock and tease someone about not having the ability to physically capture you or catch you doing something.

[if you] can't grow it, sew it phrase (e. coast sl.) new school
1. a witty retort used by females when being ridiculed or criticized for wearing a hair weave.
ex: "Don't listen to them, you can't grow it, sew it."

[you] can't lose with what I use phrase (general sl.) old school
1. a term a male uses to convince a female that she would be making the right decision if she chose to get involved with him [usually used in the context of a pickup line].

[someone who] can't think pass go phrase (general sl.) new school
1. a way to say that someone isn't smart or makes stupid decisions.
See also: [someone who's] **dumber than a bag of rocks)**
ex: "You gonna listen to him, that fool can't think pass go."

[you] can't touch this phrase (southern sl.) old school
1. a way to tease or mock one's opponent about not having the ability, talent, or skills to compete with or do better than him/her.

[when one] can't win for losin' phrase (general sl.) old school
1. a way to express dismay when things don't workout like one thought they would.
ex: "Man I can't win for losin', I lost my job on my day off."

[I] can't write a book if I can't have/take a look phrase (general sl.) old school
1. a way to try to get someone to let you have a look at something he/she doesn't want you to see; "let me see/ take a look."

[to] **cap** [someone] v. (criminal sl.) old & new school
1. to shoot someone. (var. [to] **put a cap in/up in** [someone])
ex: "The cops capped'em for no reason."

caps n. (e. coast sl.) old school
1. gold caps for one's teeth. See also: **fronts**
ex: "Where'd you get your caps done?"

[to] **car jack** [someone] v. (w. coast sl.) old & new school
1. to remove someone from his/her vehicle using force or violence
during the commission of stealing the vehicle. (var. [to get] **jacked
for** [one's] **whip/car/ wheels**)
*ex: "You can get a hundred years for car jackin' these days, and
you can forget about it if someone gets hurt."*

[to] **carry** [someone] v. (e. coast sl.) new school
1. to help, give assistance, or support someone when that person is
struggling or incapable of helping himself/herself; to allow
someone to lean on you.
ex: "I carried your sorry ass for years."

[to] **carry** [someone] v. (e. coast sl.) new school
1. to treat someone bad, unfairly, like that person doesn't deserve
any respect. (var. [to] **carry** [someone] **greazy**)
*ex: "I seen how you used to carry ya man." "Why you tryin' to
carry me like that?"*

[to] **carry** [someone] **like a sucker** phrase (e. coast sl.) new school
1. to treat someone bad, unfairly, like that person doesn't deserve
any respect. (var. [to] **carry** [someone] **f**ked up**)
ex: "I'm tired of you carryin' me like a sucker."

[to] **carry** [someone] **on** [one's] **back** v. (general sl.) new school
1. to help and support someone [usually financially].

ex: "I been carryin' you on my back since you came home from prison."

cash flow n. (e. coast sl.) new school
1. money.
ex: "Now let's talk about the cash flow." "It depends on the cash flow."

[one's] **cash flow** phrase (e. coast sl.) new school
1. one's financial status. 2. the way one earns/makes his/her money.
ex: "My cash flow is messed up right now." "I need to find me a new cash flow immediately."

cash rules phrase (e. coast sl.) old school
1. a way to declare that making money comes before everything else.
ex: "You know how it goes, cash rules shortie."

[to] **catch** [someone] v. (criminal sl.) old & new school
1. to rob/mug someone. (var. [to] **catch** [someone] **out there,** [to] **catch** [someone] **for** [his/her] **sh****)
ex: "They tried to catch ya man at the car wash."

[to] **catch a bad one** phrase (general sl.) old & new school
1. to have something unpleasant happen to oneself or to another [usually resulting in physical injury or ending up in a very bad situation].
ex: "Keep that up and sooner or later you gonna catch a bad one."

[to] **catch a body** phrase (criminal sl.) old & new school
1. to be directly or indirectly the cause of another's death. 2. to be charged with causing the death of another.
ex: "Ya manz an'nim caught a body down south."

[to] **catch a cap** v. (criminal sl.) old & new school
1. to receive a gunshot wound. (var. [to] **catch a cap in** [one's] **ass**)

ex: "Keep doin' what you doin' sooner or later you gonna catch a cap in ya ass."

[to] **catch a case** phrase (criminal sl.) old & new school
1. to be charged with a crime that one has to appear in court for and face the possibility of going to jail. (var. [to get] **cased up**)
ex: "We caught a case together back in the day." "You can catch a case for not paying child support now."

[to] **catch a contact** v. (drug sl.) old & new school
1. to feel a slight high from breathing the secondhand smoke of someone smoking marijuana. (var. [to] **catch a contact** [high])
ex: "Don't go in there unless you wanna catch a contact." "If you go in there be prepared to catch a contact."

[to] **catch a fit** v. (general sl.) old & new school
1. to explode in anger when upset, annoyed, or offended [usually causing an unpleasant scene].
ex. "I'm leaving cause you know he gonna catch a fit if he sees me here with you."

[to] **catch a heart attack** phrase (general sl.) old & new school
1. to become terribly upset about/over something. (var. [to] **have a heart attack** [over/about something])
ex: "You don't hafta catch a heart attack."

[to] **catch a slug to the mug** phrase (criminal sl.) new school
1. a way to refer to a gunshot wound to the head.

[to] **catch a vic** phrase (criminal sl.) old school
1. to mug/rob someone.
ex: "They went out early and caught two vics."

[to] **catch feelin's** phrase (e. coast sl.) new school
1. to get upset or angry when someone teases or taunts you.
ex: "You know she easy to catch feelin's."

[to] **catch hell** [from someone] v. (general sl.) old & new school
1. to feel the wrath of someone's anger or feeling of discontentment. (var. [to] **catch it** [from someone])
ex: "Every time I come here I hafta catch hell."

[to] **catch it** phrase (e. coast sl.) old & new school
1. to be the recipient of a violent assault.
ex: "Don't be the first one to catch it." "He about to catch it fa real."

[to] **catch** [someone] **outta pocket** v. (general sl.) old & new school
1. doing something wrong. 2. not alert; unprepared.
ex: "Don't ever let me catch you outta pocket again."

[to] **catch rec** v. (e. coast sl.) new school
1. to ridicule or make jokes about someone. (var. **catch rec on** [someone])
ex: "Lets go over there and catch rec on ya man and his girl." "They caught rec on ya lil sister shoes."

[to] **catch rec** v. (e. coast sl.) new school
1. to do something that one enjoys to do. 2. to give an outstanding performance.
ex: "Yo, go get the basketball so we can catch some rec."

[to] **catch** [someone] **sleepin'** v. (general sl.) old & new school
1. to catch someone not being alert, preoccupied or not paying attention.
ex: "You ain't never gonna catch ya man sleepin'."

[to] **catch** [someone] **slippin'** v. (general sl.) old & new school
1. to observe someone not being alert or paying attention to what he/she is doing [often causing that person to make a mistake or to perform poorly]. (var. [someone who's] **slippin'**)
ex: "I better not catch you slippin'."

[to] **catch some/that steel** v. (prison sl.) new school
1. to be stabbed with a makeshift weapon/knife.
ex: "Ya man was about to catch some steel over the t.v."

[to] **catch the vapors** phrase (e. coast sl.) old school
1. to become caught up in another's success, fame, glamour, hype, or popularity [when previously that person didn't draw any attention].
ex: "Shortie definitely gonna catch the vapors when I blow off this."

catz n. (general sl.) old & new school
1. a way to refer to males in the plural context.
ex: "Catz ain't feelin' that son." "Tell them catz I said chill."

caught out there phrase (criminal sl.) old & new school
1. to be mugged/robbed.
ex: "Some dude caught'em out there for the watch."

caught out there phrase (general sl.) old & new school
1. a way to refer to an unplanned pregnancy.
ex: "Shortie caught me out there."

caught up phrase (general sl.) old & new school
1. to be involved in a situation one finds extremely hard to walk away from or find a solution to. (var. [to be] **caught up in** [some] **bullsh**/foolishness/dumb sh****)
ex: "How you let yaself get caught up in that?"

caveman style adj. (e. coast sl.) new school
1. to do something carelessly or without much concern for the outcome; recklessly.
ex: "We comin' through that joint caveman style."

[a] **cell gangster** n. (prison sl) old & new school
1. an inmate who only talks tough or threateningly from behind the safety of a locked cell door.

ex: "You got a lot of cell gangsters in the County Jail."

[a] **cellie** n. (general sl.) old & new school
1. a cellular phone. (var. [a] **cell**)
ex: "Just call me on my cellie later."

[one's] **celly** n. (prison sl.) new school
1. the person one shares a cell with in prison. (var. [one's] **bunky**)
ex: "We been cellies for two years."

[a] **cereal killer** adj. (e. coast sl.) new school
1. a witty way to mock someone who is talking tough by using a parody to compare that person with a real serial killer, only this "cereal killer" isn't dangerous.
ex: "You know he ain't nothin' but a cereal killer."

cess n. (drug sl.) old & new school
1. a type of marijuana.

chalk it up phrase (general sl.) old & new school
1. a way to tell someone that something is over; the end is inevitable so its time to give up/submit. (var. **chalk it up as a lost**)
ex: "Chalk it up son, she gone."

[a] **champion lover** adj. (general sl.) old school
1. someone who is exceptionally good in bed. (var. [a] **champion bubbler**)
ex: "Rumor has it that you're a champion lover."

[to have] **champagne taste and beer pockets** phrase (general sl.) old school
1. to have a desire to live a lavish lifestyle yet being unable to afford the finer things in life [often leading one to pretend that he/she can afford to]. (var. [to] **wanna drink Crystal with Budwiser money**)

change n. (general sl.) old & new school

1. money.
ex: "He asked to borrow some change from me too."

[someone who] **changes with the weather** phrase (general sl.) old & new school
1. one whose personality is unpredictable or exhibits moodiness. (var. [to] **change with the weather**)
ex: "I don't know about her, she be changin' with the weather."

channel check phrase (prison sl.) new school
1. a way to ask someone to turn the television in search of a good program [sometimes used as a demand]. See also: **phone check**
ex: "Its time for a channel check." "Let me get a channel check."

charge it to the game phrase (w. coast sl.) new school
1. a way to tell someone he/she will have to accept, deal with, or handle something that he/she is complaining about/sees as unfair.
2. a way to say, "that's the way it is" "there's nothing you can do."
ex: "She rollin' with me now, charge it to the game."

[someone who's] **charged** adj. (drug sl.) old & new school
1. intoxicated and/or high from an illegal drug [usually marijuana]. See also: **zooted**
ex: "I knew they was charged when I seen them."

[someone who's] **charged** adj. (general sl.) old & new school
1. hype; excited.
ex: "It doesn't take much to get them catz charged."

[to] **chase** [someone] **down** v. (general sl.) old & new school
1. to pursue someone.
ex: "Look, I'm not about to chase you down for 'my' money." "I'm tired of chasin' you down."

[someone who's a] **cheapskate** adj. (general sl.) old school

1. extremely frugal; one who tries to spend the least amount of money possible.
ex: "Your friends said you were a freakin' cheapskate."

[a] **cheat sheet** n. (southern sl.) new school
1. a sheet of paper with information written on it to give someone a edge/advantage during a test or while gambling.
ex: "I hope you brought your cheat sheet."

cheaters never win and winners never cheat phrase (general sl.) new school
1. a way to respond to or mock someone who accuses you of cheating. 2. a way to chastise someone who is trying to circumvent a rule.

[to] **check** [someone] v. (general sl.) old & new school
1. to verbally chastise someone who has upset or offended you; to set someone straight. (var. [to] **put** [someone] **in check/smash**)
ex: "I had to go over there and check this chick about flirtin' with my man."

[to] **check for** [someone] v. (e. coast sl.) old & new school
1. to visit, call, or write someone. (var. [to] **check** [someone])
ex: "I checked for you twice today." "I'mma about to go check my girl."

[to] **check in** v. (prison sl.) old & new school
1. to request placement in the protective custody unit of a prison [often because one is scared or forced to seek protection from other inmates].
ex: "That sh** sounds tough, but I heard you checked in when you was in the pen."

[to] **check** [someone] **in** v. (prison sl.) new school
1. to force an inmate into protective custody through fear and intimidation. (var. [someone who] **checked in**, [someone who's] **a check in**)

ex: "When they found out he was hot, they checked 'em in."

[to] **check** [someone] **out** v. (general sl.) old & new school
1. to observe or watch someone [usually from a distance or discreetly].
ex: "Check out Ms. Thang."

check this/it phrase (general sl.) old & new school
1. a term used to get another's attention [often used when interrupting or trying to get one's point across]. 2. a hip way to say, "listen to this/me" "hear this/me out". (var. **check this/it out, check it-check it**) See also: **bust it**

check yaself phrase (e. coast sl.) old & new school
1. a way to advise someone he/she needs to take a look at his/her erratic behavior or actions [usually used in the context of a warning]. (var. **watch/dig yaself, check yaself before you wreck yaself, check yaself then rest yaself**)
ex: "I think you really need to check yaself."

chedda n. (e. coast sl.) old & new school
1. money.
ex: "I know one thing, they better have my chedda."

cheeba n. (drug sl.) old school
1. marijuana. (var. **cheeb**)
ex: "I bet ya momz and pops smoked cheeba back in the days."

cheech and chong n. (drug sl.) new school
1. marijuana.
ex: "Who brought the cheech and chong?"

cheese n. (e. coast sl.) old & new school
1. money.
ex: "That's all the cheese you brought with you?"

[someone whose] **cheese is on squeeze** adj. (e. coast sl.) new school
1. without money; destitute.
ex: "Kid, your cheese been on squeeze for the longest."

[someone who's] **cheesin'** v. (general sl.) old & new school
1. someone who has a very big smile or grin.
ex: "You cheesin' for a reason, what do you want?"

[something that's] **cheesy** adj. (general sl.) old & new school
1. something that is of poor quality or poorly put together; tacky and inexpensive.
ex: "She had the nerve to show up in this cheesy ass outfit."

[a] **chef** n. (drug sl.) old & new school
1. someone whose specialty is taking powder cocaine and turning it into crack through a cooking process. (var. [to] **chef** [for someone])
ex: "We lookin' for a new chef." "She used to chef for my manz an'nim."

[to] **chef up** v. (drug sl.) old & new school
1. the act of turning powder cocaine into crack cocaine through a cooking process.
ex: "I was in the crib chefin' up when I got the call."

Chester the molester n. (general sl.) old & new school
1. a male who likes to date females who are much younger than him.
ex: "You have a Chester the molester livin' in every project."

chicken stalkers n. (w. coast sl.) new school
1. males who are always on the hunt to meet females. (var. **chicken hawks**)

chickenheads n. (e. coast sl.) new school

1. females who are easily manipulated, impressed, willing and eager to believe anything a male tells them [usually as a result of having low self esteem].
ex: "I'm not messin' with them chickenheads." "Why it take so long for me to peep you was a chickenhead?"

chickens n. (e. coast sl.) new school
1. females [who are not necessarily "chickenheads"].
ex: "There posed to be madd chickens at the party."

chill phrase (general sl.) old & new school
1. a way to tell someone to calm down, relax, or take it easy [often used in the context of advice, a suggestion, or a demand]. 2. a way to tell someone to wait for you or wait a moment [often used in the context of advice, a suggestion, or a demand]. (var. **chill out, take a chill pill**)
ex: "Why don't you chill 'til we find out what happened." "Chill here while I go inside." "Are y'all gonna chill for me?"

[to] **chill** [with someone] v. (general sl.) old & new school
1. to spend time with someone; to hang out with someone.
ex: "Yeah I was chillin' with them yesterday." "We haven't chilled in a long time."

chill phrase (general sl.) old & new school
1. a way to tell someone to stop bothering you or to leave you alone; "stop it" "quit it". (var. **chill out**)
ex: "Chill man, I'm on the phone." "Come on man chill."

Chill Town J.C. n. (e. coast sl.) old school
1. Jersey City, N.J.

[someone who's] **chillin'** adj. (general sl.) old & new school
1. relaxing; taking it easy. 2. not participating or indulging in. 3. acting in a nonchalant way. 4. someone who's financially secure; living an above average lifestyle. 5. happy.

ex: "I was chillin' on the couch until you woke me up."
"Y'all go right ahead, me, I'm chillin'." "I seen ya manz new
house, homeboy chillin'."

[I'm] **chillin' like a bug on the ceilin'** phrase (southern sl.) new
school
1. a witty way to respond to someone's inquiry about your
welfare or well being; "I'm fine" "I'm doing okay" "I'm doing
very well". (var. [I'm] **chillin' like a villian**)
ex: "You know me, I'm chillin' like a bug on the ceilin'."

[to] **chin check** [someone] phrase (e. coast sl.) new school
1. a term used to threaten another with hitting him/her on the chin
[usually when that person has offended or challenged you]. (var.
[to] **check** [someone's] **chin**)
ex: "Don't make me chin check you kid."

[to] **chinch off** [someone] v. (general sl.) old school
1. to freeload off of someone.
ex: "You been chinchin' off me for too long."

[someone who's] **chinchie** adj. (general sl.) old school
1. extremely frugal; cheap.
ex: "I hate a chinchie ass dude."

ching ching! interj. (general sl.) new school
1. a way to mock or taunt one's opponent after you have scored a
point against him/her or when he/she has to pay you for a wager
he/she lost against you [ching ching is the sound of a cash register
opening].

[to] **chip** [someone] **up** v. (e. coast sl.) new school
1. to beat someone up.
ex: "I thought I was gonna hafta chip her ex-boyfriend up for a
minute."

[jewelry that's] **chipped up** adj. (e. coast sl.) new school

1. a piece of jewelry [a watch, ring, chain, or pendant] that has lots of diamonds encrusted. (var. **chipped out**) See also: [jewelry that's] **iced out**, [to] **flood** [one's jewelry]
ex: "The bracelet came chipped up already."

chips n. (e. coast sl.) new school
1. money.
ex: "Everybody out here tryin' to make a few chips."

chips n. (e. coast sl.) new school
1. diamonds.

Chocolate City n. (general sl.) old & new school
1. Washington D.C.

Chocolate Tye n. (drug sl.) new school
1. a type of marijuana that taste and smells like real chocolate when smoked.

[to] **choke** v. (general sl.) new school
1. to become paralyzed with fear from pressure causing one to hesitate or not perform in his/her fullest capacity when needed. (var. [to] **choke up**)
ex: "Two minutes left in the game and ya man choked."

choke n. (drug sl.) new school
1. marijuana.

[to] **choke** [someone] **out** v. (e. coast sl.) new school
1. to strangle or chock someone [possibly until one passes out]. 2. the act of putting someone in a headlock, stranglehold, or chokehold. See also: [to] **yolk** [someone]
ex: "I'm the one who saved you when he was chokin' ya ass out."

[to] **chop** [someone] v. (prison sl.) old & new school

1. to slash someone with a razor blade [usually across the face requiring stitches to close wound]. See also: **a buck fifty**, [to] **rip** [someone]
ex: "Asia got chopped in the skatin' rink on Wednesday."

[someone who's] **chopped** adj. (e. coast sl.) old & new school
1. unattractive; ugly. (var. [someone who's] **chopped up**, [something that's] **chopped**)
ex: "His old girl is chopped."

[a] **chopper** n. (southern sl.) new school
1. an AK-47 assault rifle.
ex: "Them boys in Magnolia famous for totin' them choppers."

chrome n. (criminal sl.) new school
1. a chrome plated firearm.
ex: "I seen 'em tuck the chrome in his pocket, time to jet."

[a vehicle that's] **chromed out** phrase (w. coast sl.) old & new school
1. a vehicle that has expensive chrome rims.

chronic n. (w. coast sl.) old & new school
1. marijuana.
ex: "You'll find the best chronic on the West coast."

[a] **chronic liar** adj. (general sl.) old & new school
1. someone who lies for no reason, lies all the time, or lies to get attention.
ex: "I have a cousin who's just a chronic liar."

[someone who's a] **chump** adj. (general sl.) old & new school
1. someone who lets people take advantage of or run over him/her because he/she is scared to stand up for himself.
ex: "Don't be a chump for no one." "I know that chump."

[to] **chump** [someone] v. (general sl.) old & new school

1. to belittle or disrespect someone making him/her feel defenseless, weak, or cowardly. (var. [to] **chump** [someone's] **face**)
ex: "Now I know you not about to let that broad chump you." "I seen the way she chumped you."

[to] **chump** [someone's] **style** v. (general sl.) old school
1. to do something that ridicules or calls another's character into question.
ex: "Yo, why you tryin' to chump my style duke?"

[a] **chumpy** n. (e. coast sl.) old school
1. a female.

chunky adj. (e. coast sl.) new school
1. jewelry [a watch, ring, chain, or pendant] that has lots of diamonds encrusted in it. 2. the wearing of lots of jewelry. (var. **heavy**)
ex: "Ya peoples came to the party kinda chunky kid."

[someone who's] **chunky** adj. (general sl.) old & new school
1. someone slightly overweight [not necessarily fat].
ex: "That broad ain't fat, she's just a lil chunky."

[I'm] **chunky but not funky** phrase (general sl.) old & new school
1. a witty way for someone to declare that he/she is a little overweight but the weight doesn't look that bad on him/her.

[a] **C.I.** n. (criminal sl.) new school
1. a confidential informer.
ex: "I have a strange feelin' main man a C.I."

C.I.'s n. (e. coast sl.) old & new school
1. cigarettes. (var. **C.I. germs**)
ex: "Do you know how much one C.I. cost?" "I stop smokin' C.I.'s years ago."

[to] **claim a set** v. (w. coast sl.) old school
1. to proclaim one's membership to a particular street gang. (var.
[to] **claim** [one's] **set**)
ex: "I don't claim no set homie."

[to] **clap** [someone] v. (criminal sl.) old & new school
1. to shoot someone. (var. [to] **clap at** [someone], [to] **clap**
[someone] **up**)
ex: "Ain't nobody gonna clap nobody in here."

[to] **clap them flamers** v. (criminal sl.) new school
1. to shoot one's gun.
ex: "They always been known to clap them flamers."

[the] **claps** n. (sexual sl.) old school
1. a sexual transmitted disease.

classic soldiers n. (southern sl.) new school
1. Reebok Classics sneakers. See also: **fifty-four elevens**
ex: "Catz still wearin' the classic soldiers."

[to] **clean house** v. (general sl.) old & new school
1. to win all the money from a group of people one is gambling
against. 2. to take everything. 3. to throw everyone out of one's
dwelling or place of business.
*ex: "I'mma clean house tonight I can feel it." "I said they cleaned
house when they broke in." "When I get home I'm cleaning
house."*

[to] **clean** [a male's] **pipe** v. (sexual sl.) new school
1. the act of giving a male oral sex. (var. [to] **clean** [a male's] **rifle**)

[to] **clean** [something] **up** v. (general sl.) old & new school
1. to fix or attempt to fix a statement or action that has offended or
has been misinterpreted by someone.
ex: "I wanna see how you clean this up."

[someone who's a] **clepto** adj. (general sl.) old school
1. someone who steals for the sake of stealing; a thief.
ex: "One of your clepto friends stole my ring."

[one's] **click** n. (general sl.) old & new school
1. one's group of friends.
ex: "I know I'm down with my click."

[to] **click** [with someone] v. (general sl.) old & new school
1. to get along with or feel a certain connection with someone the first time you meet that person.
ex: "The first time we talked we just clicked."

[to] **click on** [someone] v. (criminal sl.) old & new school
1. to chamber a round or cock the hammer back of a firearm while pointing it threateningly at someone. See also: [to] **back** [someone] **down**
ex: "I thought she was playin' 'til she clicked on us."

[to] **click up** v. (general sl.) old & new school
1. to gather up one's friends for the purpose of support when one is faced with a threat of being confronted by someone or another group. See also: [to] **form voltron**
ex: "When you see them clickin' up it means trouble."

[to] **clock** [someone] v. (general sl.) old & new school
1. to watch, observe, or pay extremely close attention to someone [usually discreetly and without that person's approval]. See also: [to] **sweat** [someone]
ex: "You shoulda seen the way she was clockin' you."

[to] **clock** [financially] v. (e. coast sl.) old & new school
1. the act of making money [usually illegally]. (var. [to] **clock paper/money/dollars/a grip**)
ex: "We clocked about two gee's." "We been clockin' all night."

[to] **clock N.Y. figures** phrase (e. coast sl.) new school

1. the act of making large amounts of money [usually illegally].
(var. [to] **clock major figures**)
ex: "We about to clock N.Y. figures kid."

[to] **clock some zee's** phrase (general sl.) old school
1. to be asleep; sleeping.
ex: "I'm goin' home to clock me some zee's."

closed mouth don't get fed phrase (southern sl.) old & new school
1. a way to inform someone that he/she has to speak up or let
someone know he/she is hungry in order to get fed/something to
eat.
*ex: "You shoulda said something, closed mouth don't get fed
around here."*

[to] **clown** v. (w. coast sl.) old & new school
1. to be disruptive, loud, and/or cause a unpleasant scene when
upset. 2. to do something humorous, outrageous, or zany.
*ex: "Oh, I'm about to clown now." "Tell your silly friends to stop
clownin'."*

[to] **clown** [someone] v. (w. coast sl.) old & new school
1. to ridicule or make someone the target of a joke.
*ex: "Why you always tryin' to clown me?" "Them females
clowned ya brother all night."*

[a] **clown ass** [person] adj. (general sl.) old & new school
1. someone not taken seriously, looked upon as being a jokester, or
one who does ridiculously dumb things.
ex: "Oh boy, here comes your clown ass cousin again."

clubbin' v. (general sl.) old & new school
1. the act of going to a dance club or more than one dance club in
one night.

cluck clucks n. (general sl.) new school
1. a group of silly acting females.

ex: "Them cluck clucks ain't ridin' with me."

[a] **clucker** n. (general sl.) new school
1. a silly acting female.

[a] **c-note** n. (w. coast sl.) old school
1. a one hundred dollar bill.
ex: "I put down about two c-notes on that ring."

[a] **C.O.** n. (prison sl.) old & new school
1. a correctional officer; a jail/prison guard.
*ex: "You only find a couple C.O.'s that keep sh** real."*

[to] **co-sign** [something] v. (e. coast sl.) new school
1. to give one's approval. 2. to agree with something someone
says when you know that person is wrong. (var. [to] **sanction**
[something])
ex: "How can you co-sign that garbage?"

[someone who's a] **co-signer** adj. (e. coast sl.) new school
1. someone who would agree to anything another person says
whether its wrong or right.
ex: "If you lookin' for a co-signer, I'm not the one."

[someone who's] **coachin' from the sidelines** phrase (e. coast sl.)
new school
1. one who is giving unwanted and unsolicited advice about a
matter that doesn't concern him/her, one who is being a instigator.
See also: [someone who's] **background coachin'**
ex: "Ya momz good for coachin' from the sidelines."

[to] **cock block** [someone] v. (general sl.) old & new school
1. to purposefully try to hinder someone from achieving something
[usually because one is jealous].
*ex: "That cat always tryin' to cock block." "I caught ya peoples
tryin' to cock block my moves."*

[a male who's] **cock diesel** adj. (e. coast sl.) old & new school
1. someone with a physically strong or powerful build.
ex: "When he came home from prison he was cock diesel."

[someone who's] **cock weasel** adj. (e. coast sl.) new school
1. someone who looks weak because he/she has a skinny body
frame; to look frail. See also: [someone who's] **crack diesel**
*ex: "No matter how much you workout you always gonna be cock
weasel."*

[one's] **co-dee** n. (criminal sl.) old & new school
1. one's codefendant; one's partner in crime or in wrong doing.
2. a way to refer to one's friend.
ex: "I met ya co-dee in Sing Sing."

[to] **cold** [do something] v. (general sl.) old & new school
1. to do something with disregard for the consequences 2. to do
something boldly or callously. See also: [to] **out right** [do
something]
ex: "He cold lied on you." "She cold slapped the sh** out of'em."

[to] **cold bust** [someone] v. (general sl.) old & new school
1. to catch someone in the act of doing something wrong or
deceitful.
ex: "Shut up cause you cold busted."

[someone who's] **cold chillin'** v. (general sl.) old school
1. someone who is enjoying himself/herself to the best of his/her
ability; the state of feeling good. 2. to look one's best. (var.
[someone who's] **cold lampin'**)
ex: "When I seen'em he was cold chillin'."

[to] **cold sh** on** [someone] v. (general sl.) old & new school
1. to out perform someone. 2. to totally disrespect someone.
*ex: "I'mma cold sh** on ya man next time." "Ya man tried to
cold sh** on me son."*

[someone who's a] **cold trick** adj. (w. coast sl.) old & new school
1. someone who is extremely easy to take advantage of, tricked, or suckered. 2. a way to emphasize how gullible one is when it comes to spending money on men/women.
ex: "Word on the block is, youse a cold trick."

[to] **come at** [someone] v. (e. coast sl.) new school
1. to approach or confront someone [often aggressively or with an attitude]. See also: [to] **step to** [someone]
ex: "Don't come at me like that again."

[to] **come at** [someone] **sideways** v. (e. coast sl.) new school
1. to approach someone the wrong way, disrespectfully, or in an offensive manner. (var. [to] **come at** [someone] **f**ked up/with that bullsh****)
ex: "You can't come at shortie sideways yo."

come back n. (drug sl.) old school
1. a secret ingredient mixed with powder cocaine when manufacturing crack cocaine that weakens the quality but enlarges the quantity of crack produced.
ex: "A key of come back used to be dirt cheap."

[to] **come clean** phrase (general sl.) old & new school
1. to tell the truth; to be honest about something, (var. [to] **come clean** [about something])
ex: "She finally came clean yesterday."

[to] **come correct** v. (general sl.) old & new school
1. to approach a person or a situation seriously or with no ill intent.
2. to have whatever it is one is supposed to have or expected to have when he/she arrives to settle a deal.
ex: "Look, as long as you comin' correct you won't have no problems in here."

come correct v. (general sl.) old & new school

1. a matter of fact way to tell someone that he/she better be at his/her best when the two of you meet in some sort of competition or confrontation [usually used to taunt or warn].
ex: "All I know is, if you step to me you better come correct."

[to] **come home** phrase (prison sl.) old & new school
1. to be released from prison.
ex: "You know I'm about to come home right?" "Yeah he came home and went right back two months later."

[to] **come home on that penitentiary sh**** phrase (prison sl.) old & new school
1. to exhibit the mannerisms, callous behavior, and cold demeanor one adapts while in prison when he/she is released from prison. (var. [to] **come home on that up-north/jail sh****)
ex: "I hope you don't come home on that penitentiary sh**."

come on with the/that bullsh** [man] phrase (general sl.) new school
1. a term used to express one's annoyance or reluctance to believe what someone is saying or trying to convince one of [usually when one feels that person is embellishing]. (var. **come on** [man] **with that/the bullsh****)

[to] **come out** [one's] **clothes** phrase (e. coast sl.) old & new school
1. to get undressed. (var. [to] **come up outta** [one's] **sh****)
ex: "Ain't nothin' you can say to make shortie come out them clothes." "I came out my clothes with the quickness."

[to] **come out** [one's] **mouth** phrase (general sl.) old & new school
1. to say something that offends or can be conceived as a threat/disrespect. (var. [to] **come outta** [one's] **face**)
ex: "I would never let'er come out her mouth like that about you." "Watch the way you come out ya mouth with me or about me."

[to] **come out the side of** [one's] **mouth/neck** phrase (general sl.)
old & new school
1. to say something sarcastic, disrespectful, and/or belligerent. 2. to
tell a blatant lie.
*ex: "You should have heard the way he came out the side of his
neck about you."*

[to] **come outta left field** [when talking to someone] phrase (e.
coast sl.) new school
1. to say something that is or was totally unexpected, uncalled for,
or completely out of the realm of the conversation [often
something stupid or uninformed].
*ex: "We was talkin' and all of a sudden he came outta left feild
with some crazy mess."*

[to] **come this close** phrase (general sl.) old & new school
1. a way to emphasize how close one was; extremely close.
ex: "I came this close to leavin' without you."

[to] **come through** v. (general sl.) old & new school
1. to arrive or show up. 2. to visit.
*ex: "We probably come through about two." "I came through but
you had already left for the day."*

[to] **come through like loose doo-doo** phrase (e. coast sl.) new
school
1. to be a savior for someone in his/her time of need. 2. the
opposite of letting someone down or disappointing someone. (var.
[to] **come through** [for someone])
*ex: "Have faith, my man gonna come through like loose doo-doo."
"She came through like loose doo-doo. "*

[to] **come up** v. (general sl.) old & new school
1. to acquire something one will benefit from; to gain financially.
(var. [to] **come up on** [something])
*ex: "We gonna come up with this." "We came up on that idea we
had."*

[to] **come up** [with someone] phrase (general sl.) old & new school
1. to grow up with someone as friends.
ex: "We both came up around the same neighborhood."

[a] **come up** phrase (general sl.) old & new school
1. a plan or idea on how to obtain something of value or benefit [often using means that aren't always legal or honest].
ex: "I found us a nice lil come up." "I need a come up reeeal quick."

[to] **come up** [with someone] **from the dirt/mud** phrase (general sl.) old & new school
1. to grow up with someone from childhood. 2. to have started something with someone where there was nothing, now the two of you have something tangible as a result of your efforts.
ex: "Yeah me and that cat came up from the dirt."

[to] **come up short** phrase (general sl.) new school
1. to fall short of proving oneself, one's claim, boast, or threat.
2. to not have enough of what it takes.
ex: "This fool about to come up short this time." "I don't know who, but somebody comin' up short."

[to] **come with the heat** phrase (general sl.) new school
1. to come with ones best. 2. to come with something outstanding or unique that sets something or someone apart. (var. [to] **bring the heat**)
ex: " You know you hafta come with the heat to win."

commissary n. (prison sl.) old & new school
1. the place where inmates buy their food items and other personal goods. (var. [the] **store**)
ex: "When ya commissary day?"

[the] **concrete jungle** n. (e. coast sl.) new school
1. prison. 2. housing projects.

ex: "Its dangerous livin' in the concrete jungle."

[one's] **connect** n. (drug sl.) old & new school
1. the person one buys his/her drugs from; a drug supplier.
ex: "I heard they busted your connect."

[someone who's] **connected like spider webs** phrase (e. coast sl.)
new school
1. someone who knows a lot of people who are in positions to or
have the resources to help. (var. [someone who's] **connected like a
chain link fence**)
ex: "You know he been connected like spider webs for years."

convo n. (general sl.) old & new school
1. conversation.

[one's] **convo** n. (general sl.) old & new school
1. one's ability to converse or hold a intelligent conversation. See
also: [one's] **talk game**
ex: "Hate to say it but ya man's convo is weak dawg."
"I wasn't tryin' to have a long convo with you."

coochie n. (sexual sl.) old & new school
1. a covert word for vagina. See also: [to] **beat up the coochie**
ex: "I bet she has some good coochie."

[to] **cook** [someone's] **beef** v. (e. coast sl.) new school
1. to physically assault someone as a result of an ongoing dispute
or feud
ex: "You don't want me to cook your beef."

cooked n. (drug sl.) old & new school
1. crack cocaine. (var. **cooked up**)
ex: "I told you I wanted the cooked."

[a] **cookie** n. (drug sl.) old school

1. 1-3 ounce quantity of crack cocaine flattened in resemblance to a real cookie.
ex: "They wanted to cop three cookies, but I thought they was frontin'."

[something that's] **cool** phrase (general sl.) old & new school
1. something that is "agreeable" "fine" "acceptable" "not a problem" [sometimes used mockingly when things aren't really "agreeable" "fine" "acceptable" "not a problem"].
ex: "It's cool dawg I can handle it."

[when someone is] **cool** adj. (general sl.) old & new school
1. a way to say that someone is a good or stand up person. 2. someone who is fine, content, or satisfied with something/some kind of agreement or arrangement.
ex: "I know'em he's cool." "I'm cool with that if you are."

[to be/get] **cool** [with someone] v. (general sl.) old & new school
1. to be friends or become friends with someone.
ex: "How did y'all get so cool?" "We been cool since Public School."

[someone who's] **cool** adj. (general sl.) old & new school
1. someone who is a hip individual.
ex: "You think you so cool."

cool out phrase (general sl.) old school
1. a way to ask, advise, or demand that someone relax, calm down, or take it easy.
ex: "Why don't you cool out 'til we find out what the deal is."

[someone who's] **cool people** adj (general sl.) new school
1. a real good friend. 2. a pleasant person with a nice personality. 3 a stand up individual.
ex: "I didn't know ya shortie was cool people like that."

cool points n. (e. coast sl.) new school

1. an imaginary point system that allots points or takes away
points in the way of recognition, praise, or respect when someone
does something that is considered wrong, right, hip, or not hip.
*ex: "I gotta take two cool points from you for actin' like that with
ya girl."*

[I'm/we] **cooler than 2 Eskimos chillin' in a igloo with the air
conditioner on** phrase (southern sl.) old school
1. a way for one to profess how hip he/she is or how good of
friends he/she is with someone.

[someone who's] **coolin'** v. (general sl.) old school
1. someone who is relaxing, taking it easy, or not doing anything
that requires working.
ex: "I'mma be coolin' over here when y'all finish."

[I'm] **coolin'** adj. (general sl.) old school
1. a way for one to declare that he/she is doing fine when someone
acquires about his/her well being or welfare.
ex: "I'm coolin' just got over a cold."

cooty n. (sexual sl.) old & new school
1. a term female's use to refer to their vagina.
ex: "He won't never get a whiff of this cooty again."

[to] **cop** [something] v. (general sl.) old & new school
1. to acquire something [usually by the way of purchase].
ex: "I'm about to cop that new S600."

[to] **cop** v. (criminal sl.) old & new school
1. to accept guilt and the consequences that guilt brings then
attempt to offer an excuse or explanation for one's wrong doing.
(var. [to] **cop out, cop a plea, cop deuces**)
ex: "You must be crazy if you think I'mma cop to this."

[to] **cop a attitude** phrase (general sl.) old & new school
1. to express one's displeasure with someone either

verbally or through one's body language.
ex: "Why you coppin' a attitude with me, he the one that dissed you."

[to] **cop a squat** phrase (general sl.) old & new school
1. to sit down.
ex: "Lets cop a squat right over there."

cop and go [cop and go] phrase (drug sl.) old & new school
1. a term used to hurry someone along while he/she is making a drug transaction [usually used with a sense of urgency to get the drug transaction over and to avoid a crowd].
ex: "Cop and go y'all we don't have all day."

[to] **cop them things/thangs** v. (drug sl.) old & new school
1. to buy kilograms of cocaine.
ex: "Yeah they came by and copped two of them things."

[when something is] **copastedic** adj. (general sl.) old school
1. something is fine, agreeable, or satisfactory with someone or between two parties.
ex: "That sounds real copastedic." "That wasn't copastedic at all."

[someone who's a] **cornball** adj. (e. coast sl.) old & new school
1. someone not hip; looks and acts like a nerd.
ex: "Where you meet these cornballs at?"

cornball sh** adj. (general sl.) old & new school
1. anything not cool or hip; anything non-entertaining when it's supposed to be. 2. anything one finds displeasing.
ex: "What's this cornball sh** you got goin'?" "I ain't come here for this cornball sh**."

[to] **count dough** v. phrase (e. coast sl.) school
1. the act of making large amounts of money.
ex: "Dig homie, my whole click count dough."

cousin n. (e. coast sl.) new school
1. a way to address or refer to someone whose name you do not know or whose real name you do not want to use in front of others. 2. a term of endearment among friends; friend. (var. **cuz, cuzo**)
ex: "Cousin stayin' here or leavin' with us?" "What the deal with cousin?"

[someone who's a] **crab** adj. (e. coast sl.) old & new school
1. extremely petty and without morals. 2. one who is not cool or hip. 3. a low life individual.
ex: "What you doin' with this crab?" "You know him, I heard dukes was a crab."

[someone who's] **crabbin' it** phrase (general sl.) old & new school
1. one who acts extremely petty and frugal with his/her money or possessions which makes that person appear to have no class. (var. [to do] **crab sh****)
ex: "When you go out with him, he gonna be crabbin' it." "I hate when you do that crab sh**."

crack n. (drug sl.) old & new school
1. a smokable form of cocaine. See also: **crizz, jacks**
ex: "I advise you to stay away from that crack."

[to] **crack** [on a female] v. (sexual sl.) old & new school
1. the act of hitting on or hinting toward a sexual encounter with a female. (var. [to] **crack** [for some])
ex: "I'm about to crack on shortie." "When you gonna crack for some?"

[someone who's] **crack diesel** adj. (e. coast sl.) new school
1. someone who has a extremely skinny body frame or physique.
ex: "Tell ya lil crack diesel girlfriend to get out my face."

[to] **crack for** [something] v. (general sl.) old & new school
1. to ask someone for something. (var. [to] **crack on** [someone], [to] **crack on** [someone] **for** [something], [to] **crack**)

ex: "When you gonna crack for the car keys?" "Did you crack on ya momz about the money?"

[to] **crack it up** phrase (drug sl.) old & new school
1. to go on a crack cocaine smoking binge; to use all one's money to buy and smoke "crack". (var. [to] **crack up** [all one's] **money**)
ex: "I'm not giving you money for you to go out there and crack it all up."

[to] **crack on** [someone] v. (general sl.) old & new school
1. to ridicule someone; to make someone the brunt or target of one's humor.
ex: "I can crack on you all night." "I didn't come over here for your friends to be crackin' on me."

[to] **crack up** v. (general sl.) old & new school
1. to laugh; to find something funny.
ex: "I cracked up when I heard that." "This is gonna crack you up."

[someone who's] **cracked out** adj. (drug sl.) old & new school
1. one who's appearance and character has been totally destroyed as a result of being addicted to crack cocaine.
ex: "Him of all people wound up being cracked out."

[a] **crackhead** n. (drug sl.) old & new school
1. someone who is addicted to the smokable form of cocaine.
ex: "She turned out to be the biggest crackhead on the block."

[a] **crackhead dinner** phrase (e. coast sl.) old & new school
1. a twenty-five cent (25¢) juice and a twenty-five cent (25¢) bag of potato chips or Lil Debbie cake.

[a] **crackhead soup** n. (e. coast sl.) old & new school
1. a cup of "Oodles of Noodles".

[something that's] **crackin'** adj. (general sl.) new school

1. an event or place that is filled with excitement and energy. 2. hip; happening.
ex: "It's always crackin' in here on Friday nights."

[someone who's a] crash test dummy phrase (e. coast sl.) old & new school
1. someone who will/would try anything without considering the consequences. 2. one who lives or does things recklessly. (var. **[someone who's a] car crash dummy**)
ex: "How are you gonna take advice from this crash test dummy?"

[to let someone] crawl up [your] leg phrase (southern sl.) new school
1. the act of gambling with someone who has far less money than you to start with and then let that person win a large sum of money from you.
ex: "I'd never let you crawl up my leg." "That's what you get for lettin' that bum crawl up ya leg."

[you] crazier than a blind gunfighter phrase (southern sl.) new school
1. a playful or sarcastic way to express disbelief or doubt about something someone says or does. (var. **[you] crazier than a blind bullfighter**)
ex: "Me go in there, you crazier than a blind gunfighter."

[you] crazy?! interj. (general sl.) old & new school
1. an enthusiastic way to express one's disbelief, shock, or doubt.
2. a way to declare one opposition to something someone says.
(var. **[you] must be crazy**)
ex: "I ain't leavin' you crazy, I been here all day." "Crazy, tell her to leave."

crazy adj. (general sl.) old & new school
1. a way to emphasize a lot of something. See also: **dumb, madd, stupid**

ex: "Dawg had crazy rocks in his watch." "Crazy people showed up."

[something that's] **crazy** adj. (general sl.) old & new school
1. outstanding; unique; the best of its kind. 2. different. 3. unbelievable.
ex: "That kid got the crazy flow." "You wanna hear somethin' crazy?"

[you] **crazy as all out doors** phrase (e. coast sl.) new school
1. a sarcastic way for one to express disbelief, shock, doubt, or one's unwillingness to go along with something. (var. [you] **crazy as a muthaf**ka**)
ex: "You must be crazy as all outdoors, if you think I'm tellin' her what really happened."

cream n. (e. coast sl.) old & new school
1. money.
ex: "Where you think they hid the cream?"

[to] **cream** [for something] v. (e. coast sl.) new school
1. to want something very badly or desperately.
ex: "I been creamin' to get me a new car."

[someone who's] **creased up** adj. (southern sl.) new school
1. someone who is wearing clothes or an outfit that looks like its just been ironed or came from the dry cleaners.
ex: "Where you goin' lookin' all creased up?"

[to] **creep** v. (general sl.) new school
1. to have a secret romance/love affair with someone while one is intimately involved with someone else; the act of cheating on one's spouse or lover. (var. [to] **creep with/on** [someone], [to] **creep around/out** [on someone])
ex: "I have a strange feelin' you been creepin'."

creepin' on a come up phrase (criminal sl.) new school

1. the devising of a discreet plan to acquire money [usually illegally]. See also: [a] **come up**
ex: "We just out here creepin' on a come up."

[one's] **cribo** n. (general sl.) old & new school
1. the place where one dwells. (var. [one's] **crib**)
ex: "Call me at my cribo later." "I'm about to take honey to the crib."

crillz n. (drug sl.) new school
1. a covert word for crack cocaine. (var. **crizz, crillzack, crizzack**)
ex: "My moms found out about me sellin' crillz."

[one's] **crimey** n. (e. coast sl.) old & new school
1. one's best or closet friend 2. the person who one does wrong with. 3. one's codefendant in a crime.
ex: "When did y'all two become crimeys?" "I didn't know that was ya crimey."

Cris n. (general sl.) new school
1. Crystal brand champagne.

Cris poppin' v. (general sl.) new school
1. the act of drinking bottles of Crystal brand champagne.

critical adj. (general sl.) old & new school
1. extremely serious. 2. dangerous. (var. [when things are/are about to get] **critical**)
*ex: "I'm tellin' you right now, sh** was critical last night."*

[a] **crooked I sipper** n. (e. coast sl.) new school
1. someone who drinks St. Ives brand malt liquor.

Crooklyn n. (e. coast sl.) new school
1. Brooklyn, N.Y.

[a] **cross** [out] **artist** n. (general sl.) new school

1. a disloyal or untrustworthy friend or love one who would betray you for his/her own personal gain without the least consideration to another's feelings.
ex: "That cat too much of a cross artist to have around us like that."

[to] **cross** [someone] **out** v. (general sl.) new school
1. to betray a friend or love one for one's own personal gain with no regards to the relationship one shares with that person.
ex: "I told you sooner or later slim was gonna cross you out."

[someone who's a] **crow-dad** adj. (e. coast sl.) old school
1. extremely unattractive; very ugly.

[a] **crowd mover** n. (criminal sl.) new school
1. a firearm that makes a very loud noise when fired.

[someone who's a] **crudball** adj. (e. coast sl.) new school
1. a low life and dishonest person; an untrustworthy character who is shameless or petty; unscrupulous.
ex: "I know you not thinkin' about goin' out with that crudball?"
"Are the only people you know crudballs?"

[someone who's] **cruddy** adj. (e. coast sl.) old & new school
1. unscrupulous; petty; immoral; untrustworthy.
ex: "I just realized dukes was madd cruddy."

[you] **cruisin' for a bruisin'** phrase (general sl.) old school
1. a way to warn someone that he/she is making you mad and that he/she is very close to feeling your wrath.

[someone who's a] **crumb Louie** adj. (e. coast sl.) old & new school
1. an extremely cheap or frugal person. 2. one who pretends to be financially secure but who really isn't.
ex: "Man, get ya crumb Louie ass out my face."

crumb snatchers n. (general sl.) old & new school
1. little kids; small children.
*ex: "Went over there and she had a house full of crumb
snatchers."*

crumbs n. (general sl.) old & new school
1. a small amount of money. 2. people one considers unimportant
or insignificant.
*ex: "We just barely makin' crumbs here." "I used to help all them
crumbs."*

[something that's] **crunk** adj. (southern sl.) new school
1. outstanding; unique, the best of its kind 2. enjoyable, fun, or
entertaining.
*ex: "Ludacris new ablum is crunk." "They say ya party was
crunk."*

crunk v. (southern sl.) new school
1. hyped; hyped up; excited.
ex: "They about to get crunk in here."

[to] **crush** [someone] v. (sexual sl.) new school
1. the act of having sex.
ex: "I heard you crushin' my ex-girl."

[to] **cry** v. (general sl.) old & new school
1. to complain or whine when one doesn't or can't get his/her way;
to express one's discontent about not being treated fairly.
*ex: "Thing about you is, you cry all the time." "Stop cryin' all the
time."*

[to] **cry like a** [lil] **bit**** v. (general sl.) old & new school
1. a term used to signify one's complaining, whining, or actual
crying tears [usually when one acts like he/she is tough].
ex: "He in his room cryin' like a bit**."

cryin' v. (general sl.) old & new school

1. laughing extremely hard. (var. **dyin', dyin' laughin'**)
ex: "Yo, I was cryin' when I heard that."

curiosity killed the cat [but/and] **satisfaction brought'em back**
phrase (general sl.) old & new school
1. a sarcastic way to respond to someone who used the term
"curiosity killed the cat" in a attempt to scold you for being nosy
or wanting information.

[to] **curse** [someone] **out** v. (general sl.) old & new school
1. to berate someone with profanity. (var. [to] **cuss** [someone] **out**)
*ex: "Don't you know I had to curse out his sister for not mindin'
her business."*

custies n. (drug sl.) old school
1. customers; the people who are the customers of drug dealers.
ex: "She used to be one of my custies."

cut n. (drug sl.) old & new school
1. any ingredient added to an illegal drug to strengthen, weaken or
stretch the amount.
ex: "Some drug dealers use rat poison as a cut."

[to] **cut** v. (sexual sl.) new school
1. a covert way to say the word "f**k" as in sexual intercourse.
(var. [to] **cut** [female])

[one's] **cut buddy** n. (southern sl.) old & new school
1. one's friend; a term of endearment among friends.
ex: "We been cut buddies for years."

[to] **cut into** [someone] v. (e. coast sl.) new school
1. to meet or befriend someone for the purpose of what you can
gain from that person.
ex: "I don't let catz just cut into me like that."

[someone who's] **cut like that** adj. (e. coast sl.) new school

1. someone extremely qualified or more than capable; to be exceptionally good; the best. See also: [someone who's] **built like that**
ex: "I didn't know ya man was cut like that." "Main man, you not cut like that."

[to] **cut** [someone] **off** v. (general sl.) old & new school
1. to end one's relationship and/or communication with someone. (var. [to be/get] **cut off**)
ex: "I been cut that lame off." "You need to cut honey off for good."

[to] **cut** [someone] **off** v. (general sl.) old & new school
1. to interrupt someone [often doing so rudely].
ex: "How many times I hafta tell you about cuttin' me off."

[to] **cut** [someone's] **throat** v. (general sl.) old & new school
1. to betray and/or undermine someone's plan, effort, and/or goal for one's own personal gain. (var. [to do] **cut throat sh****)
ex: "You the one who's always tryin' to cut somebody throat." "That was real cut throat sh** you pulled." "For now, I'm cuttin' throats."

[to] **cut up** v. (southern sl.) new school
1. to cause an unpleasant scene by being loud, disruptive, or rowdy. 2. to do something that is extremely funny or zany. See also: [to] **show out**
ex: "Promise me you not about to cut up in here."

[someone who's a] **cut up** adj. (southern sl.) new school
1. someone who likes to cause unpleasant scenes for the slightest or smallest of reasons. 2. someone who acts silly or zany.
ex: "You always hafta be the cut up when we go out."

cuz-mo n. (e. coast sl.) new school
1. a term of endearment among friends; friend.
ex: "What's poppin' cuz-mo?"

d

daddy n. (southern sl.) new school
1. a term of endearment among friends; friend. 2. a way to address someone whose name you do not know or do not want to use around other people.
ex: "Its about three o'clock daddy, what you wanna do?"

[to] **daddy long stroke** [a female] phrase (sexual sl.) old school
1. a term males use to boast about their love making skills and stamina. (var. [to] **long stroke** [a female])
ex: "I took shortie home last night and gave'er the daddy long stroke." "I'll put this daddy long stroke on you."

[one's] **daily grind/hustle** phrase (general sl.) old & new school
1. the thing one does everyday to earn money [legally or illegally].
ex: "I can't right now, I'm headed to my daily grind."

daisy dukes n. (southern sl.) old school
1. short pants that are cut very high and fit very tight. (var. **punanny shorts**)
ex: "You not goin' nowhere with me, wearin' them daisy dukes."

[to] **dam near** [do something] v. (general sl.) old & new school
1. to almost or come close to. (var. [something that's] **dam near**)
*ex: "I dam near lost my job cause of you." "That sh** dam near ruined my chance."*

[the] **damage** [for something] n. (general sl.) old & new school
1. the price or cost of something.
ex: "How much is the damage on that?"

[to] **damage** [someone] v. (e. coast sl.) new school

1. to physically assault someone [usually causing bodily injury]. See also: [to] **punish** [someone]
ex: "I told you my big brother was gonna damage you."

dang! interj. (southern sl.) old & new school
1. an enthusiastic way to respond to something shocking, unbelievable, or surprising [also used in exasperation when realizing one has made a mistake].
ex: "She still messin' with that dude, dang!"

dank n. (drug sl.) old school
1. marijuana.

dap n. (southern sl.) old & new school
1. a handshake or touching of clinched fists between two people when greeting or departing company or as a sign of respect, approval, being in agreement, and friendship. (var. [to give/receive] **dap** [from someone])
ex: "Give me some dap on that." "What, I can't get no dap?" "Give ya boy some dap."

[to] **dash** v. (general sl.) old & new school
1. to leave; depart from.
ex: " I was thinkin' about dashin' at two."

dawg n. (general sl.) new school
1. a term of endearment among friends; friend. (var. [one's] **dawgs**) See also: **where my dawgs at?**
ex: "Tell dawg I said what up." "Yeah, that's my dawg."

[someone who's] **dead** adj. (general sl.) old & new school
1. no longer a part of; out of the picture.
ex: "You dead, you took too long." "This your last chance, mess up this time you dead."

[something that's] **dead** adj. (e. coast sl.) old & new school

1. over; finished; resolved. 2. something that is not open for further discussion; final. (var. [to] **dead/deaded** [something])
ex: "I thought y'alls beef was dead." "Its time you dead all those bad feelin's."

[to] **dead** [someone] v. (e. coast sl.) new school
1. to refuse or deny someone something. 2. a stern way to say "no". (var. [to] **deaded** [someone])
ex: "You dead on that." "I'm thinkin' about deadin' shortie." "I already said you dead on that."

[something that's] **dead** adj. (general sl.) old & new school
1. something that isn't entertaining or enjoyable when its supposed to be; boring.
ex: "The party was dead so we left early."

dead and stinkin' adj. (e. coast sl.) old & new school
1. abandoned; forgotten about. 2. to be in a very bad and/or dangerous situation. (var. [to leave someone] **dead and stinkin'**)
ex: "When I went to prison shortie left me dead and stinkin'." "Them catz down there dead and stinkin'."

dead and stinkin' adj. (e. coast sl.) old & new school
1. without money; destitute.
ex: "I left shortie in the hotel dead and stinkin'."

dead ass adj. (e. coast sl.) old & new school
1. without money, destitute. (var. **dead broke**)
ex: "I wish I could but I'm dead ass." "I'm dead ass broke right now."

[to] **dead** [one's] **girl/shortie/man** v. (e. coast sl.) new school
1. to end an intimate relationship with one's girlfriend, boyfriend, or lover.
ex: "I deaded shortie two months ago."

dead presidents n. (e. coast sl.) new school
1. money. See also: **chips, scrilla**
ex: "I'm just tryin' to make some dead presidents."

dead serious adj. (general sl.) old & new school
1. extremely serious; not playing or joking around. (var. **dead up** [serious])
ex: "Yo man, I'm dead serious, bring my car back."

[someone who's] **dead to the world** phrase (general sl.) new school
1. a term used to describe someone being in a deep sleep.
ex: "Call back later, she's dead to the world."

[someone who's] **dead to the world** phrase (prison sl.) new school
1. one who has been abandoned by his/her friends/loved ones while incarcerated.
ex: "I been dead to the world my whole bid."

deal'em jake my hands ache phrase (southern sl.) new school
1. a way to mock or tease one's opponent in a card game when its his/her turn to deal the cards.

[something that's] **death** (pron. def) adj. (e. coast sl.) old school
1. outstanding; unique, the best of its kind. See also: [something that's] **fly**
ex: "That was death the way she sang that." "The whole show was death." "Those jackets are death."

[a] **d-boy** n. (drug sl.) old & new school
1. a street-level heroin dealer; a drug dealer of hard narcotics.

[someone whose looks are] **decent** adj. (e. coast sl.) new school
1. fairly attractive but less than gorgeous; mediocre.
ex: "She ain't all that, but she decent."

[something that's] **decent** adj. (e. coast sl.) new school
1. mediocre 2. less than outstanding.
ex: "His style ain't nothin' to brag about, its decent."

dee n. (drug sl.) old & new school
1. heroin. (var. **boy**)
ex: "He got caught with two bags of dee."

[to travel] **deep** adj. (e. coast sl.) old & new school
1. to travel with or in a large group. (var. [to] **roll deep,** [to be]
deep up in [somewhere])
ex: "We comin' down there deep." "Everywhere they go they be deep."

dee's n. (criminal sl.) old & new school
1. detectives; undercover police. (var. [a] **d.t.**)
ex: "The dee's already snatched ya man."

deez n. (w. coast sl.) new school
1. twenty inch Dayton rims for a car.
ex: "I'm coppin' some deez next week."

delf n. (e. coast sl.) new school
1. by oneself; alone; solo. (var. [to] **go for delf**) See also: **self, dolo**
ex: "I'm lookin' out for delf for now on." "I'm doin' this for delf kid."

[to] **demo** [someone] v. (e. coast sl.) old school
1. to beat someone up badly. (var. [to] **catch a demo**)
ex: "Yo, I was about to demo this cat."

[a] **demo** n. (drug sl.) old school
1 a cigarette or marijuana joint laced with "crack" cocaine. (var.
[a] **hype**)
ex: "I caught ya man smokin' a demo."

desperation moves phrase (general sl.) new school
1. things one does because he/she is desperate; a last resort.
ex: "I'm about to pull a desperation move in a minute."

[a] **dezzie** n. (criminal sl.) new school
1. a 9 millimeter Desert Eagle.
ex: "Police knocked'em with the dezzie." "I think that dezzie got a body on it."

[one's] **d**k beaters** n. (general sl.) old & new school
1. one's hand or hands.
ex: "Don't put them d**k beaters on me."

diesel n. (drug sl.) new school
1. heroin. See also: **boy**
ex: "He o.d.'d on that diesel."

[something that's] **diesel** adj. (e. coast sl.) new school
1. outstanding; unique; the best of its kind. See also: [something that's] **fire**
ex: "That whole way y'all put that together was diesel."

diesel n. (e. cast sl.) new school
1. strong alcohol or marijuana.
ex: "Who got the diesel?"

[a female who's] **diesel** adj. (general sl.) old & new school
1. a female who has a big butt or breasts worthy of praise.
ex: "Both of them sisters are diesel."

[a male who's] **diesel** adj. (general sl.) old & new school
1. a male who has a physically strong physique [usually as the result of body building]. See also: [a male who's] **cock diesel**
ex: "He was diesel 'til he started smokin' crack."

different strokes for different folks phrase (general sl.) old & new school
1. a way to tell someone that everyone has his/hers own way of doing things, looking at things, or feelings about things and everyone isn't the same.

[to] **dig** [something/someone] v. (general sl.) old & new school
1. to like, admire, or envy.
ex: "I really used to dig that cat." "I been diggin' you since public school."

[to] **dig** [something someone says] v. (general sl.) old & new school
1. to understand or relate to. 2. to like.
ex: "Can you dig where I'm comin' from?" "I can dig that."

dig... phrase (general sl.) old & new school
1. a term used as an opening to a statement, boast, explanation, excuse, or when one is trying to get his/her point across/heard. (var. **dig, I'mma tell you like this..., dig right.., dig, let me say this...**)
ex: "Dig, I'm the only one that knows how this goes." "Dig, I'mma tell you like this, just come back later."

[to] **dig** [a female's] **back out** v. (sexual sl.) new school
1. the act of having sex [usually a male term].
ex: "I'm takin' shortie home and dig'er back out."

[to] **dig off into** [someone] v. (prison sl.) new school
1. the act of stabbing someone.
ex: "They was about to dig off into ya man 'til they found out y'all was cool."

[to] **dig** [someone's] **pocket** v. (criminal sl.) old & new school
1. to reach into someone's pants pocket and take his/her possessions discreetly or by force; to pickpocket someone. (var. [to] **dig pockets**)
ex: "They caught'em down in mid-town tryin' to dig pockets."

[one's] **digits** n. (general sl.) old school
1. one's phone number.
ex: "She wants your digits."

dillznick (prop. dills nick) n. (e. coast sl.) new school
1. a covert way to say "d**k"; penis. (var. **dillz**)
ex: "Tell ya people to get the dillznick."

[to] **dime on** [someone] v. (criminal sl.) old & new school
1. to inform on someone; to reveal one's wrongdoings. (var. [to]
drop a dime on [someone])
ex: "Yeah, that kid dimed on his whole crew."

dime pieces n. (general sl.) old & new school
1. good looking females.
ex: "I don't kick it with nothin' but dime pieces."

[a] **dime sack** n. (drug sl.) old & new school
1. a ten dollar bag of drugs [usually marijuana].
ex: "My moms found my last dime sack."

dingbats adj. (general sl.) old & new school
1. females who act silly and naive.
ex: "Dude came to my house with a bunch of dingbats."

[to] **dip** v. (general sl.) old & new school
1. to leave [sometimes unexpectedly, discreetly, and/or in a hurry].
(var. [to] **dip out/out on** [someone], [to] **dip away/away from**
[someone/something])
*ex: "We about to dip cuz, you comin'?" "I had to dip out the
back door."*

[to] **dip into** [something] v. (general sl.) old & new school
1. to involve oneself in someone else's affairs for the purpose of
being nosy.
ex: "You the one always dippin' into everybody's business."

dipped adj. (general sl.) old & new school
1. dressed extremely well.
ex: "They all came dipped to my party." "I never seen you dipped like that."

dirt n. (drug sl.) new school
1. bad marijuana. See also: **bap**
ex: "Just don't bring back no dirt."

dirty (pron. durty) n. (w. coast sl.) new school
1. a term of endearment among friends; friend. 2. a way to address someone whose name you do not know or do not want to use in front of others.
ex: "I'm talkin' to you dirty."

[someone who's] **dirty** adj. (criminal sl.) old & new school
1. someone in possession of something illegal [usually drugs and/or guns].
ex: "Let me know right now if you dirty."

[someone who's] **dirty** adj. (general sl.) old & new school
1. unscrupulous; low down; petty, without morals or values.
ex: "You a dirty dude." "That was some dirty sh** you pulled."

dirty bird n. (southern sl.) new school
1. fried chicken or chicken in general.
ex: "I think we havin' that dirty bird tonight."

dirty foots n. (southern sl.) new school
1. females guys only want to be with at night for the purpose of having sex. 2. females that males have sex with but who aren't girlfriends. See also: **hood rats**
ex: "We about to go pickup a couple dirty foots at the Waffle House."

[the] **Dirty South** n. (southern sl.) new school
1. any southern state in America.

[to] **dis** [something] v. (general s1.) old & new school
1. to critique negatively. 2. to express dislike for something verbally or through action.
ex: "They dissed the whole video."

[to] **dis** [someone] v. (general sl.) old & new school
1. to disrespect someone verbally or through one's actions. 2. to reject someone's advances; to brush someone off. (var. [to] **dis the hell/sh** out of** [someone], [to] **dis** [someone] **hard/bad**)
ex: "You think I should go over there and dis'em?" "She dissed the sh** out of ya boy."

[to] **dis the program** phrase (general sl.) old new school
1. to disrespect and betray one's friendship. 2. to do the opposite of what you told someone you was going to do leaving that person feeling betrayed.(var. [to] **dis the whole program)**
ex: "I can't believe she dissed the program."

[to] **dish-out** v. (general sl.) old school
1. to contribute financially; to make payment towards.
ex: "How much I have to dish-out this time?"

[to] **disrespect** [someone's] **game** v. (e. coast sl.) new school
1. to show no respect for someone's talent or abilities. (var. [to] **dis** [someone's] **game**)
ex: "I'm tired of catz keep disrespectin' my game."

dividends n. (general sl.) old & new school
1. money.
ex: "Are you gonna have the dividends to cover that?"

dizzy [females] adj. (general sl.) old & new school
1. females who act silly, naive, and/or generally confused about
simple things.
*ex: "You know some dizzy broads." "Tell them dizzy chicks we not
comin'."*

[to] **do** [oneself] v. (e. coast sl.) new school
1. to do the things that are important to one's own self; to look out
for one's own welfare and well being and interests; to worry about
and tend to one's affairs. See also: **do you**
*ex: "I'm just tryin' to do me." "Let me do me." "I'mma do
me for now on."*

[to] **do** [someone] v. (general sl.) old & new school
1. to beat someone up badly. 2. to kill someone.
ex: "He gonna make me do'em." "He didn't mean to do that cat."

[to] **do** [someone] v. (sexual sl.) old & new school
1. the act of performing oral sex on someone.
ex: "You do me, and I'll do you." "Did he do you?"

do a bear sh** in the woods? phrase (southern sl.) new school
1. an emphatic way to answer "yes" to a question that leaves no
doubt as to your thoughts or point.

[to] **do a switch up change up** v. (general sl.) old & new school
1. to change one's mind, behaviour, attitude or direction suddenly
and without notice or explanation.
*ex: "Just when he thought he had me, I did a switch up change up
and said I had to go home."*

[to] **do** [something] **ass backwards** phrase (general sl.) old school
1. the act of doing something wrong because one didn't take
his/her time, didn't wait/listen to instructions, or failed to heed to
advice.
ex: "You always doin' somethin' ass backwards."

[to] **do big things** phrase (e. coast sl.) new school
1. to do something outstanding or extremely exceptional [often used as praise or encouragement]. (var. [someone who's] **doin' big things/somethin' big/somethin' real big/it real big/it big**)
ex: "Ya man doin' big things in ATL." "Son, I wanna do big things too son."

[a] **do boy** adj. (w. coast sl.) old & new school
1. a follower; flunky. 2. someone who does the biddings of others in order to fit in or be liked. See also: [to] **son** [someone]
ex: "Stop lyin' you was my do boy in jail."

[to] **do dirt** v. (general sl.) old & new school
1. to do something that is wrong and/or deceitful.
ex: "You don't do dirt where you live."

[when you] **do dirt, you get dirt** phrase (e. coast sl.) new school
1. a way to warn or advise someone that when you do wrong expect wrong to be done to him/her.

Do Dirty n. (southern sl.) new school
1. a name used to refer to someone who is low-down, unscrupulous, or sneaky.
ex: "That's ya man Do Dirty for you."

[to] **do** [someone] **dirty** v. (general sl.) old & new school
1. to betray a friend or loved one [for one's personal gain or as the result of jealousy]. 2. to be unfaithful to one's mate.
ex: "She did you real dirty." "Just don't do me dirty."

[to] **do** [some] **dumd sh**** v. (general sl.) old & new school
1. to commit an act that is unbelievabley ridiculous, petty, not well thought out, or highlights one's lack of common sense/intelligence. (var. [to] **do** [some ol'] **dumb sh****)
ex: "Ya man went and did some real dumb sh** today."

do fries come with that shake? phrase (general sl.) old school
1. a term males use to express admiration for a female who has a
big butt or the way a female's butt moves when she walks.

[to] **do** [someone] **greazy** v. (e. coast sl.) new school
1. to be unfaithful to one's lover, mate, or significant other. 2. to
treat someone unkind. (var. [to] **treat** [someone] **greazy**)
*ex: "I think she doin' you greazy." "I would never do you greazy
like that."*

do I look like Boo-Boo The Fool? phrase (southern sl.) new
school
1. a witty way to question someone who you feel is trying to con,
manipulate, or tell you something untrue.

[to] **do** [something] **in the blind** v. (general sl.) new school
1. to do something without having enough information
on how to or the risk involved in doing it.
*ex: "You need to tell me the truth cause I'm not doin' nothin' in
the blind."*

[to] **do some dopefiend sh**** phrase (general sl.) new school
1. to commit an extremely petty act. (var. [to] **do some** [real]
crackhead sh**)
*ex: "Ya man an'nim did some real dopefiend sh** when we went
out to eat with these chicks."*

[to] **do** [someone] **some justice** v (general sl.) old & new school
1. to do someone a favor; to be helpful to someone. 2. the act of
being just to someone. (var. [to] **do/show** [someone] **justice**)
*ex: "When you gonna do me some justice?" "I need you to
do me some justice."*

[to] **do** [someone] **somethin'** v. (general sl.) old & new school
1. to hurt someone as a result of a physical confrontation. 2. the act
of bringing harm to another.
ex: "I heard you tryin' to do me somethin' son."

[to] **do somethin'** [real] **big with** [a female] adj. (sexual sl.) new school
1. a boast made by a male when bragging about his real or imagined sexual conquest with a particular female. (var. [to] **do somethin'** [real] **special with** [a female])
ex: "I'd do somethin' special with Star Jones kid, that's my word!"

do somethin' for the kid/ya homie/ya peoples phrase (general sl.) new school
1. a hip way to request a favor from a friend or love one [usually a financial favor].
ex: "I need you to do somethin' for the kid."

[to] **do** [something] **standin' on** [one's] **head** phrase (e. coast sl.) old & new school
1. to do something with ease [usually used as a boast or a term of encouragement].
ex: "I can do this standin' on my head." "I did that time standin' on my head."

do the dam thing phrase (e. coast sl.) new school
1. an enthusiastic way to encourage or praise someone for doing something bold, gutsy, and spontaneous. (var. [well] **do the dam thing** [then])

[to] **do the knowledge** v. (e. coast sl.) old & new school
1. to think about or give something thought; to figure out something. (var. [to] **do the math**)
ex: "Just do the knowledge first." "That's what she told me, so you do the knowledge."

[to] **do the nasty** v. (sexual sl.) old & new school
1. a convert term females use for having sex. (var. [to] **do the booty**)
ex: "All he comes over for is to do the nasty."

[to] **do** [one's] **thing** v. (general sl.) new school
1. to perform outstanding; to do one's very best. (var. [to] **do**
[one's] **thing to the fullest**)
ex: *"I hafta admit, you went up in there and did ya thing."*

[to] **do** [one's] **thing** [with a female] v. (sexual sl.) new school
1. to perform outstandingly during sex [usually a male boast].
ex: *"You know I took shortie to the crib and did my thing kid."*

do what I say, not [say] **what I do** phrase (general sl.) old &
new school
1. a term used to reprimand someone for pointing out that you
indulge in the same kinds of behavior or acts that you are
demanding that he/she don't partake in.

do you phrase (e. coast sl.) new school
1. a hip and witty way to encourage someone to do what is
important to him/her, or not to worry about anything other than
one's self.
ex: *"All I can tell you is, do you." "You always do you, so this time
is no different."*

do you kiss your mother with a mouth like that? phrase (e. coast
sl.) new school
l. a way to reprimand someone about his/her use of profanity or
foul language.

[something that] **does** [someone] **some justice** phrase (general sl.)
old & new school
1. something that enhances one's appearance or performance.
(var. [something that] **does** [one] **justice**)
ex: *"Try this on, it should do you some justice."*

[someone who] **doesn't hold any/no cut cards** phrase (southern
sl.) old & new school
1. one who says what's on his/her mind without regards to

offending or upsetting others.
ex: "I'mma tell you right now, I don't hold no cut cards for nobody."

[someone who] **doesn't miss a beat** phrase (general sl.) old school
1. a way to recognize or describe one who doesn't miss anything going on around him/her; one that is aware.
ex: "You don't miss a beat do you?"

[to] **dog** [someone] v. (general sl.) old & new school
1. to treat someone badly. 2. to beat someone up badly. 3. to talk badly about someone. (var. [to] **dog** [someone] **out**)
ex: "She dogged ya homeboy." "You be doggin' him."

dog food n. (dru,g sl.) old school
1. a covert way to refer to illegal narcotics.
ex: "How much dog food do they need?"

[one's] **dogs** n. (general sl.) old & new school
1. one's feet or toes. 2. shoes or sneakers
ex: "Don't step on my dogs."

[the person one is] **doin'** v. (sexual sl.) old & new school
1. refers to the person one is having sex with; one's sexual partner.
ex: "Why you worryin' about who I'm doin'?" "Tell me you not doin' my man."

[someone who's] **doin' a** [big] **number** phrase (prison sl.) new school
1. one who is doing an extremely long prison sentence.
ex: "Somebody told me he was doin' a number."

[someone who's] **doin' bad** adj. (general sl.) old & new school
1. one who's destitute; without money; struggling financially. See also: [someone who's] **shootin' bad**
ex: "He been doin' bad since you left."

[someone who's] **doin'** [some/that] **bullsh**** v. (general sl.)
old & new school
1. someone who is exhibiting untrustworthy and deceptive
behavior; to act slyly or cunningly. (var. [someone who's] **doin'
that** [same] **ol' bullsh****)
*ex: "You can't keep doin' that bullsh**." "You always doin' some
bullsh**, that's why I don't mess with you."*

[someone who's] **doin' dirtball bad** adj. (e. coast sl.) new school
1. one who is experiencing extreme financial hardships or is
extremely destitute.
ex: "That whole lil click doin' dirtball bad now."

dolo adj. (e. coast sl.) new school
1. by oneself; alone; solo.
ex: "Tell'er I comin' dolo this time."

dome n. (sexual sl.) new school
1. oral sex.
ex: "The dome wasn't all that."

[one's] **dome** n. (general sl.) old & new school
1. one's head. (var. [one's] **dome piece**) See also: [one's] **grill**
ex: "It hit'em in his dome and he passed out."

[a] **don dada** n. (e. coast sl.) old school
1. the head of an organization 2. the person in charge or the leader;
the boss.
ex: "Here comes the don dada right now."

[you] **done bumped ya head** phrase (southern sl.) new school
1. a way to express disbelief, surprise, or shock when someone
does something or tries to convince you of something outrageous
or ridiculous.
*ex: "I Know you done bumped ya head comin' here without callin'
me first."*

[to get] **done up** v. (e. coast sl.) old & new school
1. to beat someone up badly.
ex: "I'd advise you to keep walkin' kid, before you get done up."

[a females] **donkey** n. (southern sl.) new school
1. a way to refer to a female's butt.
ex: "Did you see the donkey on that girl?"

**don't assume, cause when you do, you make an <u>ass</u> out of <u>you</u>
and <u>me</u>** phrase (general sl.) old & new school
1. a way to respond to someone who says that he/she "assumed"
something. 2. a way to tell someone not to "assume" anything.

don't be scurred phrase (southern sl.) new school
1. a way to tell someone not to be scared [usually used
when one is hesitant or a way to prod].
ex: "You the one that wanted to come, don't be scurred now."

[you] **don't believe sh** stink** phrase (general sl.) old & new
school
1. something you tell someone who fails to take your advice or
warning seriously [used in the context of a warning]. (var. [you]
don't believe sh** stink 'til you smell it/its in your face)
ex: "Don't say nothin' he don't believe sh** stink."

don't believe the hype phrase (e. coast sl.) old school
1. a way to tell someone not to believe something. 2. a way to say
that something is not true or has been exaggerated.

don't count mines phrase (general sl.) old & new school
1. a way to tell someone not to worry about your finances or
financial situation. (var. **let me count mines, can I count mines?**)
*ex: "Worry about yours, don't count mines." "Don't count mines,
I said I didn't have it."*

don't even try it! phrase (general sl.) old & new school
1. a playful or sarcastic way to tell someone not to attempt to con, deceive, convince, or manipulate you. 2. a term used to express disbelief or skepticism of another's sincerity.
ex: "Look shortie, I know it was you so don't even try it."

don't get me started phrase (general sl.) old & new school
1. a way to warn someone that if he/she pushes you, you'll say what is on your mind, what you have been refraining from saying, or you will voice your opinion. (var. **don't get** [him/her/them] **started**)
ex: "You don't wanna get me started." "I'm tellin' you right now, don't get me started."

don't get me to lyin' phrase (southern sl.) new school
1. a witty way to say, "I don't know".

don't get that/it twisted phrase (e. coast sl.) new school
1. a matter of fact way to tell someone not to be "misconstrued" or "confused" as to your intention, meaning, or claim [leaving no room for doubt or question to your seriousness]. (var. **don't get that/it f**ked up**)
ex: "I still know how to make things happen don't get that twisted."

don't go there phrase (general sl.) old & new school
1. a term used to tell someone not to say something he/she knows will unleash bad feelings or memories [usually something from one's past]. 2. a playful or sarcastic way to dismiss one's excuse or explanation [usually cause you feel its a lie]. (var. **don't even go there**)
ex: "Don't go there we already talked about this." "I'm warnin' you don't even go there."

don't hate phrase (general sl.) old & new school
1. a hip and witty way to dismiss someone who's being jealous or overly envious of someone who deserves praise and recognition

[usually used in response to someone's undeserved negative remark towards another]. See also: [to] **hate on** [someone]
ex: "Don't hate cause I still got it goin' on."

don't hate the player hate the game phrase (e. coast sl.) new school
1. a hip and witty way to dismiss someone who's being jealous or overly envious of you when that person has said something to criticize your behavior, character, performance, or boastfulness. (var. **hate the game don't hate the player**)
ex: "If your girl wants to be with me don't hate the player hate the game."

[you] **don't have the sense that God gave you** phrase (general sl.) old & new school
1. a way to reprimand someone who makes a silly mistake or says something ridiculous.

don't knock it/somethin' 'til you try it phrase (general sl.) old school
1. a way to advise someone not to criticize something he/she has never tried or indulged in.

don't knock the hustle phrase (e. coast sl.) new school
1. a way to tell someone not to criticize how you choose to make money or take advantage of situations. 2. a way to tell someone to stop being jealous of you.
ex: "I ain't takin' nothin' from you, so don't knock the hustle."

[to] **don't know** [someone] **from Adam** phrase (general sl.) old & new school
1. a way to say that someone is a stranger; that one doesn't know someone. (var. [to] **don't know** [someone] **from a hole in a wall/from a hole in a doughnut/ from a can of paint/from nowhere**)
ex: "He said he knows me, I don't know that cat from Adam."

[you] don't know the half phrase (general sl.) old & new school
1. a way to tell someone that he/she doesn't know everything, all the details, or the whole truth; there's more to the story. (var. **[you] don't even know the half of it**)
ex: "You come in here yellin' and stuff, and you don't know the half."

[you] don't know your ass from your elbow phrase (southern sl.) old & new school
1. a way to tell someone that he/she doesn't know what he/she is doing or talking about [usually used as an insult].

[I] don't know what kinda/type of time [he/she/they/ya manz/you] **on** phrase (e. coast sl.) old & new school
1. a term used to express uncertainty about one's actions, intentions, or motives.

don't let that go to your head phrase (general sl.) old & new school
1. a way to tell someone to not let something cause him/her to become over confident and cocky.
ex: "Just because you pretty, don't let that go to your head."

don't let the groundhog be ya mailman phrase (southern sl.) new school
1. a sarcastic way to respond to someone who is hurling empty threats at you, talking tough to you, or challenging you [usually used as a warning].

don't let ya mouth write a check ya ass can't cash phrase (general sl.) old & new school
1. a witty way to warn someone not to make threats that he/she can't back up or back out of [often used in a confrontational situation]. (var. **don't let ya mouth get ya ass in trouble**)

don't make me go to that ass phrase (general sl.) old & new school
1. a playful way to threaten someone with a physical beating [often used in response to an offending remark or unwanted comment].

don't meet me there, beat me there phrase (southern sl.) new school
1. a way to tell someone to be somewhere before you get there.

[I] don't mess with [you/him/her/them] **like that** phrase (e. coast sl.) new school
1. a playful or sarcastic way to deny being someone's friend [usually used when denying one's request for a favor or preferential treatment].
ex: "You know I don't mess with you like that."

[you] don't miss a meal phrase (general sl.) old & new school
1. a way to tease someone about eating too much or the fact that he/she is gaining weight.
ex: "Word up Joe, you don't miss a meal."

[you] don't move me phrase (general sl.) old & new school
1. a way to tell someone that he/she does not scare you. 2. a way to respond to one who is hurling empty threats or talking tough to you. (var. [that] **don't move me**)
ex: "Say what you wanna say, you don't move me."

don't play me like that phrase (general sl.) old & new school
1. a sarcastic way to tell someone not to take you for a fool when you feel that person is trying to deceive you or convince you of something totally unbelievable. See also: [to] **play** [someone]
ex: "Don't play me like that son, we too cool for that."

don't play me like that phrase (general sl.) old & new school
1. a way to respond to someone's doubt or wrongful assessment of

your character, actions, intentions, dedication or motives.
ex: "I already told you, don't play me like that."

don't play me, play lotto [you stand a better chance] phrase (e. coast sl.) old & new school
1. a playful or sarcastic way to tell someone to stop trying to con, deceive, or lie to you in an attempt to take advantage of or manipulate you. (var. **don't try me try lotto**)

don't play yaself phrase (general sl.) old & new school
1. a matter of fact way to warn someone not to do something or not to try something. See also: [to] **play** [oneself]
ex: "Don't play yaself when you get there." "I hope you don't play yaself."

don't play yaself or you'll find yaself by yaself phrase (general sl.) old & new school
1. a matter of fact way to warn someone not to do something or not to try something. (var. **don't play yaself or you'll find yaself** [by yaself] **pickin' up yaself**) See also: [to] **play** [oneself]

don't player hate, congratulate phrase (e. coast sl.) new school
1. a hip and witty way to tell someone not to be jealous or over envious of someone who deserves praise and recognition. (var. **don't player hate, participate**) See also: [to] **player hate**

don't put me with that phrase (general sl.) old & new school
1. a way to tell someone not to accuse or implicate your involvement in something.
ex: "I been here all day, don't put me with that."

don't say I never gave you nothin' phrase (general sl.) old & new school
1. a playful or sarcastic comment made when giving a friend or family member something [often reluctantly].

don't start nothin' won't be nothin' phrase (general sl.)
old & new school
1. a playful or sarcastic way to warn someone not to start any
trouble or not to misbehave.

don't sweat that phrase (general sl.) old & new school
1. a way to tell someone not to worry about something or let
something upset or bother him/her. See also: [to] **sweat**
[something]
ex: "I told you don't sweat that." "Look duke, don't sweat that."

don't talk about it, be about it phrase (e. coast sl.) new school
1. a matter of fact way to tell someone to do what he/she says
he/she is going to do instead of just talking about it. 2. a way to
call someone's bluff about something he/she says he/she is going
to do.

don't talk me to death phrase (e. coast sl.) new school
1. a playful or sarcastic way to tell someone to stop talking about
what he/she is going to do, and do it. 2. a way to tell someone to
show you that he/she means business.

don't try me try the bear phrase (southern sl.) new school
1. a hip and witty way to tell someone not to attempt to con,
deceive, or convince you of something that sounds totally
unbelievable.

don't worry, ya momma like it phrase (general sl.) old school
1. a playful or sarcastic way to respond to someone's
criticism or negative remark. (var. **ya momma like it**)

don't you hear/see grown folks talkin'? phrase (general sl.)
old & new school
1. a way to reprimand someone for interrupting your conversation.
2. a way to tell someone that you don't want him/her in your
conversation.

[something that's] **doo-doo** adj. (e. coast sl.) old school
1. big in size, 2. big and gaudy jewelry.
ex: "Doo-doo gold rope chains were in style in the 80's."

[something that's] **doo-doo** adj. (e. coast sl.) old & new school
1. something that is bad quality or poor in performance.
ex: "His live show is doo-doo."

Doo-Doo Brown n. (e. coast sl.) old school
1. a name for someone who has poor hygiene and/or who looks haggard and unkempt 2. another name for bum.
ex: "Ain't that ya man Doo-Doo Brown?"

[someone who's a] **doo-doo picker** adj. (e. coast sl.) old school
1. low down, petty, without morals or values. (var. [someone who's a] **doo-doo pickin'** [type of person])
ex: "I been stopped hangin' out with them doo-doo pickers."
"Here comes your doo-doo pickin' cousin again."

[a] **doo-rag** n. (general sl.) old & new school
1. a nylon head wrap for men.

door knockers n. (e. coast sl.) old school
1. really big gold earrings.

dope n. (drug sl.) old & new school
1. heroin. 2. any kind of illegal narcotic.
ex: "They look for people bringin' dope in all kinds of stuff."

[someone who's] **dope** adj. (general sl.) old school
1. is the best at what he/she does; performs outstandingly; one whose skills excel his/her peers [often used as a praise or boast].
ex: "Now, the way she did that was dope." "I can't help it, I'm just dope."

[something that's] **dope** adj. (general sl.) old school
1. outstanding; unique; the best of its kind.
ex: "Now that was dope." "You don't get no doper than that right there."

[a] **dope boy** n. (drug sl.) old & new school
1. a young male who sells illegal drugs [wholesale or retail].
ex: "Her moms found out her boyfriend was a lil dope boy."

[the] **dope d**k** n. (sexual sl.) old & new school
1. a term used to describe a man's penis when he is having sex while under the influence of heroin which greatly increases the length of time before he will reach an orgasm. (var. [to] **hit** [a female] **with the dope d**k**, [to] **give** [a female] **the dope d**k**)
ex: "A man can have sex for hours when he has the dope d**k."

[a] **dope sack** n. (drug sl.) old school
1. a single bag of heroin retailed at about ten to twenty dollars [sometimes used when referring to a bag of marijuana].
ex: "She flushed his last dope sack down the drain."

[something that's] **doped out** adj. (general sl.) old & new school
1. something that is or has been enhanced in a way that makes it look or perform better than it did in its original form.
ex: "I seen a doped out Lexus truck."

[a] **dopefiend ass** [person] adj. (general sl.) old & new school
1. one who is addicted to crack or heroin. 2. one who will lie, cheat, or steal to get what he/she wants, like someone who is on drugs. (var. [a] **dopefiend ass** [muhf**ka])
ex: "I don't wanna talk to ya dopefiend ass cousin."

[a] **dopefiend move** phrase (general sl.) new school
1. any petty act that is meant to deceive another out of a small amount of money or something of no significant value. (var. [a] **crackhead move**)
ex: "I'm already hip to your dopefiend moves."

[a] **dopefiend story** phrase (general sl.) new school
1. any story that is meant to deceive another out of a small amount of money or something of no signficant value. (var. [a] **crackhead story**)
ex: "He came back with the madd dopefiend story."

[someone who's] **dopefiend sweet** adj. (e. coast sl.) new school
1. extremely easy to deceive, manipulate, or take advantage of. See also: [someone who's] **sweet like bear meat**
ex: "When that C.O. first got here, he was dopefiend sweet."

[something that's] **dopefiend sweet** adj. (e. coast sl.) new school.
1. a food or beverage that's extremely sweetened.
ex: "You know he likes his Koolaid dopefiend sweet."

dosier (pron. doe sher) n. (drug sl.) old school
1. marijuana.

double 4's n. (criminal sl.) old & new school
1. a forty-four (44) magnum handgun.(var. **four-fours**, [a] **four-four**)
ex: "You ever see the hole them double 4's make?"

[to] **double up** v. (general sl.) old & new school
1. to increase an amount of something to twice its original amount [usually used in the increasing of a wager or portion]. (var. [to] **double up on** [someone])
ex: "If you think you can make the shot double up then." "You ready to double that up on me?"

dough n. (general sl.) old & new school
1. money. See also: **loot, papes, scratch**
ex: "She took all the dough I had left."

[a] **dough boy/girl** n. (w. coast sl.) old school
1. a drug dealer.
ex: "This is where all the dough boys hang out."

[to have] **dough mammy** adj. (southern sl.) new school
1. to be rich; wealthy.
ex: "Her pops got dough mammy."

doughnuts n. (drug sl.) old school
1. a covert way to refer to pieces of crack cocaine.

[a] **dove** n. (w. coast sl.) old & new school
1. a twenty dollar bill.
ex: "Let me hold a dove 'til later."

[a] **dove sack** n. (drug sl.) old & new school
1. a twenty dollar bag of marijuana.

down adj. (general sl.) old school
1. hip; cool. (var. [someone who's] **down**)
ex: "She thinks she's down." "He tryin' to act like he's down."

[to] **down** [someone] v. (general sl.) old & new school
1. to sharply criticize someone [usually leading one to feel discouraged and/or unhappy]. See also: [to] **knock** [someone]
ex: "What you get out of downin' people?" "Stop downin' me, and tell me somethin' I can learn from."

[to be] **down** [with something/someone] v. (general sl.) old & new school
1. to be a willing participant; to be involved with something. 2. to be in allegiance with someone no matter what the circumstances; to be a real friend to someone. (var. [to be] **down** [for something/someone])
ex: "Are you gonna be down with this?" "She been down with me from the start."

[a] **down** [ass] **broad/chick/female** adj. (general sl.)
old & new school
1. a female whose character is unwavering even under pressure
and who will show unwavering support to a friend or love one
even if it means putting herself in harms-way.
ex: "I found me a down ass chick this time."

[someone who's] **down by law** adj. (e. coast sl.) old school
1. hip; cool. 2. one whose participation is mandatory.
*ex: "Ya man thinks he's down by law." "You know I'm down by
law."*

[we] **down like four flat tires** phrase (w. coast sl.) old & new
school
1. a term of endearment among friends that professes a strong
feeling of friendship.

[to be] **down with the program** phrase (general sl.) old school
1. to be a willing and knowledgeable participant to a plan, scheme,
or deception.
ex: "As long as you down with program we cool."

[to] **drag** [someone] v. (general sl.) new school
1. to beat someone up badly. 2. to treat someone cruelly and mean.
3. to intentionally stall, delay, or prolong someone. (var. [to] **drag**
[someone] **down through there/through the mud**)
*ex: "She almost made me drag'er ass." "Your girlfriend tryin' to
drag my boy." "I know you tryin' to drag me."*

[the] **drag game** phrase (e. coast sl.) new school
1. the intentional act of prolonging, delaying, or stalling. (var. [to]
put [one's/the] **drag game down**)
*ex: "You don't hafta use ya drag game on me." "That's a nice lil
drag game you got."*

[one's] **dragon** n. (general sl.) old & new school
1. one's bad breath.
*ex: "You need to kill that dragon." "She looked good 'til
I got a whiff of her dragon."*

[to] **drain** [one's] **monster** v. (general sl.) old & new school
1. a term males use to express his need to urinate. (var. [to] **take a
leak**)
ex: "Stop the car so I can drain my monster."

drama n. (general sl.) old & new school
1. situations related to arguments, problems, or confrontations; on
going dispute. 2. controversy and conflicts in one's life caused by
external factors. (var. **strama**) See also: **issues**
*ex: "That whole family stay in some drama." "She came with too
much drama for me."*

[a] **drama queen** n. (general sl.) old & new school
1. a female who is always in the middle of controversy or disputes.
ex: "That chick right there is a straight drama queen."

[to] **drap** [someone] v. (prison sl.) new school
1. to slash someone on the face or neck with a razor blade causing
a long scar [often requiring stitches to close wound]. See also: **a
buck fifty**
ex: "Ya man almost got drapped for his sneakers on the Island."

[someone who's] **drapped** adj. (e. coast sl.) new school
1. someone who is wearing a lot of expensive jewelry. See also:
[someone who's] **heavy**

[to] **draw** [someone's] **card** v. (e. coast sl.) old & new school
1. to reveal someone's secret; to expose someone. (var. [to] **pull**
[someone's] **card**)
*ex: "Don't make me draw ya card dawg." "You should have been
there, she pulled his card in front of everybody."*

dred n. (general sl.) old & new school
1. a name used in reference to someone who has a dredlock hair style and/or is of Jamaican descent. (var. **rude boy, star**)
ex: "Drop by and see the dred before you get here."

[to] **drill** [a female] v. (sexual sl.) new school
1. a male term for having sex. (var. [to] **pound** [a female])
ex: "Did you drill her friend yet?"

drive phrase (southern sl.) new school
1. a way to give someone the authority or permission to do something or continue to do something.
ex: "Keep drivin' I'll let you know when I want the phone back."
"Go ahead and drive dawg."

[someone who's] **drivin'** adj. (southern sl.) new school
1. the person who's in control for the moment. (var. [someone who's in the] **drivers seat**, [someone who's] **drivin' the car**)
ex: "Let me do this, I'm drivin' now."

dro n. (e. coast sl.) new school
1. bright green marijuana grown under water; good marijuana.

[a] **drop** n. (general sl.) old & new school
1. a convertible automobile. (var. [a] **drop top**)

[to] **drop** [someone] v. (general sl.) old & new school
1. to knock someone out or down during a fight.
ex: "He got dropped in the first round." "I was about to drop her ex-boyfriend."

[to] **drop a bomb on** [someone] v. (general sl.) old & new school
1. to reveal a startling revelation to someone when he/she is unsuspecting of what's to come.
ex: "When you gonna drop the bomb on shortie?" "Yo, shortie cold dropped the bomb on me while I was locked down."

[to] **drop a dime on** [someone] v. (criminal sl.) old & new school
1. to inform on someone; to reveal one's secret or wrongdoing to someone with authority.
ex: "They said you dropped a dime on my man."

drop it like its hot phrase (southern sl.) new school
1. an enthusiastic way to tell someone to turn something loose or hand something over.
ex: "Drop it like its hot duke, its my turn."

[to] **drop** [something] **on** [someone] v. (general sl.) old & new school
1. to tell someone something [usually something important or meaningful].
ex: "Let me drop this on you for a minute." "Did she drop it on you yet?"

[to] **drop science** v. (e. coast sl.) old school
1. to give meaningful advice or thought provoking information people can learn from. (var. [to] **kick science/knowledge**)
ex: "I like the way he dropped the science."

[a] **drop shot** n. (southern sl.) old school
1. a female who is very easy to have sex with.
ex: "Don't bring them drop shots to my party."

[to get] **drug** v. (southern sl.) old & new school
1. to be treated extremely cruel by someone you care about. 2. to lose miserably. 3. to be badly beaten up.
ex: "When I was with her, she drug me." "I heard your team got drug in the finals." "Stop lyin', you got drug."

[to] **dry snitch** v. (criminal sl.) old & new school
1. to tell or inform on someone discreetly by giving subtle hints or clues. (var. [to] **dry snitch** [to/on someone])
ex: "My lil brother in there dry snitchin' to my momz."

[a] **dub sack** n. (drug sl.) old & new school
1. a twenty dollar bag of marijuana.

dubs n. (w. coast sl.) old & new school
1. twenty inch rims for an automobile. See also: **sittin' on dubs**
ex: "That joint'll look phat with dubs on it."

[to] **duck** [someone] v. (general sl.) old & new school
1. to purposefully hide from or avoid someone.
ex: "Tell'em I know he duckin' me."

[to] **duck rec** v. (e. coast sl.) new school
1. to back out of or not show up for a prearranged event that involves you competing against another.
ex: "All that trash you talked and when the day comes you duck rec."

duckets n. (general sl.) old school
1. money.
ex: "When can I come over and get them duckets?"

[someone who's] **duckin' them people** phrase (general sl.) old & new school
1. someone who is purposely hiding from or trying to avoid someone he/she owes or is in trouble with [usually the police or one's probation/parole officer]. (var. [someone who's] **duckin' them folks**)
ex: "When you gonna stop duckin' them people?" "You can't duck them folks forever."

dude n. (general sl.) old & new school
1. a way to refer to someone whose name you do not know or do not want to use as a sign of disrespect.
ex: "Tell dude he has to leave." "Who bought dude in here?"

dudes n. (general sl.) old & new school
1. a way to refer to males in general. See also: **catz**
ex: "Dudes be actin' like they can't get it."

[to] **duff** [someone] **up** v. (e. coast sl.) new school
1. to beat someone up.
ex: "I thought I was gonna hafta duff ya boyfriend up for a minute."

Duke Booty n. (e. coast sl.) old school
1. a nickname used when making reference to someone who isn't considered to be hip or cool.
ex: "Let leave Duke Booty here."

dukes n. (e. coast sl.) old & new school
1. a way to refer to someone whose name you do not know or do not want to use as a sign of disrespect. (var. **duke**)
ex: "If dukes is ya people, then you drive 'em."

[a] **dula** (pron. do luh) n. (e. coast sl.) old school
1. someone who is a follower; a flunky. (var. **son dula**)
ex: "Who him, that used to be my dula back in the days."

[something that's] **dumb...** adj. (general sl.) old & new school
1. a term used to emphasize one's description or observation of something. 2. a lot of something; a large amount. See also: **madd**
ex: "He brought her the dumb big diamond ring." "They had dumb food left over."

[someone who's] **dumb as a bag of rocks** phrase (general sl.) new school
1. someone not considered to be smart. (var. [someone who's] **dumb as dirt/as a brick**)
ex: "As good as he looks, he's dumb as a bag of rocks."

dumb dumbs n. (criminal sl.) old & new school
1. hollow point bullets.

[to] **dumb out** v. (e. coast sl.) new school
1. to cause an unpleasant scene by yelling, shouting,
and/or hurling profanity to express one's anger or dissatisfaction.
(var. [to] **dumb out on** [someone]) See also: [to] **spaz**
*ex: "I'm about to dumb out in here." "Shortie dumbed out for no
reason."*

dummies n. (drug sl.) old & new school
1. fake pieces of crack cocaine packaged to fool a buyer into
thinking he/she has purchased the real thing.

[a] **dummy move** phrase (e. coast sl.) new school
1. an act done to deceive or trick someone. (var. [the] **dummy
move**)
*ex: "She thought I was gonna fall for the dummy move." "I'm
about to make this dummy move on her pops."*

[to] **dump on** [someone] v. (criminal sl.) old & new school
1. to shoot at someone.
*ex: "Them fools tried to dump on me while I was drivin' through
the hood."*

[a female who has] **dumps like a truck** phrase (southern sl.) new
school
1. a female with a very big butt
ex: "I definitely like my ladies to have dumps like a truck."

dun n. (e. coast sl.) new school
1. a term of endearment among good friends; a close friend.
*ex: "Them my duns from Farragut projects." "That used to be my
dun, 'til he ratted on me."*

Duncan Hines [over/about something] adj. (prison sl.) new school
1. emotional or sensitive. (var. [to get] **Duncan Hines on**
[someone])
ex: "I know you not about to get Duncan Hines in here."

dunny n. (e. coast sl.) new school
1. a name used to mock and/or dismiss someone as being
unimportant.
ex: "I ain't gonna tell you again dunny."

dust n. (drug sl.) old & new school
1. the illegal drug known as PCP or angel dust.
ex: "I know people that went crazy after smokin' dust."

[to] **dust** [someone] v. (general sl.) old & new school
1. to out run someone. (var. [to] **leave** [someone] **in the dust**)
ex: "I let her catch up a lil then I just dusted her."

[to] **dust** [someone] **off** v. (general sl.) old & new school
1. to beat one's opponent convincingly. (var. [to] **dust** [someone's]
ass off)
ex: "You can get next, after I dust ya man off."

[to] **dust** [something] **off** v. (general sl.) old & new school
1. to finish off a food or drink item.
*ex: "You mind if I dust this off?" "You can dust that off if you
want."*

dusted adj. (drug sl.) old & new school
1. the state of being high on the illegal drug known as PCP or
angel dust.
*ex: "I swear your cousin looked dusted when I seen'em on the
train."*

Dutch Master n. (drug sl.) old & new school
1. the brand name of the cigar sometimes used to roll marijuana in.
(var. [a] **dutch**) See also: [a] **philly blunt**

[when someone is] **dyin'** [for/to get something] adj. (general sl.)
old & new school
1. to want something desperately.
ex: "I know you dyin' to get in my pants." "I'm just dyin' to take you out on a date."

dyin' [laughing] adj. (general sl.) old & new school
1. to laugh extremely hard.
ex: "I was dyin' when I heard that." "She had me dyin'."

dynamite sticks n. (general sl.) new school
1. cigarettes. See also: **cancer sticks, joes**
ex: "She lit up a dynamite stick, and I kicked'er out my car."

e

[to] **ear hustle** v. (e. coast sl.) new school
1. to eavesdrop [often repeating what one hears falsely claiming to be the source of information]. See also: [to] **burglarize** [someone's] **conversation**
ex: "Don't say nothin' she in here tryin' to ear hustle." "There you go ear hustlin' again."

early! n. (e. coast sl.) new school
1. a term used as an exclamation point at the end of one's boast, boisterous claim, tough talk, or threat [leaving no doubt to one's seriousness].
ex: "That's how you pimp fa real shortie, early!"

[an] **early bird** n. (general sl.) old school
1. one who departs earlier then an event is scheduled to end; one who goes to bed extremely early.
ex: "Why you always hafta be the early bird?"

[an] **earth** n. (e. coast sl.) old & new school
1. a female whole is a member of the Five Percent Nation [usually the girlfriend of male member]
ex: "That's his new earth."

ease up phrase (general sl.) old school
1. a way to say, "calm down", "slow down", or "relax".
ex: "You need to ease up homie, talkin' like that."

[a female who's] **easy access** adj. (sexual sl.) old school
1. easy to have sex with. 2. extremely promiscuous.
ex: "How you know shortie ain't easy access?"

[to] **eat** [something] v. (general sl.) new school
1. to accept something grudgingly.
ex: "I'mma eat that this time."

[to] **eat** [someone's] **food** v. (e. coast sl.) new school
1. to assault someone with the intent to cause great bodily
harm or death. 2. to take one's possessions with the use of
violence.
ex: "Them catz talkin' about eatin' ya food."

[to] **eat off** [someone] v. (general sl.) old & new school
1. to use someone's resources, connections, or success to support
or sustain you financially.
*ex: "Them catz been eatin' off me for years." "I let you eat off me
for too long."*

[to] **eat off** [something] v. (general sl.) old & new school
1. to reap financial security from a goal, idea, plan, or successful
endeavor.
ex: "This is something that we can eat off for years."

[a] **eight-ball** n. (drug sl.) old & new school
1. 3 ½ grams of cocaine.
ex: "She can sniff an eight-ball by herself."

eight-ball n.(general sl.) old school
1. Old English Malt Liquor.
ex: "He talking like that cause he's full of that eight-ball."

[an] **el** n. (drug sl.) old & new school
1. a cigar that has been or is about to be unrolled and emptied of its
original tobacco, refilled with marijuana, and then re-rolled.
ex: "They did about three els on the way here."

[an] **elbow** n. (prison sl.) new school
1. a life sentence in prison without the possibility of parole. See
also: [an] **"L"**

ex: "Her baby father is the one who got her an elbow." "We lookin' at an elbow if we blow trial."

emphatically non-cipher! interj. (e. coast sl.) old school
1. an enthusiastic way to disagree or voice one's strong opposition. 2. a way to say, "absolutely not", "no", "that's not right" [often used when denying].
ex: "That's emphatically non-cipher, Hip-Hop started in the Bronx."

[to] **empty out** v. (criminal sl.) old & new school
1. to repeatedly fire one's gun [usually until the gun is emptied]. See also: [to] **dump on** [someone]
ex: "Police tried to empty out on my manz, and he didn't even have a weapon."

ends n. (general sl.) old & new school
1. money.
ex: "When can I get them ends you owe me?"

enough said! interj. (general sl.) new school
1. an enthusiastic way to emphasize that one's position, declaration, or thought is undoubtedly correct and without need for further discussion or questioning [often used to terminate discussion on a subject].
ex: "You heard it for yourself, enough said!"

equal n. (drug sl.) new school
1. marijuana.

[a] **equalizer** n. (criminal sl.) new school
1. a firearm; a lethal weapon.
ex: "You know he keeps an equalizer on'em."

even Stevens phrase (general sl.) old school
1. to be even with someone after you have exacted revenge on that person for wronging you. 2. the act of paying someone back something that is owed to him/her.
ex: "I'm satisfied now, we even Stevens."

everybody and their mother... phrase (general sl.) old & new school
1. a way to emphasize a large number of people when referring to the number of people one is talking about.
ex: "Everybody and their mother gonna want one now." "Seemed like everybody and their mother was there."

everything ain't for everybody phrase (e. coast sl.) new school
1. a way to tell someone something is none of his/her business or is a secret. 2. a way to mock someone who is trying to get you to tell him/her something. 3. a way to tell someone to "stop being nosy" "you don't need to know".

[when] **everything is everything** phrase (e. coast sl.) old & new school
1. a way to express that things are, "satisfactory", "fine", "okay", or "cool". (var. [when] **everything is up to par**)
ex: "When I called she said, everything is everything."

[when] **everything is love/love-love/lovely** adj. (general sl.) old & new school
1. fine; o.k.; satisfactory; well.
ex: "Is everything love with y'all?"

[to] **expose** [someone] v. (e. coast sl.) new school
1. to reveal something about someone that he/she is trying to hide [usually used in reference to one's character or capabilities]. See also: [to] **put** [one's] **business out in the street**
ex: "Say somethin' slick and I'mma expose you in front of all ya peoples."

eye candy n. (e. coast sl.) new school
1. an attractive female.

[to] **eye hustle** v. (e. coast sl.) new school
1. to watch slyly [for the purpose of being nosy]; to spy or steal a look.
ex: "Look at them chickens over there eye hustlin'."

[a] **eye jammy** n. (e. coast sl.) old & new school
1. a black or swollen eye [usually resulting from being punched in the eye].
ex: "I heard ya girl's the one who gave you the eye jammy."

[one whose] **eyes are bigger than his/her belly** phrase (general sl.) old & new school
1. a way to refer to someone who cannot eat the amount of food he/she ordered or placed on his/her plate.

f

fa real though (pron. doe) phrase (southern sl.) new school
1. a way to express being in agreement with or being able to relate to something someone says. 2. a way to affirm or reaffirm one's statement leaving no room for doubt that one meant what he/she said. 3. a way to emphasize one is telling the truth. (var. **fa real-fa real**)
ex: "Fa real though, I never liked'em in the first place."

fa sheezy phrase (w. coast sl.) new school
1. a hip way to say, "for sure" or "yes". 2. a witty way to affirm or reaffirm one's position or thought leaving no room for doubt or question. (var. **fa shizzle**)
ex: "Fa sheezy, we all gonna be there." "That's fa shizzle."

fa shizzle my nizzle phrase (w. coast sl.) new school
1. a witty way to say "for sure my friend" or "yes my friend". (var. **fa sheezy my neezy**)
ex: "Fa shizzle my nizzle I'll be to pick you up around seven o'clock."

fa the longest phrase (general sl.) old & new school
1. a way to refer to a long period of time. 2. a way to say, "for a long period of time", "for a very/real long time". (var. **fa ever**)
ex: "I been tryin' to tell you this fa the longest." "They been gone for the longest."

face n. (sexual sl.) new school
1. oral sex. (var. [to] **give** [someone] **face**) See also: **brains**

[a] **face card** n. (e. coast sl.) new school
1. a new one hundred dollar bill with the big face. See also: **big faces**

ex: "I gave'er a face card and told'er to beat it."

face down, ass up phrase (criminal sl.) new school
l. a command to get face down on the ground heard during the commission of a armed robbery. See also: **all I wanna see is assholes and elbows**

facety adj. (general sl.) old & new school
l. arrogant; insolent; disrespectful; to have a bad attitude.
ex: "Why you always actin' so facety?"

[to] **fade** [someone] v. (w. coast sl.) old & new school
l. to out perform or do better than. 2. to beat someone up; to physically confront someone.
ex: "You can't fade me." "Ya man was about to get faded up in here."

[a female who's] **faded off the licks** adj. (e. coast sl.) new school
l. intoxicated; drunk.
ex: "I'm the one who drove them home cause her and her friends was faded off the licks."

fair exchange ain't no robbery phrase (e. coast sl.) old & new school
l. a way to express that something is or was a fair trade, deal, or agreement.
ex: "I got what I want, you got what you want, fair exchange ain't no robbery."

[someone who's] **fake** adj. (e. coast sl.) new school
l. one who pretends to be something that he/she is not [usually tough, wealthy, intelligent, authoritative, or extremely hip]. 2. one who never means what he/she says [usually willing to say anything to get his/her way]. (var. [someone who's a] **fake ass** [person])
ex: "I never realized how fake you was." "Get ya fake ass out my house."

[to] **fake a move** phrase (e. coast sl.) old & new school
1. to go back on one's word. 2. to lie; to pretend to be someone
you are not. 3. the act of making numerous excuses. 4. to do the
opposite of what one said he/she was going to do. (var. [to] **fake a
move on** [someone], [to] **fake the funk**, [to] **fake the funk on**
[someone]) See also: [to] **play** [someone] **to the left**
*ex: "We came all the way out here and she faked a move." "I'm
about to fake a move on this cat."*

fake it, 'til you can make it phrase (southern sl.) new school
1. a way to encourage someone to pretend/act like he/she knows
how to do something or knows what is going on.

fake ones n. (e. coast sl.) new school
1. people who pretend to be one's friend but who really aren't.
ex: "He turned out to be one of them fake ones."

[to] **fake** [someone] **out** v. (general sl.) old & new school
1. to deceive or con someone; to lie. 2. to do the opposite of what
one promised or was predicted to do. (var. [the] **fake out**)
*ex: "I think shortie tryin' to fake us out." "Word up son, that's the
fake out for sure."*

[someone who's] **fakin'** adj. (e. coast sl.) new school
1. pretending. 2. making outrageous claims, boasts, promises. 3.
trying to come across as tough or dangerous [but falling short of
doing so]. 4. not serious or dedicated to what he/she is saying or
doing. (var. [someone who's] **fakin' jacks**, [someone who's]
fakin' like bacon)
ex: "I already know you fakin'." "Stop fakin' jacks."

[a] **fakin' Jamaican** adj. (general sl.) old & new school
1. one who pretends to be of Jamaican decent by imitating the
Jamaican accent. See also: [an] **impasta rasta**

[to] **fall-back** v. (e. coast sl.) new school
1. to take some time [usually to re-evaluate or reflect upon].

2. to take it easy; relax.
ex: "I told shortie she need to fall-back I'm not ready for a relationship." "I knew it was time for me to fall-back then."

fall-back phrase (e. coast sl.) new school
1. a term used to dismiss someone who is annoying, harassing, or pestering you.
ex: "Fall-back man, I already told you I'd take care of it."

[to] **fall off** phrase (general sl.) old & new school
1. to show a decline in one's performance, ability, or financial status; to lose stature. 2. a way to negatively critique one's present performance compared to past performances. (var. [to] **fall off like a bad bag of dope**)
ex: "I'd be the first to tell you, if you fallin' off."

[to] **fall out with** [someone] v. (general sl.) old & new school
1. to have an argument, disagreement, or confrontation with someone [that could possibly lead to the breakup of a friendship/relationship with that person]. (var. [to] **fall out over/about** [something])
ex: "I'm not about to fall out with you because of something she said." "They fell out over the same guy."

[to] **fall up in** [somewhere] phrase (general sl.) new school
1. to arrive; to make an appearance. (var. [to] **fall up in there/in the spot**)
ex: "We probally fall up in there around six." "We fell up in the spot and got madd love."

fam n. (e. coast sl.) new school
1. a term of endearment among friends and/or family members; friend. 2. an abbreviation for the word "family". (var. **family**, [one's] **fam/family/fam-do**)
ex: "What's up fam?" "Where you goin' fam?" "That's my fam." "I can't say no to family."

[a] **fashion dred** adj. (e. coast sl.) old & new school
1. someone who wears a dredlock hair style for fashion opposed to cultural or religious beliefs. (var. [a] **Soul Train dred**)
ex: "All these catz in here are fashion dreds."

fast you past, slow you blow phrase (general sl.) old school
1. a way to mock or tease someone for not being quick, or tardy enough causing him/her to miss out on an opportunity.

[someone who's] **fatal** adj. (general sl.) old & new school
1. overly infatuated or in love with someone so deep that it causes him/her to display erratic behavior and/or violent tendencies towards the person he/she has the infatuation or love for.
ex: "Somethin' told me that broad was fatal when I first met'er."

[to] **fatten** [someone] **up** phrase (prison sl.) new school
1. to give someone a larger quantity of food than he/she is supposed to receive [usually used in the context of a request].
ex: "Fatten me up homeboy." "You think you can fatten me up next time?"

[something that's] **faulty** adj. (southern sl.) new school
1. poor in quality or performance [used as a negative critique or insult].
ex: "Everything about ya game is faulty."

fed adj. (general sl.) old & new school
1. to have had enough of one's actions or behavior one finds upsetting or bothersome. (var. [to be] **fed up with** [someone/something]/[someone's] **sh**/bullsh****)
ex: "I'm fed with all ya lies."

[someone who's a] **Fed** n. (criminal sl.) new school
1. someone who is a informer for a law enforcement agency; a snitch. (var. [someone who's been] **deputized**, [someone who's] **police, po-po, five-o**)
ex: "Stay away from that cat, he a Fed now."

[the] **Feds** n. (criminal sl.) old & new school
1. any Federal law enforcement agent or agency [D.E.A., F.B.I., U.S. Marshals, U.S. Attorney, U.S. District Court].
ex: "The Feds picked my man up for a drug conspiracy."

[the] **Feds** n. (prison sl.) old & new school
l. Federal prison.
ex: "The most famous rumor about the Feds is the one about there being swimming pools."

[to] **feed** [someone something] v. (general sl.) old & new school
1. to give someone information that isn't true in an attempt to incite, anger, or up set that person; to lie to someone.
*ex: "I believed all that stuff you was feedin' me." "Don't feed me that bullsh**."*

[to] **feed into** [something] v. (general sl.) new school
1. to let something that was intentionally meant to upset, anger, bother, or make you emotional, succeed in making you react in the way intended. 2. to let someone antagonize you in a way that causes you to respond.
ex: "Just ignore 'em, don't feed into his mess." "I'm not about to feed into nonsense."

[to] **feed off** [someone] v. (general sl.) old & new school
1. to be inspired, motivated, or influenced by one's character or actions.
ex: "We posed to feed off each other."

[to] **feel** [something] v. (general sl.) old & new school
1. to like. 2. the ability to relate and understand. 3. to be in agreement with. 4. to feel moved or influenced by. (var. [to] **feel** [someone], [to] **feel** [someone] **on** [something])
ex: "Yo, I'm feelin' that." "Can you feel what I'm sayin'?" "I was really feelin' that speech." "I definitely feel you on that."

[to] **feel a way** [about something] v. (e. coast sl.) new school

1. to be upset, bothered, or angered. 2. to have an unpleasant or uneasy feeling. (var. [to] **feel some kinda way** [about something]) *ex: "She might feel a way if I bring you." "I could tell you felt some kinda way having to tell'em."*

feel me phrase (general sl.) new school
1. a term one uses in the attempt to get someone to listen to, relate to, or pay attention to something he/she is saying or trying to convince one of.
ex: "Feel me on this." "Feel me, and then tell me what you would have done."

[you] feelin' froggy? phrase (southern sl.) old & new school
1. a way to question someone who appears to want to physically confront you while at the same time prodding him/her into a fight. (var. [if] **you feel like a glass, break,** [if] **you feel like a frog leap**)
ex: "All we want to find out is, are you feelin' froggy?"

felines n. (general sl.) new school
1. females.

[to] fess up v. (general sl.) old & new school
1. to admit or confess; to take the blame or responsibility. (var. [to] **fess up to** [something])
ex: "Be quiet, stupid, he already fessed up."

fetti n. (W. coast sl.) new school
1. money.
ex: "They toss around madd fetti every time they come in here."

fever n. (general sl.) old & new school
1. a term used for the number "five" in any game that requires the tossing of dice.
ex: "You need to roll fever to win this game."

fever in the funk house phrase (general sl.) old & new school

1. an enthusiastic chant for luck when one is tossing the dice and the number he/she wishes to make is the number five.

[to] **fiend** [for something] adj. (e. coast sl.) new school
1. to want something desperately. See also: **jonesin'**
ex: "My man fiendin' to go out with you." "She fiendin' for a ride on ya bike."

[a] **fiend** n. (drug sl.) old & new school
1. someone addicted to an illegal drug [usually refers to a person addicted to crack cocaine]. (var. [a] **dopefiend**, [a] **junky**)
ex: "Boy you better get them fiends out my house." "Don't be havin' them fiends knockin' on my door."

[a] **fiend book/movie** n. (sexual sl.) new school
1. a pornographic book or movie. See also: **shorteyes**
ex: "My girl gets mad when she finds my fiend books."

[a] **fiend monster** n. (sexual sl.) new school
1. someone who owns and/or spends a great deal of time reading or watching pornographic material.

[to] **fiend off of** [someone] v. (sexual sl.) new school
1. to use someone or the thought of someone as the focus of one's lust or sexual fantasy. (var. [to] **fiend on** [someone], [to] **get** [one's] **fiend on**)
ex: "He been in there fiendin' off that picture all day." "I'm about to go in there and get my fiend on."

[to] **fiend** [someone] **out** v. (criminal sl.) old & new school
1. the act of putting someone in a choke hold, headlock, or strangle hold [usually in the commission of a mugging] possibly causing the person to pass out. (var. [to] **dopefiend** [someone], [to] **put the fiend/dopefiend on** [someone]) See also: [to] **yolk** [someone]
ex: "Two dudes fiend 'em out and took 'is watch."

[a] **fifth** n. (criminal sl.) old & new school

1. a 45-caliber handgun.
ex: "Jake found a loaded fifth under the seat."

fifty-four elevens n. (e. coast sl.) new school
1. Reebok Classics for women [which cost $49.99 and with tax the cost is $54.11].
ex: "When I met you, you was wearin' a beat up pair of $54.11's and now you think you all that."

fifty 'leven times phrase (southern sl.) old & new school
1. a witty way to refer to the numerous amount of times someone did something. (var. **fifty million times**)
ex: "She had to call me about fifty 'leven times."

fight or take flight phrase (southern sl.) new school
1. a way to tell someone either he/she fights or runs away.
ex: "What you gonna do, fight or take flight?"

figures n. (general sl.) new school
l. money.
ex: "Just make sure them figures right." "I need my figures by tomorrow."

filthy adj. (e. coast sl.) new school
1. extremely rich.
ex: "Them catz was filthy back in the days."

find you some business phrase (southern sl.) new school
1. a way to tell someone to stop bothering or pestering you. 2. a way to say, "leave me alone", "get away from me", "stop annoying me". (var. [you] **need to find you some business/something to do**)

finders keepers, losers weepers phrase (general sl.) old & new school
1. a term used to tease someone who has lost something that you have found and refuse to give back.

[someone who's] **finished** adj. (criminal sl.) old & new school
1. someone who is facing or has been sentenced to a very long prison term [usually 20 years-life without parole].
ex: "They went down to VA got caught up and now they finished."

[something that's] **fire** adj. (e. coast sl.) new school
1. outstanding; unique; the best of its kind. (var. [something that's]
on fire/barbecue)
ex: "50 whole CD is on fire."

[to] **fire** [someone] v. (general sl.) old & new school
1. to end an intimate relationship abruptly. See also: [to] **kick**
[someone] **to the curb**
ex: "Shortie started talkin' crazy, so I fired'er."

fire launchers n. (criminal sl.) new school
1. a firearm. (var. **flame throwers**)

[to] **fire on** [someone] v. (southern sl.) old & new school
1. to hit or punch someone [usually when one isn't expecting to be hit or punched]. See also: [to] **snuff** [someone]
ex: "She just fired on my ex-girl for no reason."

[to] **fire** [someone] **up** v. (general sl.) new school
1. to beat someone up.
ex: "I came this close to firin' his ass up."

[to] **fire** [something] **up** v. (general sl.) new school
1. to light a cigarette or marijuana joint/"blunt" and proceed to smoke. See also: [to] **burn**
ex: "Let's fire the last one up before we go inside."

[a] **fish market move** phrase (e. coast sl.) old & new school
1. acts that are deceitful, sneaky, and/or petty. 2. acts that are meant to cheat people. (var. [to try/make/pull a] **fish market move**)
ex: "That was a real fish market move you tried."

fish scale n. (drug sl.) old & new school
1. a type of powder cocaine that resembles the scales of a fish. (var. **mother of pearl**)

fiteen (pron. fit een) n. (e. coast sl.) old & new school
1. fifteen (15).
ex: "She looks older than fiteen." "He scored about fiteen."

[a] **fitted** n. (general sl.) new school
1. an athletic baseball cap. See also: [a] **throwback**
ex: "I copped this vintage Yankee fitted."

fitty n. (e. coast sl.) old & new school
1. fifty (50).
ex: "I need about fitty dollars to get that.." "I lost fitty."

five-o n. (criminal sl.) old & new school
1. police; law enforcement agents. 2. one who informs on others to the police.
ex: "Let's go, here comes five-o."

[someone who's] **five on it** adj. (drug sl.) new school
1. under the influence of marijuana; "high".
ex: "You can't tell me shes's not five on it lookin' like that."

[to] **fix** [one's] **mouth/face to say** [something] v. (general sl.) new school
1. to have the audacity to say something.
ex: "I can't even see how you have the nerve to fix ya mouth to say something to me like that."

fix ya face phrase (general sl.) new school
1. a playful or sarcastic way to tell someone to take the shocked, amazed, puzzled look off his/her face [usually used when taunting one's opponent].
ex: "Fix ya face dawg, better luck next time."

fixin' phrase (southern sl.) old & new school
1. getting ready to; about to; preparing to. (var. **fin, fittin'**)
ex: "We fixin' to leave in a hour." "Where you think you fixin' to go?"

flags n. (e. coast sl.) new school
1. colored bandannas. See also: **soldier rags**

flam adj. (e. coast sl.) new school
1. flamboyant.
*ex: "You the one come in here tryin' to act all flam and sh**."*

[a] **flamer** n. (criminal sl.) new school
1. a firearm; handgun.
ex: "They never found the flamers."

[something that's] **flamin'** adj. (e. coast sl.) new school
1. outstanding; unique; the best of its kind. (var. [something that's]
flamin' hot) See also: [something that's] **blazin'**
ex: "Them catz came through with some bikes that was flamin."

flarge adj. (e. coast sl.) new school
1. a way to put emphasis on one's financial wealth or worth; rich.
ex: "He ain't broke no more, that cat is flarge." "When you flarge you can do them type of things."

[to] **flash the burner on** [someone] v. (criminal sl.) new school
1. the act of making one's firearm visible in an attempt to scare or intimidate someone.
ex: "When I got on the elevator, grandmomz flashed the burner on me just to let me know."

flat broke adj. (general sl.) old & new school
1. without money; destitute. See also: **broke as a joke**
ex: "This time of the week, I'm always flat broke."

[a] **flatfoot hustle** n. (e. coast sl.) old & new school

1. any means of making money that consist of being out on the street for long periods of time.

[a] **flat leaver** phrase (general sl.) old school
1. one who abruptly leaves the company of someone to be in the company of someone else; to rudely depart one's ompany. (var. [to] **flat leave** [someone])
ex: "I'm not goin' anywhere with you, cause you a flat leaver." "She'll flat leave you in a heartbeat."

[to] **flat out** [do/say something] v. (general sl.) old & new school
1. to boldly do or say something with disregard to what the consequences may be; to be direct and straightforward.
ex: "I flat out told'er her breath stink." "I told'em flat out, this is not going to work."

[someone with] **flavor** (pron. flava) adj. (general sl.) old school
1. stylishness. 2. one who has an air of self confidence that enhances his/her character.
ex: "You never seen flavor like this, before you met me." "I'm the one with all the flavor around here."

[to] **flex** v. (general sl.) old & new school
1. to flaunt one's material wealth or possessions in order to bring attention to oneself. (var. [to] **flex on** [someone]) See also: [to] **profile**
ex: "They all was out there flexin' their new cars."

[to] **flex on** [someone] v. (general sl.) old & new school
1. to act tough and/or aggressively when one is with his/her friends because one feels his/her friends will back him/her up in a confrontation.
ex: "Remember you tried to flex on me when you was with ya boys?"

[to] **flex with** [someone] v. (e. coast sl.) old & new school

1. to be friends with and socialize with someone on a regular basis. (var. [to] **chill with** [someone])
ex: "I used to flex with them catz back in the days."

[a] **flick** n. (general sl.) old & new school
1. a picture or movie.
ex: "How did the flicks come out?" "That was a real good flick."

[to] **flick it up** [with someone] v. (general sl.) old & new school
1. the act of taking a picture or numerous pictures. 2. to see more than one movie at a movie theater.
ex: "Don't go nowhere, we about to flick it up." "You tryin' to flick it up tonight?"

[to] **flip** [something] v. (drug sl.) old & new school
1. the act of selling one's drugs. See also: [to] **bubble** [something]
ex: "How long you think its gonna take to flip this?" "Once I can flip this we outta here."

[to] **flip** v. (criminal sl.) old & new school
1. to become a cooperating witness for the State or the Government against someone one committed a crime with in a deal for leniency. (var. [to] **flip on** [someone], [to] **flip the script** [on someone])
ex: "Word is, ya man about to flip." "He the one who flipped on L."

[to] **flip** [something] v. (general sl.) old & new school
1. to take something and change it from its original form and make it better. 2. to do something that is almost impossible to imitate or duplicate.
ex: "I liked the way she just flipped the whole song." "See if he can flip it like this."

[to] **flip** v. (general sl.) old & new school

1. to change one's mood, personality, or attitude suddenly and without any apparent reason. 2. to betray one's friendship and trust. 3. to cause an unpleasant scene by becoming loud and disruptive when one is upset or angry. (var. [to] **flip on** [someone], [to] **flip the script**, [to] **flip the script on** [someone], [to] **flip like pancakes/a light switch**)
ex: "I don't know why she flippin' like that." "Duke just flipped for no resaon."

[a] **flip artist** adj. (general sl.) old & new school
1. someone with constant mood swings and/or an unpredictable way of treating his/her friends. 2. one who holds no loyalty towards friendship and will betray a friend for his/her own personal gain.
ex: "He's cool, but he's also a flip artist so you better be on point."

[to] **flip burgers** phrase (general sl.) old & new school
1. to work for a fast food restaurant.
ex: "He said he'd flip burgers if he had to, he done with the streets."

[someone who's in] **flip mode** adj. (general sl.) old & new school
1. a way to describe someone's disposition when he/she is going through one of his/her mood swings. (var. [someone who's on/in] **flip mode status**)
ex: "As soon as she opened the door she went in to flip mode."

[to] **flip** [one's] **money** v. (general sl.) old & new school
1. to use one's money to purchase something that he/she is going to sell in order to make more money and buy more of what he/she is selling.
ex: "What I need to do to flip this money?" "I thought you was gonna help me flip my money."

[to] **flip sh** around** v. (general sl.) old & new school

1. to change the facts, truths, or events around when explaining a story/situation to benefit one's self [often putting the blame on someone else if possible].
ex: "I don't hafta flip sh** around I'm gelling you the truth."

[the] **flip side of** [something] phrase (general sl.) old & new school
1. the advantages of something compared to the disadvantages of something. 2. the other side of a story or situation. (var. **the other half**)
ex: "You might get away, but the flip side is you get caught and go to jail." "Now listen to the flip side."

[to] **flip weight** v. (drug sl.) old & new school
1. the act of selling ounce quantities to kilogram quantities of an illegal drug. (var. [to] **flip them things**)
ex: "They got large flippin' weight outta town."

[to] **flood** [a piece of jewelry] v. (e. coast sl.) new school
1. to have a large amount of quality diamonds added to a piece of jewelry [a watch, ring, pendant, or chain]. (var. [to] **flood** [something] **out**)
ex: "I'mma flood my shortie watch for her birthday."

[to] **flood the block** phrase (drug sl.) new school
1. the act of having numerous individuals selling drugs for the same person in the same area [making it hard for rival drug dealers to make money]. (var. [to] **flood** [one's] **block with work**)
ex: "What makes you think you can just flood the block like that?"

[to] **floss** v. (w. coast sl.) new school
1. to flaunt one's material wealth or possessions in order to bring attention to oneself. (var. [to] **floss on** [someone]) See also: [to] **highside**
ex: "People get jealous when we come through flossin'."

[a] **flossaholic** adj. (southern sl.) new school

1. one who is addicted to spending large amounts of money and showing off his/her material wealth [jewelry, cars, etc].
ex: "The money turned ya man into a flossaholic."

flossy adj. (w. coast sl.) new school
1. a way to describe someone who is flaunting his/her material wealth [jewelry, cars, etc].
ex: "Ya peoples came through actin' a lil flossy."

[one's] **flow** n. (general sl.) old & new school
1. one's unique ability to communicate or express himself/herself verbally. 2. the unique way a rapper delivers his/her rhymes.
ex: "She said ya flow was weak." "Where you get that whack ass flow?"

flow n. (e. coast sl.) new school
1. money. See also: **cash flow**
ex: "I'm tryin' to get my flow right."

[a] **flunky** adj. (general sl.) old & new school
1. someone who does the biddings of others to receive acceptance and recognition; a follower.
ex: "If you lookin' for a flunky, I'm not him."

[to] **fly** [something] v. (e. coast sl.) old & new school
1. to open up an establishment for business [usually as a front to sell illegal drugs from]. (var. [to] **fly a spot**)
ex: "I'm thinkin' about flyin' me a barbershop in N.C."

[something that's] **fly** adj. (general sl.) old & new school
1. outstanding; unique; the best of its kind. 2. stylish; hip; trendy. (var. [something that's] **fly as hell/ as I don't know what**)
ex: "I read the book, the movie gonna be fly."

[someone who's] **fly** adj. (general sl.) old school
1. stylish; hip; trendy. 2. one who as an overrated opinion of his/her self worth or stature; conceited. (var. [a] **fly guy/girl**)

ex: "All her friends are fly." "I can't stand them fly guys."

[to] **fly** [someone] **a kite** v. (prison sl.) old & new school
1. to send someone a correspondence through the mail [usually letter is sent to or from someone incarcerated].
ex: "When the last time you flew your brother a kite?"

[to] **fly** [someone's] **head** v. (e. coast sl.) old & new school
1. to beat someone up [usually used as an offhanded threat]. (var. [to] **fly that head**)
ex: "I was about to fly ya ex-girl's head." "Somebody gonna fly that head one day."

folk n. (w. coast sl.) old & new school
1. a term of endearment among friends; friend. (var. [someone who's] **folk/folks**)
ex: "Tell folk I said get at me." "That's folks cuz, show some respect."

[one's] **folks** n. (w. coast sl.) old & new school
1. one's group of friends. 2. members of the same gang.
ex: "When it goes down I'm ridin' with my folks." "All these catz in here are folks."

food n. (drug sl.) old & new school
1. a covert way to refer to drugs.
ex: "I'm bringin' the food with me when I come."

fool n. (w. coast sl.) old & new school
1. a term of endearment among friends; friend. 2. a way to refer to someone whose name you don't know or don't want to use in front of others.
ex: "Where you been fool?" "Why you trippin' fool?"

[a] **fool ass** [person] adj. (general sl.) old & new school

1. one whose actions and character project an image of utter foolishness, one not to be taken serious, or one who is considered a clown.
ex: "Tell me, who gonna listen to this fool ass news dude tryin' to dis Luda?"

foolery n. (e. coast sl.) new school
1. fake or imitation jewelry. 2. inexpensive jewelry trying to pass as expensive jewelry. (var. **foolry**)
ex: "Main man came to the club with a neck full of that foolery."

foolio n. (w. coast sl.) new school
1. a way to refer to someone who is acting foolish, silly, or immature.
ex: "Look at ya man foolio over there."

foot soldiers n. (e. coast sl.) old & new school
1. the people who do the biddings of others or take orders from other people [usually refers to the people who are out selling drugs for someone else]. (var. [one's] **foot soldiers**)
ex: "I lookin' for a few good foot soldiers."

[a] football number adj. (prison sl.) new school
1. 15, 20, 25 or more yearson a prison sentence. (var. **football numbers**)
ex: "He's in the Feds doin' a football number."

for a pretty female, you have a ugly attitude phrase (e. coast sl.) new school
1. a playful or sarcastic way to reprimand an attractive female displaying a nasty attitude or arrogant disposition.

for every action, there's a reaction phrase (general sl.) new school
1. a way to warn or advise someone to consider the consequences and/or repercussions of a negative action.

[to] **form voltron** v. (e. coast sl.) old school
1. the coming together of a group of friends and/or family members to confront a crisis and/or to show support for one in the group. (var. [to] **form**, [to] **form on** [someone])
ex: "As soon as they started formin' voltron, I left."

[a] **forty** n. (general sl.) old & new school
1. a forty ounce of beer.
ex: "Its your time to get the forties."

Forty One Shortie n. (southern sl.) new school
1. a nickname for a female who drinks a lot of alcohol or has the appearance of a female who drinks an excessive amount of alcohol.

[someone who's] **foul** adj. (general sl.) old & new school
1. extremely dishonest, unloyal, unscrupulous, petty or untrustworthy; one without morals.
ex: "I already told you he was foul." " Youse a foul dude."

[a] **foul move** phrase (general sl.) old & new school
1. an act that is dishonest, unscrupulous, petty or betrays the loyalty to a friend or love one. (var. [to] **pull a foul move**)
ex: "That was a real foul move I never expected that from you."

[someone who's a] **fraud** adj. (e. coast sl.) old school
1. one who is pretending to be more important and/or more tough than he/she really is. (var. [someone who's a] **fraud ass** [dude/broad/muhf**ka])
ex: "Wait 'til she finds out you a fraud." "After all these years you still a fraud."

[to] **freak** [something] v. (general sl.) new school
1. to take something and change it from its original form and make it better. 2. to do something that is almost impossible to imitate or duplicate.

ex: "I'm about to freak the Benz with the new 22 inch Mo Mo's."
"I was freakin' catz on the basketball court."

[to] **freak** [someone] v. (sexual sl.) old & new school
l. the act of having uninhibited sex in a way one has never
experienced. (var. [to] **freak the sh** outta** [someone])
ex: "If I ever get the chance I'mma freak shortie."

[someone who's a] **freak for pain** phrase (e. coast sl.) new school
1. someone who will lose, get hurt emotionally, or have his/her
pride stepped on repeatedly but will not give up or give in. See
also: [a] **pain freak**
ex: "You hafta be a freak for pain to still be with her."

[someone who's] **freakalicious** adj. (w. coast sl.) new school
1. someone who has a kinky look about him/her. 2. one who is into
kinky sex.

Fred, Bob, and Issac n. (e. coast sl.) new school
1. a covert way to refer to the Federal Bureau of Investiagtions;
F.B.I. (var. **Fred Bobinizer**)
ex: "You know Fred, Bob, and Issac been here for you."

freebase n. (drug sl.) old school
l. a smokable form of cocaine. 2. the act of smoking the smokable
form of cocaine. (var. [to] **freebase**) See also: **crack, jums**

[to] **freestyle** v. (general sl.) old & new school
1. to rhyme or rap sensibly without preparing or using material that
has already been used or heard before; the ability to rhyme or rap
spontaneously. (var. [to] **bust a freestyle**)
ex: "Most of these new school rappers can't freestyle or their
freestyles be trash."

[something that's] **fresh** adj. (general sl.) old school

1. outstanding; unique; the best of its kind. 2. stylish, hip, and trendy. (var. [something that's] **funky fresh**) See also: [something that's] **the joint**

ex: "The way they did that was fresh." "Where'd you get that fresh lookin' jacket?"

[to] **freeze** [one's] **wrist** v. (e. coast sl.) new school
1. to purchase a diamond encrusted watch or bracelet to be worn as a show piece.

ex: "I'm thinkin' about freezin' shortie's wrist for her birthday."

[a female's] **friend** n. (general sl.) old & new school
1. a way to refer to a female's menstruation cycle or "period".

ex: "My friend didn't come this month."

frienemies (pron. frien na mies) n. (e. coast sl) new school
1. people who pretend to be one's friend but who are not; friends who are jeasouls or envious [often looking for ways to destroy reputations of relationships].

from a to z phrase (general sl.) old & new school
1. everything; from the beginning to the end; the details.

ex: "I wanna know what happened from a to z."

from day one phrase (general sl.) old & new school
1. from the beginning/start [often used as a prelude to reprimanding someone about something you already warned, advised, or told him/her previously].

*ex: "From day one I knew he wasn't sh**."*

from here on out phrase (general sl.) old & new school
1. from now on; beginning now.

ex: "You on your own from here on out."

[something that went] **from sugar to sh**** phrase (southern sl.) new school

1. a way to emphasize a situation that went from good to bad [usually without really knowing why].
ex: "Our relationship went from sugar to sh** in a matter of no time."

from the door phrase (general sl.) old & new school
1. from the very beginning; to begin with; at the start. (var. **from the git go/gitty up/jump**) See also: **out the gate**
ex: "I explained that to you from the door."

[something done] **from the heart** adj. (general sl.) old & new school
1. sincerely. (var. [something that's] **from the heart**)
ex: "Look dawg, I did that from the heart."

[people who are] **from the same rib** phrase (e. coast sl.) new school
1. a term of endearment among friends who alike.
ex: "You and me dawg, we from the same rib."

[I'm] **from the Ville, never ran never will** phrase (e. coast sl.) old & new school
1. a term used by people who live in places where the name of the place ends in "ville" declare or boast of being tough.
ex: "We from Brownsville, never ran never will."

from the womb to the tomb phrase (w. coast sl.) new school
1. a way to profess one's undying loyalty to a friend or family member. 2. a way to declare that one will stick with and support a friend regardless of the situation or consequences.
ex: "I'm not goin' nowhere, I'm with you from the womb to the tomb."

[to] **front** v. (general sl.) old & new school
1. to pretend; to act more important than one really is. 2. to flaunt one's material wealth or possessions in attempt to get attention. 3. to lie; to go back on one's word; to do the opposite of

what one said he/she was going to do. 4. the act of having an
excessively high opinion of one's worth and stature. (var. [to]
front on [someone])
*ex: "Ya peops be frontin'." "I seen'em at the club frontin' big
time." "You don't hafta front for me."*

[to] **front** [someone something] v. (general sl.) old & new school
1. to give someone something on consignment or credit.
ex: "How much you think you can front me?" "I need you to front
me something 'til next week."

[the] **front end of** [something] phrase (general sl.) old & new
school
1. at the beginning; first. See also: [the] **tail end** [of something]
ex: "I wasn't here for the front end of the speech."

[a] **fronto leaf** n. (drug sl.) old & new school
1. a leaf that cigars are wrapped in that people use to re-wrap
marijuana in. See also: **blunts**

fronts n. (e. coast sl.) old & new school
1. teeth. 2. gold caps for teeth. (var. **gold fronts**)
ex: "He got one of his fronts knocked out."

frustrate'em and aggravate'em phrase (southern sl.) new school
1. a term used to annoy and taunt one's opponent during
competition [usually used when one's opponent seems frustrated
and upset].

[to] **f**k** [someone] **outta** [something] v. (general sl.) old & new
school
1. to cheat or use deception to steal another's possessions. (var. [to]
f**k [someone], [to] **f**k** [someone] **over**)
ex: "I still say we got f**ked outta them tickets."

[to] **f**k** [some] **sh**** **up** v. (general sl.) old & new school
1. to mess something up; to disrupt or destroy an action.

(var. **f**k** [something] **up**)
ex: *"You always the one who gotta f**k sh** up for everybody."*

f**k the dumd sh** phrase (general sl.) old & new school
1. a term of exasperation when fed up with listening to another's
empty threats, tough talk, taunts, or challenges and ready to resolve
matters confrontational if necessary.
ex: *"Man look, f**k the dumb sh** what you wanna do?"*

f**k what you heard! phrase (southern sl.) new school
1. a matter of fact way to affirm or reaffirm one claim, position,
or boast leaving no room for doubt, question, or further discussion.
ex: *"I stayed right there, f**k what you heard!"*

[to] **f**k with** [someone/something] v. (general sl.) new school
1. to like, admire, or envy.
ex: *"I f**ks with sex and the city." "I been f**kin' with them catz
since their first album."*

[to] **f**k with** [someone] v. (general sl.) old & new school
1. the act of playing with someone [usually in a way that confuses
or fools that person into thinking you are serious].
ex: *"Chill man, I was only f**kin' with you." "Stop f**kin' with
me like that." "I'm not f**kin' with you this time."*

[to] **f**k with** [someone] v. (general sl.) old & new school
1. to have a formal or close friendship with someone.
ex: *"I don't f**k with them catz no more." "You still f**k with
shortie?"*

f**k you think?!/thought?! phrase (general sl.) old & new school
1. an exclamation when expressing disbelief that someone could
question or doubt your abilities, intentions, or actions.
ex: *F**k you think, I wasn't gonna say nothin'." "You know I
heard, f**k you thought?!"*

f**ked adj. (general sl.) old & new school

1. a way to emphasized being in deep trouble. 2. to feel in a state of hopelessness. 3. to be deceived and taken advantage of. (var. [to be] **f**ked /f**ked up**) See also: [to be] **sh** outta luck**)
ex: "You realize we f**ked right?" "Yo man, I'm f**ked I lost the money."

[someone who's] **f**ked up** adj. (general sl.) old & new school
1. without money; destitute.
ex: "I know you wanna see me f**ked up." "I'm f**ked up right now, call me later."

f**ked up adj. (general sl.) old & new school
1. drunk; intoxicated. 2. high from an illegal drug.
ex: "I'm tellin' you, she looked like she was f**ked up." "You was f**ked up last night."

[to be] **f**ked up about** [something] adj. (e. coast sl.) new school
1. to be emotionally distraught, shaken, or upset. (var. [to be] **f**ked up over** [something])
ex: "I was f**ked about that for three days." "I think she's f**ked up over what she heard."

[to be] **f**ked up in** [something] v. (general sl.) old & new school
1. to find oneself involved in an extremely bad situation or circumstances.
ex: "I'm f**ked up in this 'cause of you."

[to be] **f**ked up in the game** phrase (general sl.) old & new school
1. to find oneself involved in an extremely bad sitaution or circumstances. 2. to have lost one's financial wealth and stature [often leaving one without the resources to recoup]. (var. [someone who's] **f**ked up in the ballgame**)
ex: "He was f**ked up in the game when he got outta prison."

[to be] **f**ked up over** [someone] v. (e. coast sl.) new school

1. a way to describe being in love [even if that love causes one pain or distress]. (var. [to] **have** [someone] **f**ked up over you)**
ex: "I was f**ked up over shortie for two years." "I'm still f**ked up over shortie."

[to be] **f**ked up with** [someone] v. (e. coast sl.) new school
1. infuriated. 2. annoyed or pissed off.
ex: "I don't wanna talk, cause right now I'm a lil f**ked up with you."

[someone who's] **f**kin' with that sh**** phrase (drug sl.) old & new school
1. a term used to make reference to someone's crack cocaine usage. (var. [someone who] **f**ks with that sh****, [someone who] **f**ks/f**kin' around** [with that sh**])
ex: "I didn't know shortie was f**kin' with that sh**."

fugly adj. (w. coast sl.) new school
1. a covert way to say "f**kin' ugly".
ex: "That was real fugly of you."

[to] **funk up** [someone's] **house** v. (general sl.) old & new school
1. to cause an unpleasant odor/stench in someone's house because one hasn't bathed. (var. [to] **stink up** [someone's] **house**)
ex: "I don't want them people in here funkin' up my house."

[to look/smell] **funky** adj. (general sl.) old & new school
1. to smell badly; odorous.
ex: "Get ya funky ass away from me."

[something that's] **funky** adj. (general sl.) old & new school
1. outstanding; unique; the best of its kind. 2. a song with a nice sounding groove and beat.
ex: "We hafta give the people somethin' funky."

[someone who's] **funny style** adj. (e. coast sl.) new school

l. someone whose personality is inconsistent and subject to mood swings. (var. **funny style** [people])
ex: *"You been real funny style lately." "If you come, don't bring your funny style friends with you."*

[a] **4 fifth** n. (criminal sl.) old & new school
1. a 45. caliber handgun. (var. [a] **4 pound**)

40 Belows n. (e. coast sl.) old & new school
1. a style of boot made by Timberland Shoes. See also: **Tims**

52 n. (prison sl.) old school
1. a unique style of street boxing.
ex: *"This kid from Marcy was the nicest cat out with the 52."*

52's n. (southern sl.) old & new school
1. a deck of regular playing cards.

[the] **52 fake out** n. (e. coast sl.) old & new school
1. the lie or deceiving act that one uses to take advantage of or trick someone out of something. (var. [the] **fake out**)
ex: *"Shortie tried the 52 fake out on me dawg."*

[to want/request] **5 minutes** phrase (e. coast sl.) old & new school
1 a term used to express one's desire to have a fist fight with someone.
ex: *"What's up, my man tryin' to get 5 minutes with your man."*

G

"G" n. (e. coast sl.) old & new school
1. a term of endearment among friends; friend. 2. a way to address someone whose name you don't know or don't want to use in front of others.
ex: "Look here G, I've heard it all before." "What time you got G?"

[someone who's a] **"G"** n. (w. coast sl.) old & new school
1. someone who acts like a thug or criminal; a tough street individual. 2. an abbreviation for the word "Gangster". See also: [an] **O.G.**
ex: "Everybody wanna act like a G." "All the real G's are dead, youngin'."

[the] **"G" code** n. (w. coast sl.) old & new school
1. the unwritten rules and codes of ethics which thugs, criminals, or "street" toughs are supposed to live by.
ex: "Catz today don't respect the G code."

[to] **gaffle** [someone] v. (w. coast sl.) old school
1. to take one's possessions through trickery or by force; to mug or rob someone. (var. [to] **get gaffled**) See also: [to] **jack** [someone]
ex: "They got gaffled for the truck comin' through the drive-thru."

game n. (general sl.) old & new school
1. the lie, con, or deceptive tactic one uses to deceive, manipulate, take advantage of, convince, or confuse someone; an excuse or explanation that isn't true but made to sound very convincing. (var. [to] **game** [someone], [to] **game** [someone] **out of** [something]) See also: [to] **run game on** [someone], [to] **spit game at** [someone]

ex: "That sounds like game to me." "I heard you tried to game my girl the same way."

[to have] **game** adj. (general sl.) old & new school
1. to possess the ability to deceive, manipulate, or lie convincingly; the ability to con people without them realizing they have been conned.
ex: "You have madd game with you."

[the] **game don't stop** n. (general sl.) old & new school
1. a way to declare or boast that one's ability to deceive, manipulate, or lie convincingly hasn't been or can't be diminished even when in a situation that seems impossible to get away with this type of behavior. (var. [the] **game don't stop cause you locked, the game ain't dead the players are scared**)

game is meant to be sold, not to be told phrase (general sl.) old & new school
1. a way to advise against giving away information without receiving some sort of compensation for it. 2. a way to mock someone who seeks information from you and you refuse to give it to him/her.

game recognize game phrase (general sl.) old & new school
1. a term used to inform someone you are aware of his/her attempt to deceive you, manipulate you, or lie to you.

[someone who's] **game tight** phrase (general sl.) old & new school
1. someone who possess a unique ability to deceive, manipulate, or lie convincingly.
ex: "Be careful cause shortie is game tight." "You think you game tight."

[something that's] **gangsta** adj. (e. coast sl.) new school
1. bold and daring; has a "street" feel or edge to it. (var. [someone who's] **gangsta**)

ex: "That was real gangsta what you did." "It don't get any gangsta than that."

[one's] **gangsta** adj. (e. coast sl.) new school
1. one's tough, bold, and daring side of his/her character.
(var. [to] **get gangsta on** [someone])
ex: "I'm positive that none of y'all wanna see my gangsta in here."

[to] **gank** [someone] v. (w. coast sl.) old school
1. to take someone's possession using trickery or by force; to mug or rob someone.
ex: "Shortie tried to gank me for everything."

[something that's] **garbage** adj. (general sl.) new school
1. of poor quality or poorly put together.
ex: "The music they puttin' out now, is garbage."

[something that's] **garbeano** adj. (e. coast sl.) new school
1. poor in quality or performance; unsatisfactory. (var. [something that's] **garbo**) See alao: [something that's] **trash**
ex: "His old sh** was slammin', that sh** he puttin' out now is garbeano."

[to] **gas** [someone] v. (e. coast sl.) old & new school
1. to give a false sense of confidence, courage, or pride; to flatter falsely. (var. [to] **gas** [someone] **up**, [to] **gas** [someone] **to the fullest**, [to] **gas** [someone's] **head/head up**, [to] **put gas in** [someone's] **tank**) See also: [to] **soup** [someone] **up**
ex: "It don't take much to gas shortie." "Watch how easily I can gas shortie up."

[the] **gas face** adj. (e. coast sl.) old school
1. a silly, shocked, embarrassing, or dumb founded expression.
ex: "He just stood there with the gas face, when he seen my new boyfriend."

212

[to] **gas** [something] **up** v. (general sl.) old & new school
1. to lie; to exaggerate.
ex: "We might need to gas the story up a lil." "She told you the gassed up version."

[someone who's] **gassed** adj. (general sl.) old & new school
1. one who holds an overrated opinion of his/her personality, abilities, or worth; to exude a false sense of confidence or cockiness.
ex: "All them broads got ya man gassed." "I don't know who got you gassed dawg."

[a] **gat** n. (w. coast sl.) old & new school
1. a firearm; handgun.
ex: "There's no gats allowed in here." "Tell'em to put the gat away."

[a] **gate** n. (drug sl.) old & new school
1. an establishment where marijuana is sold from.
ex: "That gate been there for years."

gators n. (w. coast sl.) old & new school
1. alligator shoes; shoes made of alligator material.

gats and bats n. (w. coast sl.) old & new school
1. a way to refer to the guns and night-sticks that police officers carry.

[a] **gauge** n. (criminal sl.) old & new school
1. a 12-gauge shotgun. See also: [a] **shotty**
ex: "You can't hide the gauge under there."

G'd up phrase (w. coast sl.) old & new school
1. to be dressed in one's gang colors [usually to show contempt for a rival gang]. (var. [someone who's] **G'd up)**
ex: "We goin' to that party G'd up homie."

gear n. (general sl.) old & new school
1. clothes; clothing.
ex: "I need me some new gear." "I don't wear that type of gear anymore."

[to] **gee off** v. (criminal sl.) old & new school
1. to make a large sum of money [usually as a result of doing something illegal].
ex: "I heard ya people uptown gee'd off." "I'm about to gee off, cousin."

[a] **gee pack** n. (drug sl.) old & new school
1. a prepackaged amount of drugs valued at a thousand dollars and sold at the retail level. See also: [a] **pack**
ex: "Off this gee pack, you take two hundred." "She lost two gee packs."

gee's n. (general sl.) old & new school
1. thousand dollar amounts of money; a large amount of money.

[a] **geek monster** n. (drug sl.) old school
1. someone who is addicted to cocaine.
ex: "Dawg a geek monster on the low."

geeked up adj. (drug sl.) old school
1. the state of being high from cocaine; hyperactive. See also: **wired**
ex: "I don't care what nobody says, she looked geeked up to me."

[to] **geese** [someone] **up** v. (e. coast sl.) old school
1. to give a false sense of confidence, courage, or pride; to flatter falsely. (var. [to] **geese** [someone's] **head up**)
ex: "She geesed'em into thinkin' she was really in love with'em."

[to be] **geographical** adj. (prison sl.) new school

1. the act of liking or disliking someone or something based upon the city or state someone or something originates from. (var. [to be] **on geographical time**, [someone who acts] **geograhical**)
ex: *"Catz from Brooklyn are real geographical." "I'm not on that geographical time."*

germs n. (e. coast sl.) old & new school
1. cigarettes.
ex: *"Let me get one of your germs."*

[to] **get a nut** v. (sexual sl.) old & new school
1. to have an orgasm. (var. [to] **get** [one's] **nut**) See also: [to] **bust a nut**
ex: *"Females wanna get a nut too, you know."*

[to] **get a pass** v. (general sl.) new school
1. to receive an exemption from a potentially dangerous situation or confrontation because someone you know is providing you with protection this one time.
ex: *"Lil homie you gonna get a pass on this one, next time you on your own."*

[to] **get** [one's] **ass busted** v. (general sl.) old & new school
1. to be beaten up badly.
ex: *"You better go save ya partner, he about to get his ass busted."*

[to] **get at** [someone] v. (e. coast sl.) new school
1. to contact someone for the purpose of having a discussion or meeting; to talk to someone.
ex: *"Tell ya manz to get at me." "I wanna get at your girlfriend."*

[to] **get at** [someone] v. (e. coast sl.) new school
1. to approach or confront someone [usually with the intent to cause that person great bodily harm]. 2. to assault someone [usually violently].
ex: *"Them catz tried to get at ya man last night."*

get back phrase (general sl.) old & new school
1. revenge; pay back; retaliation.
ex: "Lets play another round so I can get some get back."

[to] **get bit/bite** v. (criminal sl.) old & new school
1. to be arrested; caught.
ex: "I knew we was about to get bit and then the cops walked right by us."

[to] **get Bruce Lee on** [someone] phrase (southern sl.) new school
1. a playful way to threaten someone with beating him/her up using karate. (var. [to] **get Bruce Lee on** [someone's] **ass**)
ex: "Don't make me get Bruce Lee y'all." "I'm about to get Bruce Lee on ya ass."

[to] **get buckwild** v. (general sl.) old school
1. to demonstrate disruptive or destructive behavior. 2. to lose self control. (var. [to] **go buckwild**)
*ex: "We went up in there and got buckwild." "Sh** about to get buckwild in here tonight."*

[to] **get buckwild** v. (sexual sl.) old & new school
1. the act of having uninhibited and unrestrained sex; to get "freaky".
ex: "Behind closed doors shortie get buckwild."

[to] **get busy** phrase (sexual sl.) old school
1. the act of having sex. See also: [to] **knock** [someone's] **boots**
ex: "My momz walked in just before we was about to get busy." "We got madd busy last night."

[to] **get busy** phrase (general sl.) old school
1. to do something outstandingly or exceptionally well.
ex: "Yo, duke got busy on the mike." "I'mma show you how to get busy."

[to] **get busy** v. (general sl.) old school

1. to physically assault or fight someone.
ex: "What, y'all tryin' to get busy?" "You fight one and that whole family comin' to get busy."

[to] **get caught on a humbug/humble** phrase (criminal sl.) old & new school
1. the act of being caught and arrested as the result of a minor encounter with law enforcement or simply by chance.
ex: "They wasn't even lookin' for me, I got caught on a humbug."

[to] **get** [one's] **d**k wet** v. (sexual sl.) old & new school
1. a male term for sexual intercourse.
ex: "She know you just tryin' to get your d**k wet." "When's the last time you got your d**k wet?"

[to] **get down** [a certain kind of way] v. (e. coast sl.) old & new school
1. to do things in one's unique style of doing things when referring to his/her actions or behavior. (var. [the way someone] **gets down**)
ex: "Dig shortie, you know how I get down." "Nah, I don't get down like that."

[to] **get down and dirty** v. (general sl.) old & new school
1. to use unscrupulous, deceptive, immoral tactics to achieve one's objective. (var. [to] **get down and dirty on** [someone])
ex: "We might hafta get down and dirty this time kid."

[to] **get down for** [someone] v. (general sl.) old & new school
1. to actively show support for someone [even if it means jeopardizing one's own safety and/or security]. (var. [to] **get down with** [someone])
ex: "I like y'all, but I still hafta get down for my home team."

[to] **get down for** [one's] **crown** phrase (e. coast sl.) old school
1. to stick up for or defend the reputation of one's neighborhood [physically if necessary].

ex: "When I was young I always got down for my crown."

get down or lay down phrase (e. coast sl.) new school
1. a way to advise or warn someone he/she has a choice to join with you and if he/she refuses to do so the consequences will be harsh.

[to] **get** [a female's] **draws** v. (sexual sl.) old & new school
1. a term males use for having sex. (var. [to] **get in** [a female's]
draws, [to] **get the draws)**
ex: "How long did it take you to get the draws?" "Shortie ain't lettin' you get in them draws."

[to] **get** [one's] **drink on** phrase (general sl.) new school
1. a hip way to say that one intends to drink an excessive amount of alcohol.
ex: "I know me-myself, I came to get my drink on."

[to] **get** [one's] **face blown** v. (prison sl.) old & new school
1. to have one's face slashed with a razor [often requiring stitches to close wound].
ex: "He got his face blown for runnin' his mouth too much."

[to] **get fly** [on someone] v. (general sl.) old & new school
1. to exhibit a rude, conceited, or obnoxious attitude [often using sarcasm or offending language]. 2. the act of dismissing someone and their importance.
ex: "She tried to get real fly on me in front of her friends."

[to] **get** [one's] **freak on** v. (sexual sl.) new school
1. to indulge in uninhibited sex; to have kinky sex. 2. a term for having sex.
ex: "I thought we came here to get our freak on." "I'm out here to get my freak on."

[to] **get** [one's] **fronts knocked out** phrase (e. coast sl.) old & new school

1. to have one's teeth knocked out [usually as a result of being punched or kicked in the mouth].
ex: "I'm the one who knocked ya fronts out the last time."

[to] **get got** v. (criminal sl.) old & new school
1. to have one's possessions taken through trickery or force; to be mugged or robbed.
ex: "It looks like you was about to get got dawg, if I didn't show up." "Anybody can get got tough guy."

[to] **get** [one's] **grill/mouth/jaw wired** phrase (general sl.) old school
1. to have one's jaw broke [usually as the result of being beat up].
ex: "Don't leave outta here with ya grill wired."

[to] **get** [one's] **grown-man on** phrase (e. coast sl.) new school
1. to act savvy, sophisticated, and mature; to exude extreme self-confidence.
ex: "I was in there gettin' my grown-man on 'til you showed up."

[to] **get** [one's] **hands dirty** v. (drug sl.) old & new school
1. to make hand-to-hand drug sale transactions. 2. to commit crime. See also: [to do] **hand-to-hand combat**
ex: "That's the thing, you scared to get ya hands dirty."

[to] **get** [one's] **head cracked** v. (e. coast sl.) new school
1. to lose miserably. (var. [to] **get** [one's] **head split/split to the white meat**)
ex: "I got my head cracked down in Alantic city this weekend."

get high n. (drug sl.) old school
1. any illegal narcotic. (var. **get right**)
ex: "Her momz busted her with the get high." "Shortie and her friends don't mess with get high."

[to] **get** [one's] **hustle on** phrase (general sl.) new school

l. the act of earning one's money whichever way one does
[usually refers to some sort of shady/illegal activity].
ex: "I'll holla, I'm about to go get my hustle on."

[to] **get in** [someone's] **sh**** v. (general sl.) old & new school
1. to chastise, scold, or reprimand someone. (var. [to] **get in**
[someone's] **ass**)
ex: "You need to get in his sh** this time."

[to] **get in the wind** phrase (general sl.) old school
1. to leave; depart from.
ex: "We about to get in the wind after this song."

get in where you fit in phrase (southern sl.) new school
1. a hip way to advise or encourage someone to join in or be
a part of an activity when and where he/she feels most
comfortable, able to adjust to, or benefit from.
*ex: "Just get in where you fit in kid." "I'm tryin' to get in where I
fit in."*

[to] **get** [one's] **issue** phrase (e. coast sl.) new school
1. to receive what one is guaranteed, owed, or promised in the exact
amount.
*ex: "All I'm tryin' to do is get my issue." "When I'mma get my
issue outta you?'*

[to] **get it in** v. (sexual sl.) new school
1. to have sex. 2. to indulge in uninhibited sex.
*ex: "We was gettin' it in 'til about three in the morning."
"I heard shortie be gettin' it in."*

get it in blood phrase (e. coast sl.) new school
1. a matter of fact way to tell someone to get something from you
the best way he/she knows how [usually used mockingly,
sarcastically, or playfully]. (var. **get it like Tyson got the title**)

ex: "I'm not payin' you nothin' get it in blood."

get it right phrase (southern sl.) old & new school
1. a matter of fact way to tell someone not to make any mistakes about what you are saying, claiming, or boasting about leaving no room for doubt [often used sarcastically]. (var. [you] **better get it right**)
ex: "You heard what I said, get it right."

[to] **get lovey-dovey** [on someone] v. (general sl.) old & new school
1. to express loving affection towards someone of the opposite sex.
ex: "Shortie wanted to get all lovey-dovey and I was like, yo, I'm out."

[to] **get** [one's] **mack on** phrase (general sl.) new school
1. to use one's unique ability to meet and interact with the opposite sex with the intention of finding people whom he/she may become intimate with in the future. (var. [to] **lay/put** [one's] **mack down**) See also: [one's] **mack game**
ex: "Later for that, I'm about to get my mack on in here."

[to] **get** [one's] **man** phrase (e. coast sl.) new school
1. to exact revenge, retaliate, or settle a score with someone [usually in a physical confrontation]. 2. the act of achieving or completing one's goal.
ex: "This is how you get ya man." "That cat went up in there and got his man."

[to] **get** [one's] **man** phrase (prison sl.) new school
1. to have an orgasm. See also: [to] **bust a nut**
ex: "Its been awhile since I got my man."

get mines phrase (general sl.) old & new school
1. a bold and straightforward way to tell someone to get something that belongs to you. (var. **get mines to me/to the house, get mines or get missin', get that to me**)

ex: "I'm not tryin' to hear that, get mines."

get missin' phrase (general sl.) new school
1. a bold and straightforward way to dismiss someone [usually after being offended, disrespected or wronged].
ex: "All I know is, y'all better get missin' before they get back."

get naked phrase (e. coast sl.) old & new school
1. a term used to reclaim a clothing item or piece of jewelry from a friend or love one who has borrowed your possessions without asking. 2. a way to command someone to hand over his/her possessions [usually heard in a robbery situaion].
ex: "I know that's not my sweater, get naked."

[to] **get** [something] **off** [on someone] v. (general sl.) old & new school
1. the act of getting away with something [usually when it seemed almost impossible to get away with]. 2. to sell something.
ex: "I need to get this off quick." "Can you help me get this thing off?"

get off my bra strap phrase (general sl.) old school
1. a sarcastic way females tell someone to stop being jealous of them. 2. a female's response to someone who is trying to criticize her when there's no need to. (var. **get off my jock/jock strap/balls**)
ex: "Y'all need to get off my bra strap."

[to] **get on** phrase (general sl.) old & new school
1. the act of moving into a position where one is able to earn money, reach a goal or become successful.
ex: "How long did it take for you to get on?" "I'mma get on with my man an'nim."

[to] **get on** [someone's] **bad nerve** phrase (southern sl.) new school

l. to be extremely frustrating, aggravating, or annoying. (var. [to] **get on** [someone's] **nerve/last nerve/ good nerve**)
ex: "She just forever gettin' on my bad nerve."

[to] **get on** [one's] **feet** phrase (general sl.) old & new school
1. to become financially self sufficient and acquire the necessary things one needs to be independent of other people's help.
ex: "You can stay here until you get on your feet."

[to] **get on** [one's] **job** phrase (e. coast sl.) new school
1. the act of putting forth the effort to do a better job. 2. a stern way to advise or encourage someone to take his/her intimate relationship more seriously before he/she loses his/her partner.
(var. **get on ya job**)
ex: "You better get on ya job or you gonna lose ya girl." "I'm about to get on my job right now."

[to] **get on some bullsh**** phrase (e. coast sl.) new school
1. to become unscrupulous, untrustworthy, or scandalous [usually after one feels he/she has been wronged, disrespected, or manipulated]. (var. [to] **get on that bullsh****)
ex: "I'm about to get on some bullsh** in a minute."

[to] **get on some funny actin' sh**** v. (general sl.) old & new school
1. to exhibit moody, unpleasant, or attitude towards a friend or love one for no reason, when annoyed, wronged or angered. (var. [to] **start actin' funny**)
ex: "You always got on that funny actin' sh**."

[to] **get** [one's] **ones up** v. (e. coast sl.) new school
1. to earn/make more money; to increase one's income substantially. (var. **get ya ones up**)
ex: "I'm just tryin' to get my ones up kid."

get out! phrase (general sl.) old & new school

l. an enthusiastic way to express shock, disbelief, or one's skepticism. (var. **get outta here!, get outta town!, get the f**k outta here!**) See also: **shut up!**
ex: "Get out..... she told you that?"

get out my pocket phrase (general sl.) new school
1. a way to tell someone to stop worrying about your finances. (var. **why you all in my pockets?**)
ex: "Get out my pocket and let me worry about that."

[to] **get out on** [someone] v. (southern sl.) new school
1. to get the best of someone [usually used in the context of a physical confrontation].
ex: "I know you not gonna let her get out on you like that." "Watch how I get out on this clown."

get out the mustard and catch up phrase (general sl.) old school
1. a way to tell someone to hurry up or move faster.

[to] **get outta pocket** [with someone] v. (general sl.) old & new school
1. to talk disrespectful or extremely rude for no reason.
ex: "Ya shortie got outta pocket with me, you need to check'er."

[to] **get played** v. (general sl.) old & new school
1. to be tricked, conned, or manipulated out of something. 2. to be ridiculed, out-witted, or taken advantage of by someone you trusted; to be suckered. (var. [to] **get played like a muhf**ka**)
ex: "Tell ya man he about to get played by shortie."

[to] **get right** phrase (general sl.) old & new school
1. to do the right thing; to make an effort to do better.
ex: "When you gonna get right?" "Don't you think its time for you to get right?" "I been tryin' to get right all my life."

[to] **get right** phrase (sexual sl.) old & new school
1. to have sex.

ex: *"Me and shortie finally gonna get right." "How long should I make'em wait before we get right?"*

[to] **get right** v. (drug sl.) old & new school
1. the act of getting high from an illegal drug.
ex: *"They in your basement gettin' right." "Lets get right before we go to the club."*

[to] **get rolled on** v. (general sl.) old & new school
1. to be approached or confronted threateningly by two or more people.
ex: *"I hate to say it but you about to get rolled on up in here."*

[to] **get** [one's whole] **sh** wired/rearranged** phrase (e. coast sl.) old & new school
1. a term used to describe a jaw that has been broken and then wired to help it heal.
ex: *"Messin' with me all you gonna do is get ya whole sh** wired."*

[to] **get slick out the mouth** phrase (e. coast sl.) old & new school
1. to say something disrespectful, sarcastic, or spiteful to someone either directly or covertly. (var. [to] **pop slick**, [to] **get fly out the mouth** [on/with someone])
ex: *"I'm not about to sit here and let you keep gettin' slick out the mouth with me."*

[to] **get smoke in** [one's] **lungs** phrase (southern sl.) new school
1. a witty way to refer to the act of smoking cigarettes.
ex: *"I think he's outside gettin' smoke in his lungs."*

get somewhere phrase (southern sl.) old & new school
1. a sarcastic way to tell someone to get away from you [usually used when one is annoying you]. (var. **get you some business, find you someplace to go**)
ex: *"Can you just get somewhere please?"*

[to] **get stupid** [on someone] v. (general sl.) old & new school
1. to explode in anger when upset, wronged, or disrespected
[often causing an unpleasant scene].
*ex: "Why you pick now to get stupid on me?" "What, you tryin'
to get stupid?"*

[to] **get** [one's] **swerve on** phrase (w. coast sl.) new school
1. to enjoy oneself. 2. to cosume alcohol.
ex: "I'm tryin' to get my swerve on tonight."

get that bullsh** out ya life phrase (e. coast sl.) new school
1. a sarcastic or playful way to reprimand someone who says
and/or does something that you don't like or can't agree with.
ex: "You need to get that bullsh** out ya life."

get the bozack phrase (e. coast sl.) old school
1. a sarcastic and/or disrespectful way to dismiss someone who's
making empty threats, talking tough, or being disrespectful. (var.
get the d**k)
ex: "Tell them chumps I said get the bozack."

get the d**k/dilznick phrase (e. coast sl.) old school
1. a derogatory way to dismiss someone who has said
something to offend you.
ex: "Get the d**k fool, I ain't tryin' to hear that."

[to] **get the drama poppin'** v. (e. coast sl.) new school
1. to begin a physical confrontation [usually a violent one].
ex: "They tryin' to get the drama poppin'?"

[to] **get the drop on** [someone] phrase (criminal sl.) old & new
school
1. to catch someone by surprise [leaving him/her defenseless
against a firearm or lethal weapon].
ex: "Its gonna be hard to get the drop on'em."

get the f**k outta here phrase (general sl.) old & new school
1. a way to respond to something shocking, ridiculous, suprising or unbelievable. 2. a way to express doubt.

[to] **get the f**k up outta** [somewhere] phrase (general sl.) old & new school
1. to leave from in a hurry. 2. to depart.
ex: "I'm about to get the f**k up outta here."

get the hell on phrase (general sl.) old & new school
1. a sarcastic way to tell someone to get away from you [usually used when one is annoying you]. 2. a stern way to tell someone to leave [usually used as a warning].
ex: "You need to get the hell on." "Look homes, you and your friends need to get the hell on."

[to] **get** [one's] **thing off** v. (southern sl.) new school
1. the act of achieving one's short term goal.
ex: "We might be able to get our thing off this weekend."

[to] **get** [one's] **thing off** v. (sexual sl.) new school
1. to have an orgasm. 2. to have sex.
ex: "You come around only when you want to get your thing off." "He don't know, but I be usin' him to get my thing off too."

get to steppin' phrase (general sl.) old & new school
1. a straightfoward way to command someone to leave. 2. a playful or sarcastic way to dismiss someone.
ex: "Yo shortie its time for you and ya friends to get to steppin'."

[to] **get too familiar** [with someone] phrase (prison sl.) new school
1. the act of trying to get too friendly and personal too fast.
ex: "You aiight, but ya manz gettin' too familiar."

[to] **get up** [with someone] v. (general sl.) old & new school
1. to meet or have contact with someone of the opposite sex with the intention of getting to know that person intimately.

ex: "Tell ya friend I'm trying to get up with her." "I been trying to get up with you for a long time."

[to] **get up** [with someone] v. (general sl.) new school
1. to have a physical confrontation with someone [usually a violent one].
ex: "Somebody said you tryin' to get up with me."

get up, before you get hit up phrase (e. coast sl.) new school
1. a playful way to command someone to get out of your chair or seat.
ex: "I'mma tell you one more time, get up, before you get hit up."

[to] **get up in** [a female] v. (sexual sl.) new school
1. a male term for sexual intercourse.
ex: "If shortie comes, I'm tryin' to get up in her." "Tell ya friend I'm tryin' to get up in'er."

[to] **get up in** [someone] v. (general sl.) new school
1. to out perform one's rival or opponent. (var. [to] **get all up in** [someone])
ex: "Man I got up in them catz for two games."

[to] **get up in** [someone's] **face** v. (general sl.) old & new school
1. to approach or confront someone in a loud, aggressive, and threatening manner.
ex: "Next time you get up in my face, I'mma slap the cowboy sh** out of you."

[to] **get up off** [something] phrase (e. coast sl.) new school
1. to give someone something.
ex: "When you gonna get up off some of that money you got stashed?" "Tell her to get up off that phone number."

[to] **get up on** [something] v. (general sl.) new school
1. to learn more about; to familiarize oneself with. 2. to participate in the latest hip trend.

ex: "You need to get up on this new diet I read about."

[to] **get up on** [someone] v. (e. coast sl.) new school
1. to gain an advantage over one's rival or opponent.
ex: "How you let that clown get up on you like that?"

[to] **get up on** [someone] v. (general sl.) new school
1. to approach someone of the opposite sex with the intentions of getting to know that person intimately.
ex: "How can I get up on ya girlfriend?"

[to] **get** [one's] **weight up** phrase (e. coast sl.) new school
1. to excel. 2. to do better financially.
ex: "Boy I'm about to get my weight up."

[someone who's] **gettin' it** adj. (e. coast sl.) old & new school
1. someone who is earning large amounts of money; wealthy; rich.
(var. [someone who's] **gettin' money/money like the Feds/paid**)
ex: "He went to prison, came out, and started gettin' it." "Them catz is gettin' it now."

[someone who] **gets down** adj. (e. coast sl.) old & new school
1. someone who will never back down from a fight or run from a dangerous confrontation; someone who is fearless. (var. [to] **get down**)
ex: "I seen 'em get down before." "Them catz get down dawg, don't sleep."

[a female who] **gets her knees dirty** phrase (sexual sl.) old school
1. a female who gives oral sex to a male.
ex: "He started a rumor about you gettin' ya knees dirty."

[to] **get what** [one's] **hands call for** phrase (general sl.) old & new school
1. to get what one deserves [whether good or bad].
ex: "You keep it up, you gonna get what ya hands call for."

[to] **get** [one's] **wig tore off** phrase (criminal sl.) new school
1. a term used to refer to being shot in the head; a head injury [usually as a result of a violent act].
ex: "I stopped him from gettin' his wig tore off."

[to] **get wishy washy** v. (general sl.) old school
1. to become sentimental or emotional.
ex: "Look at you gettin' all wishy washy now."

[to] **get with** [someone] phrase (general sl.) old & new school
1. the coming together of two people of the opposite sex for the purpose of having an intimate relationship or a meaningless sexual interlude. (var. [to] **get up with** [someone])
ex: "I been wantin' to get with you for a long time."

[I'll] **get with you** (pron. wit choo) phrase (general sl.) new school
l. a sarcastic way to dismiss someone while he/she is trying to explain or offer an excuse that sounds extremely ridiculous, unbelievable, stupid. 2. a way to tell someone you will talk to him/her later.
ex: "After what you said, I'll get with you." "You thought I was stupid, get with you."

get ya grind on phrase (w. coast sl.) new school
1. a way to encourage someone to make or earn his/her money the best way he/she knows how. (var. **get ya paper/money/ shine on/paper right/hustle on**)
ex: "Don't pay them no attention, get ya grind on."

get ya weight up! phrase (e. coast sl.) new school
l. a hip and witty way to dismiss a challenge by someone who one feels isn't ready or able to pose a serious challenge or threat that needs to be answered. 2. a way to encourage someone to exert more effort if he/she wants to see better results.

get yours phrase (general sl.) old & new school

1. a way to encourage someone to reach for a goal that he/she thinks he/she deserves or is trying to achieve.
ex: "Don't let me stop you dawg, get yours."

[a] **ghetto bird** n. (w. coast sl.) old & new school
1. a police helicopter.
ex: "Ain't no out runnin' them ghetto birds."

ghetto fabulous adj. (e. coast sl.) new school
1. outrageously extravagant. 2. to live a lifestyle that surpasses the standard of living of one's community; to live lavishly in the ghetto.
ex: "Ghetto fabulous is drivin' a Benz and still livin' in the projects with ya moms."

[a] **ghetto pass** n. (general sl.) new school
1. a fictitious pass given to someone who is not from the inner city/urban community but who socializes with people who do and through that contact has become fluent and familiar with inner city/urban etiquette.

ghost adj. (e. coast sl.) new school
1. nowhere to be found; to abandon someone. 2. to leave or depart. (var. [someone who's] **ghost**, [to] **get ghost**)
ex: "I'm about to be ghost dawg." "Shortie was ghost."

gimmie phrase (general sl.) old & new school
1. a way to say, "give me" [usually used in the context of a request].
ex: "Gimmie some of that when you done." "When you gonna gimmie that back?"

gimmie got you here phrase (general sl.) old & new school
1. a witty way to respond to one who uses the term "gimmie" when asking for something [means when one's parent said "gimmie" to the other parent the two of them had sex and a child as a result]. 2. a way to tell someone "no".

gimmie me phrase (e. coast sl.) new school
1. a way to demand someone give you what you are owed or what belongs to you.
ex: "Yo, just gimmie me and I'm outta here." "Nah, you gonna gimmie before I get outta here."

[a male's] girl n. (general sl.) old & new school
1. a male's girlfriend.
ex: "I'm thinkin' about makin' her my girl."

girl n. (drug sl.) old & new school
1. powder cocaine
ex: "He couldn't stay away from the girl and wound up losing everything."

girlfriend n. (general sl.) old & new school
1. a term of endearment among female friends; friend. 2. a term females use when expressing their agreement, praise, or respect for one another.
ex: "Girlfriend we need to talk".

girlies n. (general sl.) old school
1. females. (var. [a] **girly**)
ex: "We invited madd girlies."

give'em a lollipop, he looks like a all day sucker phrase (southern sl.) new school
1. a way to tease someone who has been fooled, tricked, or conned.
2. a witty way to ridicule someone for making a fool out himself/herself.

give'em a rope and he wanna be a cowboy phrase (general sl.) old & new school
1. a way to insult someone who has gained a higher position of authority and is abusing his/her authority or new status.

[to] give [someone] a case v. (criminal sl.) old & new school

1. to cause someone to be arrested and charged with a crime. See also: [to] **catch a case**
ex: *"You ever put ya hands on me, I'm givin' you a case." "His dumb ass is the one that gave us a case."*

[to] **give** [someone] **a case** v. (e. coast sl.) new school
1. to blame someone [usually without basis]. 2. to accuse someone [without sufficient evidence].
ex: *"I can't let you give me this case."*

[to] **give** [someone] **five feet** v. (e. coast sl.) old & new school
1. to give someone room; to move back [usually used when frustrated that someone is standing too close].
ex: *"Yo my man, can a fella get five feet please?" "Hold up cuz, you gonna hafta give me five feet."*

[to] **give** [someone] **his/her props** v. (general sl.) old & new school
1. to give someone the recognition, praise, respect, or complimentary acknowledgment that he/she deserves.
ex: *"We all hafta give you your props for that."*

[to] **give it to** [someone] **raw** phrase (general sl.) old & new school
1. to tell someone the truth; to be honest and up front with someone even if it means hurting his/her feelings. (var. [to] **give it to** [someone] **uncut/raw and uncut**)
ex: *"Give it to me raw, I can take it." "I had to give it to them raw and uncut."*

[to] **give it up** phrase (prison sl.) new school
1. the act of intentionally or unintentionally exposing one's private parts [in a picture, movie, or in real life]. See also: [to] **set it out**
ex: *"Shortie was definitely givin' it up on the front cover of that Rap magazine."*

[to] **give it up for/to** [someone] v. (e. coast sl.) new school
1. the act of giving someone a verbal acknowledgment, praise,

or recognition.
ex: "I wanna give it up to my momz for holdin' a fella down."

[to] **give** [someone] **play** v. (general sl.) old school
1. to give someone an opportunity to pursue an intimate relationship with you. (var. [to] **give** [someone] **a/ some play**)
ex: "I was thinkin' about givin' you a play."

give the baby somethin' to do phrase (southern sl.) new school
1. a witty way to tell someone to stop complaining, whining, or being a sore loser. (var. [if] **you keep cryin' what the baby gonna do?**)

[to] **give** [someone] **the blues** v. (general sl.) new school
1. to annoy, aggravate, or frustrate someone; the act of upsetting someone.
ex: "Everytime I see shortie, she gives me the blues."

[to] **give** [someone] **the boot** v. (general sl.) old school
1. to end a intimate relationship with someone [usually as a result of that person doing something to wrong you].
ex: "He don't even know his girl about to give 'em the boot."

[to] **give** [someone] **the business** v. (e. coast sl.) new school
1. to physically assault someone [often causing great bodily injury or death].
ex: "Let's get outta here 'fore I hafta give this clown the business."

[to] **give** [someone] **the game** v. (general sl.) old & new school
1. to teach or show someone a way to deceive, trick, fool, con, or take advantage of someone or a situation. (var. [to] **give the game up**, [to] **give up the game**)
ex: "I just can't give you the game like that." "They all in there givin' up the game."

[to] **give** [someone] **the mumps** v. (e. coast sl.) new school

1. to physically assault someone causing large lumps and bruises on that person's face. See also: [to] **lump** [someone] **up**
ex: "He gave ya ex the mumps for dissin' you."

give ya man [over there] **some pom-poms** phrase (e. coast sl.) new school
1. a sarcastic way to ridicule or insult someone who is cheering for your opponent.

gladiator school n. (prison sl.) old & new school
1. an extremely violent prison or jail.
ex: "I did my first bid in gladiator school."

[a] **glass d**k** n. (drug sl.) old school
1. a crack cocaine pipe.
ex: "He usin' that glass d**k again."

[to] **go against the grain** phrase (e. coast sl.) old & new school
1. to wrong or betray one's friend, loved one, or friendship; to become disloyal.
ex: "After all I did for you, how could you go against the grain like that?"

[to] **go all out** v. (general sl.) old & new school
1. to do something without regards to the consequences. 2. the act of taking an action to the fullest extent. 3. to follow through with something even if it leads to trouble or a bad situation.
ex: "Are you prepared to go all out?" "You know we gonna hafta go all out with this right?"

[to] **go all out for/with** [someone] v. (general sl.) old & new school
1. the act of showing one's undying support and loyalty even if it means one will bring harm or trouble to his/her ownself.
ex: "Don't worry about that, I'm goin' all out with you." "You didn't think I'd go all out for you, did you?"

[to] **go all the way** phrase (criminal sl.) old & new school
1. to proceed with having a jury trial for one's criminal charges instead of opting for a plea bargin. (var. [to] **go all the way to the door**)
ex: "They already decided to go all the way." "If we go all the way to the door with this I know we can win."

[to] **go at** [someone] v. (general sl.) old & new school
1. to approach or confront someone. 2. to challenge. See also: [to] **step to** [someone]
ex: "You can't go at shortie like that." "The last person who tried to go at me, lost two beans."

[to] **go at it** [with someone] v. (general sl.) old & new school
1. to have a confrontation with someone [usually a loud and/or physical one].
ex: "Trust me, you don't wanna go at it with me." "I am not trying to go at it with you over this."

[to] **go down** [on someone] v. (sexual sl.) old & new school
1. to perform oral sex on another. (var. [to] **go downtown/down south** [on someone])
ex: "How you gonna go down on someone you just met?"

[to] **go for** [something] phrase (general sl.) old & new school
1. to accept something. 2. to allow something without putting forth an argument or fight [even when one is in doubt or suspicious].
ex: "I know you not about to go for that?" "I'll go for anything right now." "Yo, he went for it."

[to] **go for bad** phrase (e. coast sl.) old & new school
1. to act and/or talk tough in an attempt to scare and intimidate others.
ex: "Dude just goes for bad." "Since when ya boy start goin' for bad?"

[to] **go for fried ice cream** phrase (general sl.) old & new school

1. to believe something no matter how dumb or ridiculous.
ex: "You go for that, you'll go for fried ice cream."

[to] **go for self** v. (e. coast sl.) old & new school
1. to go at things alone. (var. [to] **go solo**, [to] **go dolo**, [to] **go for delf**)
ex: "Next time I go, I'm goin' for self."

go for yours phrase (general sl.) old & new school
1. a way to encourage someone to do something, to take a chance, or to give something a try.
ex: "Its about time you go for yours." "I see you thinkin' about goin' for yours."

[to] **go hard** phrase (e. coast sl.) new school
1. the act of choosing to do something the hard way or most complicated way for the purpose of proving one's toughness. 2. to rebut and/or refuse help even when one really needs help. 3. to do something in disregard to the consequences.
ex: "This time I'm goin' hard." "We gonna hafta go real hard to get this money."

go 'head with that bullsh** phrase (general sl.) old & new school
1. a stern way to warn someone to stop playing because you are not in the mood for games, taunting, or being threatened. (var. **go 'head** [now])

[to] **go off** v. (general sl.) old & new school
1. to yell, shout, and/or hurl profanity to express one's discontent or displeasure with something or someone. 2. to cause an unpleasant scene. (var. [to] **go off on** [someone])
ex: "I was about to go off in here." "I had to go off on my boss."

go on with ya bad ass phrase (southern sl.) new school
1. a playful or sarcastic way to encourage someone to do something. 2. a way to praise, compliment, or recognize one's accomplishment or outstanding performance.

[to] **go out** v. (criminal sl.) old & new school
1. to become a witness or informant against a friend or family member; to cooperate with authorities in the investigation of another. (var. [to] **go out on** [someone])
ex: "You think he gonna go out?" "I heard she's about to go out on her peoples." "They said you went out."

[to] **go out like a sucker** phrase (general sl.) old & new school
1. to take the cowardly way out of a situation [often without regards to how it may effect others]. 2. to accept being taken advantage of, manipulated, or deceived without attempting to standup for oneself.
ex: "He went out like a sucker takin' his girl back when he found her cheatin' on'em."

[to] **go the other way** [on someone] v. (general sl.) new school
1. to do the opposite of what one is suspecting or confident that you will do. 2. to switch direction or subject suddenly and without explanation. (var. [to] **go sideways** [on someone])

[to] **go the police route** phrase (criminal sl.) old & new school
1. to seek police intervention with a problem one has with someone else.
*ex: "Ya bit** ass man went the police route."*

[to] **go the sucker/bit** route** v. (general sl.) old & new school
1. to take the cowardly way out of a situation. (var. [to] **take the sucker/bit** route**)
ex: "He gonna go the sucker route instead of telling the truth to shortie."

[to] **go there** [with someone] v. (general sl.) old & new school
1. to use another's personal issues against him/her knowing that it will hurt that person's feelings.
ex: "We don't need to go there." "Why you hafta go there with me?"

[to] **go to** [someone's] **ass** v. (general sl.) old & new school
1. to beat someone up; to physically assault someone. (var. [to] **go upside** [someone's] **head**)
ex: "Don't make me go to your ass in here." "I'm about to go to Ms. Thing's ass."

[someone who's] **God body** n. (e. coast sl.) old & new school
1. a memebr of the Five Percent Nation. (var. [someone who's] **G.O.D., [a] God, righteous**)
ex: "Ya man turned God body in prison." "When the last time you seen the God?"

[a] **God u now** n. (e. coast sl.) old & new school
1. a covert way to refer to a gun [by taking the underlined letters in "God u now" and putting them together they then spell "gun"].
(var. [a] **God u**)
ex: "The police went lookin' for the God u now."

[someone who's] **goin' through it** phrase (e. coast sl.) new school
1. a way to describe one's depressive or stressful behavior; to exhibit signs of emotional turmoil.
ex: "I can tell you goin' through it."

[a situation that's] **going to get ugly** phrase (general sl.) new school
1. unpleasant.
ex: "I'm leavin' cause it's going to get ugly in here."

[a] **gold digger** n. (general sl.) old school
1. a female who only likes to date males with money with the intention of getting them to spend large amounts of money on her.
ex: "My mother always said you was a gold digger." "Every female in her family is a gold digger."

gold fronts n. (general sl.) old school
1. gold caps for one's teeth. (var. **fronts, gold grill**)
ex: "His gold fronts rotted his teeth."

[someone who's] **gone** adj. (drug sl.) old & new school
1. someone who is completely consumed by his/her addiction to drugs that his/her appearance is extremely haggard and unkempt and the person will do anything to get money to buy drugs.
ex: "I seen shortie last month, and she gone dawg."

[to be] **good** phrase (general sl.) old & new school
1. a way to express one doesn't want or need any more of what someone is offering. 2. a way to say one is, "satisfied", "okay", "cool", "all right", or "fine'.
ex: "Thanks anyway, but I'm good." "See if they good over there." "Y'all good with that?"

[when someone is] **good for** [something] adj. (general sl.) old & new school
1. someone who can be trusted to pay back or return something that he/she receives on credit, consignement, or on the approval of another [someone is either good or not good for something].
ex: "Come on man, you know I'm good for it." "She never said you wasn't good for it this time."

Good Gawd! interj. (general sl.) old school
1. a witty and enthusiastic way to express shock, surprise, or bewilderment.
ex: "Good Gawd, what the hell's goin' on here?"

good googily moogily! phrase (general sl.) old school
1. an enthusiastic way to respond to something surprising, shocking, or unbelievable.
ex: "Good googily moogily, that's a ugly child."

good lookin' phrase (general sl.) old & new school
1. a way to say, "thank you". 2. a way to express appreciation. (var. **good lookin' out**)
ex: "Good lookin' I need a hand with that." "That was good lookin' dawg."

[someone who's] **good people** adj. (e. coast sl.) new school
1. a way to describe someone as being a good and decent person; someone trustworthy. (var. [someone who's] **good peoples**)
ex: "Money and his brother Brain from Farragut Projects always been good people." "Ya man said, y'all was good people."

[one who's] **good with the hands** adj. (general sl.) old & new school
1. someone who knows how to fight/box extermely well. (var. [one who's] **good with these**, [to be] **nice with the hands**)
ex: "He posed to be real good with the hands."

goonie goo-goo lookin' [females/broads] adj. (general sl.) old school
1. females that are goofy looking and acting. 2. silly and immature acting females.

[to] **gorilla** [someone/something] v. (w. coast sl.) old & new school
1. to take something from someone using force, intimidation, or violence; to bully someone. See also: [to] **house** [someone]
ex: "They tried to gorilla us for the court."

gorilla cookies n. (w. coast sl.) old & new school
1. an imaginary cookie that tough guys/girl supposedly eat to make them tough.
ex: "Ya man act like he been eatin'em gorilla cookies again." "I think he ran out of his gorilla cookies."

[to] **gorilla grill** [someone] v. (w. coast sl.) new school
1. to look at someone with a mean or tough expression. (var. [to] **give** [someone] **the gorilla grill**)
ex: "I'm not gonna put up with all this gorilla grillin'."

gorillas adj. (w. coast sl.) old & new school
1. tough guys; bullies; "street toughs". See also: **rillas**
ex: "I keep a couple gorillas around me."

[a female who] **got a/the madd phat ass** adj. (general sl.) old &
new school
1. a female with an extremely large butt.
ex: "Now tell me she ain't got the madd phat ass."

[you] **got alotta sh**/bullsh** with you** phrase (e. coast sl.) new
school
1. a term used to reprimand someone's deceptive, dishonest, or
unscrupulous behavior or thoughts.

[someone who's] **got it goin' on** phrase (general sl.) old & new
school
1. someone who is very attractive. 2. someone who performs or
does something outstandingly or unique. 3. someone who is
wealthy and/or successful. (var. [someone who] **has it goin' on,**
[to] **have it goin' on**)
*ex: "Shortie over there got it goin' on." "I ain't know you got it
goin' on like that." "I seen ya boy and he don't have it goin' on no
more, what's up with that?"*

[someone who] **got it like the Feds** phrase (e. coast sl.) new school
1. one who possess or has access to a large amount of money or
drugs; one who has a large quantity.
*ex: "Talk to ya manz an'nim, I heard they got it like the Feds
now."*

[I] **got my ear to the ground** phrase (southern sl.) new school
1. a way to tell someone you are waiting to hear or receive
information. (var. [I] **got my ears open**)
*ex: "I got my ear to the ground, soon as I hear something I'll let
you know."*

[I] **got places to go and people to see** phrase (general sl.) old &
new school
1. a witty way to explain one's departure.
ex: "I wish I could stay, but I got places to go and people to see."

[one who's] **got the game and gone with it** phrase (general sl.)
new school
1. a term used to point out how someone has excelled in something
that he/she just recently learned how to do. 2. to become better in
something than the person who taught it to you [usually used
when evaluating one's performance or capability].
ex: "You taught'em well, he got the game and gone with it."

[you] **got the right plan, but the wrong man** phrase (southern sl.)
new school
1. a witty way to tell someone he/she has a good idea
but you are not interested. 2. a sarcastic way to tell someone you
want no parts of his/her plan or scheme.

[you] **got too much sh** with you** phrase (general sl.) new school
1. a term used to reprimand someone for being a con artist,
unscrupulous, or a deceiver. (var. [you] **got too much bullsh****
with you)

gots to be more careful phrase (southern sl.) new school
1. a term used to express shock or surprise when one realizes that
he/she has made a mistake or error.

gotta phrase (general sl.) old & new school
1. a way to say, "have to" or "must".
ex: "I gotta get some of that."

[I] **gotta go see a man about a dog** phrase (general sl.) old school
1. a witty way to explain one's departure.
*ex: "Meet me later, cause right now I gotta go see a man
about a dog."*

[you] **gotta pay the cost to be the boss** phrase (general sl.) old &
new school
1. a term used to explain that one has to be able to take the good
with the bad and/or be willing to work hard to become successful.

[one's] gover'ment name phrase. (e. coast sl.) old & new school
1. one's name on his/her birth certificate apposed to the religious name, nickname, or alias one chooses for himself or herself.
ex: "I don't go by my gover'ment name." "That just my gover'ment name."

grands n. (general sl.) old & new school
1. large amounts of money. 2. thousand dollar amounts of money.
ex: "They said they was gonna pay us a couple grands." "All I seen was grands and I was ready."

[to] grand stand v. (general sl.) old & new school
1. to flaunt one's possessions or financial wealth in the attempt to get attention. 2. to act more important than one is. 3. to cause an unpleasant scene needlessly.
ex: "They come here every weekend grand standin'."

granny panties phrase (general sl.) new school
1. big female underwear or draws.
ex: "I peeked in her drawer shortie had like five pairs of granny panties, I started buggin'."

gravy n. (general sl.) new school
1. money.

[someone who's] greazy adj. (e. coast sl.) new school
1. one who is deceitful, untrustworthy, sneaky, or without morals and loyalty. (var. [to act] **greazy**) See also: [someone who's] **cruddy**
ex: "It don't pay to be greazy." "Them Brownsville chicks are real greazy."

[someone who's] green adj. (general sl.) old & new school
1. naive; unfamiliar with the procedure.
ex: "You was green 'til you met me."

greenery n. (drug sl.) new school

1. a covert word for "marijuana".
ex: "She likes her greenery when she gets home from work."

[one's] **grill** n. (general sl.) old & new school
1. a person's face, mouth, teeth, or head. (var. [one's] **grill piece**)
ex: "The ball smashed'em right in the grill."

[to] **grill** [someone] v. (general sl.) new school
1. to look or stare at someone with a mean expression.. See also:
[to] **ice grill** [someone]
ex: "Yo, dude over there grillin' ya girl dun."

[to] **grill** [someone] v. (general sl.) old & new school
1. to repeatedly field the same questions to someone; inquire about
the same information over and over again.
*ex: "You better be ready cause you know your girl gonna
grill you when you get home."*

[someone who's] **grimy** adj. (e. coast sl.) new school
1. one who is deceitful, untrustworthy, sneaky, or without morals
and loyalty. See also: [someone who's] **shystee**
ex: "I don't hang with them catz no more cause they madd grimy."
*"That's that grimy sh**."*

[to] **grind** phrase (general sl.) old & new school
1. to make money [usually refers to the selling of drugs]. (var. [to]
get [one's] **grind on**) See also: [to] **clock dollars**
ex: "I been out grindin' all night."

[one's] **grind** n. (general sl.) new school
1. the way one makes or earns his/her money.
ex: "I need to find me a new grind." "This the only grind I know."

[one's] **grip** n. (w. coast sl.) old & new school
1. money.
*ex: "I don't tell you what to do with your grip, don't tell me what
to do with mines."*

[a] **grip** n. (criminal sl.) new school
1. a firearm; gun.
ex: "I refused to carry a grip."

[a] **grip** n. (general sl.) old & new school
1. a wad of cash. See also: [a] **knot**
ex: "Did you see the grip he pulled out?"

grip n. (e. coast sl.) new school
1. a term of endearment among friends; friend. 2. way to address someone whose name you don't know or don't want to use in front of others. See also: **money**
ex: "Ayo grip, I already told you she wasn't here."

[a] **grit** [on one's face] adj. (e. coast sl.) new school
1. a mean or tough expression on one's face [usually in the attempt to intimidate or appear tough]. 2. a scowl.
ex: "Duke got a hellava grit." "Every time I see you, you got this grit on your face what up with that?"

[to] **grit on** [someone] v. (e. coast sl.) new school
1. to look or stare at someone with a mean or tough expression. See also: [to] **mean mug** [someone]
ex: "They grit on you cause they jealous."

grow up? grow up?... when I see you it makes me wanna throw up phrase (general sl.) old school
1. a witty way to respond to someone who tells you to "grow up".

grub n. (general sl.) old & new school
1. food.
ex: "What kind of grub she cook?"

[to] **grub** v. (general sl.) old & new school
1. to eat. (var. [to] **get** [one's] **grub on**)
ex: "I'm about to go in here and grub." "What time we gettin' our grub on?"

guard ya grill phrase (e. coast sl.) new school
1. a way to warn or advise someone to protect himself or herself during a physical confrontation. See also: **protect ya neck**

[something that's] **gully** adj. (e. coast sl.) new school
1. bold and daring. 2. something that has a "street" feel or edge to it.
ex: "G-Unit clothin' line is the gulliest sh** out there right now."

[someone who's] **gully** adj. (e. coast sl.) new school
1. a tough guy/girl; a "street tough"; a "thug". 2. to be "gangsterish". 3. bold and daring.
ex: "Shortie madd gully dawg." "Brooklyn catz been gully from way back."

[a male's] **gun** n. (sexual sl.) old & new school
1. a covert way to refer to a penis.
ex: "She said his gun was shootin' blanks."

[a] **gun** n. (prison sl.) old & new school
1. a makeshift knife or lethal weapon.
ex: "I used to carry my gun to the shower with me when I was in prison."

[to] **gun butt** [someone] v. (criminal sl.) old & new school
1. to hit someone in the head with a firearm.
ex: "I watched the police gun butt ya man after they chased'em down."

[to] **gun** [someone] **down** v. (sexual sl.) new school
1. to have an orgasm while masturbating to a thought, picture, or fantasy of someone.
ex: "I gun her down twice a week."

Gun Smoke n. (e. coast sl.) new school
1. Brooklyn, N.Y. See also: **Brooklawn, Bucktown**
ex: "Don't ever trust them catz from Gun Smoke."

h

[one's] **H.B**. n. (sexual sl.) new school
1. an abbreviation for [**hump buddy**]; a term used to refer to
someone who one is involved with sexually but not emotionally.
(var. [one's] **F.B.** [f**k buddy])
*ex: "Oh that's just my H.B." "I told'em we were only hump
buddies, and he got mad."*

hafta phrase (general sl.) old & new school
1. a way to say, "have to" or "must".
ex: "I hafta get outta here." "Do you hafta do that?"

[to] **hail** [someone] **up** phrase (general sl.) old & new school
1. to give verbal recognition to someone.
ex: "Tell'em we hailed'em up when you see'em."

half a man n. (e. coast sl.) new school
1. fifty dollars ($50.00¢).
ex: "I sent'em a half a man for his birthday."

half a "o-z"/ "o" n. (drug sl.) old & new school
1. a half once of cocaine.
ex: "That's the second half a o-z he lost this week."

[to] **half-ass f**k with** [someone] v. (e. coast sl.) new school
1. to have a less than cordial friendship or interaction with
someone. (var. [to] **half-ass mess with/like** [someone])
ex: "Yeah, I half-ass f**ks with ya man every now and then."

[a male who's] **half-man half-amazin'** adj. (e. coast sl.) new
school
1. a male whose performance or abilities excel past his peers [often
used as a boast or praise].
ex: "I'm the one who's half-man half-amazin'."

[to] **half step** phrase (general sl.) old & new school
1. the act of putting forth less than one's full effort [usually effecting one's performance].
ex: "We don't have no time for half steppin'."

[someone who's] **half-way decent** adj. (general sl.) old & new school
1. one whose looks are just above average.
ex: "All her friends are half-way decent."

[something that's] **half-way decent** adj. (general sl.) old & new school
1. mediocre; just above average.
ex: "If its half-way decent I'mma cop one." "She brought back something that was half-way decent."

[a] **ham sandwich/sammich** n. (w. coast sl.) old school
1. a Cadillac Brougham.

hamburger helper phrase (e. coast sl.) old school
1. extra income earned to supplement one's main source of income.
ex: "That part-time job is only hamburger helper."

[a] **hammer** n. (criminal sl.) new school
1. a firearm; gun. 2. a empty handgun.
ex: "Y'all gonna hafta leave them hammers outside."

[one's] **hand skills** phrase (general sl.) old & new school
1. one's ability or inability to fist fight/box.
ex: "I think he wants to test ya hand skills." "You seen I got hand skills."

[to go] **hand-to-hand** v. (drug sl.) old & new school
1. the act of selling drugs retail in an open air drug market personally interacting with and making the sales to customers.
(var. [to do] **hand-to-hand combat**)

ex: "You hafta be real careful when you out there doin'
hand-to-hand." "I seen females doin' hand-to-hand combat."

[one's] **handle** adj. (general sl.) old & new school
1. one's unique ability to dribble a basketball.
ex: "She has the best handle on the team."

handle it! (pron. han'le it!) interj. (e. coast sl.) old & new
school
1. a playful or sarcastic way to tell someone to accept something
that he/she is complaining to you about.
ex: "Best thing I can tell you is handle it!"

handle that! (pron. han'le dat!) phrase (e. coast sl.) new school
1. a demanding way to prod someone into handling or confronting
a situation when that person is showing signs of hesitancy.
ex: "Instead of being out here, you need to get in there and handle
that!"

handle ya business phrase (e. coast sl.) new school
1. a way to encourage someone to do something that he/she is
showing a sign of hesitancy about doing; a term used to prod. (var.
handle yours)
ex: "You don't need me to tell you, handle ya business." "When
you gonna handle ya business?"

[to] **hang up** phrase (prison sl.) old & new school
1. to commit suicide by hanging oneself.
ex: "Things are never that bad you hafta hung up."

[to] **hang up** [one's] **guns** phrase (criminal sl.) old & new school
1. to quit [usually used as a vow to stop committing crime].
ex: "I know its time for me to hang up my guns now." "I thought
you was hangin' up ya guns."

[to] **hang with** [someone] v. (general sl.) old & new school

1. to spend time socializing and going places with a friend or love one. (var. [to] **hangout with** [someone])
ex: "I been stop hangin' with them clowns."

[he's] **happier than a fat lady on a broke scale** phrase (southern sl.) new school
1. a witty way to express another's happiness or elation. (var. [She's] **happier than a fat cop in a all night doughnut shop**)

[someone who's] **hard** adj. (general sl.) old & new school
1. tough; a "street" tough; a thug. (var. [to act] **hard**)
ex: "You think you so hard." "There's always someone harder than you."

hard n. (drug sl.) old & new school
1. crack cocaine.
ex: "The Feds found two ounces of hard in her bag."

hard adj. (sexual sl.) old & new school
1. a way to refer to an erection. (var. [a] **hard on**)

hard head makes a soft ass/behind phrase (general sl.) old & new school
1. a term used to warn someone who won't or doesn't like to listen to advice, warnings, or common sense just before he/she is getting ready to do something he/she should not do.

[someone who's] **hard headed** adj. (general sl.) old & new school
1. someone who won't and doesn't like to listen to advice, warnings, or common sense.
ex: "She's not stupid, she's just hard headed."

hard heads n. (general sl.) old & new school
1. young "street" toughs who won't or don't like to listen to advice, warnings, or common sense.
ex: "Don't invite them hard heads to your party."

[a] **hard knock life** phrase (e. coast sl.) new school
1. a life filled with many problems and struggles stemming from the lack of having the financial means to acquire the things one needs to live comfortably.
ex: "Growin' up in a hard knock life is critical."

[it's] **hard on the boulevard** phrase (general sl.) new school
1. a way to express how tough and dire one's financial situation is [used to emphasize being destitute]. (var. [when its] **hard on the yard**)
ex: "Yo dawg, I wish I could but things are hard on the boulevard right now."

[a] **hard rock** n. (general sl.) old school
1. a "street" tough; a thug.
ex: "Why ya man thinks he's a hard rock?"

[he was] **harder than Chinese arithmetic** phrase (sexual sl.) new school
1. a witty way to describe an erection.
ex: "Man, shortie had me harder than Chinese arithmetic."

[someone who] **has a body** phrase (criminal sl.) old & new school
1. one who has caused or being accused of causing the death of another.
ex: "Somebody said he has a body."

[someone who] **has buck in him/her** adj. (general sl.) new school
1. one who demonstrates a tendency to be rebellious.
ex: "Shortie got a lil buck in her." "You ain't got no buck in you."

[a male who] **has his** [girl/shortie] **on house arrest** phrase (e. coast sl.) new school
1. a male who pressures his girlfriend not to go out socially [in an attempt to limit her interaction with others]. (var. [a female who's] **on house arrest/home confinement**)

ex: "Shortie, I know you tired of that cat havin' you on house arrest."

[someone who] **has it bad** phrase (e. coast sl.) old & new school
1. one who has a real or imaginary addiction causing him/her to display behavior that is irrational and/or self destructive. (var. [to] **have it bad**)
ex: "Ya boy started messin' with them drugs and now he's got it bad." "When I was with shortie I had it bad, I didn't want her goin' nowhere."

[someone who] **has no heart** phrase (general sl.) old & new school
1. one who is cowardly
ex: "I knew you didn't have no heart."

[someone who] **has no hustle** [in him/her] phrase (general sl.) old & new school
1. one who lacks the ingenuity, drive, and imagination to create ideas to make money [also used to point out one's laziness]. (var. [someone who] **has no hustle game**, [someone who doesn't] **have a hustlin' bone in** [his/her] **body**)
ex: "You ain't never gonna have nothin' cause you don't have no hustle in you."

[a female who] **has that come-back** phrase (sexual sl.) new school
1. a female whose sex is so satisfying it is guaranteed to make a male come back for more. (var. [a female with] **that come-back**)
ex: "I'm tellin' you, shortie got that straight come-back, joe."

[a female who] **has/gives the bomb head** adj. (sexual sl.) new school
1. a covert way to evaluate a female's ability to perform oral sex as being exceptional/outstanding.
ex: "I bet you shortie got the bomb head."

[a male who] **has the magic stick** phrase (sexual sl.) new school

1. a male who has the ability to satisfy a woman sexually demonstrating stamina, endurance, and skill in the bed. See also: [a] **magic stick**
ex: "Shortie not goin' nowhere cause she know I got the magic stick."

[to] **hate on** [someone] v. (general sl.) new school
1. to refuse to give recognition or praise to someone who has earned and deserves it because one doesn't like or is jealous of that person; to look for something negative to say about someone who deserves praises, respect, and admiration. (var. [to] **hate**, [someone who's a] **hater**) See also: [a] **player hater**
ex: "You just hatin' on 'em cause he blew up." "It don't pay to hate, dawg."

[to] **hate** [someone] **with a passion** phrase (general sl.) new school
1. to truly dislike or despise someone. (var. [to] **hate** [something] **with a passion**)
ex: "Growin' up, I hated that cat with a passion."

hater aid n. (e. coast sl.) new school
1. an imaginary drink people who "hate on" other people drink to make them so openly jealous of others.
ex: "I see you been drinkin' that hater aid again."

[to] **haul ass** v. (general sl.) old & new school
1. to leave; depart in a hurry; to run.
ex: "I don't know what happened but when she seen you, she hauled ass."

[to] **have a big cheese smile on** [one's] **face** adj. (general sl.) old & new school
1. a witty way to describe one's broad smile or look of elation.
ex: "I open the door, homeboy standin' there with a big cheese smile on his face."

[to] **have a complex** [about something] phrase (e. coast sl.) old & new school
1. to have a real or imaginary insecurity [usually that one is very self-conscious about]. (var. [someone who] **has a complex**)
ex: *"I think ya man got a complex." "You not one of them catz who has a complex are you?"*

[to] **have a thing for** [someone] phrase (e. coast sl.) new school
1. to like; to be infatuated with. (var. [to] **have a thing for** [something]) See also: [to be] **big on** [someone]
ex: *"I heard your girlfriend got a thing for one of my manz."*

[to] **have** [one's] **back** phrase (general sl.) old & new school
1. to offer one's undying support [even if it means putting one's own self in jeopardy].
ex: *"Whatever you want to do I got your back."*

[to] **have beef** [with someone] phrase (general sl.) old & new school
1. to have serious problems with someone. See also: **beef**
ex: *"Yo, you got beef with me?" "We got beef?"*

[to] **have** [one's] **body under pressure** phrase (sexual sl.) new school
1. to be sexually aroused by one's mere presence, thought, or flirtatious behavior.
ex: *"The way you keep my body under pressure isn't good for my relationship."*

[to] **have** [something] **comin'** phrase (general sl.) new school
1. to be on the receiving end of something that is owed, promised, mandatory, or yours by matter of right.
ex: *"You have that comin' regardless."*

[to] **have** [someone] **f**ked up in the game** phrase (general sl.) new school
1. to be confused about, wrong, or mistaken when it comes to

someone's intentions or thoughts. 2. to have an advantage or edge over someone. (var. [to] **have** [someone] **f**ked up in the ball game**)
ex: "You got me f**ked up in the game, if you think I'mma apologize." "She got me f**ked up in the game right now."

[to] **have hate in** [one's] **blood** phrase (general sl.) new school
1. someone who is always quick and ready to express jealous and envious feelings towards someone who deserves praise and admiration. (var. [someone who] **has hate in** [his/her] **blood**)
ex: "You just sayin' that cause you have hate in ya blood."

[to] **have** [someone] **in his/her feelin's** phrase (general sl.) new school
1. to make someone mad, upset, and/or angry.
ex: "Stop playin' cause as soon as I start, I'mma have you in your feelin's."

[to] **have larceny in** [one's] **heart** phrase (e. coast sl.) old & new school
1. to be unscrupulous in one's actions and character. (var. [someone who] **gets larceny in his/her heart**)
ex: "You hafta be careful with them catz, they all have larceny in their hearts." "It don't pay to have larceny in ya heart."

[to] **have love for** [someone/something] v. (general sl.) old & new school
1. to have an affinity for someone or something.
ex: "I'mma aways have love for you homie."

[to] **have money comin' out the ass** phrase (general sl.) old & new school
1. to be extremely wealthy; rich. (var. [to] **have major paper**)
ex: "Them catz got money comin' out the ass now."

[to] **have no love for** [someone] phrase (general sl.) old & new school
1. to dislike someone.
ex: "You know I don't have no love for the other team."

[to] **have no rap for** [someone] phrase (general sl.) old & new school
1. to have nothing to say to someone [usually because one has wronged, disrespected, or offended you].
ex: "Yo son, word up, I ain't got no rap for them broads maaan."

[to] **have** [someone] **on joke time** phrase (e. coast sl.) new school
1. to look at or perceive someone as being foolish or not serious. (var. [someone who's] **on joke time**)
ex: "I honestly think y'all have me on joke time around here."

[to] **have** [someone] **open** phrase (general sl.) old & new school
1. to have someone extremely infatuated with/over you [usually because of something special you do]. (var. [to] **have** [someone] **open like 7-11**) See also: [to] **dig** [someone]
ex: "Shortie got you open." "I know you tryin' to get me open."

[to] **have that/a monkey on** [one's] **back** phrase (drug sl.) old & new school
1. to have an addiction to some form of hard narcotic.
ex: "Just by the way she look, you can tell she got that monkey on her back."

[to] **have the munchies** phrase (general sl.) old & new school
1. to have a craving for junk or snack food.
ex: "They came to my house two in the mornin' from the club with the munchies."

[to] **have the nerve...** phrase (general sl.) old & new school
1. to have the audacity or gall to say or do something.
ex: "And do you know this creep had the nerve to ask me to pay for dinner."

[to] **have the ups on** [someone] phrase (general sl.) old & new school
1. to hold an advantage over someone.
ex: "How'd you let him get the ups on you?"

[to] **have** [someone] **twisted** phrase (general sl.) new school
1. to be confused about, wrong, or mistaken when it comes to someone's intention or thoughts. (var. [to] **have** [someone] **confused/mixed up/mixed up with someone else**)
ex: "You got me twisted." "I'm the one who got who twisted?"

[to] **have it out with** [someone] v. (general sl.) old & new school
1. to have an argument, fight, or confrontation with someone.
ex: "Sooner or later me and you gonna have it out."

[to] **have** [one's] **way** phrase (e. coast sl.) new school
1. to have the ability to do what one wants against his/her opponent. (var. [to] **have** [one's] **way with** [someone])
ex: "I be havin' my way when I play ya brother." "I'm about to have my way with this chump."

[someone who's] **havin' a baby** phrase (general sl.) old & new school
1. one who is expressing displeasure loudly and angrily. (var. [to] **have a baby/fit** [on someone])
ex: "When I told her, she just started havin' a baby."

[to] **hawk** [someone] v. (general sl.) old & new school
1. to watch/observe someone closely. (var. [someone who's a] **hawk**)
ex: "I can't go anywhere without him hawkin' me."

hay n. (w. coast sl.) new school
1. marijuana.

haze n. (drug sl.) new school
1. marijuana. (var. **purple haze**)

he ain't no gorilla, he just got the suit on phrase (southern sl.) new school
1. a witty way to dismiss someone who's acting or talking tough.

[to] **head** [somewhere] v. (general sl.) old & new school
1. to go somewhere. 2. to travel in a certain direction. (var. [to be] **headed** [in a certain direction], [to] **head over** [somewhere])
ex: "I'm about to head home."

head n. (sexual sl.) old & new school
1. oral sex.
ex: "She never had head."

[a] **head crack** adj. (e. coast sl.) old & new school
1. an instant winner [usually used to taunt others that one is gambling against in any game one can win instantly].
ex: "This is where I come up with a head crack."

head games phrase (genera sl.) old & new school
1. the lies, deceptions, and unscrupulous mind games that people play in attempts to take advantage of or manipulate someone.
ex: "Tell ya peoples I ain't in for all the head games." "Don't come at with them head games."

[to] **head out** v. (general sl.) old & new school
1. to leave; to depart.
ex: "What time y'all wanna head out?" "We was just about to head out."

[a female's] **head piece** phrase (sexual sl.) old & new school
1. a term used to refer a female's ability or inability to perform oral sex. (var. [a female's] **head game**)
ex: "How's shorties head piece?" "I heard her head game is all that."

headquarters n. (general sl.) old school
1. a name used to refer to someone who has a big head.

ex: "Here comes ya man headquarters." "You think headquarters can hook me up with a friend?"

[to go] **head up** v. (general sl.) old & new school
1. to compete or go up against someone one-on-one without other people interfering. (var. [to] **go head up**)
ex: "We can go head up in here." Just let me know when you ready to go head up."

heads n. (general sl.) old & new school
1. people; a way to refer to a group of people.
ex: "Madd heads posed to be there." "I didn't realize so many heads was into this."

heads n. (drug sl.) old & new school
1. a way to refer to people who smoke and/or are addicted to crack cocaine.
ex: "I seen ya moms hangin' out with some heads from up the block."

heads up phrase (general sl.) old & new school
1. a warning shouted to alert people that something is falling or about to fall from somewhere above.

[a female who's] **healthy** adj. (general sl.) old & new school
1. a female with a big butt and large breast.
ex: "...She aiight, but shortie over there, she's healthy."

[someone who has] **heart** adj. (general sl.) old & new school
1. one who is brave and courageous; daring.
ex: "Ya man don't have no heart." "It don't take heart to do that."

[someone who's your] **heart** adj. (general sl.) old & new school
1. a beloved friend of loved one.
ex: "You my heart shortie." "Son used to be heart 'til he snaked me."

[someone whose] **heart pumps koolaid** phrase (general sl.) old school
1. one who is afraid or scared and cowardly. (var. [someone whose] **heart pumps Kool Aid all day long**)
ex: "Stay here if ya heart pump koolaid."

heat n. (criminal sl.) old & new school
1. a firearm; gun. See also: **iron**
ex: "I hope you not bringin' no heat."

[something that's] **heat** adj. (general sl.) new school
1. outstanding; unique; the best of it's kind.
ex: "I can't even front son, that is definitely heat."

heated adj. (general sl.) old & new school
1. angry; mad; upset.
ex: "Yo, that sh** had me heated." "You could tell he was heated about that."

[someone who's] **heavy** adj. (general sl.) old & new school
1. someone who is wearing a lot of expensive jewelry.
ex: "They came to the party madd heavy."

[something that's] **hella proper** adj. (w. coast sl.) new school
1. outstanding; unique; the best of its kind.
ex: "That house I'm about to buy my momz is hella proper."

hellava phrase (southern sl.) old & new school
1. a term used to emphasized ones description or assessment [of something or someone].
ex: "You know youse a hellava dude." "That's one hellava walk you got there."

Hell if I care phrase (southern sl.) old & new school
1. a matter of fact way to say "I don't care" or "I could care less".
ex: "You ain't never gotta come back, Hell if I care."

Hell if I know phrase (general sl.) old & new school
1. a hip way to say "I don't know" [usually used when one is stumped for an answer]. (var. **Damn if I know**)
ex: "Hell if I know, I never got that far."

Hell nah! phrase (southern sl.) new school
1. a negative way to respond to something shocking, surprising, or unbelievable. (var. **oh, Hell nah**)
ex: "Hell nah, I know she didn't tell you that."

Hells Yeah! interj. (general sl.) new school
1. an enthusiastic way to answer "yes" or "you bet" to a question [usually pertaining to wanting to do something].
ex: "Hells Yeah I want to go with y'all."

[to] **help** [someone] **get on his/her feet** phrase (general sl.) old & new school
1. to lend someone assistance who is struggling financially until he/she can earn and/or save enough money to become financially independent [usually giving that person money or a place to live]. See also: [to] **get on** [one's] **feet**
ex: "Can you help me, 'til I get on my feet?"

[to] **hem** [someone] **up** v. (criminal sl.) old & new school
1. to rob someone.
ex: "They said you got hemmed up for the watch."

hemmed up phrase (criminal sl.) old & new school
1. arrested; caught; to be detained by law enforcement agents. 2. to be delayed.
ex: "Police hemmed my man up for nothin'." "Looks like we gonna be hemmed up for a while."

Henny n. (general sl.) new school
1. Hennesy brand of cognac. (var. **Henny Rock**)
ex: "Shortie drinks a lil Henny every once in a while."

herb (pron. 'erb) n. (drug sl.) old school
l. marijuana.
ex: "Smokin' herb is whack."

[to] **herb** (pron. her-b) [someone] v. (e. coast sl.) old & new school
l. to bully, manipulate, or take advantage of someone using
intimidation, deception, or praying on one's weaknesses [often
taking advantage of that person's need to feel accepted]; to treat
someone like a sucker.
ex: "Ya man got herbed in prison." "Can't you see they tryin' to
herb you?"

[a] **herb** (pron. her-b) adj. (e. coast sl.) old & new school
l. one who is easily manipulated, intimidated, and/or taken
advantage of because of his/her need to feel accepted. 2. one who
is not cool, hip, or trendy.
ex: "Don't tell that herb to come over here." "You know they got
that cat on herb status, right?"

Hershey n. (e. coast sl.) new school
l. a type of marijuana that tastes and smells like chocolate when
smoked.

he say, she say phrase (general sl.) old & new school
l. rumors and innuendo that people spread then deny spreading
and/or blame someone else for spreading.
ex: "I don't get involved with the he say, she say."

[to] **hide heat** phrase (criminal sl.) new school
l. to carry a concealed firearm. (var. [to] **hold heat**)
ex: "When you get on a plane now, you won't know who's hidin'
heat."

high as a kite phrase (general sl.) old school
l. a way to describe being intoxicated and/or high from an illegal
narcotic.
ex: "She came to the party high as a kite."

[to] **high beam** [someone] v. (southern sl.) new school
1. to flaunt one's diamond encrusted jewelry in front of others to get attention or to show off. See also: [to] **floss on** [someone]
ex: "I was high beamin' them fools at the club."

high maintenance [females] adj. (e. coast sl.) new school
1. females with expensive tastes, needs, and wants. (var. **high maintenance** [chicks, shorties, broads])
ex: "I ain't tryin' to kick it, if you one of them high maintenance chicks."

[something that's] **high-power'd** adj. (general sl.) old school
1. outstanding; unique; the best of its kind.
ex: "The T-connection was high-power'd back in the days."

[a] **high roller** adj. (general sl.) old school
1. someone who has and spends large amounts of money freely.
ex: "The high rollers don't get here 'til at least two in the mornin'."

[to] **highside** v. (w. coast sl.) new school
1. to act like or pretend to be better than everyone because of one's financial status, position of authority, fame or success. See also: [to] **act brand new**
ex: "Last time he came through the hood, he was highsidin' the peoples."

[a] **high top** n. (general sl.) old school
1. a haircut that was popular in the 1980's. (var. [a] **high top fade**)

[someone who's] **hikin' it** [somewhere] phrase (general sl.) old & new school
1. walking. (var. [to] **hike it** [somewhere])
ex: "Y'all better start hikin' it cause y'all can't ride with me."

[to] **hip** [someone] v. (general sl.) old & new school

1. to inform or reveal information to someone that he/she was not aware of; to bring something to someone's attention. (var. [to] **hip** [someone] **to** [something]) See also: [to] **put a bug in** [someone's] **ear**
ex: "Be quiet while I try to hip you to what went down."

Hip-Hop n. (e. coast sl.) old & new school
1. an Urban youth culture which originated in the Bronx N.Y. in 1979-1980 where DJ's would play different records and MC's would rhyme along with and over the beat of the record being played.

Hip-Hop kids n. (general sl.) old & new school
1. people who are a part of, follow, and help create the trends of the Hip-Hop culture.
ex: "You have Hip-Hop kids all over the world now."

[to] **hit** [someone] v. (general sl.) old & new school
1. to give, lend, or share something with someone. (var. [to] **hit** [someone] **off**, [to] **hit** [someone off] **with something**)
ex: "Once I hit you with this that's the last of it."

[someone who's] **hit** adj. (general sl.) new school
1. in trouble or in a bad situation. 2. without money; destitute. See also: **dead and stinkin'**
ex: "I hate to say it, but ya man hit." "I'm hit right now."

[to] **hit** [someone] v. (sexual sl.) old & new school
1. the act of having sex. (var. [to] **hit**, [to] **hit that up**, [to] **hit the skins**) See also: [to] **bone** [someone]
ex: "I heard you hit her sister." "She let you hit that yet?" "I was just about to hit."

[to] **hit a lick** phrase (criminal sl.) old & new school
1. to take, steal, or pilfer something that will bring someone quick cash; to commit robbery. (var. [to] **hit a nice lil lick**)
ex: "We about to hit this lick, you down?"

[a male who'd] **hit anything** [moving] adj. (sexual sl.) old & new school
1. a male who will have sex indiscriminately with any female he can.

[to] **hit** [someone] **dead in the face/eye/mouth** phrase (general sl.) old & new school
1. the act of hitting someone in the face/eye/mouth with a punch or object that was thrown. (var. [to] **hit** [someone] **dead in** [his/her] **sh****)
ex: "Do that again, I'mma hit you dead in the mouth."

[to] **hit** [a female] **from the back** v. (sexual sl.) old & new school
1. a male term for having sex with a female "doggie style" (var. [to] **hit it from the back**)
ex: "She asked me to hit 'er from the back."

[to get] **hit in the head** phrase (southern sl.) new school
1. to lose one's money gambling; to take a lost on a bet. 2. sentence to a long prison term. (var. [to get] **banged in the head**)
ex: "I been gettin' hit in the head all week."

[to] **hit** [someone] **in the head** phrase (criminal sl.) new school
1. to testify against a friend or family member in a court of law [as a result the friend or family member usually is sent to prison for a long period of time].
ex: "You know he ain't no good, he hit his own cousin in the head."

[to] **hit it and quit it** phrase (sexual sl.) old & new school
1. to engage in a meaningless sexual liaison or one night stand.
ex: "I know all you wanna do is hit it and quit it." "I told you he was gonna hit it and quit it."

[someone who's] **hit like monkey/puppy sh**** phrase (southern sl.) new school

1. one who is in extremely bad trouble. 2. a way to emphasize being without money or destitute.
ex: "If I can't explain this, I'm hit like monkey sh**."

[to] **hit** [someone off] **love/lovely/love love** v. (general sl.) old & new school
1. to be extremely generous when giving someone something; to give an abundance of.
ex: "When I hit the bricks Heav hit me love son."

[to] **hit** [someone] **off** v. (sexual sl.) old & new school
1. to have sex. 2. to perform oral sex on someone. (var. [to] **hit off**)
ex: "I would hit you off but you might tell somebody."

[to get] **hit off** v. (general sl.) old & new school
1. to receive something.
ex: "We about to get hit off in a minute." "When the last time you been hit off?"

[to] **hit** [something] **on the head** phrase (general sl.) old & new school
1. to assess or answer correctly.
ex: "You hit that right on the head."

[to] **hit** [someone] **on the hip** v. (general sl.) old & new school
1. to beep, text message, or phone someone on their cellular phone or pager.
ex: "Just hit me on the hip when you've made up your mind."

[to] **hit** [a female] **on the regular/reg** v. (sexual sl.) new school
1. to have sex with a particular female on a regular basis.
ex: "Dawg was hittin' his wife on the regular." "He used to hit that on the reg."

[to] **hit** [a female] **raw** v. (sexual sl.) old & new school
1. to have unprotected sex. (var. [to] **hit raw**, [to] **hit** [a female] **raw dawg**)

ex: " I can't believe you hit shortie raw. "

[to] **hit the bricks** phrase (prison sl.) new school
1. to be released from jail or prison. (var. [to] **hit the streets**) See also: [to] **touchdown**
ex: "I hit the bricks real soon." "Its all about you and me when I hit the bricks. "

[to] **hit the hammer** phrase (prison sl.) new school
1. the touching of clinched fists to solidify a deal, wager, or arrangement [represents the giving of one's word]. (var. [to] **hit the rock**)
ex: "Lets hit the hammer before we begin. "

[to] **hit the highway** phrase (general sl.) old & new school
1. to travel somewhere one has to use a highway to reach his/her destination; to depart on a long road trip; to leave. (var. [to] **hit the highway on** [someone])
ex: "Tell dawg we about to hit the highway." "I hit the highway on them chickenheads. "

[to] **hit the mall** phrase (general sl.) old & new school
1. to make a trip or visit to a shopping mall.
ex: "The best day to hit the mall is Saturday. "

[to] **hit the pipe** v. (drug sl.) old & new school
1. to smoke crack cocaine using a glass pipe. (var. [someone who] **hits the pipe**)
ex: "Talk to him before he starts hittin' the pipe. "

hit the water, it don't hit back phrase (prison sl.) new school
1. a witty way to tell someone to bathe.

[to be/get] **hit up** phrase (criminal sl.) old & new school
1. to be shot; wounded by gunfire. (var. [to] **hit** [someone] **up**)
ex: "How many times did he get hit up?" "Somebody tried to hit'is ass up. "

[to] **hit** [someone] **up** [for something] v. (general sl.) old & new school
1. to ask someone for something; to make a request.
ex: "Hit'em up and see what he says."

[to] **hit** [someone] **up** v. (general sl.) old & new school
1. to contact someone through any means of communication.
ex: "I was just about to hit you up about that thing we talked about earlier."

[to] **hit** [someone] **with** [a line/lie/excuse/explanation] v. (general sl.) new school
1. the attempt to use a line, lie, excuse or explanation convincingly.

[to] **hit** [someone] **with a package** v. (drug sl.) old & new school
1. to give someone a certain amount of illegal drugs to sell retail. (var. [to] **hit** [someone] **off with a package**) See also: [a]
package)
ex: "I seen when he hit you with that package."

[to] **hit** [someone] **with some bullsh**** phrase (general sl.) new school
1. to tell someone something that is a lie, decptive, or a con in attempt to offer an excuse or explanation. (var. [to] **hit** [someone] **with some** [ol' / the] **bullsh****)
ex: "I couldn't believe shortie tried to hit me with some bullsh**."

[to] **hit** [someone] **with the real** phrase (general sl.) new school
1. to be blunt, open, and honest with someone. (var. [to] **hit** [someone] **with the realz/the really real/ the real deal**)
ex: "I just hit shortie with the real and told' er I wanted to see other people."

[something that's] **hittin'** adj. (general sl.) old & new school
1. outstanding; unique; the best of its kind; exemplary.
ex: "That sh** gonna be hittin'."

hittin' switches v. (w. coast sl.) old & new school
1. the act of using the hydraulic system one has installed in his/her automobile to make the car go up and down or tilt sideways.

[a] **hold card** phrase (e. coast sl.) old & new school
1. a secret [that usually can destory one's reputation].
ex: "Don't make me expose ya hold card." "I peeped'is hold card a long time ago."

[to] **hold court in the streets** phrase (criminal sl.) old & new school
1. to have a violent confrontation with law enforcement officials that are trying to arrest and bring one back to prison [usually used as a vow not to be brought back to prison without a fight]. (var. [to] **hold court**)

[to] **hold** [someone] **down** v. (general sl.) new school
1. to cover for, fill in for, or offer support for someone when needed. (var. [to] **hold it down** [for someone])
ex: "Go 'head and leave I'll hold you down." "Can you hold it down 'till I get back."

[to] **hold** [something] **down** v. (general sl.) new school
1. to secure or retain something. (var. [to] **hold** [something] **down** [for someone])
ex: "Hold down a spot for me when you get there."

hold it down phrase (general sl.) new school
1. a way to tell someone to take care of himself/ herself when departing comapany.
ex: "Y'all hold it down, and I'll call y'all later."

[someone who's] **holdin'** phrase (general sl.) new school
1. one who has, has access to, or earns large amounts of money; rich, wealthy.
ex: "People keep sayin' Mike ain't holdin', I got 'em still holdin'

*some paper." "Bullsh** ain't nothin' ya man Russell holdin'
for real."*

[to] **hold** [one's] **nuts** phrase (southern sl.) new school
1. to wish someone bad luck or failure. 2. to wish for the opposite
of what another is wishing for. (var. [to] **hold** [one's] **nuts on**
[someone])
ex: "Look at them bammas over there holdin' their nuts."

[to] **hold** [one's] **own** phrase (general sl.) old & new school
1. to sustain the pressure one is under or may be facing.
ex: "Look, I can hold my own, what about you?"

[to] **hold** [one's] **own** phrase (general sl.) old & new school
1. to have the ability to shoulder one's own responsibilities,
situations, or challenges. (var. [to] **carry** [one's] **own weight**)
*ex: "Look here homes, I can hold my own wherever I go." "I been
holdin' my own this long, why do I need you?"*

[you] **hold the tail while I milk this cow** phrase (southern sl.) old
& new school
1. a way to respond to someone who is trying to give you
instructions on how to do something he/she knows little or nothing
about. 2. a way to say, "let me do this".

hold tight phrase (general sl.) old & new school
1. a way to tell someone to wait, give you a moment, or be patient.
ex: "Hold tight, they'll be here."

hold up phrase (general sl.) old & new school
1. a term used to interrupt or stop someone from saying anything
further [usually because one is skeptical/confused].
ex: "Hold up man, what did you mean by that?"

[to] **hold water** phrase (general sl.) old & new school
1. to have the ability to keep a secret. (var. [to] **hold** [one's] **water**)

ex: "I doubt if she can hold water."

hold ya head phrase (e. coast sl.) old & new school
1. a way to tell someone to calm down, take it easy, or to remain in control of their emotions. (var. [to] **hold** [one's] **head**)
ex: "You hafta learn how to hold ya head sometimes."

[someone who's] **holdin'** v. (drug sl.) old & new school
1. someone who is in possession of drugs packaged for retail sale.
ex: "Which one of y'all is holdin'?"

holler (pron. holla) phrase (southern sl.) new school
1. a playful or sarcastic way to cut someone off verbally [usually signaling one is through with talking or listening] while one is leaving the presence of that person [often used dismissively]. 2. a way to say "goodbye" or "see you later". (var. **I'll holler** [at you])

[to] **holler** (pron. holla) **at** [someone] v. (southern sl.) new school
1. to talk; to communicate. 2. the act of getting better acquainted. (var. [to] **holler**)
ex: "I been tryin' to holler at you for a while." "When can I holler at you?" "Tell'er I want to holler." "I heard you holler'd at my boy last night."

holler (pron. holla) **at ya boy/girl** phrase (southern sl.) new school
1. a witty way to tell a friend or love one to get [back] in contact with you [usually used at the end of a written or verbal communique].
ex: "Next time you in town, holler at ya boy." "Holler at ya girl when you know something."

holler back phrase (southern sl.) new school
1. a hip way to tell someone to contact you at a another time [usually used when departing ways]. (var. **holler back youngin'**)
ex: "All you hafta do is holler back when you think you ready."

holler if you hear me phrase (southern sl.) new school

1. an enthusiastic way to ask someone to say something if he/she agrees, approves, or can relate to what you are saying.
ex: "We don't kick it with scrubs, holler if you hear me."

[to] **holler on** [someone] v. (criminal sl.) new school
1. to inform on a friend or love one to law enforcement or testify against them in a court of law.
ex: "He's the same dude that holler'd on us."

hollow heads n. (criminal sl.) old & new school
1. bullets that are hollowed tipped. See also: **dumb dumbs**
ex: "The hollow heads explode in you."

homeboy n. (general sl.) old & new school
1. a term of endearment among friends; friend. 2. a way to address someone whose name you don't know or don't want to use in front of others. (var. **homegirl, homie, homie stromie, hometeam, home slice**)
ex: "I wouldn't do that homeboy." "And I thought you was my homeboy."

home grown n. (drug sl.) old school
1. weak marijuana.
ex: "Don't nobody want none of that home grown."

homes n. (general sl.) old & new school
1. a way to address someone whose name you don't know or whose name you don't want to use [usually used as a way to dismiss someone's importance].
ex: "If homes is goin' I'm not comin'."

[one's] **homie** n. (w. coast sl.) old & new school
1. one's friend. 2. males who are from the same city, state, or neighborhood as you.
ex: "You always gonna be my homie." "I want you to meet ya homies."

[a] honeycomb hide-out n. (general sl.) old & new school
1. the house, apartment, or place where you and your friends frequent and/or gather the most.
ex: "Its time for me to find us a new honeycomb hide-out."

[a] honey dip n. (general sl.) new school
1. an attractive and/or sexy looking female.
ex: "That's a nice lil honey dip you got there youngin'."

honey spots n. (general sl.) new
1. places where good looking females congregate.
ex: "I found this down low honey spot."

honeys n. (general sl.) old & new school
1. females; a group of females.
ex: "There was madd honeys there."

hoochie wear/gear phrase (southern sl.) new school
1. clothing that females wear which reveals too much of their cleavage and buttock areas of their body. (var. [a] **hoochie outfit**)
ex: "You not goin' nowhere with me, with that hoochie gear on."

hoochies n. (southern sl.) old & new school
1. females who wear clothes that reveal too much of their body and/or private part for the purpose of getting attention from men. 2. females who are very promiscuous. (var. **hoochie mommas**) See also: **ashy feets**
ex: "Who told that hoochie she was invited?"

[one's] hood n. (w. coast sl.) old & new school
1. one's neighborhood. 2. a neighborhood in the inner city. (var. **the hood**)
ex: "We had fun comin' up in my hood."

[a] hood divorce phrase (general sl.) new school

1. the unofficial separation of a married couple where they are legally married but date other people; a divorce without the paperwork.
ex: "They was hood divorced for two years."

hoodfellas n. (e. coast sl.) new school
1. the "street" individuals from one's neighborhood who know how to make money illegally.

[a] **hood rat** n. (general sl.) new school
1. a neighborhood female who sleeps around with many different males from the same neighborhood.
ex: "He don't live around here, so he don't know she's a straight hood rat."

hood rich n. (e. coast sl.) new school
1. to have the financial means that allows one to live flamboyantly above the median income range for one's neighborhood [often refusing to move/live anywhere else].

[a] **hoody** n. (general sl.) old & new school
1. a hooded sweat shirt or sweat jacket [favored by young "street" toughs].

[to] **hook off on** [someone] v. (e. coast sl.) new school
1. the act of punching someone when he/she least expects it [usually wanting to be the first to strike].
ex: "She just came in the room and started hookin' off."

[to] **hook** [someone] **up** v. (general sl.) old & new school
1. to do a favor for someone; to show someone preferential treatment. (var. [to] **hook** [something] **up for** [someone], [to] **hook** [someone] **up with** [something])
ex: "Thanks for hookin' that up."

[to] **hookup** v. (general sl.) old & new school

1. to meet or get together with someone [usually refers to a intimate gathering between two people]. (var. [to] **hookup with** [someone])
ex: "I been tryin' to hookup with you for a long time."

[one's] **hookup** n. (prison sl.) new school
1. one's personal contact information [address, phone number, etc.]
ex: "Did she leave her hookup before she left?"

[to] **hook** [someone] **up with** [someone] v. (general sl.) old & new school
1. to introduce two people of the opposite sex to each other with the intention of them becoming intimately involved; to play matchmaker.
ex: "I'mma try to hook you up with my cousin."

[something that's] **hooked** adj. (general sl.) old & new school
1. outstanding; unique; the best of its kind. (var. [something that's] **hooked up**)
ex: "His new crib is hooked."

hookers n. (general sl.) old & new school
1. a playful way to refer to females [not used in the context of a female literally being a prostitute].
ex: "Find out what them hookers gonna do."

[a] **hooptie** n. (w. coast sl.) old & new school
1. an old and battered automobile.
ex: "My moms first car was a hooptie."

[to] **hop in** [someone's] **whip** v. (general sl.) old & new school
1. to get into someone's car. (var. [to] **hop outta a whip**)
ex: "Word up son, shortie hopped right in his whip."

hops n. (e. coast sl.) old school

1. a term of endearment among friends; friend. 2. a way to address someone whose name you do not know or do not want to use in front of others.
ex: "You hafta wait in the car hops."

[someone who has] **hops** adj. (general sl.) new school
1. one who has the ability to jump extremely high.
ex: "That new kid got madd hops."

[a] **horn** n. (general sl.) old & new school
1. a telephone. See also: [a] **jack**
ex: "I need to use your horn."

horse hair n. (general sl.) old & new school
1. synthetic hair used by females to enhance the length of their real hair. 2. a weave.
ex: "Ya Shortie horse hair looks nice on her."

[something that's] **hot** adj. (general sl.) old & new school
1. outstanding; unique; the best of its kind. (var. [something that's]
red hot, burnin' hot)
ex: "That new remix is hot dun."

[someone who's] **hot** adj. (general sl.) old & new school
1. one who is very attractive, sexy, and/or has a very nice body.
ex: "I met this hot lil chick yesterday."

[someone who's] **hot** adj. (criminal sl.) new school
1. one who has cooperated with law enforcement agents in an investigation of a friend or love one or has testified in court against a friend or love one.
ex: "We just found out ya boy is hot."

[a female who's a] **hot ass** adj. (general sl.) old & new school
1. a female who is extremely flirtatious and/or promiscuous.
ex: "Go in there and sit your lil hot ass down." "She growin' up to be a hot ass."

hot balls n. (criminal sl.) new school
1. bullets. (var. **hot ones**)
ex: "You be cryin' if you got hit with one of these hot balls."

hot boys n. (southern sl.) new school
1. young "street" individuals who make large amounts of money and live the reckless life of "thugs".
ex: "Them broads like messin' with them hot boys, 'til a hot boy goes to jail, them broads is gone."

Hotlanata n. (southern sl.) new school
1. Atlanta, GA.

[a] **hot rock** n. (general sl.) new school
1. a basketball. (var. [a] **pill**)
ex: "He shot the hot rock at the buzzer and won the championship."

[something that's] **hot to death** adj. (general sl.) old & new school
1. outstanding; unique; the best of its kind.
ex: "That outfit he wore to the awards was hot to death."

[someone who's] **hot to death** adj. (general sl.) old & new school
1. one who is very attractive and/or sexy.
ex: "I remember when she was lil, now she's hot to death."

[someone who's] **hotter than fish grease** phrase (criminal sl.) new school
1. someone who is being sought after by the police; a wanted criminal; a fugitive. 2. someone who has testified or cooperated with law enforcement agents against a friend or family member.
ex: "You can't come around here, you hotter than fish grease."

[a] **hottie** adj. (general sl.) old & new school
1. someone who is extremely good looking and/or has an extremely nice body.
ex: "There posed to be some real hotties out here tonight."

[to] **hound** [someone] v. (general sl.) old & new school
1. to nag, annoy, and/or aggravate someone. 2. to repeatedly field the same questions at someone. 3. to watch someone extremely close. (var. [someone who's a] **hound**)
ex: "This cat been houndin' me all night."

[to] **house** [someone] v. (e. coast sl.) old school
1. to take someone's possessions by force, intimidation, or through manipulation; to bully someone out of something. (var. [to] **house** [someone] **for his/her sh****, [to] **house** [someone's] **sh****)
ex: "I can't believe you let'em house you."

how you? n. (general sl.) old & new school
1. a hip way to greet someone. 2 a way to say "how are you doing?"
ex: "Peace son, how you?"

how you livin'? phrase (general sl.) old & new school
1. a term used to question one's character or actions when you observe him/her doing someone wrong, strange, or questionable. 2. a way to express shock, disbelief, or surprise. 3. a way to inquire about one's well being. (var. **is that/ that's how you livin'?**)
ex: "How you livin' pa?" "All I wanna know, is that's how you livin'?"

[a] **hucklebuck** n. (southern sl.) new school
1. in a losing position; at a very bad disadvantage; a situation very hard to get out of.
ex: "I can't leave now, these chumps got me in hucklebuck and I'm down five hundred."

humongus adj. (general sl.) old & new school
1. extremely big [usually used to describe a female's butt].
ex: "Shortie butt is humongus."

humpbacks n. (prison sl.) new school
1. cigarettes.

ex: "I quit smokin' them humpbacks years ago."

hump day n. (general sl.) old & new school
1. Wedensday; the middle of the week.

[someone who's] **hungry** adj. (e. coast sl.) new school
1. in desparate need of or want for something [usually money, success, or fame].
ex: "When catz get hungry, that's when the larceny starts comin' out."

[a] **hun'ned** n. (e. coast sl.) old & new school
1. one hundred. 2. numerations of hundreds. (var. **hun'neds)**
ex: "He had to do a hun'ned pushups." "You still owe me a couple hun'ned."

hurt adj. (general sl.) old & new school
1. without money; destitute. (var. [someone who's] **hurtin'**)
ex: "Yo, them catz hurtin' since you been away."

[to] **hurt** [someone's] **heart** phrase (general sl.) old & new school
1. to do something to someone that causes that person heartache, grief, pain, sorrow, emotional turmoil. (var. [something that] **hurts** [someone] **to** [his/her] **heart,** [someone who] **hurts** [someone] **to** [his/her] **heart)**
ex: "She hurt my heart when she told me that." "Seein' you like this, hurts me to my heart."

[not] **hurtin' for nothin'** phrase (general sl.) new school
1. to have everything one can possibly need or want; to have the financial ability to live comfortable.
ex: "I don't need your sh** I ain't hurtin' for nothin'." "I don't ask cause I'm not hurtin' for nothin'."

[someone who] **hurts you to your heart** phrase (general sl.) old & new school

1. someone who causes you extreme emotional anguish or pain. (var. [something that] **hurts you to your heart**)
ex: "She hurt me to my heart when she told me the truth about dude."

[to] **hustle** v. (general sl.) old & new school
1. to make money using one's ingenuity [usually acts or means that aren't necessarily legal].
ex: "I been out here hustlin' all day." "I need you to help me work this hustle."

[one's] **hustle** n. (general sl.) old & new school
1. the way one makes and/or earns his/her money legally or illegally. (var. [a] **hustle**])
ex: "I'm not about to let you come in here and mess up my hustle." "You gonna hafta find your own hustle."

[to] **hustle** [someone] v. (general sl.) old & new school
1. the act of conning someone.
ex: "You know better than try to hustle me." "That's all part of the hustle." "Your hustle is weak."

[to] **hustle backwards** phrase (e. coast sl.) old & new school
1. to have no tangible results from one's illegal activity because one squanders his/her ill gotten gains. (var. [someone who's] **hustlin' backwards**)
ex: "If you don't have nothin' to show for your time in the game, you hustlin' backwards."

hustlers n. (general sl.) old & new school
1. people who con other people for money or things of value. 2. drug dealers; people who earn large amounts of money through illegal activities.

hustlers ends phrase (e. coast sl.) new school
1. large amounts of money.
ex: "She wanted a cat with hustlers ends."

hydro n. (drug sl.) new school
1. bright green marijuana grown under water; good marijuana. (var. **'dro**)

[one's] **hydro flow** adj. (e. coast sl.) new school
1. one's unique and/or superior way of talking, rhyming, and/or charming someone of the opposite sex.
ex: "Once I hit her with this hydro flow, she was on me."

[a] **hype** n. (drug sl.) old & new school
1. a cigarette or marijuana joint/"blunt" laced with crack cocaine.
ex: "She smoked one hype and was hooked."

i

I ain't! interj. (southern sl.) old school
1. a playful or sarcastic way to put emphasis on your refusal to do something that someone is asking you to do; a way to say, "no" or "no I'm not".

I ain't f**kin' with you [no more] phrase (general sl.) old & new school
1. a matter of fact way to tell someone you don't want anything to do with him/her [sometimes used insincerely when one is annoyed, angry, or frustrated with a friend or love one].
ex. "I already told you, I ain't f**kin' with you no more."

I ain't gonna sh**, shave, or bathe 'til I see better days phrase (prison sl.) new school
1. a way to vow not to do anything until one's situation or circumstances improve [usually used when dissatisfied].

I ain't got... phrase (general sl.) old & new school
1. a term used in prelude to expressing one's doubt [usually about what someone else will do or not do].
ex: "I ain't got her comin' back." "I ain't got it rainnin."

I ain't got nothin' but love for you phrase (e. coast sl.) old school
1. a friendly way to mock someone who is complaining to you about your treatment towards him/her.

I ain't mad at you phrase (w. coast sl.) new school
1. a friendly or sarcastic way to inform someone you do not have a problem with his/her decision or comment [even if you don't mean it]. 2. a way to say something is okay.
ex: "If you wanna talk to my ex, I ain't mad at you."

I ain't never been scared of nothin' standin'/walkin' on two feet phrase (e. coast sl.) old & new school
1. a way to respond to one's claim that you are scared of him/her or of a certain individual.

I ain't no killer, but don't push me phrase (w. coast sl.) new school
1. a playful way to warn someone to stop taking you lightly when it comes to standing up for yourself. 2. a way to tell someone you will fight/defend yourself if you are forced to.

I ain't stutter (pron. stutta) phrase (general sl.) old & new school
1. a playful or sarcastic way to say, "you heard me", "you heard what I said", "I don't have to repeat myself", "I meant that", "I made myself clear", when someone is pretending to not have heard you or not understand what you are talking about. (var. **I ain't stutter, utter, or mutter**)

I ain't the herb (pron. her-b) **you lookin' for** phrase (e. coast sl.) old & new school
1. a term used to warn and/or advise someone you are not the type of person who won't stand up for himself/ herself, that can be easily taken advantage of, lead to believe something ridiculous or unbelievable. (var. **I ain't the one you lookin' for**)

I ain't the one, and we dam sure ain't the two phrase (general sl.) old school
1. a term females use to dismiss males who are being rude or disrespectful when trying to come on to them.

I ain't the one to gossip phrase (general sl.) old & new school
1. a term used as a disclaimer right before or right after one relays a rumor he/she has heard.

I always get me phrase (general sl.) new school
1. a way to affirm one's claim that he/she always gets what he/she wants.

I bullsh** you not phrase (general sl.) old & new school
1. a term used to express ones sincerity, seriousness, attempt to sound honest.
ex: "I bullsh** you not dawg that was her."

I call you son not cause you mine, I call you son cause you shine phrase (e. coast sl.) new school
1. a term of endearment among friends [usually used to express friendship].

I can do bad by myself phrase (general sl.) old & new school
1. a term used to inform someone you don't need him/her if he/she is unable or unfit to contribute or help out [usually used in reference to an intimate relationship].
ex: "You need to get your act together cause I can do bad by myself."

I can go with that phrase (general sl.) new school
1. a hip way to reach an agreement or consensus about something.
(var. **I can get with that, I can go/get** [with you on] **that**)
ex: "That sounds about right, I can go with that."

I can show you better than I can tell you phrase (southern sl.) new school
1. a playful or sarcastic way to respond to someone who is questioning or doubting your abilities or claims [usually used confrontationally or challengingly].

I can't call it phrase (general sl.) old & new school
1. a way to respond to one's verbal greeting or verbal inquiry as to your well being (var. **I can't make no noise/complain/kick up no dirt, I can't call it and if I call it I might spoil it**)

I can't kick a field goal if I had three legs phrase (southern sl.) new school

1. a way to express one's bad luck or misfortune.

I can't stand that [epithet] phrase (general sl.) old & new school
1. a term used to emphasize one's dislike for another [use a insult, derogatory term or phrase to describe such person].
ex: "I can't stand that bit** ass cousin of yours."

I can't tell phrase (southern sl.) new school
1. a playful or sarcastic way to express doubt or question one's claim, boast, threat, or character [usually used to put one on the spot or as a way to force one to affirm himself/herself].
ex: "I can't tell you goin' in there." "You gonna do what to me, I can't tell."

I can't tell I said somethin' wrong, my mouth/lip/nose ain't bleedin' phrase (southern sl.) new school
1. a way to respond to someone who has accused you of saying something to him/her which was offensive or disrespectful. (var. **I can't tell I said somethin' wrong, my mouth/lip/nose ain't swollen, I can't tell I said somethin' wrong, my teeth still in my mouth/I still got all my teeth**)

ice n. (general sl.) old & new school
1. diamonds.

[to] **ice grill** [someone] v. (e. coast sl.) new school
1. to look or stare at someone with a mean and/or tough expression. (var. [to] **hit** [someone] **with the ice grill/grilly**) See also: [to] **mean mug** [someone]
ex: "You be tryin' to act all friendly and sh** and people still give you the ice grill."

[jewelry that's] **iced out** adj. (general sl.) new school
1. jewelry that has many diamonds encrusted in it [a watch, ring, pendant, or chain]. (var. [jewelry that's] **iced down/icy**, [to] **ice** [something] **out**)

ex: "I'm about to give Shortie this iced out bracelet for her birthday."

I could sell a weekend cruise to a man on death row phrase (southern sl.) new school
1. a witty term one uses to profess his/her ability to be a fast and/or slick talker. (var. **I could sell birth control to a nun/contact lenses to a blind man/life insurance to a dead man**)

I'd kiss a fly in a bow tie phrase (southern sl.) new school
1. a way for one to express his/her desperation to meet and/or go out with someone of the opposite sex on a date. (var. **I'd kiss a pig in a wig**)

I do what I do, like I'm doin' it for T.V. phrase (e. coast sl.) new school
1. a witty way to boast about being the best at what one does [also used to taunt one's opponent].

I does this phrase (general sl.) new school
1. a term one uses to affirm or reaffirm his/her boast, claim, or declaration when someone verbally challenges or questions his/her word [usually used to exude a air of confidence when responding to someone's doubt]. (var. **I do/ does this for a livin'**)

I don't care where you go… but you gots to get up outta here phrase (general sl.) old & new school
1. a no-nonsense way to tell someone that he/she has to leave/go, he/she can't stay any longer, or its time go; a term used to put or throw someone out of a place of business or one's dwellings. See also: **let ya feet meet the street**

I don't get down like that phrase (general sl.) old & new school
1. a term one uses to defend his/her character when being accused of wrongdoing and deception. 2. a way to inform someone you do

not indulge or part take in a certain action. See also: **that's not my style**
ex: "Don't bring ya drugs around me, cause I don't get down like that."

I don't give a fat baby's ass… phrase (southern sl.) old school
1. a witty or sarcastic way to tell someone "I don't care…..", "I could care less….." or "so what!" [usually used when dismissing someone's excuse or explanation].
ex: "I'm goin', I don't give a fat baby's ass what you say."

I don't need to cheat you to beat you phrase (general sl.) new school
1. a witty way to respond to someone's allegation that you are cheating him/her during a game or competition.

I don't need you, let the welfare feed you phrase (e. coast sl.) old & new school
1. a sarcastic way to dismiss someone's usefullness or importance to you. (var. **I don't need'em, let the welfare feed'em)**

I don't play like that phrase (general sl.) old & new school
1. a way to inform someone that you don't or didn't appreciate his/her off brand comment or attempt to be funny [usually used when one feels offended].
ex: "I'mma tell you right now, I don't play like that."

I don't play [them] **sex games** phrase (prison sl.) new school
1. a matter of fact way to respond to sexual comments, jokes, or innuendo directed at you from someone of the same sex [used to convey one's serious displeasure].
ex: "Dig homes, I don't play sex games."

I don't play them kind/type of games phrase (general sl.) new school
1. a matter of fact way to respond to someone's offhanded remark, comment, or innuendo [used to convey one's serious displeasure].

ex: "I'm only gonna tell you once, I don't play them kind of games."

I don't run on gas phrase (general sl.) old & new school
1. a term used to reject one's insincere attempt to encourage, prod, or manipulate you using fake flattery or praise.
ex: "Spare me the bullsh**, I don't run on gas."

I don't trust you as far as I can see you, and I need glasses phrase (southern sl.) new school
1. a term used to express one's distrust of another.

I don't turn down nothin' but my collar phrase (southern sl.) old & new school
1. a way for one to declare that he/she isn't ashamed to accept a handout, charity, or help. 2. a way to inform someone you don't say no or refuse anything offered to you.

I'd rather clothe you, than feed you phrase (general sl.) old & new school
1. a witty way to comment on ones large appetite. 2. a playful way to tell someone it would cost less to buy his/her clothes then it would cost to buy him/her food.

I'd rather tell you than smell you phrase (prison sl.) new school
1. a witty way to tell someone he/she needs to bathe or that he/she stinks.

[someone who's] iffy adj. (general sl.) old & new school
1. a way to describe someone who is unpredictable or inconsistent with his/her behavior or personality. See also: [someone who's] **sometimin'**

if...? if my aunt had balls she'd be my uncle phrase (general sl.) new school
1. a term used in response to someone who uses "if" as part of

his/her explanation, excuse, denial, or afterthought. (var. **if...?** if **"if" was a fifth, we'd all be drunk**)

if I had it, I'd make you take it phrase (southern sl.) new school
1. a way to tell someone you don't have what it is he/she is asking for but if you did have it you'd gladly give it him/her. (var. **if I had it I'd smack you with it**)

if I had it you could get it, cause I'd love to see you with it phrase (e. coast sl.) old & new school
1. a witty way to tell someone you don't have what it is he/she is asking you for but if you did have it you'd gladly give it to him/her.

if I had your hand, I'd chop mines off phrase (e. coast sl.) new school
1. a modest way to respond to someone's praise of your success or general well being. 2. a way to relay to someone that he/she is doing better than you financially.

if I'm lyin' grits ain't groceries phrase (southern sl.) old & new school
1. a witty or sarcastic way to tell someone you are telling the absolute truth or that you absolutely know what you are talking about [usually used as a way to affirm or reaffirm one's truthfulness]. (var. **if I'm lyin' I'm flyin'**)

if I need to hit you, I don't need to be with you phrase (general sl.) old & new school
1. a term males use to affirm their stance against striking a female.

if I seen you drownin' in the middle of the ocean, I'd throw you a metal/iron life saving jacket phrase (southern sl.) new school
1. a sarcastic way to tell someone you would never do anything to help him/her. (var. **if I seen you on fire in the middle of the**

street/on the side of the road I wouldn't piss on you to put
you out)

if I tell you a duck can pull a truck, just hook the muhf**ka up
phrase (e. coast sl.) new school
1. a witty way to respond to someone who is questioning whether
or not you can do what you say you can do/get done. 2. a way to
say, "believe me", "I'm sure/positive". (var. **if I tell you there's
cheese on the moon, just bring crackers**)

if it ain't broke, don't fix it phrase (general sl.) old & new school
1. a way to instruct someone to leave things the way they are.

if it don't make dollars, it don't make sense phrase (e. coast sl.)
old & new school
1. a hip way to say if something doesn't involve reaping a financial
gain then doing it is a waste of time.

if it wasn't for bad luck, I wouldn't have no/any luck phrase
(general sl.) old & new school
1. a term used to express exasperation or dispair.

if lookin' good was a crime, you'd be a felony phrase (general
sl.) old & new school
1. a term used to flatter and/or compliment someone about his/her
good looks or appearance. (var. **if lookin' good was a crime,
you'd be a felony, cause right you dressed to kill**)

if the board don't call, I'm headed for the wall phrase (prison
sl.) new school
1. a term prisoners use to express a desperate desire to go home.

if you can "huh" you can hear phrase (general sl.) old & new
school
1. something you tell someone who answers "huh" to your
question or inquiry. 2. a way to say, "you heard me".

if you don't know, you better ask somebody phrase (general sl.) new school
1. a boisterous way to respond to someone who has called your character, abilities, or talents in to question while at the same refusing to give you the recognition or praise that you deserve. (var. **if you don't know now you know**)

if you had brains, you'd be dangerous phrase (general sl.) old & new school
1. a covert way to tell someone he/she is stupid [usually after that person has said or done something stupid].

if you knew better, you'd do better phrase (e. coast sl.) new school
1. a way to reprimand someone who has said or done something stupid or ridiculous. 2. a covert way to tell someone he/she is stupid.

if you nervous, join the service phrase (general sl.) old & new school
1. a way to taunt and tease someone about being scared or showing hesitancy about doing something. (var. **if you scared buy a dog/get in my pocket**)

if you owe me, you know me phrase (e. coast sl.) old school
1. a witty way to verbally put pressure on someone who owes you money when you see him/her with some money.

if you smell somethin', its him/her cause [he/she] **some sh**** phrase (southern sl.) new school
1. a way to taunt and tease your opponent after you have beaten him/her in competition or after he/she has made an error while competing against you.

if your name ain't delicate, stay the hell out of it phrase (e. coast sl.) new school
1. a witty or sarcastic way to tell someone to mind his/her business, stay out of your affairs, or keep his/her opinions, or thoughts to himself/herself.

if your nose ain't snotty, you beggin' somebody phrase (general sl.) old school
1. a witty way to reprimand someone who is always begging, in need of, or asking to borrow something.

if you'd signify, you'd/you'll testify phrase (southern sl.) new school
1. a way to tell someone that if he/she could tell such an outrageous lie he/she could easily testify or inform on a friend or love one in a court of law or to law enforcement agents.

[to] ig [someone] v. (general sl.) old & new school
1. to ignore someone; to purposely not pay attention to someone. 2. the abbreviation for the word "ignore".
ex: "You can't ig me forever." "Just ig them."

I got a weight problem....I can't wait to eat phrase (general sl.) old & new school
1. a humorous way to acknowledge one's own weight problem or the gaining of weight.

I got money like the mint, the gover'mint phrase (general sl.) old school
1. a way to boast about having lots of money. See also: [someone who has] **long money**

I got my mind on my money and my money on my mind phrase (w. coast sl.) new school
1. a witty way to confirm that one is thinking about his/her money or a way to make money.

I got that/this phrase (general sl.) old & new school
1. a way to assure someone that you will take care of something for him/her or assure him/her that you are in control of a situation.

I got that ass phrase (general sl.) old & new school
1. a way to alert and/or inform someone he/she has been caught doing something [usually something wrong].
ex: "I got that ass now, you not goin' nowhere."

I got you phrase (general sl.) old & new school
1. a way to assure someone you will take care of something or that he/she is in good hands [usually used to ease one's fears or insecurity].
ex: "Don't worry about nothin' dawg, I got you." "I got you on this."

I gotta get me phrase (general sl.) old & new school
1. a way to tell someone you have to get what belongs, is owed, or promised to you. (var. **I gotta get mines**)
ex: "I gotta get me before we leave."

I hear that phrase (general sl.) old & new school
1. a term used to acknowledge, agree with, or express one's ability to relate to something someone says. See also: **word up, you know thats right, ain't that the truth?**

I hear you talkin' phrase (general sl.) old & new school
1. a sarcastic way to mock someone's tough talk or empty threats and challenges.

I just act like this phrase (southern sl.) new school
1. a way to tell someone you are not as dumb or stupid as he/she thinks you are [usually used when someone tries to tell you something utterly ridiculous]. (var. **I just look like this/this way**)
ex: "Shortie I just act like this, so you need to stop."

I keep it real like a piece of blue steel phrase (e. coast sl.) old school
1. a term used to affirm or reaffirm that one doesn't lie and/or pretend to be someone he/she is not [usually used to exude confidence]. See also: [to] **keep it real**

I keeps it real phrase (general sl.) old & new school
1. a matter of fact way to pronounce one's steely character, unflinching or unwavering stance. 2. a way to pronounce one's honesty.

I like you, don't make me love you to death phrase (e. coast sl.) new school
1. a sarcastic way to respond to someone who has said and/or done something ridiculous or stupid.

I love you like a play cousin phrase (southern sl.) new school
1. a witty and playful way to dismiss a friend or love one who is complaining about the way you treat him/her or complaining about you not being fair.

[something that's] ill adj. (general sl.) old & new school
1. outstanding; unique; the best of its kind. 2. strangely or outrageously different.
ex: "That new video was ill." "Them some ill ass sneakers you got on, what's the name?"

[someone who's] ill adj. (general sl.) old & new school
1. obnoxious; rude; sarcastic. 2. upset; angry; mad. 3. one who says or does outrageously funny things. (var. [to say/do something] **ill**, [to act] **ill**)
ex: "When we got there these broads was actin' real ill towards us." "Tell'er she's makin' me ill." "That was some ill stuff she did."

ill chicks adj. (general sl.) new school
1. females with bad attitudes or who act and talk sarcastic,
obnoxious, or rude. See also: **bee-otch**
ex: "Dude brought a bunch of ill chicks to my party."

[the] **ill thing** [was/about it was]... phrase (general sl.) old & new
school
1. a way to say, "the odd/crazy/weird/funny/strange thing
was/about it was..."
*ex: "The ill thing was, I never seen'er before today." "That's what
the ill thing about it was, you feel me?"*

Illadelphia n. (e. coast sl.) new school
1. Philadelphia, PA. (var. **Illadelph**)
ex: "We goin' down to Illadelphia for the weekend."

I'll be that phrase (general sl.) old & new school
1. a sarcastic way to accept someone's name calling while showing
that person he/she can't upset you.
ex: "I'll be that, but you better ask ya momz about me."

I'll beat the blood out you phrase (general sl.) old & new school
1. a playful way to threaten someone with a bad physical beating.
See also: [to] **beat the blood out of** [someone]

I'll beat the cowboy sh outta you** phrase (e. coast sl.) new
school
1. a witty and playful way to threaten someone with beating
him/her up. (var. **I'll beat the horse sh** outta you**)

I'll break my foot off in ya ass phrase (general sl.) old & new
school
1. a witty and/or sarcastic way to threaten someone with a
physical beating.

I'll cut you everywhere but loose phrase (southern sl.) old &
new school
1. a playful way to threaten someone with harm. (var. **I'll cut you
too short to sh**/from asshole to elbow**)

I'll hit you faster than anything they got in a gun store phrase
(e. coast sl.) new school
1. a witty way to threaten someone with hitting him/her as fast as
you can/so fast that he/she won't realize it. (var **I'll hit you so fast
the black eye'll get there before the punch** [does])

**I'll hit you so hard when you wake up your clothes'll be outta
style** phrase (e. coast sl.) new school
1. a playful way to threaten someone with hitting him/her as hard
as you possibly can. (var. **I'll hit you so hard the first child you
have will come out with a black eye**)

I'll make you famous phrase (general sl.) old & new school
1. a way to respond to someone's threat, challenge, or tough talk so
that person knows you are not afraid of him/her.

[a female's] **ill/bomb nana** adj. (e. coast sl.) new school
1. a covert way to describe how good a vagina felt or feels during
sex [also used as a boast or claim].
ex: "I willin' to bet all three sisters have the ill nana."

[to] **ill on** [someone] v. (general sl.) old & new school
1. to explode in anger when offended or disrespected [often
exhibiting disruptive behavior and /or spewing foul language].
(var. [to] **ill out on** [someone])
ex: "Oh, I thought I was gonna hafta to ill on her for a minute."

I'll plant my foot so far up your ass, you'll sh sneakers for a
year** phrase (e. coast sl.) new school

1. a witty and playful way to threaten someone with a physical beating. (var. **I'll plant my foot so far up your ass you'll swear I was a farmer**)

I'll run through you like exlax phrase (e. coast sl.) new school
1. a witty way to taunt one's opponent about being able to do whatever you want against him/her during competition.

I'll slap fire from your ass phrase (e. coast sl.) new school
1. a witty and playful way to threaten someone with slapping him/her as hard as you possibly can. (var. **I'll slap the taste out your mouth**)
ex: "Say that again, and I'mma slap fire from your ass."

I'm about to be Elroy and jet son phrase (e. coast sl.) new school
1. a witty way to tell a male friend or love one you are about to leave or depart.

I'm being real with you [homie] phrase (w. coast sl.) old & new school
1. a term used to convey one's sincerity. 2. a way to say "I'm telling [you] the truth" or "I'm being serious with you." "I'm laughin', but I'm being honest with you."

I'm cool phrase (general sl.) old & new school
1. a way to say, "no thank you" or "I don't need or want any". 2. a way to respond to someone's inquiry about your well being that lets that person know you are fine or okay. (var. **I'm good**)
ex: "Ask them, me, I'm cool." "I'm cool with that if you are."

I'm fire, pour some water on me, I'm out phrase (southern sl.) new school
1. a witty way to tell a friend or love one you are leaving. (var. **I'm gone, I'm outta here**)

I'm hungrier than a hostage phrase (e. coast sl.) new school
1. a witty way to express how hungry one is.

I'm in it for the reason, not the season phrase (e. coast sl.) new school
1. a witty way to explain your involvement in something has a specific purpose and goal. (var. **I'm not in it for the season, I'm in it for the reason**)

I'm in it to win it phrase (general sl.) old & new school
1. a term used to express one's determination and resolve to succeed or see something through to the end.
ex: "I can't speak for y'all, but I'm in it to win it this time."

I'm in the cut like bandaids phrase (southern sl.) new school
1. a way to profess one's patience or easy going ways.

I'm just the man standin' next to the man phrase (southern sl.) old & new school
1. a modest way to respond to someone who has praised you as being "the man" [usually used when trying to give another recognition].

I'm not even gonna do you like that phrase (general sl.) old & new school
1. a way to tell someone you are going to take it easy on him/her, not keep him/her in suspense or not going to play games with him/her. (var. **I'm not even gonna do that to you**)

I'm not feelin' you [on that] phrase (general sl.) old & new school
1. a way to inform someone that you are not or can not relate to or understand something that he/she says, does, or feels.
ex: "I heard what you said, but I'm not feelin' you."

I'm not feelin' you like that phrase (general sl.) new school
1. a term used to tell someone you do not like him/her enough to become intimately involved with him/her [usually used to rebuff one's advances]. (var. **I'm not feelin'** [ya boy/girl/friend/man] **like that**)
ex: "We can still be friends, I'm just not feelin' you like that."

I'm not new to this phrase (e. coast sl.) old & new school
1. a way to inform someone that you have experience or knowledge about something that he/she is trying to tell you about or act like that he/she knows more than you about. (var. **I'm not new to this, I'm true to this, I'm not new to this f**k around and leave you black and blue to this**)

I'm not stupid, I just look that way phrase (southern sl.) new school
1. something you tell someone who you know is trying to con or deceive you. (var. **I'm not slow I just look this way**)

I'm not talkin' too fast, you listenin' too slow phrase (e. coast sl.) new school
1. a witty way to respond to someone's claim that you are talking too fast or trying to fast talk him/her.

I'm not the one phrase (general sl.) old & new school
1. a way to inform someone you are not someone easily pushed around or scared to standup for himself [usually used when someone is trying to deceive or take advantage of you.]. (var. **I'm not that guy/female you lookin' for**)
ex: "They know I'm not the one."

I'm on some real sh** phrase (general sl.) old & new school
1. a term used to profess one's seriousness towards a situation or his/her actions. (var. **I'm on that real sh****[homie])

I'm out phrase (general sl.) old & new school
1. a way to say "I'm leaving." (var. **I'm out this piece/bit****)
ex: "I'll see y'all later, I'm out."

I'm out like shout phrase (general sl.) old & new school
1. a hip way to announce one's intention to depart.
ex: "I'm out like shout, I gotta get up early in the morning."

I'm out there phrase (general sl.) new school
1. a way to inform someone that you are too deeply involved in a situation for you to turn back or change the events [usually used as an explanation].
ex: "I don't know how this happened, but I'm out there."

I'm serious, you delirious phrase (general sl.) old & new school
1. a way to affirm or reaffirm one's position or thought when someone isn't taking him/her serious.

I'm so bad I kick my own ass twice a day phrase (southern sl.) new school
1. a witty way to profess one's toughness.

I'm so broke I can't pay attention phrase (general sl.) old & new school
1. a way to emphasize being without money; extremely destitute [usually as a response to someone who asks you for money]. (var. **I'm so broke I can't rub two nickles together**)

I'm so broke, if water was 50 cents a gallon I couldn't buy myself a sip phrase (southern sl.) new school
1. a way to emphasize being without money; extremely destitute [usually used as a response to someone who asks you for money].

I'm so cool I sweat ice cubes phrase (general sl.) old & new school
1. a way to profess having a "cool" or "hip" personality.

I'm that cat ya momz warned you about phrase (general sl.) new school
1. a male's boisterous way to proclaim his toughness, thugishness, or "bad boy" personna to a female.

I'm scaaared of you! phrase (general sl.) old & new school
1. a witty way to mock being afraid of someone when he/she has said something tough, bold, provocative, uncharacteristic, threatening, or boisterous.

I'm true to this phrase (general sl.) old & new school
1. a way to affirm or reaffirm one's dedication to something. (var. **I'm true to this like Brutus/like Newmark and Lewis**)
ex: "How many times I'mma tell you I'm true to this?"

I'mma phrase (general sl.) old & new school
1. a way to say, "I'm going to".
ex: "I'mma see you later about this."

I'mma tell you some good sh** phrase (general sl.) new school
1. a term used as a prelude to telling someone something matter of factly [usually used to emphasize one's seriousness]. (var. **I'mma tell you like this…., let me tell you some good sh**…**)
ex: "I'mma tell you some good sh**, don't come back around here."

I'mma plant my foot so far up your ass you gonna swear I was startin' a garden phrase (southern sl.) new school
1. a witty and playful way to threaten someone with a physical beating.

I'mma sew ya butt cheeks together and feed you exlax phrase (e. coast sl.) new school
1. a witty and playful way to threaten someone with harm. (var. **I'mma sew your eyes open and feed you sleepin' pills**)

I'mma slap the camel sh** outta you phrase (general sl.) new school
1. a witty and playful way to threaten someone with slapping him/her as hard as you possibly can.

I'mma hit you with somethin' proper phrase (general sl.) old & new school
1. a way to let someone know you are going to be very generous when you give him/her something.
ex: "As soon as I make this move, I'mma hit you with somethin' proper."

[an] impasta rasta n. (general sl.) new school
1. a way to refer to someone who tries to imitate and/or pretend to be of Jamaican decent. See also: [a] **fakin' Jamacian**

I need you like a fish need a raincoat phrase (southern sl.) new school
1. a witty way to tell someone you don't need or want anything from him/her [usually when someone acts like you can't do anything without him/her].

[to be] in phrase (general sl.) old & new school
1. to have the opportunity, approval, or acceptance one has been working for, wanting, or hoping for. (var. [to be] **in there, in there like swimwear, in like Flynn, in there like last year, in there like I been there**)
ex: "We in now dawg." "I'm tyrin' to be in there like swimwear."

in a heart beat phrase (general sl.) old & new school
1. a way to say, "without hesitation", "immediately", or "right away".
ex: "I would said yes in a heart beat."

in a knick of time phrase (general sl.) old & new school
1. before the last possible moment.
ex: "We got there just in a knick of time."

in a N.Y. state of mind phrase (e. coast sl.) old & new school
1. in serious thought or a serious frame of of mind.

[to be] in [one's] feelin's phrase (general sl.) new school

1. to be mad, upset, or angry.
ex: "Leave her alone, cause she already in her feelin's."

[to be] **in** [someone's] **pocket** phrase (general sl.) old & new
school
1. to owe or have someone owe you a great deal of money [usually
stemming from a gambling debt]. (var. [to be] **into** [someone])
ex: "How long you been in'is pockets?"

[to be] **in power** phrase (e. coast sl.) new school
1. to be in a position of authority, to give orders, or able to help
people become successful.
ex: "Them catz been in power since you left."

[to have someone] **in smash** phrase (e. coast sl.) old & new school
1. to have someone under your complete control, influence, or
authority. (var. [to have someone/something] **locked/locked
down/on lock/on lock down**)
*ex: "Chill dawg, I got Shortie in smash." "He had the whole team
in smash."*

[someone who's] **in the buildin'** phrase (general sl.) new school
1. an enthusiastic way to announce one's arrival or presence.
ex: "Ladies and gentlemen, Cosmic Kev is the buildin'."

in the meantime in between time phrase (general sl.) old & new
school
1. a way to say, "while we wait…", "while we have time…",
"until…".
*ex: "In the mean time in between time lets go get somethin' to
eat."*

[to be] **in the mix** phrase (general sl.) old & new school
1. involved. (var. [to be] **up in the mix**)
*ex: "When somethin' bad happens you always somewhere in the
mix."*

[someone who's] **in violation** phrase (e. coast sl.) new school
1. one who has done something to wrong or disrespect a friendship or love one. (var. [to be] **in total violation**)
ex: "Ya peoples in violation dawg."

incarcerated scarfaces n. (e. coast sl.) new school
1. individuals who are in prison for selling drugs.

indo n. (drug sl.) new school
1. a specific type of marijuana. (var. **Indonesia**)

indigo n. (drug sl.) old & new school
1. a brand of marijuana
ex: "That smell like that indigo."

[one's] **intimidation game** phrase (e. coast sl.) new school
1. one's convincing use of intimidation to get his/her way.
ex: "We already hip to your intimidation game homie, that's not gonna work around here."

I play everything from marbles to manslaughter phrase (southern sl.) new school
1. a witty way to respond to someone who asks you if you know how to play a certain kind of game.

I put myself out there phrase (general sl.) new school
1. a way to admit the cause of one's own troubles or dilemma is the result of one's foolishness.
ex: "Its too late for that, I put myself out there."

I put that on everything phrase (e. coast sl.) new school
1. a way to swear, give one's word, promise, or guarantee. (var. **I put that on my life/on everything I love/on everything/on my momz/on ma dukes/on my seeds/on my hood/on my wiz/on my miz**) See also: **that's on everything**

ex: "I'mma pay you back man, I put that on everything."

I rather be carried by six, then judged by twelve phrase
(criminal sl.) old & new school
1. a way to declare that one would rather die then face a jury trial
for criminal charges.

Iron n. (criminal sl.) old & new school
1. a handgun

Iron horse n. (general sl.) old & new school
1. a subway train

[if] **I said somethin' wrong, straighten it** phrase (southern sl.)
new school
1. a blunt way to challenge someone to do something after he/she
has accused you of saying something offensive or disrespectful.
(var. [if] **I said somethin' wrong make it right**)

I see ya work phrase (e. coast sl.) new school
1. a hip and witty way to praise someone for his/her performance,
achievement, or success. (var. **I seen ya work**)
ex: "Yeah son, I see ya work." "I seen ya work last night."

I see you by yourself phrase (southern sl.) new school
1. a way to greet someone who is in the company of another whom
you don't like or have discontent for.

I seen better butts on a cigarette phrase (e. coast sl.) old & new
school
1. a witty way to disagree with someone's praise of a female's butt.

ish phrase (e. coast sl.) new school
1. a covert way to say the word "shit".
ex: "I like that ish." "Let me hear that ish."

ism n. (e. coast sl.) new school
1. marijuana.
ex: "They bought over madd ism."

[one's] **issue** n. (prison sl.) new school
1. something one is guaranteed or supposed to get as a matter of one's right or policy. (var. [to receive one's] **issue**)
ex: "All I want is my issue." "That's your issue."

issues n. (general sl.) new school
1. unresolved personal and sometimes emotional problems which sometimes effect one's character and/or behavior.
ex: "Shortie got too many issues for me."

is that right? phrase (southern sl.) new school
1. a mockingly way to question or express skepticsm about someone's declaration, claim, boast, or vow.

is that/this some bullsh** or what?! phrase (general sl.) new school
1. a matter of fact way to express one's discontent, dissatisfaction, annoyance, disbelief, frustration, surprise or shock in response to a unpleasant surprise or unfair treatment.
ex: "Tell me, is that some bullsh** or what, I was here longer than all these people and they get promoted."

I take'em 8 to 80 cripple, blind, or crazy phrase (e. coast sl.) old & new school
1. a witty way to inform someone that you have no reservations about how a person looks when you are looking for a date. 2. a witty way to explain being with someone others may feel isn't up to standards.

it ain't easy bein' greazy phrase (e. coast sl.) old & new school
1. a witty way to respond to someone who has accused you of being deceitful, untrustworthy, or dishonest.

it ain't that kind of party phrase (general sl.) old new school

1. a way to inform someone that he/she has the wrong idea or picture concerning your actions or intentions. 2. a witty way to turn someone down.
ex: "Look man, you gonna hafta tell your friends it ain't that kind of party."

it don't pay to be that nosy phrase (general sl.) old & new school
1. a sarcastic or witty way to reprimand or criticize someone for being so nosy. See also: **that's why the graveyard full/packed now**
ex: "Look dawg, it don't pay to be that nosy, let's get outta here."

it don't take all day to figure that out phrase (general sl.) new school
1. a way to mock someone about the simplicity of figuring out the obvious. (var. **it don't take a rocket scientist to figure it out, it don't take a whole lot to figure that out**)

it gets greater later phrase (e. coast sl.) new school
1. an optimistic way to look at a bad situation or unpleasant circumstance.

it is what it is phrase (e. coast sl.) new school
1. a matter of fact way to say, "that's how things are" or "that's just the way it is" when being questioned about a controversial situation [also used in the context when one is not about to offer an explanation].

it's a beautiful thing phrase (e. coast sl.) new school
1. an enthusiastic way to describe feeling good or having a sense of euphoria when expressing feeling good about something.

it's a wrap phrase (e. coast sl.) new school
1. an enthusiastic way to announce the end of something when the ending is clear or inevitable [often used as a taunt]. 2. a way to finalize an ending. (var. **that's a wrap**)

ex: "It's a wrap now, she seen you." "Two more baskets and it's a wrap."

it's all about me phrase (general sl.) old & new school
1. a way to declare one's own self importance.
ex: "This time around dawg, it's all about me."

it's all good phrase (general sl.) new school
1. a way to say something is, "okay", "fine", "no big deal", "nothing to get upset about" [sometimes used when one is trying to hide his/her true feelings towards a situation].
ex: "It's all good, we can leave at six." "Tell Shortie she ain't never gotta call, it's all good."

its's all hood phrase (general sl.) new school
1. an enthusiastic, boisterous, or sarcastic way to say that "everything is o.k./fine/satisfactory" [often used mockingly or tauntingly]. (var. **it's all hood bee-otch**)
ex: "It's all hood, we got more comin'."

it's all on you phrase (general sl.) old & new school
1. a way to give someone the authority to make the decision. (var. **it's on you**)
ex: "I can't stop you, it's all on you."

it's been real phrase (general sl.) old & new school
1. a departing term used to convey one had a real nice time and/or enjoyed oneself.
ex: "I gotta go yo, but it's been real,"

it's better to be pissed off, than pissed on phrase (e. coast sl.) new school
1. a witty way to console someone who exacted revenge against someone who upset, disrespected, or wronged him/her. 2. a term used to encourage someone to stand up for himself/herself.

it's either my way or the highway phrase (general sl.) old & school
1. a way to inform someone he/she has no say in the decision making; a way to issue an ultimatum.

it's goin' down major/crazy phrase (general sl.) new school
1. a enthusiastic way to add hype to one's plan he/she is about to initiate or for an upcoming event. (var. **it's goin' down like the Titanic/Fat People on Roller Skates/Ice Skates**)
ex: *"You gotta be there cause it' goin' down crazy tonight."*

it's gonna get ugly phrase (general sl.) new school
1. a way to inform someone that things are going to get much worse [usually used as a way to taunt or intimidate one's opponent]. (var. **it's about to get ugly**)
ex: *"I'm leavin' cause it's gonna get ugly when she comes back."*

it's like that? phrase (e. coast sl.) old & new school
1. a way to question someone's actions or thoughts that have surprised you, confused you, or caught you off guard.
ex: *"Ayo dawg, it's like that?" "If it's like that let me know."*

it's like that phrase (e. coast sl.) old & new school
1. a matter of fact way to tell someone who is questioning you about your actions or statemnets that, "this is how it is" without the need to explain further. 2. a way to answer someone who uses the term "it's like that?" when questioning you.
ex: *"It's like that now dawg." "Yeah, it's like that between her and I."*

it's my world, you just a squirrel tryin' to get a nut phrase (general sl.) old school
1. a witty way to exude one's own self importance and/or authority. (var. **it's my world**)

it's not the beauty, it's the booty phrase (e. coast sl.) new school

1. a way to tell someone how a person looks is of no importance when you are just trying to have sex with that person. (var. **it's the booty, not the beauty**)

it's on phrase (general sl.) old & new school
1. a term used to signify the start of something [usually used as a prelude to a challenge or confrontation]. (var. **it's on like a pot of neck bones, it's on like Donkey Kong**)
ex: "It's on, and she don't even know it yet."

[when] **it's on** phrase (sexual sl.) old & new school
1. the initial moment before/between foreplay and sex is about to begin. (var [when] **it's about to be on**)
ex: "Oh snap, it's about to be on now."

it's on and poppin' phrase (southern sl.) new school
1. a term used to signify the start of something [usually used as a prelude to a challenge or confrontation]. (var. **it's on and crackin'**)
ex: "Tell Shortie it's on and poppin'."

it's only right phrase (e. coast sl.) new school
1. a way to relay that something is/was the right, fair, or just thing to do.
ex: "It's only right you come with us." "Give it back, its only right."

it's your world phrase (general sl.) old school
1. a playful or sarcastic way to appease someone who is in control, has an advantage and/or authority over you in an attempt to make that person feel important [usually used mockingly].
ex: "Its your world pa, I can't say nothin'."

it's written all over your face phrase (general sl.) old & new school
1. a way to tell someone you can tell he/she is lying, guilty, or hiding something by the expression on his/her face.

ex: "You don't hafta say nothin', it's written all over your face."

itches n. (e. coast sl.) new school
1. a covert way to say the word "bit**es."
ex: "Where them itches think they goin'?"

[the] itty bitty titty committee phrase (general sl.) old & new school
1. the fictitious name of a group whose members all have small breasts.
ex: "Your girl must belong to the itty bitty titty committee."

I used to play this for bread and meat, if I ain't win, I ain't eat phrase (southern sl.) new school
1. a witty way to boast about being an expert in a particular game or sport [usually used as a response to someone who asks you do you know how to play a certain game].

I walk with a limp and talk like a pimp phrase (e. coast sl.) old & new school
1. a witty way to declare how cool and hip one is. (var. **I walk with a limp, talk like a pimp and keep my stash/ pockets phat like the blimp**)

I want it all, brand new socks and draws phrase (southern sl.) new school
1. a way to declare you want everything or you won't be satisfied until you get everything.

I was born at night ... but not last night phrase (general sl.) old school
1. a way to express disbelief to one's claim or story.

I was out phrase (general sl.) old & new school
1. a way to say that you were laughing very hard or you found something extremely funny. 2. a way to say that you were in a deep sleep.

ex: "When I seen'em do that I was out." "He was out the whole ride."

I wish you would phrase (general sl.) old & new school
1. a term used to partly warn and partly dare someone to do something [often used tauntingly or challengingly]. (var. **boy I wish you would**)

I wouldn't give the dog a bone if he brought a rabbit home phrase (southern sl.) new school
1. a witty way to respond to someone's suggestion that you help a particular person you are dead set against helping. (var. **I wouldn't give'em a glass of water if his whole mouth was on fire**)

I wouldn't give you enough sh to make your breath stink** phrase (e. coast sl.) new school
1. a witty or sarcastic way to tell someone "no" when that person asks you for something tangible [usually used to express one's discontent for the person asking].

I wouldn't sh you, you my favorite turd** phrase (southern sl.) new school
1. a witty way to tell someone you wouldn't try to deceive or lie to him/her when that person voices concern that you are not being truthful.

I81-U812 phrase (e. coast sl.) old school
1. an incorrect phone number you give someone who is persistent about getting your number and you just want to brush him/her off or make him/her leave you alone.

j

jack interj. (general sl.) old & new school
1. nothing; anything. (var. **jack sh**/do-do/diddly**) See also:
nathin
ex: "You don't know jack about me." "I wouldn't tell them jack sh**."

[to] **jack** [someone] v. (w. coast sl.) old & new school
1. to take someone's possessions using force, intimidation, or deception. (var. [to] **pull a jack move,** [to be] **jacked**)
ex: "We got jacked for the tickets." "We about to pull a jack move to get us some free tickets."

[to] **jack** [something] **off** phrase (e. coast sl.) new school
1. to lose a strong advantage or lead during competition due to one's errors, lack of effort, and/or because of one's over confidence and cockiness. (var. [to] **jack** [something])
ex: "Ya man jacked off the game doin' dumb sh**."

[to] **jack off** v. (sexual sl.) new school
1. a male term for masturbation.
ex: "I walked in, and he was in there jackin' off."

[to] **jack** [someone] **up** v. (general sl.) old & new school
1. to grab hold of someone [usually by his/her shirt or coat lapels] in a way that he/she can not flee and in most cases cornering the person at the same time.
ex: "As soon as she started lyin' her momz just jacked her ass up."

[something that's] **jacked up** adj. (general sl.) old & new school
1. a action that is cruel, offensive, disrespectful, spiteful, or maliciously intended.
ex: "That was jacked up what you said." "They did some jacked up sh** to shortie lil brother."

jackers n. (w. coast sl.) old & new school
1. muggers; armed robbers; people who take other people's possessions by force. (var [a] **jacker**)
ex: "Be careful, the jackers are out tonight." "You always have to keep your eyes open for the jackers."

jacks n. (drug sl.) old school
1. capsules of crack cocaine.
ex: "He tried to swallow the jacks when the cops came."

[someone who's] **Ja-fakin'** adj. (general sl.) new school
1. someone that pretends to be of Jamaican decent by imitating the Jamaican accent. See also: [an] **impasta rasta**
ex: "He ain't Jamaican, he Ja-fakin'." "Get ya Ja-fakin' ass away from me."

jail house bullsh** phrase (general sl.) old & new school
1. things people say when incarcerated in an attempt to convince someone that he/she has changed, sorry, or caring.
ex: "He called talkin' that same jail house bullsh**."

jake n. (e. coast sl.) old & new school
1. code word for police or any law enforcement agent [can also refer to someone working with the police as an informant].
ex: "We got pulled over by jake twice today." "I think ya man is jake dawg."

[something that's] **jake the fake** adj. (e. coast sl.) old school
1. imitation; bogus; a cheap copy of the original [usually used in reference to clothes, jewelry, handbags].
ex: "I seen ya man rockin' jake the fake Fubu."

[someone who's] **jalepeno** adj. (prison sl.) new school
1. a way to refer to someone who has cooperated with law enforcement agents in the investigation or prosecution of a friend

or family member. 2. another way to call someone a "snitch".
(var. [someone's who's] **a jalapeno**) See also: [someone who's]
hot
ex: "The word came back that ya man jalapeno son, whassup with that?"

[to] **jam** [someone] v. (criminal sl.) new school
1. to rob someone.
ex: "He realized he was about to be jammed and took off runnin'."

[to] **jam** [someone] v. (general sl.) old & new school
1. to put someone in a bad situation; to get someone in trouble.
(var. [to] **jam** [oneself], [to] **jam** [someone] **up**)
ex: "This the second time you jammed me." "I can't keep jammin' myself up for you."

[one's] **jam** n. (general sl.) old & new school
1. one of one's favorite songs.
ex: "Turn that up, that's my jam."

[a] **jam** n. (general sl.) old school
1. a dance party.
ex: "I haven't been to a good jam in a while."

[a] **jammy** n. (criminal sl.) old school
1. a firearm; handgun.
ex: "He snuck in with the jammy."

[a female who's] **Janet Jackson material** phrase (e. coast sl.) new school
1. a female who is extremely good looking. (var. [a female who's]
Halle Berry material, [a female who's] **Janet Jackson-Halle Berry material**)
ex: " Back in the days shortie was Janet Jackson Material."

janky adj. (southern sl.) new school
1. something or someone who brings you the feeling of bad luck; an uneasy feeling.
ex: "Get your janky behind away from me." "I know I can't depend on your janky ass."

[to] **jap** [someone] v. (e. coast sl.) old school
1. to punch someone in the face, mouth or eye [usually when that person wasn't expecting to be hit].
ex: "She japped dude in the eye for feelin' her butt."

[to] **jap the sh** outta** [someone] v. (e. coast sl.) old school
1. to punch someone in the face, mouth, or eye as hard as one can [usually while that person isn't expecting to be hit]. (var. [to] **knock the hell/sh** outta** [someone])
*ex: "You missed it, homegirl japped the sh** outta dude."*

[someone who's] **jaw jackin'** v. (southern sl.) new school
1. someone who is talking tough but doesn't really want a situation or confrontation to escalate.
ex: "That's all you good for is jaw jackin'." "Quit the jaw jackin' and let's go."

[to get] **jazzy** [with/on someone.] v. (general sl.) old school
1. to address, respond, or say something sarcastic to someone. See also: [to] **get slick out the mouth**
ex: "Who you tryin' to get jazzy with?"

[to] **jef** v. (southern sl.) new school
1. to act or play the part of someone who is submissive to gain favor from someone who has authority. (var. [to] **play the jef game**, [someone who's] **jeffin'**)
ex: "Ya man in the boss office jeffin' again."

jelly adj. (e. coast sl.) old school
1. cowardly.
ex: "You and ya man is jelly."

[to] **je rk** [someone] v. (e. coast sl.) old & new school
1. to trick, deceive, sucker someone out of something.
ex: "I feel you tryin' to jerk me." "I never been jerked like this."

[to] **jerk** [someone's] **rec** phrase (e. coast sl.) new school
1. to cause one's team or teammate to lose or do poorly from lack of effort or errors. 2. to get in the way of someone's fun. 3. the failing to show up for a prearranged contest with one's opponent. (var. [to] **jerk rec**)
ex: "You on that team, cause you be jerkin' my rec."

[to] **jet** v. (general sl.) old & new school
1. to leave; depart from. See also: [to] **bounce**
ex: "We was just about to jet." "They been jetted."

[to] **jet off** v. (general sl.) old & new school
1. to leave in a hurry to avoid detection or being caught. (var. [to] **jet off** [with someone/with someone's possessions])
ex: "You better catch'em cause he about to jet off."

jew'ells n. (e. coast sl.) old school
1. jewelry. (var. **jewels**)
ex: "Dawg got his jew'ells snatched at the party in Brooklyn."

jewels n. (e. coast sl.) old & new school
1. meaningful advice or lessons; morals to a story.
ex: "I'm about to give you some real jewels right now." "Can you understand these jewels I'm givin' you?"

[something that's] **jiggy** adj. (general sl.) new school
1. outstanding; unique; the best of its kind. (var. [something that's] **jig**) See also: [something that's] **off the chain**
ex: "Tell the truth, this sh** is jiggy ain't it?"

Jim Browski n. (sexual sl.) old school
1. a covert way to refer to a penis. (var. **Jimmy**)
ex: "Make sure you put a condom on Jim Browski."

[a] **jim hat** n. (sexual sl.) old & new school
1. a condom. (var. [a] **raincoat**)
ex: "I know you brought a jim hat with you."

[a] **jit** n. (southern sl.) new school
1. a young person [usually refers to a male].
ex: "You know you jits can't come in here." "Them jits always comin' in here makin' all that noise."

[to] **jive like** [someone] adj. (e. coast sl.) new school
1. to have a less than enthusiastic or weak feeling towards someone. (var. [someone who's] **jive all right** [with you])
ex: "I used to jive like shortie." "We were jive all right back in the days."

[one's] **J.0.** n. (general sl.) old & new school
1. one's job or occupation. (var. [one's] **J.O.B.**)
ex: "Don't just come to my J.0. like that."

[to] **jock** [someone] v. (general sl.) old school
1. to admire and/or be infatuated with someone for one or two particular reasons; to be a fan of someone. (var. [to] **ride** [someone's] **jock**, [to be] **on** [someone's] **jock**)
ex: "She be jockin' the whole basketball team."

[to] **jock** [someone] **hard** v. (general sl.) old school
1. to like, admire, or envy someone to the point where one becomes a pest.
ex: "Maybe you just jockin 'em too hard."

Jody n. (southern sl.) old & new school
1. the fictitious name of the man who cheats with another man's girlfriend while he is incarcerated.
ex: "Jody musta spent the night, cause I can't get a answer on the phone."

Joe n. (southern sl.) new school
1. a term of endearment among friends; friend. 2 a way to address someone whose name you do not know or do not want to use in front of others.
ex: "Where you been Joe?" "We need to straighten this out Joe."

joes n. (prison sl.) new school
1. cigarettes.
ex: "Let me bum one of your joes from you."

[something that's] **John Blaze** adj. (e. coast sl.) new school
1. outstanding; unique; the best of its kind. See also: [something that's] **blazin'**
ex: "This book is definitely John Blaze."

[a] **Johnny pump** n. (general sl.) old & new school
1. a fire hydrant.

[a] **joint** n. (criminal sl.) old & new school
1. a firearm; handgun.
ex: "We had to hide the joint." "How many joints he lookin' for?"

[a male's] **joint** (pron. jawnt) n. (e. coast sl.) new school
1. his girlfriend or intimate female freind; his casual female sex partner. See also: [one's] **side joint**
ex: "That's my new joint over there." "I got a nice lil joint waitin' for me when I get out."

[a] **joint** n. (drug sl.) old & new school
1. a kilogram amount of cocaine.
ex. "He sold three joints to the DEA."

[a male's] **joint** n. (sexual sl.) old & new school
1. a cover way to refer to a "penis."

[a song which is someone's] **joint** phrase (general sl.) old & new school

1. a favorite song of someone's.
ex: "That used to be my joint."

[a] **joint** n. (e. coast sl.) old & new school
1. an automobile. (var. [one's] **joint**) See also: [a] **whip**
ex: "I gotta pick me up one them new joints." "Them joints are the hottest things out."

joints n. (prison sl.) old & new school
1. a way to refer to the number of years that one is facing or serving in prison.
ex: "Duke lookin' at twelve joints." "How many joints did he do already?"

[to] **jone** [on someone] v. (southern sl.) old school
1. to ridicule someone; to make someone the subject of a joke or numerous jokes. (var. [to] **jones** [on someone])
ex: "I didn't come here for ya friends to be jonin' on me." "Let's jone on ya man over there."

[someone with a] **jones** phrase (general sl.) old & new school
1. someone with a real or imaginary addiction to something or someone. See also: [a] **phone jones**
ex: "I used to have a jones for Shortie."

[someone who's] **jonesin'** adj. (general sl.) old & new school
1. to want, need, or crave something desperately. (var. [to] **jones** [for something], [to] **have a jones**)
ex: "That cat jonesin' to get her home."

[to] **joog** (pron. j'uh'g) [at someone] v. (general sl.) new school
1. to tease, taunt, or mock someone in an attempt to annoy, frustrate, or harass him/her.
ex: "He kept joogin' at'em, I told'em to stop."

[to] **jook** (pron. jux) [someone] v. (criminal sl.) old & new school
1. to take one's possessions by force; to rob someone. (var. [to]
pull a jooks)
ex: "Even thugs can get jooked." "I got the perfect jooks."

juice adj. (general sl.) old & new school
1. influence; power and connections.
*ex: "I heard you the one with the juice." "Who had the real juice
around here?"*

[to] **juice** [someone] v. (general sl.)old school
1. to con or manipulate someone out of his/her money or
possessions [usually over a long period of time].
*ex: "She been juicin' dude for years." "All you wanna do is try to
juice my homeboy."*

[to] **jump bad** v. (general sl.) old & new school
1. to display a sudden surge of toughness or willingness to get
confrontational when one doesn't normally display such behavior.
*ex: "Of all people you wanna jump bad with me?" "You can jump
bad all you want, just don't put ya hands on me."*

[to] **jump down** [someone's] **throat** phrase (general sl.) old &
new school
1. to yell, chastise, or scold someone [usually before knowing or
allowing one to explain or offer an excuse] (var. [to] **jump all
down** [someone's] **throat**)
*ex: "She's real quick to jump down your throat, so wait until later
to tell her."*

[I'll] **jump down your throat and tap dance on your liver**
phrase (southern sl.) new school
1. a witty way to threaten someone with beating him/her up. (var.
[I'll] **jump down ya throat/chest like a bad cold**)

[the] **jump-off** phrase (e. coast sl.) new school
1. the start of something big, major, or extravagant.

ex: "You not stayin' for the jump-off kid?" "When y'all havin' the jump-off?"

[something that's about to] **jump off** phrase (general sl.) old & new school
1. about to start/begin.
ex: "Its really gonna jump off when they get here." "What time this thing jumpin' off?"

[a] **jump off** n. (e. coast sl.) new school
1. a person one has sex with without any emotional or financial attachment/commitment; one's secret lover.
ex: "Shortie over there is my new jump off." "Chicks be havin' jump offs too."

jump outs n. (drug sl.) old & new school
1. narcotics police who jump out of their unmarked patrol car to chase and arrest drug dealers.

[to] **jump out the gym** phrase (e. coast sl.) new school
1. a enthusiastic way to emphasize one's jumping ability.
ex: "She was jumpin' out the gym all through college."

[to] **jump out there** phrase (e. coast sl.) new school
1. to take a chance or risk. 2. to take a guess. (var. [to] **jump out there head first**, [to] **jump head first**)
ex: "You know him, he's always jumpin' out there."

[to] **jump up in** [someone's] **face** v. (general sl.) old & new school
1. to become aggressively confrontational during a argument or when feeling disrespected.
ex: "You should have seen the way she jumped up in his face."

[a party that's] **jumpin'** adj. (general sl.) old & new school
1. extremely enjoyable.
ex: "I'm tellin' you, this party is gonna be jumpin'."

jums n. (drug sl.) old school
1. crack cocaine sold inside of capsules. (var. **jumbos**)
ex: *"When the cops came he swallowed 10 jums."*

[a female who has] **junk in her trunk** phrase (southern sl.) new school
1. a female who has a large butt.
ex: *"She definitely got a lot of junk in her trunk."*

[somewhere that's] **just a hop, skip, and a jump from here/there** phrase (general sl.) old & new school
1. somewhere that isn't far.
ex: *"We just a hop, skip, and a jump from there, so be ready by the time we get there."*

k

[to] **keep a foot on** [someone's] **neck** v. (general sl.) new school
1. to keep another oppressed or at a disadvantage.
ex: "As long as I'm in charge I'mma keep my foot on y'alls neck."

[to] **keep** [someone's] **commissary on swole** phrase (general sl.)
new school
1. to send money to someone in jail on a regular basis so that
person can purchase the things he/she needs in the prison
commissary store. (var. [to] **keep** [someone's] **commissary phat**)
*ex: "My man Heav kept my commissary on swole since he hit the
bricks."*

[to] **keep** [something] **funky/gully/gangsta** phrase (e. coast sl.)
new school
1. the act of being bold, daring, and truthful without regards to the
consequences; to speak one's mind [also used as a prelude to a
bold, daring, or truthful statement one is about to make]. (var.
[someone who] **keeps** [things] **funky/gully/gangsta**)
*ex: "That's how you keep it funky." "Nah, let's keep sh** gangsta,
I never wanted you to come with us."*

[to] **keep** [one's] **game tight** phrase (general sl.) old & new school
1. the act of maintaining the highest level of performance at all
times; to continuously practice to reach a level of excellence. (var.
[to] **keep** [one's] **sh** tight**)
*ex: "I always keep my game tight." "This is how you keep ya game
tight."*

[to] **keep** [something] **gritty** phrase (general sl.) old & new school
1. to keep an edginess or boldness to an action or behavior. (var.
[to] **keep** [something] **grimy/gutter/street**)
ex: "Paper or no paper kid, I gotta keep it gritty."

[to] **keep** [someone] **in the blind/dark** phrase (general sl.)
old & new school
l. to keep information, truth, or secrets from someone; to keep
someone unknowing. (var. [to be] **in the blind/dark**)
ex: "It was your job to keep'em in the blind."

keep it gangsta phrase (e. coast sl.) new school
1. a term used to encourage someone to be truthful regardless of
the cost as a way to show his/her toughness.
ex: "Keep it gangsta son, tell her you goin' with us."

[to] **keep it movin'** phrase (e. coast sl.) new school
1. the act of not stopping to socialize with others. 2. a way to tell
someone to keep going and/or don't stop. (var. [to] **keep it movin'
on** [someone])
*ex: "When I see them catz, I just keep it movin'." "Come on dawg,
keep it movin'."*

[to] **keep** [someone] **honest** phrase (southern sl.) new school
1. to call one's bluff for the purpose of making that person prove
that he/she is telling the truth or not trying to deceive you.
*ex: "Just to keep you honest, go in there and bring it out so I can
see it for myself."*

[to] **keep it real** phrase (general sl.) old & new school
1. the act of not pretending to be someone or something that one is
not. 2. to be truthful dispite the cost [sometimes used as a prelude
to the truth one is about to tell]. 3. the act of not comprising one's
character or position for material gain. (var. [to] **keep it real with**
[someone], [one who] **keeps it real**)
*ex: "You always keep it real with people." "To keep it real with
you, I don't like that jacket."*

keep my name out your mouth phrase (e. coast sl.) new school
l. a way to demand someone to stop talking negatively about you
and/or stop spreading lies about you.
ex: "All I'm tellin' you is to keep my name out your mouth." "You

need to keep my name out your mouth."

[to] **keep** [something] **on the hush/hush hush/down low/low/d.l./l** phrase (general sl.) old & new school
1. to keep one's actions a secret; the act of being discreet. (var. [to] **keep** [something] **up under the table/up under the hat**)
ex: "We really need to keep this on the hush." "I thought you knew to keep this up under the table."

[to] **keep** [one's] **sh** tight** phrase (general sl.) new school
1. to keep one's appearance well groomed and fashionablely dressed.
*ex: "One thing about Golden Girl she keeps her sh** tight."*

[to] **keep** [something] **stirred up** phrase (general sl.) new school
1. to constantly be the cause of confusion and/or controversy that involve and surround others. (var. [someone who] **keeps some sh** stirred up, keeps some sh** up in the air/going/floatin' around**)
*ex: "Project females keep some sh** stirred up." "Why you always keep sh** stirred up?"*

[to] **keep up with the Joneses** phrase (general sl.) old & new school
1. the attempt to keep up with, imitate, and/or follow the latest styles and trends of people who have large sums of money and/or who are hip.
ex: "An average person can go broke tryin' to keep up with the Joneses."

[a] **key** n. (drug sl.) old & new school
1. a kilogram amount of cocaine.
ex: "Duke got caught with three keys."

[a] **khaki cop** n. (prison sl.) new school
1. an inmate who is extremely friendly with the correctional staff [often giving them information about what is going on in the prison].

kick phrase (e. coast sl.) new school
1. a way to tell someone "no" when he/she asks for a cigarette [used to tease or mock someone's dependency on cigarettes].

[to] **kick** [someone something] v. (general sl.) old & new school
1. to give or loan someone money. (var. [to] **kick** [someone] **down** [some money], [to] **kick** [someone] **a bone**)
ex: "I was hopin' you could kick me somethin' 'til Friday."

[I'll] **kick a bone out ya ass** phrase (e. coast sl.) old school
1. a witty way to threaten someone with kicking him/her as hard as you can or beating him/her up [usually used in response to another's witty threat or challenge]. (var. [I'll] **kick a bone out ya back**)
ex: "Don't make me kick a bone out ya ass."

[to] **kick** [something] **around** phrase (general sl.) old & new school
1. to discuss or entertain an idea or thought. (var. [to] **toss** [something] **around**)
ex: "We kicked it around for awhile, but we gonna hafta pass."

[to] **kick dirt on** [someone] v. (e. coast sl.) new school
1. to attach something bad, negative, and/or disrespectful to someone's name, actions, or character in an attempt to destroy that person's reputation or relationships with others. (var. [to] **kick dirt on** [someone's] **name**, [to] **kick dirt about** [someone]) See also: [to] **throw salt**
ex: "Why you tryin' to kick dirt on my man?"

[someone who's] **kickin'** adj. (general sl.) old & new school
1. one who has a bad odor due to poor hygiene [usually refers to the body or breath]. (var. [someone who's] **kickin' like a Karate movie/like Bruce Lee/Hatian soccer player**)
ex: "Ya man breath be kickin'."

[to] **kick it** phrase (general sl.) old & new school
1. to talk to or with someone; the act of conversing. (var. [to] **kick it with/about** [someone]) See also: [to] **holler at** [someone]
ex: "I need to kick it with you for a minute." "I haven't kicked it with you for a long time."

[to] **kick it here and there with** [someone] phrase (general sl.) old & new school
1. to talk to or with someone sporadically. (var. [to] **kick it with** [someone] **here and there/once in a blue/once in a blue moon/every now and then/off and on**)
ex: "We kick it here and there since she went to college."

[to] **kick it with** [someone] phrase (general sl.) old & new school
1. to be intimately involved with someone. (var. [two people who] **kick it, kick it together, kick it like that**)
ex: "How long y'all been kickin' it with each other?" "I didn't know you and her were kickin' it."

[to] **kick more flavor than a Life Saver** phrase (southern sl.) old school
1. a boisterous way for one to claim to be "hip" and "cool". (var. [to] **have more flavor than a Life Saver**) See also: **flavor**

[to] **kick** [something] **off** phrase (general sl.) old & new school
1. to start or begin something.
*ex: "What time y'all want to kick this sh** off?" "It didn't kick off until late."*

[to] **kick off in** [someone's] **ass** phrase (southern sl.) new school
1. to beat someone up [usually used as a threat or a response to a threat].
ex: "I came this close to kickin' off in his ass last night."

[to] **kick out** v. (general sl.) old & new school
1. to pay the monetary cost of something. (var. [to] **kick out for** [something])
ex: "How much do we have to kick out for this?"

kick rocks phrase (southern sl.) new school
1. a witty way to command, suggest, or advise someone to leave [sometimes used to dismiss someone]. See also: **bounce, step off**
ex: "I think its time for y'all to kick rocks."

kick that sh** phrase (general sl.) old & new school
1. a way to encourage someone when he/she is singing, rapping, or saying something of importance.
ex: "Go ahead and kick that sh**." "You need to kick that kind of sh** more often."

[to] **kick the ballistics** v. (e. coast sl.) old school
1. to talk to or with someone; to converse or discuss. (var. [to] **kick the boe-boe/the willy boe-boe/the willy** [with someone])
ex.: "I was kickin' the ballistics with my man upnorth."

[to] **kick the bucket** phrase (general sl.) old school
1. a way to refer to death; the act of dying. (var. [when someone] **kicks the bucket**)
ex: "When did he kick the bucket?"

[to] **kick** [someone] **to the curb** phrase (general sl.) old & new school
1. to abruptly end a intimate relationship with someone; to break off ties to someone. See also: [to] **cut** [someone] **off**
ex: "You should have been kicked that clown to the curb."

[something that's] **kickin'** adj. (general sl.) old school
1. outstanding; unique; the best of its kind. 2. enjoyable; entertaining.
ex: "Matrix reloaded was kickin'."

kicks n. (general sl.) old & new school
1. sneakers; shoes: (var. **foot gear/wear**)
ex: "I need to get me some new kicks."

kicks n. (general sl.) old & new school
1. thrills; excitement; pleasure. (var. [to] **get** [one's] **thing off**)
ex: "Is this how you get your kicks?"

kid n. (e. coast sl.) old & new school
1. a term of endearment among friends; friend. 2. a way to address
or refer to someone whose name you don't know or don't want to
use in front of others.
*ex: "Where you know kid from?" "Ayo kid, I like the way you
handled that."*

kids n. (e. coast sl.) old & new school
1. a way to refer to males in the plural sense. See also: **catz**
*ex: "Who know them kids?" "I met these kids who said they knew
you."*

[to] **kill** [something] adj. (general sl.) old & new school
1. to do an outstanding job [usually used in the context of
evaluating one's performance].
ex: "Shortie went in there and killed it." "I'm about to kill it."

[to] **kill** [something] v. (general sl.) old & new school
1. to put an end to or stop. 2. to finish off a food or drink.
*ex: "I thought y'all killed that beef." "You know, ya'll need to kill
that." "Can I kill that for you?"*

[to] **kill** [someone] adj. (general sl.) old & new school
1. to become an overwhelming burden or responsibility to
someone [usually the burden is financial]
ex. "The two weeks they was here, they killed me."

[to] **kill** [someone's] **high** phrase (drug sl.) old & new school
1. to annoy, aggravate, or frustrate someone so bad/enough that
he/she comes out from under the influence of an illegal drug or

intoxication. (var. [to] **blow/f**k up** [someone's] **high)**
ex: "Not now maaaan, you killin' my high."

[to] **kill** [someone] **in** [something] v. (general sl.) old & new
school
1. to out perform someone. (var. [to] **kill** [someone] **at**
[something])
ex: "I killed cousin in this two days ago."

[to] **kill** [someone] **with kindness** phrase (general sl.) old & new
school
1. the act of treating someone kindly when that person doesn't
deserve it or when that person has wronged you [usually used to
hide one's own bitterness over being wronged].
*ex: "The best way to get back at them is to kill them with
kindness."*

killer Cali n. (w. coast sl.) new school
1. California.

killer weed adj. (drug sl.) new school
1. a term used to describe extremely good marijuana. (var. [that]
killer/killer weed)
*ex: "They brought some killer weed." "We lookin' for that killer
weed."*

[he/she] **kiss so much ass, his/her breath smells like sh**** phrase
(southern sl.) new school
1. a sarcastic way to criticize and/or insult someone's consistent
effort to gain favorable recognition by a boss or superior. (var.
[he/she] **kiss so much ass his/her tongue got sh** stains on it)**

[a] **kite** n. (prison sl.) old & new school
1. a letter or note sent from prison or passed between prisoners.
ex: "Did you get that kite I sent you?"

[a] **kitty** n. (sexual sl.) old & new school
1. a covert way to refer to a female's vagina. (var. [a female's]
kitty cat)
ex: "You ain't never gonna get to see that kitty."

[one's] **knife game** phrase (prison sl.) new school
1. one's keen ability and willingness to use a knife [usually
during a violent confrontation].
ex: "They heard about his knife game in the State Pen."

[to] **knock** [someone] v. (general sl.) old & new school
1. to criticize or talk badly about ones's actions or efforts [usually
when that person doesn't deserve it].
*ex: "You always lookin' for a reason to knock me." "Don't knock
me dawg."*

[to] **knock** [a female's] **boots** phrase (sexual sl.) old & new school
1. the act of having sex. (var. [to] **knock boots**, [to] **knock boots
with** [someone], [to] **knock** [a female's] **boots off**) See also: [to]
do the nasty
ex: "I'm not in a rush to knock Shortie boots."

[to] **knock** [a female] **down** v. (sexual sl.) new school
1. the act of having sex. (var. [to] **knock** [a female] **off**)
ex: "It took me almost two years to knock Shortie down."

[to] **knock** [someone] **hustle** phrase (e. coast sl.) old & new school
1. to criticize how one makes or earns his/her money [usually
refers to the earning of illegal money].
*ex: "Don't knock the hustle." "Why you tryin' to knock my
hustle and sh**?"*

[to] **knock** [someone] **in the head** phrase (criminal sl.) new school
1. to inform and/or testify against a friend or love one in court and
be the reason that person received time in prison. See also: [to]

bust on [someone]
ex: "Come to find out, my own man was gonna knock me in the head."

knock it off phrase (general sl.) old & new school
1. a playful or sarcastic way to tell someone to stop lying, stop pretending, or stop acting a certain way. See also: **stop frontin'**
*ex: "Knock it off nobody tryin' to hear that sh **."*

[to] **knock** [something] **off** v. (general sl.) old & new school
1. the act of selling something.
ex: "I can't go nowhere until I knock this off."

[a] **knock off** adj. (general sl.) old & new school
1. a piece of merchandise that is a imitation [usually costing way below what the real product costs]. (var. [merchandise that is] **Canal street sh****)
ex: "I see you went and copped a pair of those knock off Gucci bags."

[to] **knock** [someone] **off his/her square** v. (e. coast sl.) new school
1. to make someone mad or upset causing him/her to lose his/her temper and/or composure. (var. [to] **have** [someone] **off his/her square**)
ex: "You can't let this knucklehead knock you off your square."

knock [something] **out** v. (general sl.) old & new school
1. to finish up or complete. 2. to finish off a food or drink item.
ex: "I went in there and knocked it out in two hours." "You can knock this out if you want to."

[one's] **knockout game** n. (general sl.) old & new school
1. one's unique ability to knockout people during a fight.
*ex: "His knockout game is some sh** since he started smokin' crack."*

[to] **knock** [someone/something] **out the box** phrase (general sl.)
old & new school
1. to the act of replacing something or someone because of the
better quality, performance, or appearance.

[to] **knock the doors down** phrase (sexual sl.) new school
1. a male term for performing exceptionally during sex [usually
used as a boast or claim]. (var. [to] **knock the walls down/the roof
off/the dust off**)
ex: *"I'm about to take Shortie in here and knock the doors down."*

knocked phrase (criminal sl.) old & new school
1. arrested; caught doing something wrong. (var. **knocked off**) See
also: **bagged**
ex: *"I got knocked in N.C." "She the one that got us knocked off."*

knocked in the head phrase (prison sl.) new school
1. to receive a long prison sentence.
ex: *"When my man got sentenced, the judge knocked'em in the
head."*

[someone who's] **knocked out** adj. (general sl.) old & new school
1. a way to describe someone being in a deep sleep.
ex: *"He was knocked out the whole trip."*

knocked up phrase (general sl.) old school
1. pregnant. (var. [to] **knock** [someone] **up**)
ex: *"You let that sorry scrub knock you up?"*

[something that's] **knockin'** adj. (general sl.) new school
1. outstanding; unique; the best of its kind.
ex: *"Banks new joint is knockin'."*

[to] **knot** [someone] **up** v. (e. coast sl.) new school
1. to hit someone causing a noticeable bruise on the head/face/
(var. [to get] **knotted up**) See also: [to] **lump** [someone]
ex: *"You about to get knotted up in a minute, keep runnin' ya
mouth."*

[to] **know** [someone's] **style** phrase (general sl.) new school
1. a way to claim to know one's character or what he/she is about [often opposite or what he/she feels about themselves].
ex: "Stop lyin' chump I know ya style."

[you] **know that's right** phrase (general sl.) new school
1. an enthusiastic way to express being in agreement or being able to relate to a comment made by someone. (var. **I know that's right**)
ex: "You know that's right, I'm not going either."

[to] **know the half** phrase (general sl.) old & new school
1. to have a full and complete understanding of a situation or event. (var. [to] **know the whole nine**)
ex: "You talkin' and you don't even know the half."

knowledge n. (sexual sl.) new school
1. oral sex [usually received by a male].
ex: "All I can say is the knowledge is off the hook."

[to have] **knowledge of self** phrase (e. coast sl.) old & new school
1. to know, respect, and understand one's own self.
ex: "You need knowledge of self before you can advise me of anything."

knowledge self phrase (e. coast sl.) old & new school
1. a serious way to tell someone to stop and think about what he/she is doing [used to make someone aware of his/her actions].
ex: "Knowledge self dawg, you know better than that."

knucka n. (e. coast sl.) old & new school
1. a term of endearment among friends; friend. (var. [to be someone's] **knucka**)
ex: "That was my knucka back in the days."

[one's] **knuckle-game** phrase (e. coast sl.) new school
1. one's hand fighting skills.
ex: "Ya pops had a mean knuckle-game back in the days." "He ready to test your knuckle- game."

[a] **knuckle-head** n. (general sl.) old & new school
1. one who acts irresponsible and/or immature while trying to act like he/she is an adult. 2. rowdy and disruptive young people [usually refers to males].
ex: "Why you hangin' with that knuckle-head?"

knuckle up phrase (e. coast sl.) new school
1. a way to tell someone to prepare to fight or defend himself.
ex: "Knuckle up punk, we about to do this."

[something that's] **kosher** adj. (general sl.) old school
1. "agreeable","acceptable", "fine", or "okay".
ex: "Does that sound kosher to you?" "You know that's not kosher right?"

l

[a] **"L"** n. (criminal sl.) old & new school
1 a life sentence in prison without the possibility of parole. (var. [a]
L-note)
ex: *"Dukes lookin' at a "L" this time around."*

la n. (drug sl.) new school
1. marijuana. (var. **lah**)

[a] **Lac** n. (southern sl.) new school
1. a Cadillac automobile.
ex: *"He always drove a Lac."*

[to] **lace** [someone] v. (criminal sl.) new school
1. to shoot someone. (var. [to] **lace** [someone] **up**, [to be] **laced up**)
ex: *"Police laced my man with 15 shots."*

[to] **lace** [something/someone] v. (e. coast sl.) old & new school
1. the act of making someone's or something's appearance more
glamorous. (var. [to] **lace** [someone/something])
ex: *"I took Shortie to the mall and laced'er with some new gear."*
"Once I lace the crib, then I'll invite you over."

[I'm/We] **laid back, like car seats in a Caddilac** phrase (southern
sl.) new school
1. a witty way to profess one's "coolness". 2. a term of endearment
among friends to signify friendship.

[to get] **laid down** [by a judge] v. (prison sl.) new school
1. to have a judge sentence someone to an extremely long prison
sentence.
ex: *"Judge laid my man down for 20 joints."*

laid up phrase (general sl.) old & new school
1. the state of being temporarily incapacitated [usually due to an illness].
ex: "Ask the doctor how long I'mma be laid up." "I was laid up for three days with the flu."

[a] **lambo** n. (general sl.) new school
l. a Lamborghini automobile.
ex: "Buster Bust got the meanest lambo out."

[someone who's] **lame** adj. (general sl.) old & new school
1. one who is not "cool" or "hip" [often when one thinks he/she is].
2. one who is easily fooled, taken advantage of, and/or extremely gullible.
ex: "I stop goin' there cause too many lames started hangin' out there." "I can't believe I hang out with you lames."

[something that's] **lame** adj. (general sl.) old & new school
1. something which is supposed to come across as "cool", "hip", and/or entertaining, but falls extremely short of that goal; poor in performance.
ex: "That was a lame ass movie." "That book is lame compared to this one."

lame [excuses/explanations/stories/jokes/ raps/pick up lines/ ways of doing something] adj. (general sl.) old & new school
1. poor in quality, delivery, and performance. 2. ridiculously stupid or unbelievable.
ex: "That was the lamest excuse I have ever heard."

[to] **lamp** v. (e. coast sl.) old school
1. to relax; to take it easy. 2. to wait patiently. (var. [to] **lamp out**)
ex: "I was in here lampin' 'til y'all came." "I'mma lamp with my man 'til y'all get back." "We in here lampin'."

large adj. (general sl.) old & new school
1. wealthy; rich; (var. [one who's] **large like a 5 car garage, large and in charge**) See also: **flarge**
ex: "Ya man an'nim used to be large, what happened?"

lawd n. (e. coast sl.) old school
1. a term of endearment among friends; friend.
ex: "Ayo lawd, where you headed?"

lawd son phrase (e. coast sl.) old school
1. an enthusiastic way to express shock, disbelief, or exasperation.

[to] **lay** v. (general sl.) old & new school
1. to wait. (var. [to] **lay for** [someone])
ex: "I'll lay over here." "You think you can lay for me 'til I get there?"

[to] **lay down** phrase (general sl.) new school
1. to quit; give up; to concede defeat.
ex: "I don't know what happened but they just laid down." "Its time for you to lay down."

[to] **lay down** n. (prison sl.) new school
1. the act of refusing to participate in mandatory or recreational activities in a prison institution as a means of protest [usually done knowing that one will be punished by being sent to solitary confinement].

[to] **lay** [someone] **down** phrase (criminal sl.) old & new school
1. to rob someone at gun point. 2. to shoot someone with the intent to kill him/her [usually in the commission of armed robbery]. (var. [to] **lay** [someone] **down for the count**)
ex: "They came in here and laid everyone down."

[to] **lay** [something] **down** phrase (general sl.) new school
1. to set the rules or demands.

ex: "Let me lay this down for y'all." "I'm about to lay this down plain and simple."

[to] **lay gas** v. (general sl.) old & new school
1. to fart (flatulate). (var. [to] **blow gas**)
ex: "Next time you hafta lay gas, step outside."

[to] **lay in the cut** phrase (southern sl.) old & new school
1. the act of waiting [usually patiently and/or discreetly]. (var. [to] **lay in the cut for** [someone])
ex: "I'm layin' in the cut until he messes up."

[to] **lay it down** v. (general sl.) new school
1. the act of going to bed/sleep. (var. [to] **take it down**)
ex: "I don't know about you, but I'm ready to lay it down for the night."

[to] **lay low** phrase (general sl.) old & new school
1. the act of maintaining a low profile.
ex: "We can lay low here for a few days."

[to] **lay pipe** v. (sexual sl.) new school
1. a term males use to describe the act of giving a female sexual satisfaction. (var. [to] **lay pipe on pipe** [a female], [to] **pipe** [a female] **to death**)
ex: "I laid pipe on Shortie all weekend." "Call me back, I'm about to lay some pipe."

[to] **lay up for** [someone] v. (general sl.) old & new school
1. the act of waiting for someone [usually to let that person catch up to you and often used as a request]. (var. [to] **lay for/on** [someone])
ex: "Lay up for a minute." "I'mma lay up for you here." "I can't lay for you all night."

[to] **lay up with** [someone] phrase (sexual sl.) old & new school
1. to spend time [hours, days, weeks, or months] with someone in

his/her dwelling having sex; to have sex.
ex: "Who you been layin' up with this time?" "He probably somewhere layin' up with some other chick."

[to] **lay wood** phrase (sexual sl.) new school
l. a term males use to describe the act of giving a female sexual satisfaction. (var. [to] **lay wood** [on a female])
ex: "Shortie once I lay this wood on you, you'll be callin' me everyday."

lead n. (criminal sl.) old & new school
l. bullets.

lead poison phrase (criminal sl.) old & new school
1. to be wounded or die as a result of being shot.
ex: "He was found in the alley with lead poison."

[someone who's] **leakin'** phrase (criminal sl.) new school
1. bloody; bleeding; bloodied. (var. [to] **leave** [someone] **leakin'**)
ex: "They said he was leakin' all over the place." "Somebody left ya boy leakin' in the parkin' lot."

[a male who's] **leakin'** adj. (general sl.) old & new school
1. a male who is having a abnormal discharge from his penis the result of being infected with a sexually transmitted disease. See also: [someone who's] **burnin'**
ex: "I woke up this mornin' and my joint was leakin'."

leanin' adj. (e. coast sl.) new school
1. drunk; intoxicated. (var. **leant**) See also: **pissy, toasted**

[to] **leave** [someone] **for dead** phrase (e. coast sl.) old & new school
1. to abandon or forget about someone in his/her time of need.
2. to show and/or offer no support to someone.
ex: "Most your friends and some of your family will leave you for dead when you go to prison."

[to] **leave** [someone] **hangin'** phrase (general sl.) old & new school
1. to offer someone no assurances. 2. the act of dismissing one's attempt to shake your hand as a way to show discontent or disdain. 3. to have one wonder or guess as to what you are going to do. (var. [to] **leave** [someone] **out there**)
ex: "That's the second time you left me hangin'."

[to] **leave** [someone] **in the dust/wind** phrase (general sl.) old school
1. to outrun someone. See also: [to] **dust** [someone]
ex: "She left both police in the dust."

leaves n. (drug sl.) new school
1. marijuana. (var. **leaf**)

leery adj. (general sl.) old & new school
1. paranoid; unsure; skeptical. 2. scared.
ex: "Ya man startin' to make me leery about'em."

[a female who's] **legal** adj. (sexual sl.) old & new school
1. a female who meets the statutory age limit required to legally consent to sex.
ex: "You don't look legal to me shortie, let me see some ID."

less phrase (general sl.) old & new school
1. "unless".
ex: "I can't go less you pay me."

[to] **let** [something] **go** phrase (general sl.) old & new school
1. to let a unpleasant situation or confrontation end or die out without letting things escalate.
*ex: "Yo son, you need to let that go." "Why you can't learn to let sh** go?"*

[to] **let** [something] **go to** [one's] **head** phrase (general sl.) old & new school
1. to let something make one over confident and cocky.
ex: "Don't let what I said go to your head." "See what happens when you let sh** go to your head?"

[to] **let** [someone] **hold somethin'** phrase (general sl.) new school
1. the act of allowing someone to borrow something [usually money or drugs and usually used as a request].
ex: "When you gonna let ya boy hold somethin'?" "I was wondering if I can hold somethin'."

[to] **let** [someone] **live** phrase (e. coast sl.) new school
1. to allow someone the opportunity to do something [usually used to request assistance]. 2. to make it possible for someone to accomplish a goal.
ex: "I'm the one that let you live." "Let me live dawg, I need what you have."

[to] **let** [someone] **live** phrase (prison sl.) new school
1. the act of protecting or exempting someone from the pressure, fear, and/or intimidation that one can face while in prison from other inmates.
ex: "I'm the one that let your cousin live while we was in the Feds."

[to] **let** [something] **marinate** phrase (southern sl.) new school
1. to let an idea or thought sink in or be contemplated before responding.
ex: "Look, let that idea marinate for a couple days and then get back to me." "You finished lettin' that plan marinate?"

[to] **let loose** v. (criminal sl.) old & new school
1. to fire one's gun recklessly and indiscriminately. (var. [to] **let loose on** [someone])
ex: "This crazy dude let loose at his job."

let me find out phrase (e. coast sl.) new school
1. a term used to question, express doubt and skepticism. 2. a way
to respond to someone who does or says something shocking,
surprising, or unbelievable.
*ex: "He spent the night with you, let me find out." "Let me find out
you don't know how to treat your girl."*

let me get some smoke in my lungs phrase (prison sl.) new school
1. a witty way to ask someone for some of a cigarette or for a
whole cigarette. (var. **let me smoke with you, let me get one of
yours**)

let me get that phrase (e. coast sl.) new school
1. a term used to command someone to give you what he/she owes
you or has of yours that you want back. (var. **let me get that up
off you**)
ex: "Let me get that, cause I see right now you playin' games."

let me see ya head get small phrase (e. coast sl.) new school
1. a rude and sarcastic way to dismiss someone in a way that
directs that person to leave or depart. (var. **let ya head get small**)
See also: **tell ya story walkin'**
ex: "Let me see ya head gettin' small with ya smartass."

let my name taste like sh** in your mouth phrase (e. coast sl.)
new school
1. a sarcastic way to reprimand someone for talking negatively
and/or spreading rumors about you in an attempt to make that
person stop.

[to] let [one's] pants sag v. (general sl.) old & new school
1. to wear one's pants in a way in which they fall past the waist
and expose one's underwear.
ex: "Don't you think you a lil old to be lettin' ya pants sag?"

let the door knob hit you, where the good Lord split you
phrase (general sl.) old school
1. a witty way to tell someone to leave and/or respond to
someone's threat to leave. (var. **let ya feet do the walkin' and ya
ass do the talkin', introduce your feet to the street**)

let you tell it phrase (e. coast sl.) new school
1. a term used to mock another's claim, version, or opinion [also
used as sarcastic prelude when dismissing another's claim, version,
or opinion].
*ex: "Let you tell it, I was posed to lose already." "I can't find a
good man, let you tell it."*

let's blow this joint phrase (general sl.) old & new school
1. a term used to suggest or declare one's departure.

let's do this phrase (general sl.) old & new school
1. a term used to suggest or declare the commencement of a plan or
action [usually used to exude one's willingness to do something
when answering a challenge].
ex: "Its up to you, but I say let's do this."

lethal n. (drug sl.) new school
1. marijuana.
ex: "Cops found a bag of lethal in the bag."

lettuce n. (general sl.) new school
1. money. See also: **cabbage**

[a] **Lex** n. (general sl.) new school
1. a Rolex watch. 2. a Lexus automobile.

[a] **Lex dawg** n. (general sl.) new school
1. a Lexus automobile.

[a] **lick** n. (criminal sl.) old & new school
1. an idea or plan to obtain money [usually illegally]. (var. [to] **catch a lick**) See also: **a come up**
ex: "That's the lick that got us paid." "I came up with a nice lil lick if y'all interested."

[to] **lick shots** v. (criminal sl.) old & new school
1. the act of shooting a firearm. (var. [to] **lick shot at** [someone])
ex: "They just started lickin' shots for no reason."

licks n. (e. coast sl.) new school
1. alcohol; liquor.
ex: "I got sick off the licks last night."

[to] **lift** [someone] v. (criminal sl.) old & new school
1. to shoot someone. (var. [to] **lite** [someone] **up**)
ex: "Ya man was about to get lifted in there."

lifted adj. (drug sl.) new school
1. the state of being high from marijuana.
ex: "Yo, they got madd lifted on his birthday."

[to] **light somethin' up** phrase (criminal sl.) new school
1. a way to refer to a shooting or shoot-out involving numerous shots being fired.
ex: "Man I outta here, they look like they ready to light somethin' up."

[to] **light** [someone] **up** v. (criminal sl.) old & new school
1. to shoot someone. (var. [to] **light** [one's] **ass up**) See also: [to] **bust** [someone]
ex: "I heard some catz tried to light you up cross town over that chickenhead."

[to] **light** [a female's] **wrist** v. (e. coast sl.) new school
1. the act of buying a female a diamond bracelet or a watch encrusted with diamonds.
ex: "I'mma light my Shortie wrist for her birthday."

like a muhf**ka! phrase (general sl.) new school
1. a term used to emphasize one's boast, claim, description or assessment of something/events [affix term to statement].
2. a term used to signal one's agreement or ability to relate to something said.
ex: "G-Unit blew up like a muhf**ka!" "Shortie is bad like a muhf**ka!"

like da farmer said to the potata, "plant you now - dig you later" phrase (southern sl.) old & new school
1. a witty way to say "good bye" or "see you later" when departing the company of a friend or love one.

[someone who's] like that adj. (general sl.) old & new school
1. the best at what he/she does. 2. one who is extremely good looking. (var. [someone who's] **all that**)
ex: "She's like that on the court." "I didn't know you was like that."

[something that's] like that adj. (general sl.) old & new school
1. outstanding; unique; the best of its kind [usually refers to quality and performance]. See also: **all that**
ex: "I heard her sing before and she's like that."

like what?! Interj. (e. coast sl.) new school
1. a term used as an exclamation point when one is making empty threats or issuing challenges that he/she wants to be taken seriously.

like you said/sayin' somethin' phrase (general sl.) old & new school
1. a sarcastic way to dismiss an empty threat or challenge.
ex: "You actin' like you said somethin'!"

lil homie n. (w. coast sl.) old & new school
1. a term of endearment used to refer to a young person or little kid. (var. **the lil homie**)

lil momma n. (southern sl.) new school
1. a term of endearment males use to address or refer to females who are hip.
ex: "Ask lil momma to bring some of her friends."

lil Ms. Hottie pants n. (general sl.) old school
1. a way to refer to a female who exhibits flirtatious or promiscuous behavior.
ex: "Look at lil Ms. Hottie pants over there talking to your boyfriend."

[to] **link up** phrase (general sl.) new school
1. to meet with someone.
ex: "We all posed to link up over the weekend."

[to] **lipperfess** v. (e. coast sl.) new school
1. the act of talking tough in an attempt to scare and/or intimidate someone as part of a bluff. (var. [one's who's] **lipperfessin'**)
ex: "I'm really not in the mood for a whole lot of lipperfessin'."

[to] **lip wrestle** v. (southern sl.) new school
1. the act of arguing pointlessly [without fear the argument will escalate to a physical confrontation]. (var. [to] **word wrestle**)
ex: "I see right now, all you wanna do is lip wrestle."

liquid crack n. (e. coast sl.) old school
1. a brand of alcohol named "CISCO".
ex: "He was out drinkin' that liquid crack again, now he's sick as a dog."

[someone who's] **live** adj. (e. coast sl.) old school
1. one who is and/or considered to be "hip" and "cool". 2. a "streetwise" individual.

ex: "You think you live now." "Bring some live catz with you to my party."

[to] **live large** v. (general sl.) old & new school
1. to have the financial resources to live an extravagant lifestyle. (var. [someone who's] **livin' large**)
ex: "This what you call livin' large." "We livin' large now." "Bob thinks he's livin' large."

[someone who's] **livin' foul** adj. (general sl.) old & new school
1. someone who indulges in unscrupulous, shameful, or dishonest behavior. (var. [to] **live foul**)
ex: "I didn't know your people was livin' foul like that." "That's livin' foul."

[someone who's] **livin' illegal** v. (criminal sl.) new school
1. one who commits crime or is involved in things that may be shady as a way to make money. (var. [someone who's] **illegal**)
ex: "I'm tired of livin' illegal."

[someone who's] **livin' legal** (criminal sl.) new school
1. one who doesn't commit crime or indulge in things that may be shady as way to make money. (var. [someone who's] **legal**)
ex: "When I met you, you was livin' legal and now look at you."

loc n. (w. coast sl.) old & new school
1. a term of endearment among friends; friend. 2. a way to address someone whose name you do not know or do not want to use in front of others.
ex: "That was my bad loc."

[someone who's] **loc'ed out** adj. (w. coast sl.) old & new school
1. crazy; to act irrational. 2. the abbreviation for the word "loco". (var. [to] **loc out**)
ex: "Don't get messed up with them loc'ed out catz from Brownsville."

[to] **lock ass with** [someone] v. (general sl.) new school
1. to engage in a physical confrontation; the act fighting. (var. [to]
lock ass, [to] **lock up with** [someone])
ex: "Homes, you not tryin' to lock ass wit me, trust me on that."

[to] **lock** [something/someone] **down** phrase (e. coast sl.) old &
new school
1. to secure. 2. to have something or someone under one's
power/control. (var. [to] **have** [something/someone] **on lock/on
lock-down status**)
ex: "I had N.C. on lock-down for five years."

[to be in/on] **lock-down** phrase (prison sl.) new school
1. incarcerated; in prison. (var. [someone who's] **locked**)
ex: "How long he gonna be on lock-down?"

[to] **lock** [something/someone] **in** phrase (e. coast sl.) new school
1. to agree to a deal or arrangement which leaves no room for
backing out.
*ex: "The first thing we need to do is lock this thing in." "Oh that's
already locked in."*

[something that's] **locked** phrase (e. coast sl.) new school
1. guaranteed; a sure thing. 2. to have something secured. (var.
[something that's] **a lock**)
ex: "I already got that locked." "What I told you is a lock."

[as] **long as I owe you, you'll never go broke** phrase (general sl.)
old & new school
1. a witty way to respond to someone who is complaining about
the money you owe him/her.

long money phrase (general sl.) new school
1. large amounts of money. (var. [someone whose] **money is long**)
*ex: "You gonna be outta ya league, catz come here with long
money."*

long time no see phrase (general sl.) old & new school
1. a term used to acknowledge not seing a person in a long period of time when greeting him/her.
ex: "Long time no see homie, where you been?"

look at ya man [over there] phrase (general sl.) new school
1. a term used mockingly when bringing a male's ridiculous behavior to the attention of a mutual friend.
ex: "Look at ya man, he should be shot."

[to] **look cross-eyed at** [someone] v. (general sl.) old & new school
1. to look at someone strangely, with contempt, or with dislike.
(var. [to] **look at** [someone] **cross-eyed**)
ex: "Everybody started lookin' cross-eyed at you when she started talkin'."

[to] **look like** [one] **got hit in the face with a bag of nickles** phrase (general sl.) old & new school
1. a way to describe someone as being ugly or very unattractive.
(var. [to] **look like** [one] **got hit with a sock filled with rocks**)

[to] **look like** [someone] **got one foot in the grave** phrase (general sl.) old school
1. to look sickly or unhealthy.

[to] **look out for** [someone] v. (general sl.) old & new school
1. to do a favor and/or show someone preferential treatment. (var. [to] **look out**)
ex: "Next time I come through, I'mma look out for you and your peoples."

look out, for the cookout phrase (general sl.) new school
1. a way to ask someone for a favor and/or preferential treatment.
ex: "Come on dawg, I need you to look out for the cookout."

[to] **look pressed** v. (southern sl.) new school
1. worried ; stressed.
ex: "Do I look pressed to you?" "She looked real pressed when I seen her."

[to] **look sideways at** [someone] v. (e. coast sl.) new school
1. to stare at someone with a tough or mean glare. (var. [to] **look at** [someone] **sideways**)
ex: "Every time I come in here you always lookin' sideways at me, what's up?"

[to] **look stupid in the face** adj. (general sl.) new school
1. to look bewildered, shocked, or surprised. (var. [to] **look** [all] **stupid in the face**)
ex: "I left 'em standin' there lookin' stupid in the face."

lookin' at my Gucci it's about that time phrase (general sl.) old school
1. a witty way to announce one's depature or signal that it is time to leave [usually while looking at one's watch].

[a female who's] **lookin' right** adj. (general sl.) old & new school
1. a female who is attractive and fashionably dressed [enhancing her appearance]. 2. a term males used to give praise to a female's body. (var. [a female who] **looks right**)
ex: "Son, Shortie came to work lookin' right."

loose me! interj. (e. coast sl.) new school
1. a way to command someone to hand over something.
ex: "Loose me, I need to use that phone."

loosies n. (general sl.) old & new school
1. individual cigarettes sold out of the pack in neighborhood bodegas.
ex: "I think loosies cost about 25¢ now."

[someone who's] **lost in the sauce** phrase (general sl.) old school
1. confused; unable to grasp the significance of something. (var.
[someone who's] **lost)**
ex: "Its hard to talk to her, cause she's lost in the sauce."

loud pipes n. (southern sl.) new school
1. a way to refer to the removal of the muffler on a car or
motorcycle and the noise it creates.
ex: "You'll never see loud pipes on a Benz."

[to] **lounge** v. (general sl.) old school
1. to wait. 2. to take it easy. (var. [to] **lounge for** [someone], [to]
lounge out)
*ex: "I'mma lounge for my dawgs to come out." "I'mma lounge for
the rest of the day."*

lounge phrase (general sl.) old school
1. a way to ask someone to wait for you. 2. a way to encourage
someone to calm down or to take it easy when you see him/her
getting upset or impatient.
ex: "Can you lounge for me over there?"

[a] **louwinski** n. (sexual sl.) new school
1. oral sex performed on a male.
ex: "A lil louwinski never hurt nobody."

love n. (e. coast sl.) new school
1. a term of endearment among friends; friend. 2. a way to address
someone whose name you do not know or do not want to use in
front of others [also used to ease the tension between two strangers
in a altercation]
*ex: "I know love an'nim from way back." "Ayo love I ain't lookin'
for no problems."*

[to receive] **love** [from one's peers/friends/neighborhood] v.
(general sl.) new school
1. to receive respect, admiration, or praise.

ex: "Eleven years later and I still get love from my peoples."

[something that's] **love** phrase (e. coast sl.) new school
1. agreeable; fine with you; satisfactory; okay [usually used to express one's gratitude and appreciation]. See also: [to] **show** [someone] **love**
ex: "That sound like love to me."

love boat n. (drug sl.) old & new school
1. embalming fluid (P.C.P.). See also: **dust**
ex: "I know people who have lost their mind usin' love boat."

love is love phrase (e. coast sl.) new school
1. a term used to convey that everything is fine, OK, agreeable, acceptable, or satisfactory [usually used with sincerity and respect].
ex: "Love is love with us son."

[a male's] **love muscle** n. (sexual sl.) old school
1. a covert way to refer to a male's penis.
ex: "Shortie tried to kick me in the love muscle."

love, peace, and hair grease phrase (general sl.) new school
1. a witty way to say, "good bye" when departing the company of a friend or love one. (var. **love, peace, and pigs feet**)

love, sex, and welfare checks phrase (general sl.) new school
1. a witty way to say, "good bye" when departing the company of a friend or love one.

love was love phrase (sexual sl.) new school
1. a covert way to say that sex was good

[to] **low ball** [someone] v. (general sl.) new school
1. to do something to undermine someone's effort, plan, or goal.
ex: "I would never try to low ball my homies."

[a] **low budget Shortie** phrase (e. coast sl.) new school
1. a female who doesn't desire expensive gifts or living necessities to be happy, feel wanted, and/or feel important.
ex: "I'd rather deal with a low budget Shortie any day."

low-level trickin' phrase (w. coast sl.) new school
1. the act of spending a minimal amount of money on someone you are pursuing an intimate relationship with or just a one night stand.
ex: "All you hafta do is a lil low-level trickin on shortie, trust me."

low pro phrase (general sl.) old & new school
1. the state of maintaining a low profile. (var. [to] **play a low pro**)
ex: "I have to be low pro when I get out."

[to] **luck up** [on something] v. (general sl.) old & new school
1. to get lucky.
ex: "I heard you lucked up in Atlantic City over the weekend."

[to] **lump** [someone's] **meat rack** phrase (criminal sl.) new school
1. a way to refer to being shot in the head. (var. [to] **lump** [someone's] **hat rack**, [to] **put a hole in** [someone's] **helmet**)
ex: "They said someone lumped his meat rack." "They found'em in the trunk with his meat rack lumped."

lunch money adj. (southern sl.) old & new school
1. small amounts of money [usually used to insult or criticize someone's financial status].
ex: "You won't get far with this Shortie on lunch money."

[someone who's] **lunchin'** v. (southern sl.) new school
1. not paying attention; daydreaming; to be aloft.
ex: "You be lunchin' big time." "You need to stop lunchin' Shortie."

lust if you must phrase (w. coast sl.) old school
1. a witty way to tell one's boyfriend or girlfriend it's okay to look at another person of the opposite sex.

[you] **lyin' and your breath stink** phrase (general sl.) old & new school
1. a witty way to accuse someone of lying or making a bogus claim.

[someone who's] **lyin' like a bit**** phrase (southern sl.) old & new school
1. someone who is telling an extremely outrageous lie [usually on someone else or to escape blame]. (var. [someone who's] **lyin' like sh**/a summa bit****)
ex: "I'm tellin' you son, that cat lyin' like a bit**."

m

ma n. (e. coast sl.) new school
1. a. term of endearment males use to address females. 2. a term a male uses to address a female whose name he doesn't know or doesn't want to use in front of others. See also: **boo, shortie**
ex: "Dig ma, I'm tryin' to get at you about somethin'."

Ma Bell n. (general sl.) old school
1. the Telephone Co.
ex: "You should pay Ma Bell her money, then your phone would still be on."

ma duke n. (e. coast sl.) old school
1. a way to refer to one's mother; mom. (var. **ma dukes, momma duke, momma dukes, momma san**) See also: [one's] **ol' earth**
ex: "How's ma dukes doin'?" "I'm about to put ma dukes up in a house."

[a] **mack** n. (w. coast sl.) old & new school
1. a male who has the unique ability to finesse and manipulate multiple females at the same time with none of them realizing what he is truly about or up to. (var. [to] **mack**, [to] **put** [one's] **mack down,** [one's] **mack game**, [a] **mack daddy**)
ex: "You won't ever see a mack like me again." "I been mackin' since High School." "I'm a mack from way back."

[a] **mack millie** n. (criminal sl.) new school
1. a mack 10 or 11 automatic machine gun. (var. [a] **mack**)
ex: "Shortie had a mack millie water gun, that looked real as a mug."

[someone who's] **madd cool** adj. (general sl.) old & new school

1. an extremely pleasant person to be around; has a wonderful personality.
ex: "I didn't know ya momz was madd cool like that."

[someone who's] **mad as sh**** phrase (general sl.) old & new school
1. extremely mad; furious. (var. [someone who's] **mad as a muhf**ka**)
ex: "I don't know what you did, but homes is mad as sh** with you."

[to] **mad dog** [someone] w. (w. coast sl.) old school
1. to look or stare at someone with a mean and/or tough facial expression. (var. [to] **mad dog 20-20** [someone]) See also: [to] **grit on** [someone]
ex: "As soon as I walked in, catz started mad doggin' me and shortie."

madd adj. (general sl.) old & new school
1. a lot of; a large amount. 2. a term used to put strong emphasis on one's description of events, feelings, or thoughts.
ex: "They had madd honey's at the party." "I left madd early." "She got a madd attitude problem."

[a] **magic stick** n. (sexual sl.) new school
1. a covert way to refer to a penis.

mahondo n. (criminal sl.) old school
1. a verbal warning relayed through shouts from people in a high drug traffic area to alert others that the police are coming, near, or active in the area.

[a male's] **main chick/girl** phrase (general sl.) old & new school
1. the female who a male treats more special than any other female with whom he may be intimate with as well.
ex: "Shortie we cool, but you could never be my main chick."

main man n. (southern sl.) new school
1. a term or endearment among friends; friend. 2. a term used to address a male whose name you do not know or do not want to use in front of others [sometimes used to dismiss someone's importance].
ex: "What it look like main man?" "I think main man was just about to leave."

maintain phrase (general sl.) old & new school
1. a way to wish someone well when departing company, ending a letter, or ending a phone coversation.
ex: "Yo dawg maintain and I'll holler at you later." "Tell everybody I said maintain, and I'll talk to you some other time."

maintainin' phrase (general sl.) old & new school
1. a way to say one is doing fine or well when another inquires about his/her well being.
ex: "I'm maintainin' through all this." "I'm maintainin', how are you?"

[a] **major figure** n. (e. coast sl.) new school
1. a person who earns a lot of money, is important, and commands a lot of respect in his chosen profession. (var. [someone who's] **major**)
ex: "Everybody's not built to be a major figure."

[to have/make] **major figures** phrase (e. coast sl.) new school
1. to have or make large amounts of money.
ex: "Soon we gonna be makin' some real major figures." "I heard they holdin' major figures."

make a long story short phrase (general sl.) old & new school
1. a direct way to tell someone to get to the point or to the details of a story or explanation [sometimes used as a way to interrupt one who is taking too long to get to the point or the importance of a story].
ex: "How about just makin' a long story short."

[to] make funny-style moves phrase (e. coast sl.) new school
1. to demonstrate behavior or acts that are questionable, suspect, or sneaky; to act furitively
ex: "Dukes be makin' some funny-style moves."

[to] make [someone] into plant food phrase (criminal sl.) new school
1. a term used to refer to murder. (var. **[to] make [someone] into fish food**)
ex: "Somebody made dude into plant food."

make it light on yourself phrase (southern sl.) new school
1. a witty way to respond to someone who asks "what you wanna bet?" "how much you wanna bet?", or "you wanna bet something?". 2. a term used to give someone the choice of what a wager or punishment should be.

make it snappy, nappy phrase (general sl.) old school
1. a witty way to tell someone to hurry and/or move quickly.

[to] make moves phrase (e. coast sl.) new school
1. to do what is necessary to implement and achieve one's goal.
(var. **[to] make moves with [someone], [someone who's] makin' moves**)
ex: "I'm about to make some moves with ya man."

[to] make [someone] sick to his/her stomach phrase (general sl.) old & new school
1. a way to emphasize one's extreme dislike for another.
ex: "That Itch make me sick to my stomach."

[to] make the block hot phrase (drug sl.) old & new school
1. any activities that make the police frequent a area where there are drugs being sold. (var. **[someone who's] makin' the block hot, [to] hot the block [up]**)
ex: "These young catz makin' the block hot." "You keep makin' the block hot when you ride through."

[one's] **man** n. (general sl.) old & new school
1. one's male friend. (var. [one's] **manz**)
ex: "That's my man from B.K." "I'm tellin' my man what you said."

man down phrase (southern sl.) old & new school
1. a warning relayed through shouts in a high drug traffic area to alert others that the police or someone known to be or suspected of being a police informer is coming or in the area.

man listen! interj. (e. coast sl.) new school
1. a straightforward way to inform someone that you are not trying to, don't want to, or not in the mood to hear his/her excuses [usually used as a prelude for one who's about to get upset]. (var. **maaaaan listen!**)
ex: "Man listen, you can tell that to someone who wants to hear it."

Manhattan makes it, Brooklyn takes it phrase (e. coast sl.) old & new school
1. a boisterous claim among Brooklyn toughs which proclaims that Brooklyn toughs are the toughest of all five boroughs.

[to get] **manish** v. (e. coast sl.) new school
1. to talk and act tough when one is not known for being or acting tough to another's surprise. (var. [to act] **manish**)
ex: "Them catz gettin' a lil money now they startin' to get real manish."

manish adj. (general sl.) old & new school
1. a term used to describe a female who acts like a male.
ex: "Them broads actin' too manish for me."

[one's] **manz an'nim** phrase (e. coast sl.) new school
1. a hip way to refer to several of one's male friends. (var. [one's] **man an'nim**, [one's] **menz**)

ex: *"Look at what ya manz an'nim did." "Lets call ya man an'nim." "All them catz is my menz."*

[to] **map sh** out** phrase (general sl.) old & new school
1. to plan. (var. [to] **map** [something] **out**)
ex: *"I been mappin' this sh** out for a long time."*

[to] **marinate** v. (southern sl.) new school
1. to relax; to take it easy. 2. to wait.
ex: *"We all need to marinate for a few and see what happens."*

[a] **mark** adj. (w. coast sl.) old & new school
1. one who is easily fooled, taken advantage of, or gullible. 2. one who is not considered "hip" or "cool". (var. [a] **mark ass busta**)
ex: *"I'm not bringin' them marks with me." "She thinks I'm a mark."*

[to] **mark** [someone] v. (e. coast sl.) old & new school
1. to re-enact or describe the act of a shooting, stabbing, or slashing of a razor across one's face in a playful manner by pointing or using an imaginary weapon on another in one's demostration.
ex: *"Don't mark me like that."*

[to] **mash** [someone] v. (w. coast sl.) new school
1. to beat someone up [often involves several individuals beating up on one person]. (var. [to] **mash** [someone] **out**)
ex: *"I had no choice but to mash his ass."*

mashed adj. (e. coast sl.) new school
1 drunk; intoxicated. See also. **pissy, tore up**
ex: *"My pops came home mashed, talkin' junk."*

[to] **mask up** v. (e. coast sl.) new school
1. the act of donning a ski mask or bandanna before one indulges in some sort of criminal activity to hide one's face.

mass n. (e. coast sl.) new school
1. money. 2. large amounts of money. (var. **math**)
ex: "Everybody out here still tryin' to get that mass."

material n. (drug sl.) old school
1. a covert word for "drugs."

[a] **maytag** n. (prison sl.) old school
l. one who washes other peoples clothes in prison out of fear or intimidation. 2. a follower; a flunky.
ex: "Ya man was my maytag in prison." "He lookin' for somebody to be his maytag." "They made 'em into a maytag."

[to] **max out** [one's prison sentence] v. (prison sl.) old & new school
1. to do the maximum amount of one's prison sentence without being allowed parole, probation, or work release.
ex: "I kinda figured they was gonna make me max out."

[a] **McNasty** n. (sexual sl.) old & new school
1. a name males use to refer to a female who is very promiscuous or easy to have sex with.
ex: "He's not from around here, so he don't know she's a McNasty." "Yo son, he about to marry that McNasty."

McUgly adj. (e. coast sl.) new school
1. extremely ugly or unattractive.

me, myself, and I phrase (general sl.) old school
1. a way to make reference to oneself.
ex: "All I hafta worry about is me, myself, and I."

me personally... phrase (general sl.) old & new school
1. a term used as a prelude to giving one's opinion, advice, or view. (var. **me myself...**)
ex: "Me personally, I would have been jetted."

[a female with a] **mean body** adj. (sexual sl.) old & new school
1. a term used to describe a female who has a body worthy of
praise and admiration [usually a big butt or breasts].
*ex: "I don't know what happened but back in the days, shortie had
a mean body."*

[to] **mean mug** [someone] v. (southern sl.) new school
1. to look or stare at someone with a mean or tough facial
expression. See also: [to] **grit on** [someone]
ex: "Chicks was all mean muggin' me and sh**."

Medina n. (e. coast sl.) old school
1. Brooklyn N.Y.

[one's] **melon** n. (general sl.) old & new school
1. a person's head. See also: [one's] **dome**
ex: "Your lil sister got the biggest melon I ever seen in my life."

[one's] **mental** n. (e. coast sl.) old school
1. one's father.
ex: "I gotta go somewhere for my mental."

mess around... phrase (general sl.) old & new school
1. a term used as a prelude to issuing a threat or a warning. (var.
mess around and......)
ex: "Mess around, I might put you last now."

[to] **mess with** [something] v. (general sl.) old & new school
1. to like. 2. to have an indulgence for. (var. [to] **f**k with**
[something hard])
*ex: "I mess with Sex and the City, that's my show." "I messes with
those new S. Carter joints."*

[to] **mess with** [someone] v. (general sl.) new school
1. to like and admire someone; to be a fan of someone. 2. to have
an intimate relationship or friendship with someone. (var. [to] **f**k
with** [someone hard])
ex: "On the real I messes with Foxy and Kim, they rep BK son."

meth n. (drug sl.) old & new school
1. methadone. 2. Methamphetamine (speed).

M.I.A. n. (southern sl.) new school
1. Miami Fla.

M.I.A. phrase (general sl.) new school
1. missing in action.
ex: "Shortie M.I.A., she hasn't been home in two weeks."

[to] **milk** [someone] v. (general sl.) old & new school
1. to con or manipulate someone out of his/her money or possessions over a long period of time. See also: [to] **juice** [someone]
ex: "I'm tellin' you, shortie just tryin' to milk you."

[to] **milk** [a situation] v. (general sl.) old & new school
1. to prolong a situation that is to your benefit for as long as possible.
ex: "I can't blame you for milkin' this."

[an automobile that's] **milky** adj. (e. coast sl.) new school
1. a brand new automobile [often refers to a white automobile].
ex: "Homeboy pushin' the milky 500 straight out of prison." "I gotta cop somethin' milky."

mind ya business you might live longer phrase (general sl.) old & new school
1. a witty way to reprimand someone for his/her nosiness [also used as a warning].

mind yours phrase (general sl.) old & new school
1. a playful or sarcastic way to tell someone to mind his/her business or to stay out of your business [usually used in the context when one is volunteering his/her unwanted advice].
ex: "You need to mind yours son."

mineaswell phrase (general sl.) old & new school
1. an unenthusiastic way to encourage or support a decision or choice one makes.
ex: "Mineaswell, you tried everything else." "I mineaswell try it like this."

[when it's] **mink weather** phrase (e. coast sl.) new school
1. a hip way to say that the weather is cold enough for wearing a fur coat.

[a] **minute man** n. (sexual sl.) old & new school
1. a man who lacks the stamina or endurance to last for long periods of time during sex; a male who ejaculates prematurely.
(var. [a] **five minute brother**)
ex: "Word is homeslice, youse a minute man."

[one's] **miz** n. (e. coast sl.) new school
1. one's mother. (var. [one's] **miznother**)
ex: "I seen your miz on the bus this morning." "Tell ya miz I said hello."

[one's] **M.O.** phrase (e. coast sl.) new school
1. one's method of or reputation for doing something [one's "modus operandi"].
ex: "I knew its was you, cause that's your M.O."

M.O.B. phrase (e. coast sl.) new school
1. a covert term males use to remind or signal a friend that "money over broads" or money comes first/before females when that friends seems preoccupied with a female.
ex: "Lets go dawg, its M.O.B." "M.O.B. dawg, what you gonna do?"

[one's] **mob** n. (general sl.) new school
1. one's favorite sports team. 2. one's group of friends.
ex: "The Knicks always gonna be my mob." "Ask'er can I bring my mob."

[to] **mob** [someone] v. (w. coast sl.) old school
1. the act of one individual getting beat up by a group of other individuals. (var. [to] **mob on** [someone])
ex: *"Some catz tried to mob my man on his way to school."*

[a] **mobile** n. (general sl.) old school
1. a mobile phone.

Moe n. (general sl.) old & new school
1. Moet champagne. (var. **Moey**)

moist adj. (e. coast sl.) new school
1. cowardly; afraid. 2. emotional.
ex: *"I found out ya man is moist dawg."*

momma here comes that man again phrase (southern sl.) new school
1. a witty way to tease and taunt one's opponent during competition every time you score a point and/or when your winning is inevitable.

mommies n. (e. coast sl.) new school
1. females. (var. [a] **mommie**)
ex: *"There's some nice lil mommies in here tonight."*

[a] **mo-mo** n. (southern sl.) old school
1. a motel. See also: [a] **tellie**
ex: *"We stopped at the nearest mo-mo."*

[one's] **momz** n. (general sl.) old & new school
1. one's mother.
ex: *"Here come ya momz now."*

money n. (e. coast sl.) old & new school
1. a term of endearment among friends; friend. 2. a way to address someone whose name you do not know or do not want to use in front of others. (var. **money grip**)

ex: "Ayo, money said the same thing." "Who seen money leave?"

[the] **Money Earnin'** n. (e. coast sl.) old & new school
1. Mount Vernon N.Y. (var. **the Vernon, Money Earnin' Mount Vernon)**
ex: "We moved from the Money Earnin' when I was real little."

[one who has] **money like the Feds** phrase (e. coast sl.) new school
1. rich; wealthy. 2. to have or make large amounts of money.
ex: "Them catz used to have money like the Feds, until they went to the Feds."

[one who has] **money like the mint, the govermint** phrase (general sl.) old & new school
1. to have, earn, or make large amounts of money [usually used a boast or brag]. (var. [one who has] **more money than the mint, the govermint)**

money on the wood make the game go good phrase (e. coast sl.) old & new school
1. a straightforward way to inform someone that you will not accept a bet and/or gamble against him/her until you see his/her money; a way to refuse to gamble or bet someone using I.O.U.'s

money talk bullsh** walk phrase (general sl.) old & new school
1. a hip way to challenge or accept one's offer to wager money.
2. a way to declare financial compensation.
ex: "I said what I said, money talk bullsh** walk." "Look, if that's what y'all wanna do money talk bullsh** walk"

monkey ass phrase (general sl.) old & new school
1. a derogatory way to use the word "ass". (var. [a] **monkey ass** [person])
ex: "She can kiss my monkey ass." "Oh, I got something for your monkey ass."

monkey see, monkey do phrase (general sl.) old & new school
1. a playful or sarcastic way to point out someone's attempt do as
you or follow your lead.
ex: "You didn't even give it an hour and, monkey see, monkey do."

Moola n. (general sl.) old & new school
1. money
ex: "Just tell me how much moola we talkin'."

mos def phrase (e. coast sl.) new school
1. an enthusiastic way to say "yes" or "most definitely".
ex: "Are we comin', that mos def."

Mother's Day n. (southern sl.) old school
1. the first day of every month that people on public assistance
receive their government checks. (var. **the first of month, check
day**)
ex: "She'll pay you back on Mother's Day."

[to] **motivate** v. (e. coast sl.) old school
1. to leave; to depart from.
*ex: "Its time for us to motivate." "I motivated about three in the
mornin'."*

mouth almighty phrase (general sl.) old school
1. a way to refer to someone who can't keep a secret, spreads
rumors, or gossips. See also: [to] **run** [one's] **mouth**
ex: "Thanks to mouth almighty, my girl found out."

[one's] **mouth piece** phrase (general sl.) old & new school
1. one's teeth. 2. one's mouth.
ex: "How can you kiss someone with a mouth piece like that?"
"Did you smell shortie mouth piece? .... Yo!"

[to] **move** [a particular kind of way] v. (general sl.) old & new
school

1. the act of doing things a certain kind of way. 2. a way to say, "do things".
ex: "This is how we move around here." "I didn't know you was movin' like that."

[to] **move on** [someone] v. (criminal sl.) new school
1. to rob someone. (var. [to get] **moved on**)
ex: "Somebody tried to move on my peoples."

[to] **move weight** phrase (drug sl.) old & new school
1. to sell ounce quantities and more of an illegal drug; to sell drugs only in wholesale quantities. (var. [to] **sell weight**)
ex: "We wasn't into movin' weight that's how we lasted so long outta town."

move ya feet, lose ya seat phrase (general sl.) old & new school
1. a witty way to tease someone whose seat you now occupy because he/she left it unoccupied when he/she returns to reclaim his/her seat.

[something that] **moves** [you] v. (general sl.) old & new school
1. inspires. 2. intimidates; scares.
ex: "What he said kinda moved me." "Slim, what you sayin' don't move me." "What, you think that sh** moves me?"

Ms. Thing n. (general sl.) old & new school
1. a way to refer to a female who is conceited and stuck up. [sometimes reference is used unjustly].
ex: "I thought Ms. Thing wasn't comin'."

much love phrase (general sl.) old & new school
1. a genuine and sincere expression of love when departing company of a friend or love one or when ending a verbal or written communiqué.

[one's] **mug** n. (general sl.) old & new school
1. one's face.
ex: "Did you see Shortie mug?"

mug phrase (general sl.) new school
1. a covert way to use the term "motherf**ker". (var.
muthafker, mutha, muhf**ka**)
ex: "Its cold as a mug out there."

mugly adj. (e. coast sl.) new school
1. extremely ugly; unattractive.
ex: "She's cute, but her two friends are mugly."

[someone who's your] **muhf**ka** n. (general sl.) old & new school
1. one's closet and best friend [used as a term of endearment
among and in reference to friends]. (var. [one's] **muhf**ka**)
*ex: "Mister A.D., that's my muhf**ka." "Don't worry, you still my
muhf**ka."*

[someone who's a] **muhf**ka** adj. (general sl.) old & new school
1. one whose behavior is utterly unbelievable, ridiculous or stupid.
2. one who is outrageously bold or daring.
*ex: "Shortie a muhf**ka, I ain't never seen nothin' like that."
"For real dawg, youse a muhf**ka."*

[to] **munch** v. (general sl.) old & new school
1. to eat. (var. [to] **munch down on** [something])
ex: "When I walked in, they was already munchin' away."

munchies n. (general sl.) old & new school
1. junk or snack food.
ex: "I picked up some munchies for the trip."

[to] **murder** [something] v. (general sl.) new school
1. to do an extremely good job; to perform excellently or
outstandingly [usually used when evaluating one's performance].
*ex: "I'm about to murder this next song." "Ya man murdered that
sh**."*

[to] **murder** [someone] v. (general sl.) new school
1. to out perform someone; to do a better job than someone else [usually used when evaluating two peoples performance]. (var. [to] **murder** [someone] **at** [something])
*ex: "Ya homeboy murdered the other team by himself." "What you talkin' about I murdered you at that sh**."*

[to] **murder** [someone] **with** [one's] **mouth** phrase (e. coast sl.) new school
1. the act of talking tough and issuing empty threats with no intentions of following up on one's words [usually threats consist of what one is going to do to someone in a physical confrontation]. (var. [someone with a] **murder mouth**) See also: [to] **talk that murder one sh****
ex: "The only thing you gonna do is murder somebody with ya mouth." "You been murderin' me with ya mouth for the last ten minutes."

[to] **murk** v. (e. coast sl.) new school
1. to leave; to depart. (var. [to] **murk out**)
ex: "Whether you here or not I'm murkin' at six." "They been murked out."

[to] **murk** [someone] v. (e. coast sl.) new school
1. death caused by murder; homicide.
ex: "He got murked about two years ago." "Did they find out who murked ya man?"

[to] **mush** [someone] v. (general sl.) old school
1. to use one's hand to forcefully push someone's head or face back [sometimes used to dismiss someone]. (var. [to] **smush** [someone])
ex: "I'mma mush you next time I catch you lookin' over there."

mustard n. (criminal sl.) new school
1. a firearm; handgun.

ex: "You can't get in here with the mustard dawg."

mutha made'em, mutha loved'em, mutha f**k'em phrase (general sl.) new school
1. a sarcastic way to express discontent, disrespect, or general bad feelings for someone you dislike, are angry with, or who has wronged you.

my arms might be too short to box with God, but I'll knock your [punk / sucker/lame/chump] **ass out** phrase (southern sl.) new school
1. a witty way to respond to an empty threat [used to exude confidence that one will win a physical confrontation with the one issuing the empty threat].

my bad phrase (southern sl.) old & new school
1. a way to offer an apology. 2. an apologetic way to say, "my fault", "my mistake", "excuse me", "I'm sorry". (var. **my bag**)
ex: "My bad, I didn't see you in here." "That was definitely my bad."

my main sh** stain phrase (general sl.) new school
1. a witty way to acknowledge or recognize someone as being a very good friend.
ex: "You know doggone well you my main sh** stain." "Save some for my main sh** stain."

my mans pots and pans phrase (general sl.) old & new school
1. a witty way to acknowledge, recognize, and/or make reference to a specific friend; a term of endearment among friends. (var. **my man fifty grand/from the mutha land/if nobody can you can**)
ex: "Where you know my mans pots and pans from?"

[that's] **my manz an'nim** phrase (e. coast sl.) new school
1. a hip way to acknowledge, recognize, and/or make reference to a specific friend within a group of other friends. (var. [that's] **my man an'nim**)

ex: "My manz an'nim comin' to get us at twelve." "You said you know my man an'nim?"

my name ain't Eddie Spaghetti, soup me up when you ready phrase (general sl.) old & new school
1. a witty way to inform someone that his/her attempt to con, deceive, or fool you isn't working [usually used when one is told something unbelievably ridiculous]. (var. **my name ain't Joe Neckbone/Sam Sausage Head**)

my name is Bennett and I'm not in it phrase (southern sl.) new school
1. a witty way to exclude oneself from a disagreement or argument others are attempting to involve you in. (var. **my name is Les and I'm not in that mess, my name is Paul and this between y'all**)

my name is Neil and I know exactly how you feel phrase (southern sl.) new school
1. a witty way to tell someone you know how he/she feels or you can relate to how he/she feels.

my spots don't change phrase (e. coast sl.) new school
1. a way to reassure someone that you will not or have not changed towards him/her despite the misunderstanding you have had with a mutual friend.
ex: "That's between me and him, my spots don't change."

my stomach on the curb phrase (e. coast sl.) new school
1. a way to emphasize being extremely hungry. (var. **my stomach touchin' my back**)

my stomach touchin' my back like a knapsack phrase (e. coast sl.) new school
1. a witty way to express or describe one's hunger.

my word is [my] bond phrase (e. coast sl.) old school

1. a term used to solidify one's word as being good and trusting [sometimes when one's word is being doubted it reassures].

n

na phrase (general sl.) old & new school
1. a way to say, "no" [usually used when refusing or denying]. (var. **nah**)
ex: "Na dawg, I ain't say that." "Na you done had enough already."

na'mean phrase (e. coast sl.) new school
1. a way to say, "you know what I mean?", "you understand?", "can you relate to that?", "have I made myself clear?" See also: **ya dig?**
ex: "I was this close na'mean?" "You did that to yaself na'mean?"

[someone who's] **name doesn't/don't hold no weight** phrase (general sl.) old & new school
1. one whose reputation or character is not credible therefore garners no respect with his/her peers.
ex: "That's what you say, but ya name don't hold no weight around here."

[someone whose] **name rings bells** phrase (e. coast sl.) old & new school
1. someone who has a reputation for being a tough guy or "street" individual. 2. one who is very popular.
ex: "My name rings bells around here." "My name used to ring madd bells in the East."

Nap town n. (general sl.) new school
1. Indianapolis, IN.

[the] **nappy dugout** n. (w. coast sl.) old school
1. a covert way to refer to a vagina.

[a] **narrow ass/behind** [person] adj. (general sl.) old school
1. a witty way to reprimand someone who is being extremely annoying.
ex: *"Will you sit your narrow ass down somewhere."*

[a] **Nasty McNasty** n. (general sl.) old & new school
1. a female who is easy to have sex with.

nathins phrase (e. coast sl.) new school
1. a way to say, "nothing" [usually used when refusing or denying]. (var. **nathin**)
ex: *"I wouldn't give her nathins." "I'm not tellin' you nathin."*

[when a male's] **nature rises** v. (sexual sl.) old school
1. a covert way to refer to an erection.
ex: *"Shortie make a catz nature rise just lookin' at her."*

near (pron. n-air) phrase (southern sl.) old & new school
1. a way to say, "not one...." or "none...."
ex: *"Ain't near one of you give me any help." "I don't owe near person in here." "I'm not answering near question."*

[when one's] **neck glows** phrase (general sl.) new school
1. one is wearing an expensive diamond encrusted platinum or gold chain and pendant. (var. [when one's] **neck and wrist glows**)

[to] **need a check up from the neck up** phrase (general sl.) new school
1. the need to be chastised or reprimanded for doing something so unbelievable or ridiculously stupid.
ex: *"I need a check up from the neck for listenin' to you."*

[to] **need** [something] **in** [one's] **life** phrase (southern sl.) new school
1. a way to attribute one's moodiness or attitude to something that is lacking in that person's life and once that void is filled he/she will feel better.

ex: "All she need is a man in her life." "I need some money in my life."

nephew n. (w. coast sl.) new school
1. a term of endearment among friends; friend.
ex: "I'll take care of that for you nephew." "Tell nephew I'll be back."

nevermind phrase (general sl.) old & new school
1. a way to say, "forget about it" [usually used in the context of one changing his/her mind].
ex: "Nevermind now, you took too long."

never say never phrase (general sl.) old school
1. a term used to remind someone that there's always a remote possibility. (var. **you never know**)

never that! interj. (e. coast sl.) new school
1. an enthusiastic way to declare one would never do something, let something happen. 2. a way to say "no way".
ex: "You and me, never that!"

neverworry n. (general sl.) old & new school
1. a fictitious month of the year one gives to someone he/she is trying to brush off [usually used as a way to dismiss someone's advances].
ex: "Call me on neverworry 23, and I'll think about it."

never would I... phrase (general sl.) new school
1. a term used as a prelude to one declaring what he/she wouldn't do [even if that declaration is a lie]. (var. **never would I do that**)
ex: "You can trust me, never would I lie to you."

never would I jump out there phrase (e. coast sl.) new school
1. a matter of fact way to declare that one would never take a chance where he/she could be wrong, rejected, or have his/her feelings hurt.

new borns n. (southern sl.) new school
1. brand new expensive rims for a car.

[a] **new jack** n. (prison sl.) old & new school
1. someone new; a first timer.
ex: "These new jacks come in here thinkin' they know everything."

New Jeruz n. (e. coast sl.) new school
1. New Jersey.

New Yiddy n. (e. coast sl.) new school
1. New York City.

N.Y. (pron. en-y) n. (e. coast sl.) old & new school
1. a hip way to refer to New York City
ex: "You can tell he's from N.Y."

[someone who's] **nice** adj. (general sl.) old & new school
1. a way to describe someone's performance as being outstanding, excellent, and/or worthy of praise [usually used as a compliment or praise]. (var. [to be] **nice at** [something])
ex: "I didn't know you was that nice." "You nice at that sh** dawg."

nice adj. (general sl.) old & new school
1. intoxicated; high from an illegal drug. See also: **stimo, zooted**
ex: "These kinds of chicks don't get nice."

[someone who's] **nice with the hands** phrase (general sl.) old & new school
1. someone who knows how to fight extremely well. (var. [someone who's] **nice with these**)
ex: "I remember when ya man was real nice with the hands."

[someone who's] **nice with the smitties** phrase (general sl.) old school
1. someone who knows how to fight extremely well.

ex: "You wanna see how nice I am with the smitties?"

[to] **nick** v. (prison sl.) new school
1. to crave for a cigarette. (var. **nickin'**, [to] **have a nicotine fit**)
ex: "I was in there nickin' the whole time."

[a] **nickel** n. (prison sl.) new school
1. a five year prison sentence.
ex: "All I'm facin' is a nickel."

[a] **nickel** n. (drug sl.) old & new school
1. a quantity of drug retailing for five dollars. (var. [a] **nickel bag**)
ex: "That cops caught'em with three nickels."

[a] **nina** n. (criminal sl.) old & new school
1. a nine millimeter handgun. (var. [a] **nino**)

[a] **nine** n. (criminal sl.) old & new school
1. a nine millimeter handgun.
ex: "They found two nines under the bed."

[that] **ninja** n. (e. coast sl.) new school
1. a term used to refer to the H.I.V. or A.I.D.'s virus. See also: **that thing**
ex: "I dunno dawg, Shortie might have that ninja."

no bullsh**! interj. (general sl.) new school
1. an enthusiastic way to agree with someone's description, assessment, or observation. 2. a way to declare "you are absolutely right" "I can't agree with you more".
ex: "Yeah no bullsh**shortie breath do be kickin'!"

no diggy phrase (e. coast sl.) new school
1. an enthusiastic way to agree with or express one's approval and/or support. 2. a term used to affirm or reaffirm a thought or claim leaving no room for doubt. (var. **no diggity, no question, no doubt, no diggity no doubt**)

no disrespect... phrase (general sl.) old & new school
1. a term used as a prelude to giving someone an honest critique,
assessment, or thought [that may cause that person to get
offended].
ex: "No disrespect dawg, but ya girl ain't all that."

no eggies, no beggies phrase (general sl.) old school
1. a witty way to inform someone not to ask for some of your food
or drink before he/she has a chance to. 2. a way to refuse
someone's request for some of your food or drink.

no funds... no buns phrase (e. coast sl.) new school
1. a witty term females use to declare that if a male doesn't spend
money of them there's no chance of them being intimate with that
male.

[a] nobody adj. (general sl.) old & new school
1. someone unimportant. 2. one who is considered not "cool" or
"hip".
ex: "Don't hang out with that nobody."

nobody move nobody get hurt phrase (criminal sl.) old school
1. a warning issued in the commission of an armed robbery. 2. a
term used to taunt one's opponent after you score a point against
him/her or when your winning is inevitable.

noid adj. (e. coast sl.) old & new school
1. paranoid; nervous; scared. See also: **p-noid**
ex: "Your people startin' to make me a lil noid about this deal."

non cipher phrase (e. coast sl.) old & new school
1. a matter or fact way to say, "incorrect", "that's wrong/not right",
or "no" [usually matter of factly when making a point]. (var. **now
cipher**)
ex: "That's non cipher, Hip-Hop started out in the Bronx N.Y."

nookie n. (sexual sl.) old & new school
1. a term females use to refer to sexual intercourse and/or their vagina.

North Cack n. (southern sl.) new school
1. North Carolina. (var. **North Caclalacka/Cackalacky/ Click/Clicky, N.Cee**)
ex: "I'm about to make this run to North Cack."

[someone who's] **not all there** phrase (general sl.) old & new school
1. someone who exhibits a limited ability to think or rationalize which can be indenified through his/her strange and erratic behavior and/or statements.
ex: "I been sayin' she not all there for years."

[someone who's] **not built like that** phrase (e. coast sl.) new school
1. one who is lacking whatever it takes to achieve a certain task or level of excellence [usually used to dismiss one's claim or boast]. (var. [someone who] **ain't** [built] **like that**)
ex: "You just talkin', you know I know you not built like that."

[someone who's] **not havin' it** phrase (general sl.) old & new school
1. one who is not going to be pushed around, taken advantage of, intimidated, scared off, or made a fool of. (var. [someone who's] **not goin' for** [something])
ex: "You know dam well she not havin' it."

[something that's] **not in** [one's] **nature/character** phrase (e. coast sl.) new school
1. an action or behavior that is inconsistent with one's character [usually used when denying an accusation].
*ex: "That sh** right there's not in my nature dawg."*

[someone who's] **not livin' right** phrase (general sl.) new school
1. a term used to describe someone's unscrupulous, shameful, or dishonest behavior. 2. one who indulges in illegal acts.
ex: "That's what happens when you not livin' right."

not now, right now phrase (e. coast sl.) new school
1. a way to say, "immediately", "right now", "without delay" [usually used in the context of demanding someone].
ex: "You need to get over here, not now, right now."

[someone who's] **not/ain't worth a dam** phrase (general sl.) old & new school
1. undependable; untrustworthy; extremely petty.
ex: "I coulda been told you he wasn't worth a dam."

nothin' beats a failure but a try phrase (general sl.) old & new school.
1. a way to encourage someone to try. 2. a way to declare that you have decided to try something you were hesitant about.

[someone who's] **nothin' but mouth** phrase (general sl.) old & new school
1. a term used to dismiss someone as being someone who only talks tough in an attempt to scare and intimate others. 2. one who's constantly making empty threats.
ex: "I don't see how you listen to'em, you know he ain't notin' but mouth."

[someone who's] **nothin' but the truth** phrase (e. coast sl.) new school
1. a way to describe an athlete as being the best player there is in his/her sport [usually used to praise one's performance and/or talents]. (var. [someone who's] **the truth**])
ex: "Back in his days, that cat was nothin' but the truth."

nothin' comes to a dreamer but sleep phrase (general sl.) old & new school
1. a term used to advise and encourage someone not to waste or spend his/her time daydreaming.

nothin's fair to a square phrase (w. coast sl.) old school
1. a playful or sarcastic way to respond to someone's complaint of you treating him/her unfair or unequal.

now that's bad phrase (general sl.) old & new school
1. a sarcastic and negative way to criticize one's actions, statement, or behavior. (var. **that's bad**)
ex: "She stole the waitresses tip now that's bad."

Now Y n. (e. coast sl.) new school
1. New York City.

now you worryin' about the wrong thing phrase (southern sl.) new school
1. a witty way to inform someone to mind his/her business or to stop being nosy [usually used sarcastically when someone offers his/her unwanted opinion or is over inquisitive].

nunya (pron. none ya) phrase (e. coast sl.) new school
1. a way to say, "none of your.....".
ex: "I don't want nunya money." "That's nunya business anyway."

nupid adj. (general sl.) new school
1. more than stupid; extremely dumb.
*ex: "That was some real nupid sh** you pulled."*

[a] nut n. (general sl.) old & new school
1. a debt.
ex: "When you gonna pay off that nut." "I need to start payin' this nut off." "Help me pay this nut dawg."

[a] **nut** n. (sexual sl.) old & new school
1. an orgasm.

[to] **nut** v. (sexual sl.) old & new school
1. to have an orgasm. (var. [to] **nut off**)
ex: *"Soon as I started to nut, I called out another chick's name."*

[a] **nut ass** [female/broad] adj. (e. coast sl.) new school
1. a female who exhibits erratic behavior during or after a relationship has ended [usually as a result of some sort of emotional or mental condition she suffers from that her mate was not aware of]; a crazy or unstable female.
ex: *"I can't believe you brought this nut ass broad with you."*
"Where did you meet these nut ass females?"

[to] **nut up** phrase (general sl.) old & new school
1. to suddenly stop talking, sharing information, or revealing a secret.
ex: *"Shortie nutted up when I asked her about what she had seen."*

[a] **#1 stunna** adj. (southern sl.) new school
1. someone who does outrageous things to get attention when flaunting his/her expensive possessions or finacial wealth.
ex: *"Ya man tryin' to be the #1 stunna around here since you left."*

O

[a] **o/o-z** n. (drug sl.) old & new school

1. a ounce of cocaine.
ex: "She got caught on the plane with three o's in her bag."

Oaktown n. (w. coast sl.) old & new school
1. Oakland California.
ex: "Oaktown got some real playas out there."

[someone who's] **o.c.** adj. (general sl.) new school
1. a way to describe someone as being "out of control". 2.
disruptive, rowdy; to display rebellious behavior.
*ex: "Shortie been o.c. since she was about 12 or 13." "I hate to
say it, but they definitely o.c."*

[to] **O.D.** [on someone] v. (e. coast sl.) new school
1. to explode in sudden anger [usually when offended or
disrespected].
ex: "My momz O.D.'d on me in front of my girl."

off brand [people] adj. (e. coast sl.) new school
1. people considered not "cool" or "hip"; nerds; people who aren't
popular amongst their peers.

off the back phrase (general sl.) old & new school
1. a way to say, "right from the start", "to start off with", or
"before I begin". (var. **off the rip/top/out the gate**)
ex: "I need to tell you this right off the back."

[someone who's] **off the chain** adj. (general sl.) new school
1. rebellious; out of control. 2. extremely good looking. (var.
[someone who's] **off the hook**)
ex: "I hate to tell you, but ya shortie is off the chain."

[something that's] **off the chain** phrase (general sl.) new school
1. outstanding; unique; the best of its kind. 2. enjoyable; fun;
exciting. (var. [something that's] **off the hook / heezy / meter /
rector / rector scale / thermo / thermostat / meat rack / hinges**)
ex: "This book is off the chain dawg."

[we] **off the chain in this game** phrase (southern sl.) new school
1. a boisterous way to declare to be the best or an expert at
something one's does.

[something that's] **off the heezy fa sheezy** phrase (w. coast sl.)
new school
1. an enthusiastic way to say something is outstanding, unique, or
the best of its kind [usually used when agreeing with someone's
assessment]. 2. a way to state that something is or will be
enjoyable.
*ex: "That new video was off the heezy fa sheezy." "You should
have went, that trip was off the heezy fa sheezy."*

[to get something] **off the muscle** phrase (general sl.) new school
1. to take something through the use of force or intimidation. (var.
[to take something] **off the muscle**)
*ex: "We took that off the muscle." "He said he gonna get that from
you off the muscle if he has to."*

off the top of my head phrase (general sl.) old & new school
1. a way to say, "without thinking", "just guessing".
*ex: "Off the top of my head I'd hafta say we did it about three
times."*

[to do/say some] **off the wall sh**** phrase (general sl.) old & new
school
1. to do or say something out of place, irrational, that makes no
sense or comes across as crazy. (var. [to do/say] **some ol' off the
wall sh****)
*ex: "They always come in here talkin' that off the wall sh**."
"Shortie tried to tell me some ole off the wall sh** about
you."*

[something that's] **official** adj. (general sl.) new school
1. outstanding; unique; the best of its kind [also used as a stamp of approval]. (var. [something that's] **official like bone gristle/a train whistle/a missile**)
ex: "This that official sh**." "Do you want somethin' that's official or somethin' whack?"

[an] **O.G.** n. (w. coast sl.) old & new school
1. a older "street" tough/thug; an older gang member. 2. an abbreviation for the term "original gangster".
ex: "In 05-06 a lot of O.G's get out of prison."

Oh! Hell Nah! interj. (southern sl.) new school
1. a playful, sarcastic, or negative way to respond to something surprising, unbelievable, shocking [also used to voice one's disagreement or dissatisfaction].
ex: "Oh! Hell Nah!, I know you not wearin' my new sweater."

Oh no doubt phrase (general sl.) old & new school
1. an enthusiastic way to express being in agreement with another's opinion, assessment, or word of advice.
ex: "Oh no doubt, I'm already workin' on that."

Oh no you [he/she] **didn't** phrase (general sl.) old & new school
1. a playful, sarcastic, or negative way to respond to someone's actions or words one finds shocking, surprising, or unbelievable [also used to voice one's disagreement or dissatisfaction towards someone]. (var. **I know this** [insult/ derogatory statement / expletive] **just didn't...**)

Oh, now you/we full of jokes [huh]? phrase (general sl.) new school
1. a sarcastic way to question one's attempt to be funny [also used when questioning one's attempt to give you advice or opinion that sounds ridiculous to you]. (var. **now you on joke time** [huh]?)

Oh, now you eat tough man cookies? phrase (general sl.) new school
1. a sarcastic way to question someone's sudden and bold attempt to standup for himself/herself against you.

Oh snap! interj. (general sl.) old & new school
1. an enthusiastic way to express shock, surprise, or disbelief. (var. **Oh snaps!**)
ex: "Oh snap look who's here." "Oh snap, ain't that your girl?"

[an] O.J. n. (e. coast sl.) old school
1. a luxury car that is a taxi.

ol' boy n. (southern sl.) old & new school
1. a term of endearment for an older male. 2 a way to refer to one's father or fatherly figure. 3. a way to refer to an older male in the third person.
ex: "What ol' boy gonna do?" "Talk to ol' boy lately?"

[one's] ol' earth n. (e. coast sl.) old & new school
1. one's mother; mom. See also **Ma Dukes**
ex: "You shoulda listened to ya ol' earth when it came to shortie."

ol' girl n. (southern sl.) old & new school
1. a way to refer to females [usually ones's mother, female acquaintance, or girlfriend].
ex. "You know ol' girl ain't having that." "When the last time you spoke to ol' girl?"

[an] ol' head n. (e. coast sl.) new school
1. a hip way to refer to an older adult male.
ex. " You need to ask the ol' head." "What you wanna do ol' head, we can play one more game."

[one's] ol' lady/man n. (general sl.) old school
1. a hip way to to refer to one's girlfriend or boyfriend.

*ex: "You might need to ask the ol' lady first." "What ya ol'
man have to say?"*

ol' school n. (general sl.) new school
1. a way to make reference to the past. 2. anything retro.
ex: "This is that ol' school homeboy."

[an] **ol' school joint** n. (general sl.) new school
1. a song that was popular a long time ago [hearing it often
sparking a bit of nostalaga].
ex: "Turn that up, that's a real ol' school joint."

[one's] **old way** n. (general sl.) old & new school
1. one's former neighborhood.
ex:"Last time you been around the old way?"

[to be] **on** [someone] phrase (general sl.) new school
1. to be infatuated with; to like someone romantically. (var. [to be]
on [someone] **like that/ hard**) See also: [to be] **big on** [someone]
ex: "I'm telling you, she's on me." "He's on your friend hard."

[to be] **on** [something] phrase (general sl.) new school
1. to like something a lot; to be infatuated with. (var. [to be] **on**
[something] **hard/like that**)
ex: "I'm on that ol' school Hip-Hop."

[someone who's] **on** adj. (general sl.) old & new school
1. successful; in a position to attain financial security or wealth; in
a position of authority and/or with vast resources at his/her
disposal. See also: [to] **put** [someone] **on**
ex: "We gonna be on in a minute." "I'm on now."

[someone who's] **on a mission** phrase (general sl.) old & new
school
1. one who is driven by a strong desire to succeed or reach
an objective [the end result usually has something to do with

acquiring money]. 2. to be extremely dedicated to one's goal or vision.
ex: "I can't talk to you right now, cause I'm on a mission." "When I seen'er she looked like she was on a mission."

[something that's] **on a one** adj. (e. coast sl.) new school
1. outstanding; unique; the best of its kind. (var. [something that's] **on one million/one thousand**)
ex: "That meal Shortie hook'd up was on a one." "That outfit is on one million."

[he/she/you] **on a seafood diet ... everything you see, you eat** phrase (southern sl.) new school
1. a witty way to respond to someone stating that he/she is on a diet. (var. **it must be a seafood diet... cause everything you see, you eat**)

on cruise control phrase (general sl.) new school
1. taking it easy; in no rush or hurry; at a slower pace. (var. [to] **put it in cruise control**)
ex: "I'mma be on cruise control for the whole week."

[someone who's] **on different time** [then other people] adj. (e. coast sl.) new school
1. one who behaves or thinks differently then most people; to think outside the norm [usually because one has his/her own agenda that others can't comprehend]. (var. [someone who's] **on a different** [type/kind of] **time**, [someone who's] **not on the same** [type/kind of] **time** [as other people])
ex: "Its not that, we just on different time." "Ya manz an'nim on some different type of time then you."

one mo' again phrase (southern sl.) new school
1. a witty way to say "one more time".
ex: "If I hafta tell you one mo' again, you gonna know somethin'."

[someone who's] **on "e"** adj. (general sl.) old & new school
1. without money; destitute. (var. [someone who's] **pockets are on "e"**)
ex: "You have to look out this time, I'm on "e" 'til next Friday."

[someone who's] **on "E"** adj. (drug sl.) new school
1. one who is using or addicted to using the drug Ecstasy. (var. [someone who's] **on "E" hard**)
ex: "She better be careful, cause them catz on "E"."

[to receive something] **on** [one's] **face** phrase (general sl.) old & new school
1. to receive something on cosignment from another because one's credit is good [usually used in the context when requesting credit].
ex: "You think I can get that on my face?" "I can walk in there and get that for you on my face."

[someone who's] **on fire** adj. (sexual sl.) old & new school
1. infected with a sexual transmitted disease. (var. [someone who's] **burnin'**)
ex: "You need to get tested cause I heard he might be on fire."

[someone who's] **on fire** adj. (criminal sl.) new school
1. someone who has cooperated with a law enforcement agency in the investigation of another and/or testified against a friend or love one in court. See also: [someone who's] **hot**
ex: "People stop messin' with'em when they found out he was on fire."

on fire adj. (general sl.) old & new school
1. mad; angry. See also: **heated**
ex: "Yo, Shortie on fire cause you ain't call."

[someone who's] **on foot patrol** v. (general sl.) new school
1. walking. 2. one who doesn't own or have access to an automobile. See also: [someone who's] **hikin' it** [somewhere]
ex: "Them bum ass catz still on foot patrol after all these years."

[someone who's] **on front street** phrase (general sl.) new school
1. one who is going to be held responsible if things go wrong; one who is on the spot. (var. [to] **put** [oneself] **on front street/out on front street**, [to go] **on front street for** [someone]
ex: "I went out on front street for you." "You the one that put yourself out there on front street."

[something done] **on G.P.** phrase (general sl.) old & new school
1. something done for no good reason, to spite someone, or because one can or felt like it.
ex: "We went down there on G.P." "I just called on G.P. to see how you was doin'."

[someone who's] **on herb status** phrase (e. coast sl.) old school
1. someone treated with no respect, or seriousness by his/her peers [usually because he/she is perceived as not being cool, hip, or street wise].
ex: "You gonna be on herb status your whole life."

[someone who's] **on it like that** phrase (general sl.) old & new school
1. a term used to question or confirm one's unpleasant disposition, attitude, rude behavior, or dishonest ways. See also: [to] **get down** [a certain kind of way]
ex: "I didn't know you was on it like that dawg." "I know you not on it like that?"

[someone who's] **on joke time** phrase (e. coast sl.) new school
1. not serious; taking a serious situation extremely lightly or like a joke. 2. the act of playing or joking at the wrong time.
ex: "I see right now, you on joke time."

[someone who's] **on** [his/her] **knuckles** phrase (e. coast sl.) new school
1. destitute; without money. (var. [to be] **on** [one's] **knuckles / last leg/back**) See also: [someone who's] **shootin' bad**
ex: "Yo dawg, right now a fella on his knuckles."

[to be] **on** [someone] **like a cheap suit** phrase (e. coast sl.) new school
1. to watch someone extremely close; the act of following and/or crowding someone. (var. [to be] **on** [someone] **like stink on sh**/white on rice/lil hairs on the back of someone's neck**)
ex: "When we get there, I'mma be on you like a cheap suit."

on my word! phrase (general sl.) old & new school
1. an enthusiastic way to affirm or reaffirm one's thought, position, or declaration leaving no room for doubt of one's conviction to stand by what he/she has said. (var. **that's my word!**)
ex: "On my word, Shortie was there." "Everything I told you is on my word."

[to be] **on** [one's] **P's and Q's** phrase (general sl.) old school
1. paying attention, alert, prepared, ready.
ex: "I want everyone to be on their P's and Q's this time."

[someone who's] **on paper** phrase (prison sl.) new school
1. a term used to refer to having a certain amount of parole probation, or supervised release [after being release from prison].

on point phrase (general sl.) old & new school
1. alert; prepared; attentive.
ex: "We hafta be on point in here."

[a male who's] **on some bit** sh**** phrase (e. coast sl.) old & new school
1. a derogatory term used to describe a male who exhibits an unbearable amount of moodiness, sarcasm, or behavior unbecoming a male.
ex: "He on some bit** sh** cause we didn't let'em play."

[someone who's] **on some Brooklyn sh**** phrase (e. coast sl.) new school
1. the act of being cunning, deceitful, and untrustworthy. 2. to show favoritism and preferential treatment towards someone from

Brooklyn opposed to someone who isn't from Brooklyn. (var. [someone who's] **on that Brooklyn sh**/ B.K. sh****)
ex: "I don't trust them catz, cause they be on some Brooklyn sh**." "I see ya man on that Brooklyn sh**."

[someone who's] **on some chuck chillout sh**** phrase (general sl.) old school
1. taking it easy; relaxing. 2. the act of maintaining a low profile.
ex: "After this move we make, I'm goin' on some chuck chillout sh**."

[someone who's] **on some derelict sh**** phrase (e. coast sl.) old & new school
1. the act of being petty, deceitful, and untrustworthy.
ex: "Ya peoples got on some real derelict sh** last night."

[someone who's] **on some kiddie sh**** phrase (general sl.) old & new school
1. a term used to describe someone who's extremely playful, always joking around, or not to be taken serious.
ex: "Come on man let's go can't you see she on some kiddie sh**."

[someone who's] **on some other sh**** phrase (e. coast sl.) new school
1. someone who does things different then his/her peers [often leaving his/her peers lost to understand what that persons intentions or motives are]. 2. selfish. 3. one who has a hidden agenda.
ex: "It's hard to say with him he be on some other sh**."

[someone who's] **on some sh**** phrase (general sl.) old & new school
1. a way to describe someone's attitude and demeanor as being petty, unpredictable, rude, and arrogant. 2. one who is untrustworthy and deceitful for no reason. (var. [someone who's] **on some bullsh**/that bullsh****)

*ex: "I told you them catz be on some sh**."*

[someone who's] **on some** [ol'] **superman sh**** phrase (criminal sl.) old & new school
1. one who tries to be a hero in the commission of a robbery, mugging, or assault of another [putting his/her safety in harms way].
*ex: "He almost got away 'til the dude in the truck got on some superman sh**."*

[someone who's] **on somethin'** phrase (drug sl.) old & new school
1. high from an illegal narcotic [usually used as a basis to explain one's erratic behavior or actions].
ex: "You can't tell me ya man ain't on somethin'."

[someone who's] **on sucker status** adj. (e. coast sl.) new school
1. treated or thought of as someone who's easily tricked, manipulated, or made a fool of. See also: [someone who's] **on herb status**
ex: "They had ya man on sucker status in prison."

[someone who's] **on sucker time** phrase (e. coast sl.) new school
1. a term used to describe someone's actions as being unscrupulous, deceiving, shameful, or petty.
ex: "I was with them the other day, them catz on that sucker time."

[someone who's] **on swole** adj. (general sl.) new school
1. one who makes or has access to large amounts of money. (var. [someone who's] **sittin' on swole**)
ex: "They went outta town and now they on swole."

[someone who's] **on swole** adj. (general sl.) old & new school
1. to have a pumped up body building physique as a result of weight training.
ex: "When ya cousin came home from jail, that cat came home on swole."

[someone who's] **on the ball** adj. (general sl.) old & new school
1. extremely alert, informed, and prepared to step in and handle a problem if needed.
ex "I always knew you were on the ball."

[someone who's] **on the burn** phrase (general sl.) old school
1. on some type of punishment.
ex: "She can't talk to you right now cause she's on the burn for comin' home late." "I know I'mma be on the burn for a while with this report card."

on the down low phrase (general sl.) old & new school
1. discreetly; secretively. (var. [to do something or keep something] **on the d.l./the low/the q.t./quiet storm/ the L/the hush/the hush hush/the quiet tip**)
ex: "She wants to get with you on the down low."

[someone who's] **on the grind** phrase (e. coast sl.) new school
1. one who is doing whatever he\she does to make money [even if it means indulging in illegal activities]. (var. [to be] **on** [one's] **grind/hustle**)
ex: "I can't kick it with you right now, I'm on the grind." "I don't mess with you when you on your grind."

[someone who's] **on the hustlin' tip** adj. (drug sl.) old & new school
1. a term used to describe someone who is in the drug trade or involved in illegal activity to earn his/her income.
ex: "He went down to Raleigh on the hustlin' tip."

[someone who's] **on the lee low** phrase (general sl.) old school
1. one who is maintaining a low profile.
ex: "I kept tellin'em he had to be on the lee low."

on the low... phrase (general sl.) old & new school
1. a way to say, "between you and me..." [often used in prelude of revealing something secretive].
ex: "On the low, she's the one that told on you."

[something done] **on the q.t.** adj. (general sl.) old & new school
1. discreetly; furtively; secretly. (var. [something done] **on the quiet tip/storm**)
ex: "We can come back on the q.t. if you want."

on the real phrase (general sl.) old & new school
1. an enthusiastic way to affirm or reaffirm one's truthfulness or conviction to stand by what he/she has said [usually used when trying to sound convincing]. (var. **on the realz/really real/real to real, on the strength**)
ex: "Your Shortie stepped to me, on the real."

on the real… phrase (general sl.) old & new school
1. a term used as a prelude to expressing one's true feelings or thoughts. (var. **on the realz/really real/real to real, on the strength…**)
ex: "On the real, I never liked ya punk ass anyway." "On the real Shortie, you can't cook."

on the real? phrase (general sl.) old & new school
1. a way to question someone's statement and/or truthfulness. (var. **on the realz?/real to real?, on the strength?**)
ex: "On the real, that's what you heard?" "On the real dawg, I don't believe that."

[someone who's] **on the run** phrase (criminal sl.) old & new school
1. one who is a fugitive.
ex: "I was on the run for two years."

on the sneak-tip phrase (general sl.) old & new school
1. an act or action done discreetly, covertly, or furtively. (var. **on the sneak**)
ex: "I picked'er up, took'er out, and dropped'er off on the sneak-tip."

[to do something] **on the strength** phrase (e. coast sl.) new school
1. the act of doing something without looking or wanting anything
in return; to extend one's generosity.
*ex: "I took care of that for you on the strength." "You don't owe
me nothin', that was on the strength, you my dawg."*

on the strength phrase (e. coast sl.) new school
1. because one can or has the ability to. (var. [to do something] **on
the strength**)
*ex: "I should take that from you on the strength." "I went in there
on the strength just to let them know."*

[someone who's] **on the up and up** phrase (general sl.) old & new
school
l. being honest; serious. 2. one who is legitimate.
*ex: "About time you on the up and up." "On the up and up I had
nothin' to do with this."*

[day/weeks/months/years] **on the wake-up** phrase (prison sl.) old
& new school
1. a term used to calculate the amount of days, weeks, months, or
years one has left before he/she is released from prison.
ex: "Son got about 6 more months on the wake-up."

[someone who's] **on time** phrase (general sl.) old & new school
1. a term used to recognize someone who came through at the right
time or at a time of need [usually used to express one's
appreciation]. (var. [something that's] **on time**, [someone who's]
right on time)
ex: "That was on time dawg." "You on time with this."

[to be] **on that** [same] **ol' bullsh**** phrase (general sl.) old & new
school
1. to exhibit the same petty, unscrupulous, untrustworthy behavior
when one is older as one did in his/her younger years.
ex: "I see you still on that ol'bullsh**, ain't nothin' change."

[to be] **on that type of time** [with someone] phrase (e. coast sl.) new school
1. to have a friendly, cordial, or sociable relationship with someone.

[to be] **on** [someone's] **tip** phrase (general sl.) old school
1. to be overly infatuated or envious of someone. 2. to like and admire someone greatly. (var. [to be] **on** [someone's] **balls/nuts/d**k/jock/bra strap**)
ex: *"They been on my tip for years."*

[someone who's] **on top of** [his/her] **game** phrase (general sl.) new school
1. someone whose performance and actions exudes excellence and flawlessness. 2. to be the best at what one does.
ex: *"Its hard to stay on top of ya game if you use drugs." "The streets force real catz to stay on top their game."*

[to be] **on** [a certain] **type of time** phrase (e. coast sl.) new school
1. a way to refer to one's particular way or style of doing something [usually used questioningly when one is trying to figure out or understand one's behavior or unfamiliar actions].
ex: *"I didn't know you was on that type of time." "Is that the type of time you on?"*

[a] **one eyed monster** n. (prison sl.) new school
1. television set; TV.
ex: *"I know people who watch that one eyed monster all day."*

one hand can't wash by itself phrase (general sl.) old & new school

1. a term used to tell someone that you are willing to help in exchange for his/her help [usually used when trying to convince one to help]. (var. **one hand wash the other, one hand wash the other both hands wash the face**)

one love phrase (e. coast sl.) old & new school
1. a term used to express one's sincerity and/or love when ending a conversation verbally, in writing or when departing the company of a friend or love one. (var. **one**)
ex: "One love dawg, I'll talk to you soon."

one time n. (e. coast sl.) new school
1. an undercover cop; police officer. 2. a verbal warning used to alert someone the police is coming or there is police activity in the area.

one thing for certain, two things for sure... phrase (general sl.) old & new school
1. a matter of fact way to express one's confidence in his/her statement, boast, or claim leaving no doubt as to his/her words [often used as a prelude to one's statement, boast, or claim].
ex: "One thing for certain, two things for sure I can't ask your broke ass for nothin'."

ones n. (e. coast sl.) new school
1. money.
ex: "How my ones lookin'?"

[a] **onion** n. (sexual sl.) new school
1. a female's butt.
ex: "Shortie got a nice lil onion back there."

[a] **onion** n. (drug sl.) old & new school
1. an ounce of cocaine.
ex: "They came and got about four onions."

only thing bad about you is ya breath phrase (general sl.) old & new school
1. a witty way to dismiss someone's tough talk and empty threats.

oogly adj. (general sl.) new school
1. extremely unattractive; ugly.
ex: "This oogly dude tried to kick it with me at the club."

[to] **open up shop** phrase (drug sl.) old & new school
1. the opening up of a place or area for the purpose of selling drugs.
ex: " One thing about Brooklyn dudes, they'll go anywhere and try to open up shop."

opinions are like assholes, everybody has one phrase (general sl.) new school
1. a way to dismiss someone's unwanted opinion [often used as sarcasticly].

Origin n. (southern sl.) new school
1. Magnolia Housing Projects in New Orleans.

O.T. phrase (e. coast sl.) old & new school
1. an abbreviation for "out of town"; the act of traveling to another state [usually for the purpose of selling drugs].
ex: "I heard you wanna go O.T. with us."

[someone who's] **o.t. on the grind** phrase (drug sl.) old & new school
1. someone who has traveled to another state to sell drugs.
ex: "They all went o.t. on the grind three weeks ago."

[one's] **out** n. (general sl.) new school
1. one's way out of a situation or trouble. (var. [an] **out**)
ex: "That's ya out, son." "Help me kid, I need an out."

[to bc] **out** v. (general sl.) old & new school
1. to leave; depart from.
ex: "I'm out son, holler at me later." "We out dawg."

[to] **out and out** [do/say something] v. (general sl.) old & new school
1. the act of boldly doing something; to act without hesitation or regards for the consequences.
ex: "I out and out told her the truth."

[to be] **out of** [one's] **character** phrase (e. coast sl.) new school
1. the act of displaying behavior that is uncharacteristic of one's
normal behavior [usually in a bad way].
ex: "You need to talk to ya man, cause he's out of character."

out the ass phrase (general sl.) new school
1. a way to emphasize a large amount. (var. [to] **have** [something]
out the ass, [to] **pay out the ass**)
*ex: "Them catz got cars out the ass." "He had to pay Shortie out
the ass."*

[something that's] **out the window** phrase (general sl.) new school
1. no longer a consideration.
*ex: "You not goin' with me, that sh** is out the window." "Don't
even worry 'bout it cause that's out the window as far as I'm
concerned."*

[someone who's] **out there** phrase (general sl.) new school
1. totally consumed by his/her addiction, feelings for his/her lover,
or problems making him/her exhibit behavior that is irrational
and/or self destructive.
ex: "I hate to say it, but ya ex-Shortie is out there."

outta phrase (general sl.) old & new school
1. a way to say, "out of".
ex: "We about to be outta here." "Get outta my face."

outta bounds phrase (general sl.) new school
1. something said or done that was uncalled for, wrong, and/or
mean spirited.
ex: "Ya girl was definitely outta bounds for that one dawg."

[someone who's] **outta gas** phrase (general sl.) new school
1. one who is out of luck [often finding oneself in a precarious
situation]. (var. [someone who's] **sh** outta luck**)
ex: "With that judge, ya manz outta gas."

[I'm] **outta here like Belvadere with no underwear** phrase
(e. coast sl.) new school
1. a witty way to inform someone you are leaving. (var. [I'm]
outta here, [I'm] **outta here like last year**)

[someone who's] **outta pocket** phrase (e. coast sl.) new school
1. someone who has said or done something that was uncalled for,
wrong, and/or mean spirited.
*ex: "Dawg you was outta pocket tellin' Shortie something like
that."*

[an] **ou-wop** n. (criminal sl.) old & new school
1. an Israeli made Uzi machine gun.

[an] **overseer** n. (e. coast sl.) old & new school
1. a policeman, parole officer, probation officer, or correction
officer.

owe me like you know me phrase (e. coast sl.) new school
1. a witty way to demand someone pay you the money which
he/she owes you at the exact moment you happen to observe
him/her with money or receiving money.

[an] **ox** n. (prison sl.) old & new school
1. a single edge razor [usually carried in one's mouth or sneaker as
a method of concealment].

[to] **ox** [someone] v. (prison sl.) old & new school
1. to cut or slash someone with a single edge razor across the face
or neck [usually requiring stitches to close wound]. See also: **a
buck fifty**
ex: "This kid was about to ox ya man for his sneakers."

P

pa n. (e. coast sl.) old & new school
1. a term of endearment among friends; friend. 2. a way to address someone whose name you do not know or do not want to use in front of others.
ex: "Nah pa, that sh** ain't right."

[a] **pack** n. (drug sl.) old & new school
1. a quantity of prepackaged illegal drugs sold on the retail level. (var. [a] **package**)
ex: "That crackhead cousin of yours ran off with the pack."

[to] **pack heat** v. (criminal sl.) new school
1. the act of carrying a firearm. See also: **strapped**
ex: "If you packin' heat they won't let you in the door."

[a] **packed suitcase** n. (e. coast sl.) new school
1. a big butt.
ex: "When Shortie stood up and I seen her packed suitcase, I was like dammmm."

[a male who's] **packin'** adj. (sexual sl.) old & new school
1. has a well endowed penis.
ex: "She didn't believe I was packin' 'til I got with her."

[someone who's a] **pain freak** adj. (southern sl.) new school
1. someone who will lose consistently and/or miserably but won't quit or keeps coming back for more. 2. someone who stays in a painful relationship or situation that keeps causing him/her emotional anguish.
ex: "I knew you was a pain freak." "You must be some kind of pain freak."

paper n. (general sl.) old & new school
1. money. (var. **papes, papers**) See also: **dough, loot, scrilla**
ex: "All I want is the paper you owe me."

paper n. (drug sl.) old school
1. Bamboo or Easy Wider rolling paper used to roll marijuana cigarettes. (var. **Bamboo**)
ex: "Ask them if they have any paper."

papers n. (prison sl.) new school
1. little pieces of paper in which individual doses of an illegal drug are wrapped in and sold on the retail level. See also: **balloons**

pardon self phrase (e. coast sl.) old & new school
1. excuse me; I'm sorry; I apologize.
ex: "Pardon self, I didn't mean to interrupt."

parkin' lot pimpin' phrase (w. coast sl.) new school
1. the act of hanging out in the parking lot of a club before and/or after the club closes in an attempt to meet or pick up a male or female.
ex: "There was a whole lot of parkin' lot pimpin' goin' on tonight."

[to] **parlay** phrase (e. coast sl.) old school
1. to rest, take it easy, or relax. 2. to wait. (var. [to] **parlay for/on** [someone]) See also: [to] **lamp**
ex: "I'm about to go to Shortie house and parlay." "Y'all parlay while I find out what's up."

[a] **paro** n. (drug sl.) old school
1. someone addicted to powder or crack cocaine.

paro adj. (e. coast sl.) old & new school
1. paranoid; scared; nervous.
ex: "I was a lil paro about comin' back here."

partna n. (w. coast sl.) new school
1. partner. 2. a playful or sarcastic way to address a friend or adversary to let that person know you mean business or that you are serious. (var. **partnah**)
ex: "You wanna repeat that partna?" "Look here partna."

[a] **patient** n. (drug sl.) old school
1. one who smokes and is addicted to crack cocaine.
ex: "Son, you won't believe who's a patient now."

[to] **pay a nut** v. (general sl.) old & new school
1. to pay a debt.
ex: "Are you the one who has to pay this nut?"

[he/she] **pay like** [he/she] **weigh** phrase (southern sl.) new school
1. a witty way to inform someone that someone is generous with his/her money when he/she becomes involved in a intimate relationship. (var. [someone who] **pays like they weigh**)
ex: "Shortie pay like she weigh." "Them kinda of chicks always pay like they weigh."

pay like you weigh phrase (southern sl.) new school
1. a witty way to demand someone pay his/her debt immediately [usually as the result of a lost wager].

[a] **pay master** n. (prison sl.) new school
1. one who has a debt to pay [one is either a good or bad pay master].
ex: "Go ahead and lend it to 'em, he's a good pay master."

[to] **pay out the ass** phrase (general sl.) old & new school
1. to pay out a large amount of money [usually as restitution or as a way to solve a problem].
ex: "You best believe before this is over you gonna be payin' out the ass."

pay you? pay you no mind phrase (general sl.) old & new school
1. a sarcastic way to dismiss someone who is asking to you pay
him/her what you owe him/her.

PC n. (prison sl.) old & new school
1. an acronym for "Protective Custody" [the part of a prison/jail
inmates are housed in for their own safety or protection from other
inmates].
*ex: "He talk all that gangsta sh** and he went to PC the first time
he went to jail."*

PC n. (general sl.) old & new school
1. a small amount of money; petty cash.
ex: "I took my PC and left." "Ask ya momz for a lil PC."

peace phrase (e. coast sl.) old & new school
1. an term of affection used when greeting, departing, or ending a
verbal or written communique with someone.
*ex: "Peace Dawg, how you?" "Until we see each other again
peace."*

peace in the Middle East phrase (general sl.) old & new school
1. a term used to say, "good bye" or "farewell" when departing
company or ending a verbal or written communique with a friend,
love one, or acquaintance. (var. **peace to the deceased)**

peace out phrase (general sl.) old & new school
1. a hip way to say "good-bye" or "farewell" when departing the
company of a friend or loved one [also used at the end of a phone
call or letter]. See also: **one love**
ex: "Peace out dawg, I'll holler at you later."

[one's] pedigree phrase (e. coast sl.) old school
1. reputation; character; style of doing things. See also: [one's]
steelo
ex: "You better check my pedigree shortie."

peel phrase (criminal sl.) old & new school
1. a command used during a robbery which instructs the victim to hand over his/her jewelry.

[to] **peel** [someone's] **cap** v. (criminal sl.) new school
1. a way to describe someone being shot in the head. (var. [to] **peel** [someone's] **cap back/back to the white meat**, [to get one's] **cap peeled/peeled back**, [to] **peel** [someone's] **meat rack/ hat rack /onion**)
ex: "He gonna make somebody peel'is cap, watch."

[to] **peel on** [someone] v. (general sl.) old & new school
1. the act of pulling out a large wad of money and pulling off a couple of the bills for the purpose of flaunting one's money. 2. to take off one's shirt to flaunt his/her physique and/or muscles.

[to] **peep** [something] v. (general sl.) old & new school
1. to become aware of something by observing, taking notice, giving something serious thought. (var. [to] **peep** [someone's intentions], [to] **peep** [something] **out**)
ex: "I already peeped that about you." "I been peeped that."

[to] **peep** [someone's] **hold card** v. (general sl.) old & new school
1. to become aware of one's motives or secrets by observing, taking notice, or giving something serious thought.
ex: "I peeped Shortie hold card as soon as she came through the door."

peep this phrase (general sl.) old & new school
1. a term used to get someone's attention or to get someone to listen [usually used as a prelude when making someone aware of something or pointing out an observation]. (var. **peep it, peep the move**)
ex: "Yo, come over here and peep this."

penitentiary rich n. (prison sl.) new school
1. to revel in the falsehood of being wealthy because an inmate
has more material/finances than other inmates [in reality his/her
finances don't amount to anything substantial].
*ex: "He was one of them same dudes actin' like he was
penitentiary rich and when he got home he didn't have a place to
stay."*

[one's] people n. (e. coast sl.) new school
1. one's friend or group of friends. (var. [one's] **peoples, peops**)
See also: **fam**
*ex: "Them my people." "I seen ya peoples uptown." "Whassup
with ya peops?"*

[someone who's] people adj. (e. coast sl.) new school
1. someone who is a friend. (var. [someone who's] **peoples, peops**)
ex: "Are y'all still people?"

people in Hell want ice water phrase (southern sl.) old & new
school
1. a sarcastic way to say, "so what", or "I don't care" to someone
who is complaining that you refuse to give him/her that he/she
wants. (var. **people in Hell want AC**)

[to] perpetrate v. (e. coast sl.) old school
1. the act of pretending [usually to make one seem more important
than one really is]. 2. to make false claims that one is unable to
back up; to lie. (var. [to] **perpetrate a fraud**)
ex: "Ya peoples was in here last night perpetratin'."

[someone who's] perpetratin' v. (e. coast sl.) old school
1. one who exhibits an overrated sense of his/her selfworth and
pretends to be more important than everyone around him/her.
ex: "That itch be perpetratin'."

[a] **perpetrator** adj. (e. coast sl.) old school
1. one who pretends to be more important than he/she really is; one who has an overrated opinion of his/her self worth. 2. a phony.
ex: "I always knew you was a perpetrator."

[one's] **personal** n. (drug sl.) old & new school
1. a small quantity of drugs one has for his/her own personal consumption [term isn't limited to drugs].
ex: "All of that right there you welcome to, this right here, that's my personal."

[one's] **personal vic** phrase (prison sl.) new school
1. a way to refer to the person one beats in competion regularly. (var. [one's] **personal victim**)
ex: "Leave him alone, that's my personal vic."

pervin' v. (sexual sl.) new school
1. the act of lusting.
ex: "I can't believe ya lil brother was in here pervin' like that."

[to] **peter roll** [someone] v. (prison sl.) old & new school
1. winning without allowing one's opponent to score a point; to shut someone out. See also: [to] **skunk** [someone]
ex: "I make this last shot and that's a peter roll."

petro adj. (e. coast sl.) old school
1. scared; afraid; nervous. See also: **bimmie**
ex: "They all used to be petro of me."

p-funk n. (drug sl.) old & new school
1. heroin. See also: **boy**

[something that's] **phat** adj. (general sl.) old & new school
1. outstanding; unique; the best of its kind. 2. hip; trendy; stylish. (var. [something that's] **phat to death/like a muhf**ka**)
ex: "Now that was phat." "I think that's gonna be madd phat."

[a female who's] **phat** adj. (general sl.) old & new school
1. a female who has a big butt. (var. [a female who's] **phat as all outdoors, phatter than a goverment mule**)
ex: *"...She took off her jacket, Shortie was phat as all outdoors."*

[a female with a/the] **phat ass** adj. (sexual sl.) old & new school
1. a way to praisingly describe a female extremely large butt.
ex: *"Who you talkin' about, shortie with the phat ass?" "Yeah she definitely got a phat ass."*

[a] **phat back** adj. (general sl.) new school
1. a female's big butt. (var. [a] **phat bumper**)
ex: *"I'm diggin' that phat back Shortie got."*

[a] **phat sack** adj. (drug sl.) old & new school
1. a full bag of a drug selling on the retail level [usually refers to marijuana].
ex: *"I can't start my day without a phat sack."*

[a] **phat stack** n. (general sl.) new school
1. a large amount of money.

[a] **phatty girl** n. (sexual sl.) new school
1. a covert way to refer to a vagina.

[a] **phatty patty** n. (sexual sl.) new school
1. a female's butt.

[a] **PH.D** n. (e. coast sl.) new school
1. a "player hating degree" an imaginary Doctorate Degree in hating other people, failing to recognize other people's achievements or talents that are praise worthy. See also: [to] **hate on** [someone]

phone check phrase (prison sl.) old & new school
1. a blunt way to tell someone to hang up the phone because you want to use it [usually used as a command]. (var. [to] **phone check** [someone])
ex: "Let me get a phone check partna."

[a] **phone gangster** n. (prison sl.) old & new school
1. someone who talks tough and threateningly over the phone to someone incarcerated because he/she knows that person can't immediately confront him/her.
ex: "When I called her she put this phone gangster on the line."

[a] **phone jones** phrase (prison sl.) old & new school
1. the excessive use of a telephone; a phone addiction.
ex: "Shortie got a real phone jones I see."

[when a] **phone's off the hook** phrase (prison sl.) old & new school
1. someone is or attempting to eavesdrop.
ex: "Lower your voice, I think a phone's off the hook."

[someone who's] **phony** adj. (general sl.) old & new school
1. not genuine; fake; insincere. (var. [someone who's] **phony as a three dollar bill**)
ex: "Don't bring ya phony ass friends around me."

[a] **Philly** n. (drug sl.) old & new school
1. the brand name of the cigar that people use to roll marijuana in. (var. [a] **Philly blunt**)
ex: "Who got the Philly?"

picture that phrase (e. coast sl.) old school
1. a playful, sarcastic, or obnoxious way to tell someone to imagine something. (var. **picture that with a Kodak**)
ex: "Me go out with you, picture that."

[a] **pie** n. (drug sl.) old & new school
1. a kilogram of cocaine.
ex: "Pies cost about 21.5 now."

[a] **pie flipper** n. (drug sl.) new school
1. one who sells multiple kilogram amounts of cocaine.

[a] **piece** n. (general sl.) old & new school
1. a gold or platinum pendant [often diamond encrusted] to hang
on one's gold or platinum chain.
*ex: "Fat Joe got the hottest piece in Hip-Hop." "He got robbed for
the piece, in Brooklyn." "He had to pay to get the piece back."*

[to] **piece** [someone] **off** phrase (e. coast sl.) new school
1. to give someone an amount of money [regardless of how
much].
*ex: "Shortie said she gonna piece me of when she gets paid this
week."*

pieces n. (general sl.) new school
1. females.
*ex: "There was a couple good lookin' pieces in here lookin' for
you."*

[a] **pigeon** adj. (e. coast sl.) new school
1. a female who is extremely gullible and easily influenced by a
male's material wealth or by his reputation. See also:
chickenheads
*ex: "....Spot six females together and I bet you at least two of them
are pigeons."*

[a] **pill** n. (general sl.) old & new school
1. a basketball.

[someone who's a] **P-I-M-P** n. (e. coast sl.) new school
1. a term males use to boast and brag about being a ladies man and having numerous ladies that he is intimate with [this word is not used literally in reference to a real "pimp"].

[to] **pimp** [someone] v. (southern sl.) old & new school
1. to use or take advantage of someone through manipulation and deceit. (var. [to] **pimp** [someone] **out of** [something])
ex: "Ya man let Shortie pimp'em for a car payment." "I'm not about to let you pimp me player."

[to] **pimp** [something] v. (general sl.) old & new school
1. to do something stylishly.
ex: "I seen ya moms pimpin' the ride you gave'er."

pimp n. (w. coast sl.) new school
1. a term of endearment among friends; friend. 2. a way to address someone whose name you do not know or do not want to use in front of others. (var. **pimpin'**)
ex: "Call me back later pimp." "Where you and pimpin' about to go?"

pimp juice n. (e. coast sl.) new school
1. Crystal Champagne.

[something that's] **pimp sh**** adj. (general sl.) old & new school
1. anything that is flamboyant and stylish.
*ex: "That's that pimp sh**." "I'm goin' to the mall and pick up some of that pimp sh**."*

[to] **pimp slap** [someone] v. (general sl.) old & new school
1. to slap someone with the back of one's hand; to back-hand someone. (var. [to] **bit**** **slap** [someone])
ex: "Shut up before I pimp slap you."

[to] **pimp the system/game** phrase (general sl.) old & new school
1. to take advantage of a situation or opportunity that one stands to benefit from.
ex: "I pimped the system my whole bid." "You have to learn to pimp the game and not let the game pimp you."

[a] **pimped out** [automobile] adj. (w. coast sl.) new school
1. a automobile that has had its appearance enhanced by adding detailing and accessories [like t.v.'s in the head rests, expensive rims, and adding a plush interior].
ex: "Ya man showed up in a pimped out Lexus."

pimpin' ain't easy phrase (general sl.) old & new school
1. a term used to boast that manipulating or tricking someone of the opposite sex isn't always as easy as it seems [often used when caught in the act of manipulating or tricking someone or while explaining that managing a intimate relationship with two or more people can be challenging at times].

pimpin' ain't easy, it's greazy/sleazy phrase (general sl.) old & new school
1. a term used to respond to someone who uses the term "pimpin' ain't easy" that tells that person what he/she is doing is wrong.

[a] **pipe** n. (sexual sl.) new school
1. a covert way to refer to a penis. See also: **wood**

[to] **pipe** [a female] v. (sexual sl.) new school
1. a term males use for having sex. (var. [to] **put the pipe on/up in** [a female], [to] **pipe** [a female] **down/to death**, [to] **give** [a female] **the pipe/some pipe**) See also: [to] **lay pipe**

[to get one's] **pipe cleaned** v. (sexual sl.) new school
1. the act of a man receiving oral sex. See also: **brains**

[a] **pipe cleaner** n. (sexual sl.) new school
1. one who gives oral sex to a man.

[a] **pipe head** n. (drug sl.) old school
1. someone addicted to crack cocaine.
ex: "Don't be bringing them pipe head chicks to my house no more."

[a] **piss test** phrase (drug sl.) old & new school
1. a urinalysis to detect drug usage. (var. [to get] **pissed**)
ex: "I had to take a piss test for two months." "There's things you can do to beat a piss test."

pissy adj. (e. coast sl.) new school
1. drunk; intoxicated.
ex: "I was pissy the whole weekend."

pistol grippin' phrase (criminal sl.) new school
1. the act of carrying a firearm. See also: [to] **hold heat**

Pistolvania n. (e. coast sl.) new school
1. Pennsylvania.
ex: "You know them boys from Pistolvania don't play."

[to] **pitch** v. (drug sl.) old & new school
1. the act of selling crack cocaine on a retail level. (var. [to] **pitch them thangs**)
ex: "We all used to pitch in front of 202."

[to] **pitch a bit**** v. (general sl.) old & new school
1. to express one's discontent or anger through yelling and the use of foul language.
ex: "Shortie moms came home and pitched a bit**."

pitchers n. (drug sl.) old & new school
1. street level drug dealers.

[the] **PJ's** n. (general sl.) old & new school
1. Public Housing complex. (var. [the] **Projects**)
ex: "Which PJ's did you grow up in?"

[to] **plant** [someone] v. (criminal sl.) new school
1. to bury someone alive or dead. 2. a way to refer to the act of murder.
*ex: "That bullsh** gonna get you planted."*

[to] **plant a seed** phrase (general sl.) old & new school
1. to provoke or incite thought discreetly, subtly, or by hinting. (var. [to] **plant a seed in** [someone's] **mind/ head**)
ex: "Once you planted the seed, it was too late."

[to] **plant** [one's] **seed** v. (general sl.) old & new school
1. to impregnate. (var. [to] **plant** [one's] **seed in/with** [a female])
ex: "I'm tryin' to plant my seed in Shortie."

plat n. (e. coast sl.) new school
l. platinum.
ex: "His joint just went double plat."

plats n. (southern sl.) old & new school
1. braided hair.
ex: "Don't you think its time to take out the plats?"

[to] **play** [oneself] v. (general sl.) old & new school
1. to put oneself in jeopardy of losing something as the result of doing something stupid, deceitful, or wrong and getting caught [usually refers to losing trust, a relationship, or self respect]. (var. [to] **play** [oneself] **out**)
*ex: "I warned you not to play yaself." "If you do that sh**, you playin' yaself."*

[to] **play** [oneself] v. (general sl.) old & new school
1. to do or say something that brings embarrassment or ridicule to oneself. (var. [to] **play** [oneself] **out**)

ex: "I played myself by coming here."

[to] **play** [someone] v. (general sl.) old & new school
1. to trick, fool, or deceive someone in the attempt to or in the act of taking advantage of that person. 2. to manipulate someone for one's own benefit. (var. [to] **play** [someone] **out/to the left/like a sucker)**
ex: "Can't you see he played you." "I never thought you'd play me like that."

[to] **play** [someone a certain type of way] v. (general sl.) old & new school
1. to treat someone a certain type of way.
ex: "I thought we was cool and you gonna play me like that?" "I would never play you like that."

[to] **play a role** v. (general sl.) old school
1. to emulate the character of a tough guy/girl or a street thug. (var. [to] **play the role)**
ex: "Look at him over there tryin' to play a role."

play around, lay around phrase (general sl.) old & new school
1. a stern way to warn someone not to do something that bothers or upsets you [usually used when one is fed up and ready to confront that person over said behavior].

[to] **play both sides** phrase (general sl.) new school
1. to be in support of two opposing sides until it is clear which side is going to win and then throwing all your support behind the winning side.

[to] **play both sides against the middle** phrase (general sl.) old & new school
1. the act of manipulating and pitting two sides against each other until it is clear which side is going to win then throwing all your support behind the winning side.

[to] **play catch up** phrase (prison sl.) new school
1. the attempt to make up for lost time when released from prison [usually by trying to acquire things one cannot afford leading that person to resort to criminal activity].
ex: "See one thing about me, I'm not going home to play catch up."

[to] **play** [someone] **close** v. (general sl.) old & new school
1. to crowd someone. 2. the act being too familiar with someone you don't know or just met. 3. to watch someone extremely close.
See also: [to] **sweat** [someone]
ex: "Why she playin' you so close?" "You need to stop playin' me so close."

play cops n. (general sl.) old & new school
1. security guards. (var. **play police, toy cops**)
ex: "Let's go before the play cops come over here."

[to] **play dumb/stupid** v. (general sl.) old & new school
1. to act unknowing or uniformed.
ex: "He just playin' dumb."

[to] **play** [someone] **for a/the herb** phrase (e. coast sl.) old & new school
1. to treat someone like he/she is easily taken advantage of, suckered, or manipulated. 2. to treat someone like he/she isn't cool or hip; to show one no respect. (var. [to] **play** [someone] **like/for a sucker**)
ex: "I still say Shortie played you for a Herb."

[to] **play gorilla** phrase (general sl.) new school
1. to talk and act tough in an attempt to scare, intimidate, and bully others. (var. [to] **play gangster,** [to] **play like** [one] **is a gorilla**)
ex: "That's the brother who's always tryin' to play gorilla."

[to] **play** [something] **off** v. (general sl.) old & new school

1. to act nonchalant; the act of trying to appear or act normal [usually when caught, confronted, or accused of wrong doing]. *ex: "Just play it off for me... please."*

play on player phrase (general sl.) new school
1. an enthusiastic way to bid someone farewell or say "good bye".
2. an enthusiastic way to encourage someone to continue doing what he/she is doing.

[to] **play one pocket** phrase (general sl.) new school
1. to be dishonest, deceiving, or cunning.
ex: "Ya man gonna mess around and get hurt tryin' to play one pocket Dun."

[to] **play PC** v. (prison sl.) old & new school
1. to ask to be housed in "Protective Custody" in prison because one is scared of other inmates.
ex: "What up kid, catz sayin' you played PC when you was up north."

[to] **play police** v. (prison sl) new school
1. a way to describe one's inquisitiveness or nosiness in search of information or answers.
ex: "I know ya man ain't in there tryin' to play police." "They said you was out here playin' police."

[to] **play** [one's] **position** v. (e. coast sl.) new school
1. to stay within the boundaries of one's allotted or assigned position, role, or title [usually when it comes to relationships with others].

play p**sy and get f**ked phrase (general sl.) old & new school
1. a stern way to emphasize the danger of continuing to taunt or provoke you after you have spoken to someone about it before.

[to] **play** [a female] **right** v. (general sl.) old school

1. the attempt to say and do things that will enhance a male's chance to become intimately involved with a particular female.
ex: "You hafta learn how to play Shortie right."

[to] **play** [someone] **soft** v. (general sl.) old & new school
1. to do or say something to someone because you know or feel that he/she won't stand up to you, retialiate, get mad or try to stop you [often because you feel that person is cowardly].
ex: "It's no way I could let her play me soft like that." "Stop lettin' people play soft kid."

[to] **play super hero** phrase (criminal sl.) old & new school
1. to assume the role of a good Samaritan or a law enforcement agent [usually trying to stop some type of form of criminal activity].
ex: "He got those stitches in his head tryin' to play super hero."

[to] **play the block** phrase (general sl.) old & new school
1. to hang out or congregate on a street or main throughway for long periods of time [usually while there is drug dealing going on close by].
ex: "That's all he do is get up and go outside and play the block."

[to] **play the crib** phrase (e. coast sl.) old & new school
1. to stay in the house.
ex: "I know you not playin' the crib on a day like this." "I'mma play the crib today."

[to] **play the cut** phrase (southern sl.) old & new school
1. to wait patiently and/or discreetly. See also: [to] **lay in the cut**
ex: "I'm gettin' tired of playin' the cut for Shortie." "Y'all play the cut while I go inside."

[to] **play the fifty** phrase (general sl.) new school
1. the attempt to manipulate opposing sides until there is a clear winner.
ex: "You can get hurt tryin' to play the fifty with them catz."

[to] play the fool [for someone] v. (general sl.) old & new school
1. to pretend not to notice or be aware of one's mate being unfaithful in an attempt to hold on to him/her [usually until one gets fed up pretending and builds up enough courage to leave that person]. (var. **[to] play** [a female/male] **for the fool**)
ex: "Shortie think I'm a play the fool for her, she must be smokin'."

[to] play the low phrase (general sl.) old & new school
1. the act of being discreet. 2. to wait patiently and/or discreetly. 3. to maintain a low profile.
ex: "You gotta play the low when you first get out of prison."

[to] play the mall phrase (general sl.) old & new school
1. to visit the mall to socialize rather than to shop.
ex: "We thinkin' about playin' the mall for a couple hours."

play ya bunk phrase (prison sl.) old & new school
1. a sarcastic way to dismiss someone's attempt to offer an opinion or critique about a matter that doesn't concern him/her. (var. **play ya bunk chump**)
ex: "Shut up and play ya bunk."

play ya position phrase (prison sl.) new school
1. a playful or sarcastic way to order someone to stop talking and/or acting like he/she is tough.
ex: "You need to knock it off and play ya position."

play yaself phrase (general sl.) old & new school
1. a term used to warn someone not to do something that you specifically told him/her not to do [also used in the context of daring a person after you have warned him/her]. (var. **play yaself find yaself by yaself** [pickin' up yaself])
ex: "Go'head and play yaself." "I don't think you believe me, so play yaself."

[something that's] **played** adj. (general sl.) old & new school
1. not longer considered hip, cool, or trendy. (var. [something that's] **played out**)
ex: "That sh** been played."

player (pron. playa) n. (general sl.) new school
1. a term of endearment among friends; friend. 2. a way to address someone who se name you don't know or don't want to use in front of others. (var. **player player, playboy**)
ex: "I think you gonna like this player."

[a] **player** n. (general sl.) old & new school
1. someone who is hip, cool, and trendy. 2. one who is sly and cunning enough to maintain multiple intimate relationships with people of the opposite sex openly or discreetly.
ex: "Shortie I been a player all my life."

[to] **player hate** v. (general sl.) new school
1. to talk negatively about someone who deserves praise; to wrongly criticize [usually as result of one being jealous of another]. (var. [to] **player hate on** [someone], [someone who's a] **player hater**) See also: [to] **hate on** [someone]
ex: "You do too much player hatin' for me."

player player phrase (general sl.) new school
1. an enthusiastic way to greet or cheer someone on [also used as a congratulatory praise].
ex: "Go'head player player."

[to] **pluck** [someone's] **nerve** v. (general sl.) old & new school
1. to annoy, upset, or aggravate someone. (var. [to] **pluck** [someone's] **last nerve**)
ex: "This lame keep pluckin' my nerves."

[to] **plug** [someone] **in** v. (general sl.) new school
1. to introduce, arrange a meeting, or allow someone to utilize your resources and connections. (var. [to] **plug** [someone]) See also: [to] **hook** [someone] **up**

ex: "I want you to plug me in with your cousin."

[something that's] **plush** adj. (general sl.) old & new school
1. luxurious.
ex: "I got Shortie livin' up in the plush new crib."

p-noid adj. (e. coast sl.) new school
1. paranoid; nervous; scared. See also: **noid**
ex: "Weed used to make me p-noid."

[one's] **P.O.** n. (criminal sl.) old & new school
1. parole or probation officer.
ex: "I gotta see my P.O. later." "Shortie be actin' like she my P.0. and sh**."

[someone whose] **pockets got the mumps** phrase (general sl.) old & new school
1. one who is carrying a large wad of money in his/her pants pocket. 2. one who makes or has access to large amounts of money; rich; wealthy. (var. [someone whose] **pockets are on swole**)
ex: "When I was out there, my pockets kept the mumps."

[someone whose] **pockets stay/are crowded** phrase (e. coast sl.) new school
1. someone who has or keeps a large amount of money on his/her person; wealthy; rich.
ex: "His brother is the one who has the crowded pockets."

po-ice n. (e. coast sl.) old & new school
1. police; law enforcement agents. 2. someone known or suspected of being an confidential informant. (var. **po-lease**)
ex: "Tell me if you see po-ice.'

[someone who's] **police** n. (criminal sl.) old & new school
1. someone who is or suspected of being an police informant or prosecutors witness.
ex: "I'm tellin' you man, that dude is police kid."

[when] **police run down on** [someone] v. (criminal sl.) old & new
school
1. a term used to describe the aggressive way the police use to
stop someone they suspect of committing or about to commit a
crime [often a drug or weapons related crime with normally more
then one cop making the stop].
ex: "Police ran down on the whole block and I jetted."

points adj. (e. coast sl.) old & new school
1. recognition; praise; respect; notice. See also: **browny points**
ex: "I won't get no points for beatin' you."

[a] **pole** n. (sexual sl.) old & new school
1. a covert way to refer to a penis.

[a] **pole** n. (e. coast sl.) old school
1. an extremely big gaudy gold rope chain [favored by rappers and
drug dealers in the 80s]. See also: [a] **cable**

po-leeze phrase (general sl.) old & new school
1. a playful or sarcastic way to say "please" in attempt to dismiss
someone who is trying to tell you something unbelievable or
ridiculous [usually in relations to a lie or excuse].
ex: "You think I believe that, po-leeze."

[to] **politic** v. (e. coast sl.) new school
1. the act of talking with others who can further one's goal; to
converse. (var [to] **politic with** [someone])
ex: "Tell'em I'll be up the block politicin'."

politricks adj. (e. coast sl.) new school
1. the lies and deceptions that politicians use to fool the people, get
elected, or to get out of trouble. 2. politics.
ex: "See politricks at its finest."

[a] **poo putt** n. (e. coast sl.) old school
1. someone not cool, hip, or trendy; a nerd.
ex: "That whole group is a bunch of poo putts."

pootie n. (sexual sl.) old & new school
1. a covert way to refer to a female's vagina. 2. sexual intercourse.
(var. **puddie, poo-tang, pootie tang**)
ex: "He just sayin' that to get some pootie."

[to] **pop** [someone] v. (criminal sl.) old school
1. to shoot someone.
ex: "She popped her husband three times."

[to] **pop a cap** v. (criminal sl.) old school
1. to shoot one's gun. (var. [to] **pop a cap at/in** [someone])
ex: "I thought she was about to pop a cap at you."

[to] **pop a cap in** [someone's] **ass** v. (criminal sl.) old school
1. the act of wounding someone by gunfire [often used as a empty threat].
ex: "You gonna make me pop a cap in ya ass."

[to] **pop** [one's] **collar** v. (w. coast sl.) new school
1. to indicate or exude the utmost confidence and poise with a tug of one's shirt collar or lapel.
ex: "You need to pop ya collar to that."

[one's] **pops** n. (general sl.) old & new school
1. one's father.
ex: "He looks just like his pops." "I grew up with ya pops "

[to] **pop sh**** v. (general sl.) old & new school
1. to verbally challenge, taunt or sound threatening [often using insolence and/or profanity]. (var. [to] **pop sh** about/to** [someone])
ex: "You been poppin' a whole lot of sh** lately."

[to] pop the trunk [on someone] v. (w. coast sl.) old & new school
1. to go in one's trunk to retrieve a weapon [usually a handgun].
ex: "Dawg I'm out, homes about to pop the trunk on these fools."

po-po n. (criminal sl.) old & new school
1. police; law enforcement agents. 2. someone who is known or suspected of being a police informant. (var. **po-nine**)
ex: "We jetted on po-po."

popped phrase (criminal sl.) old & new school
1. arrested; caught.
ex: "She almost got us popped."

popped n. (general sl.) old & new school
1. without money; destitute.
ex: "I'm popped right now."

poppi n. (e. coast sl.) new school
1. a term of endearment females use for males they like, are friends with, or intimate with [often used as a pet name or as a tool for a female to soften a male up]. (var. **poppi chulo**)
ex: "I been checkin' you out for a while poppi." "Poppi when you gonna take me to dinner?"

poppi n. (drug sl.) old & new school
1. the covert name one uses for his/her Hispanic drug supplier.
ex: "We need to go see poppi."

poppi grande n. (e. coast sl.) new school
1. the person in charge; the boss; chief decision maker.
ex: "It's your call poppi grande, whassup?"

[one's] posse n. (e. coast sl.) old school
1. one's group of friends. See also: [one's] **crew**
ex: "Make sure you bring ya whole posse with you."

[to] **post up** v. (general sl.) old & new school
1. to wait. 2. to position oneself in a way that one can observe someone or a situation. (var. [to] **post up on/for** [someone])
ex: *"I'm going to her job and post up 'til she gets off work."*

[a] **pound** n. (drug sl.) old school
1. a kilogram amount of cocaine.
ex: *"Police set'er up to buy a couple of pounds."*

[a] **pound cake** n. (general sl.) old school
1. five dollars. (var. [a] **pound cakey**)
ex: *"I always give her son a pound cake."*

[to] **pound the concrete** phrase (general sl.) new school
1. the walking or traveling involved with one's attempt to further his/her goal.
ex: *"Yo, I been out here poundin' the concrete for you for two days."*

[a] **power move** phrase (e. coast sl.) new school
1. the act of making a strong, aggressive, and decisive move to further one's goal. (var. [to] **make a power move**)
ex: *"I made a power move today." "We about to make a big power move." "That was a power move what you did."*

power move phrase (e. coast sl.) new school
1. a witty way to offer mock congratulations when observing someone about to bathe, brush his/her teeth, or any task needing to be performed.
ex: *"Power move kid, you was startin' to stink."*

power u n. (e. coast sl.) old & new school
1. a covert way to say the word "pus**" when referring to sex or a vagina.
ex: *"I heard shortie got some good power u." "You get the power u yet son?"*

[to] **press** [someone] v. (e. coast sl.) new school
1. the act of applying pressure [sometimes through intimidation or threats]. (var. [to] **put the press on/down on** [someone], [to] **put [one's] press game down**)
ex: *"Look, you not gonna be pressin' me about this all night."*

[the] **press game** phrase (e. coast sl.) new school
1. the actual tactics one employs to pressure or put the pressure on someone. (var. [to] **put the press game on** [someone])
ex: *"I used my press game to get the keys."*

[to be] **pressed** [about/over something] adj. (southern sl.) new school
1. stressed; worried; distraught. 2. desperate; in need.
ex: *"I'm not even pressed about that." "Do I sound pressed to you?"*

pressure busts pipes phrase (general sl.) old & new school
1. a way to taunt or mock someone's inability to handle or perform under pressure [also used when someone quits under the pressure].

[something that's] **primo** adj. (e. coast sl.) new school
1. outstanding; unique; the best of its kind; top of the line.
ex: *"This that primo sh**." "Bring out the primo for my peoples."*

product n. (drug sl.) old school
1. a covert word for drugs.
ex: *"How much product did she get caught with?"*

[a] **professional** n. (sexual sl.) new school
1. a classy way to refer to oral sex given to a male.
ex: *"She said a professional was out the question."*

[to] **profile** v. (general sl.) old & new school
1. the flaunting of one's material possessions or wealth to get attention. (var. [to] **style and profile**)
ex: *"I like the way y'all be profilin'."*

project beef n. (e. coast sl.) old & new school
1. ongoing problems that often lead to physical confrontations with people from one's own housing project.
ex: "Years and years can go by, and dudes still bring up project beefs cause they don't have nothing else to do."

project females n. (e. coast sl.) old & new school
1. females who grow up in public housing complexes.
ex: "You hafta watch some of them project females."

[I] **promise you that!** interj. (general sl.) old & new school
1. a matter fact way to put emphasis on one's threat or declaration in a way that conveys one's seriousness and conviction.
ex: "She ain't never comin' back in here, promise you that!"

[something that's] **proper** adj. (general sl.) old & new school
1. outstanding; unique; the best of its kind. 2. cool, hip, and/or trendy. See also: [something that's] **hella proper**
ex: "That was madd proper."

props n. (general sl.) old & new school
1. recognition; respect; praise; a compliment. (var. [to] **give** [someone] **his/her props**)
ex: "I hafta give you your props for that." "You deserve madd props."

[a] **public pretender** n. (criminal sl.) new school
1. a criminal lawyer paid by the city or state to defend indigent inmates; a court appointed lawyer.
ex: "I told my public pretender, if it's such a sweet deal why don't he take it."

puddin' n. (e. coast sl.) new school
1. money. See also: **cheese, scrilla**

[to] **puff** [something] v. (drug sl.) new school
1. to smoke marijuana. (var. [to get] **puffed up**)
ex: "Can we puff in here?"

pull adj. (general sl.) old & new school
1. influence. See also: **juice**
ex: "Let's see how much pull you have."

[to] **pull** [a female] v. (general sl.) old & new school
1. to acquire some sort of contact information from a female when first meeting [with the possibility of starting a intimate Relationship]. (var. [to] **bag** [a female])
ex: "I pulled a badd lil shortie on the way here."

[to] **pull a jack move** v. (w. coast sl.) old & new school
1. the act of taking something from someone using trickery, deception, or intimidation; to rob someone. (var. [to] **pull a lick**)
ex: "We had to pull a jack move to get this."

[to] **pull a spin move** v. (e. coast sl.) new school
1. to mislead someone in an attempt to stall or deceive. See also: [a] **spin move**
ex: "Shortie pulled the vicious spin move when we got out there."

[to] **pull** [someone's] **card** v. (e. coast sl.) old & new school
1. to expose one's secret, intention, or true character [usually by putting that person on the spot].
ex: "Say I won't go over there and pull his card."

[to] **pull** [someone's] **coat** v. (general sl.) old & new school
1. the act of bring something to someone's attention; to inform, alert, or let someone in on a secret. (var. [to] **pull** [someone's] **coat to** [something], [to] **put a bug in** [someone's] **ear**) See also: [to] **hip** [someone]
ex: "I need to pull ya coat about Shortie."

[to] **pull out on** [someone] v. (criminal sl.) old & new school
1. to brandish a firearm on someone. (var. [to] **pull out**) See also: [to] **back** [someone] **down**

[to] **pull up** v. (general sl.) old & new school
1. to arrive. (var. [to] **pull up on the scene/set**)
ex: *"When I pull up, shortie all in duke's face like this..."*

[to] **pull up** v. (e. coast sl.) old & new school
1. to stop and rethink or re-evaluate.
ex: *"I had to pull up when I seen how things was turnin' out."*

[to] **pull** [someone] **up** phrase (e. coast sl.) new school
1. the act of approaching someone for the purpose of giving that person advise or to bring something to his/her attention; to confront someone about his/her behavior.
ex: *"You need to pull ya man up and tell'em about himself."*

[to] **pull up on** [someone] v. (general sl.) new school
1. to approach someone confrontationally. See also: [to] **step to** [someone]
ex: *"Hold up, let me pull up on this dude for a minute."*

[to] **pull up on** [a female] v. (general sl.) old & new school
1. to approach a female.
ex: *"I didn't care, I pulled up on shortie."*

[to] **pull up** [a male's] **skirt/dress** phrase (e. coast sl.) new school
1. to expose a male for being a coward [usually after he has presented an image of being a thug or "street" tough]. See also: [to] **expose** [someone]
ex: *"Don't make me come outside and pull ya skirt up duke."*

[to] **pump** [something] v. (drug sl.) old & new school
1. the act of selling drugs [usually on the retail level]. (var. [to] **pump for** [someone])
ex: *"He been pumpin' on this block for years."*

[to] **pump** [a certain kind of way] v. (e. coast sl.) new school
1. the act of doing something a unique and specific type of way. 2. to display a certain type of behavior. See also: [to] **move** [a certain kind of way]

ex: "I didn't know you pump like that." "I don't pump like that dawg."

[to] **pump sh** up** v. (general sl.) old & new school
1. to instigate a situation in an attempt to incite or cause an escalation. (var. [to] **pump** [something] **up**)
ex: "I'm tellin' you, she tryin' to pump sh** up."

[to] **pump** [someone] **up** v. (general sl.) old & new school
1. to incite; to stoke one's emotions. See also: [to] **amp** [someone] **up**
ex: "Stop tryin' to pump ya man up." "Let them catz pump you up if you want to."

[to] **pump with** [someone] phrase (e. coast sl.) new school
1. to socialize or "hangout" with someone. 2. to like someone.
ex: "I don't pump with them kinda catz no more." "I pumps with Shortie."

[to] **pump with** [something] phrase (e. coast sl.) new school
1. to like something.
ex: "I pumps with "The Basement" on B.E.T."

[to] **pump with** [something] **like that** phrase (e. coast sl.) new school
1. to exhibit unwavering support for something or someone; to like or admire. (var. [to] **pump with** [someone] **like that**)
ex: "Regardless of what, I pumps with them catz like that so watch ya mouth."

[one's] **pumpkin** n. (general sl.) old school
1. a person's head.
ex: "Half his pumpkin was missin'."

punch drunk adj. (general sl.) new school
1. a look of confusion or bewilderment [usually after losing in competition].
ex: "Ya man sittin' over there lookin' punch drunk."

[to] **punish** [someone] v. (e. coast sl.) new school
1. the act of physically assaulting someone [usually causing extensive injury].
ex: "Dun got punished."

[to] **punish** [someone] v. (e. coast sl.) new school
1. to out perform and/or beat someone mercilessly during competition [often used as a boast or taunt].
ex: "I'm about to punish ya man." "We punished that team."

[to] **punish** [a female] v. (sexual sl.) new school
1. a term males use to boast about their outstanding performance during sex.
ex: "I took Shortie home and punished'er." "I'm about to punish Shortie as soon as I hang up with you."

[to] **punish** [something edible] v. (e. coast sl.) new school
1. to eat hungrily or greedily.
ex: "I'm about to go in here and punish these nachos."

[a] **punk** adj. (general sl.) old & new school
1. someone considered to be cowardly.
ex: "Who you callin' a punk?"

[to] **punk** [someone] v. (general sl.) old & new school
1. to make someone look and/or feel cowardly or weak after belittling, intimidating, or challenging that person to a physical confrontation. (var. [to] **punk** [someone] **down**)
ex: "I know you not gonna let him punk you like that."

[a] **punk ass** [person] adj. (general sl.) old & new school
1. cowardly; easily intimidated. 2. one who lacks the courage to stand up for themselves.
ex: "I don't want ya punk ass around me."

[a] **punk ass excuse** adj. (general sl.) old & new school
1. a very weak or incredibly ridiculous excuse.

ex: "I'm tired of your punk ass excuses."

punk panties n. (prison sl.) old & new school
1. male brief underwear. (var. **tighty whities, supermanz**)
ex: " I told shorties I don't rock with the punk panties."

punnanny (pron. poo nanny) n. (sexual sl.) old & new school
1. a covert word for vagina.

purple haze n. (drug sl.) new school
1. a brand of marijuana. (var. **haze**)

[to] **push** [an automobile] v. (general sl.) new school
1. to drive.
ex: "Shortie pushin' a LS." "You think ya moms gonna let you push the jeep this weekend?"

[when/if] **push come to shove...** phrase (general sl.) old & new school
1. a way to say, "if we have to", "if things get that bad", "as a last resort", or "if there's no other choice/way."
ex: "Push come to shove, we just hafta leave early."

[to] **push somethin' phat** phrase (general sl.) new school
1. to own and/or drive an expensive or new automobile.
ex: "As soon as he got out of jail he was pushin' somethin' phat."

[to] **push that/some steel** phrase (prison sl.) new school
1. the act of stabbing someone with a homemade knife or sharp metal. (var. [to] **push that thing/thing-thing**)
ex: "Dawg, I'll push that steel if I have to."

[to] **push up on** [someone] v. (general sl.) old & new school
1. to approach someone [threateningly or flirtatiously]. (var. [to] **push up**)
ex: "I heard you was tryin' to push up on my girl."

[to] **push** [someone's] **wig back** v. (criminal sl.) new school
1. a way to describe being shot in the head [usually resulting in death]. (var. [to] **push** [someone's] **sh** back**)
ex: "When they found'em somebody already had pushed his wig back." "Catz talkin' about pushin' ya wig back."

[someone who's] **pus**** adj. (general sl.) old & new school
1. cowardly. See also: [someone who's] **sex**
ex: "That cat was pus** growin' up."

[to] **put a baby** [up] **in** [a female/shortie] v. (general sl.) old & new school
1. a male term for impregnating a female.
ex: "He wished he'd put a baby in shortie now, I bet."

[to] **put a black eye in** [the/one's] **ball game/game** phrase (e. coast sl.) new school
1. the act of purposely trying to hinder or place obstacles in someone's way to stop him/her from reaching a goal [often using rumors or lies to discredit that person]. (var. [to] **put salt** [in the/someone's] **game/ball game**)
ex: "Duke tried to put a black in my game behind my back with shortie."

[to] **put a bone on** [someone] v. (general sl.) new school
1. to tell a lie about someone in a attempt to discredit or ruin that person's reputation. (var. [to] **put a bone/bad bone out on** [someone])
ex: "You know somebody put a bone on you right?"

[to] **put a clappin' to** [someone] v. (southern sl.) new school
1. the act of shooting someone.
ex: "I heard somebody put a clappin' to ya boy."

[to] **put a foot on** [someone's] **neck** phrase (e. coast sl.) new school
1. to oppress someone; to have or keep someone at a disadvantage. (var. [to] **keep a foot on** [someone's] **neck**)

ex: "My P.O. tried to put his foot on my neck as soon as I came home."

put a "H" on ya back and handle it phrase (e. coast sl.) old school
1. a witty way to tell someone to "handle" something [usually used to dismiss someone's complaint].

[to] **put a hurtin' on** [a female] v. (sexual sl.) old & new school
1. a male term for describing satisfying a female sexually [usually used a boast]. See also: [to] **beat up the coochie**
ex: "Shortie fa real, I'll put a hurtin' on you." "I bet ya friend didn't tell you about the hurtin' I put on her the other night."

[to] **put a hurtin' on** [someone] **pockets** v. (general sl.) old & new school
1. to be or to become a financial burden to another. 2. to take advantage of someone financially.
ex: "I like shortie and everything, but she startin' to put a hurtin' on me." "The six months we was together, I made sure I put a hurtin' on his pockets."

put a straightenin' on that phrase (southern sl.) new school
1. a way to prod someone into correcting, confronting, or standing up to someone who has disrespected him/her. See also: [to] **straightenin'** [someone]
ex: "You gotta put a straightenin' on that dawg."

[to] **put** [one's] **bid in** phrase (general sl.) old & new school
1. to request an opportunity; to ask.
ex: "I'm just tryin' to put my bid in Shortie."

[to] **put** [someone's] **business out in the street** phrase (e. coast sl.) old & new school
1. to reveal someone's secret or personal affairs for the sake of gossip. (var. [to] **put** [someone's] **business out there/on front street/on the street**)

ex: "When we broke up, this lame put all my business out in the street."

[to] **put** [someone] **down** phrase (general sl.) old & new school
1. to share a piece of information with someone. (var. [to] **put** [someone] **dee**)
ex: "I need to put you down about somethin'."

[to] **put** [someone] **down** phrase (general sl.) old & new school
1. to criticize someone negatively [often when that person deserves praise]. See also: [to] **knock** [someone]
ex: "You always lookin' to put somebody down about something."

[to] **put fear in** [someone's] **heart** phrase (general sl.) old & new school
1. to scare someone through intimidation.
ex: "You don't put no fear in my heart kid."

[to] **put flavor to** [something] v. (general sl.) old school
1. to add something that enhances the quality or appearance.
ex: "I'mma show you how to put flavor to that outfit."

[to] **put foot to** [someone's] **ass** phrase (w. coast sl.) old & new school
1. to beat someone up mercilessly. (var. [to] **put foot in** [someone's] **ass**)
ex: "I started to take this clown outside and put foot to his ass."

[to] **put** [one's] **gorilla game down** phrase (w. coast sl.) new school
1. to bully someone. 2. to initimidate someone to get one's way. (var. [to] **gorilla** [someone])
ex: "Whenever I needed some loot, I'd go in there and put my gorilla game down."

[to] **put** [someone's] **head to bed** phrase (e. coast sl.) old school
1. to knock someone out. (var. [to] **put** [someone's] **head out**)
ex: "I put this cat head to bed at my man High School."

[to] **put** [someone] **in a house/crib** phrase (general sl.) new school
1. to buy or rent someone a house or apartment.
ex: "I'm about to put ol' girl in a house off this loot."

[to] **put** [someone] **in his/her feelin's** phrase (e. coast sl.) new school
1. to make someone mad.
ex: "You know all I hafta say is you stupid and I'mma put you in your feelin's."

[to] **put** [someone] **in the car** phrase (e. coast sl.) new school
1. to make something possible for someone through the use of your influence and connections; to allow someone to participate. (var.
[to] **put** [someone] **in the house/up in the house/up in there**)
ex: "I'mma put you in the car, the rest is up to you."

[to] **put** [someone] **in the mix** phrase (general sl.) old & new school
1. to involve someone [usually in some type of controversy]. (var.
[to] **put** [someone] **in some bullsh**/ in the middle of some bullsh****)
ex: "Why you always hafta put me in the mix with this nonsense?"
"We put you in the mix dawg?"

[to] **put in work** phrase (prison sl.) new school
1. to assault someone [usually causing severe bodily injury]. (var.
[to] **put** [one's] **work in**)
ex: "Ya man was known for puttin' in work upnorth."

[to] **put in work** phrase (e. coast sl.) new school
1. to perform outstandingly [usually used as a boast or compliment]. (var. [to] **put** [one's] **work in**)
ex: "You put in work this time."

[to] **put it down for** [one's peoples/peops/homies/hood] v. (general sl.) new school
1. to dedicate one's performance or effort to one's friends, love ones, or neighborhood.

ex: "I'm puttin' it down for the peoples this time.

[to] **put it on** [someone] v. (sexual sl.) new school
1. to demonstrate uninhibited sex with one's partner leaving him/her completely satisfied.
ex: "I put in on shortie somethin' terrible."

[to] **put** [one's] **mack down** phrase (general sl.) new school
1. to use one's charm and finesse when meeting someone of the opposite sex in the attempt to start a relationship with him/her.
ex: "We about to go in here and put our mack down."

[to] **put money on** [someone's] **books** phrase (prison sl.) old & new school
1. to send someone in prison money [a money order].
ex: "In ten years this cat never once put money on my books."

[to] **put** [one's] **muscle game down** phrase (prison sl.) new school
1. the use of intimidation to scare and/or pressure someone. (var. [to] **put** [one's] **gorilla game down**)
ex: "See, you don't know how to put ya muscle game down."

[to] **put** [someone] **on** v. (general sl.) old & new school
1. to give someone an opportunity to become successful through the use of your influence and connections. (var. [to] **get put on**)
ex: "I put my man on when he came home."

[to] **put** [something] **on** [someone] v. (general sl.) old & new school
1. to blame someone [usually undeservingly].
ex: "I can't let you put that on me like that."

[to] **put** [someone] **on blast** v. (e. coast sl.) new school
1. to put someone on the spot by revealing his/her secrets [usually in a attempt to ruin that person's reputation or relationship with others].
ex: "I can't believe this itch put me on blast like that on the radio station."

[to] **put** [someone] **on his/her back** v. (w. coast sl.) old & new school
1. to knock someone down or out during a fight. (var. [to] **knock** [someone] **on his/her ass**)
ex: "She put this chick on'er back."

[to] **put** [someone] **on/out on front street** phrase (e. coast sl.) new school
1. to put someone on the spot or in an awkward position [usually by exposing something that the person was trying to keep a secret]. 2. to leave or put someone in a position that the blame will fall on him/her.
ex: "I can't let you put me on front street like that."

[to] **put** [someone] **on the map** phrase (general sl.) old & new school
1. to make someone famous, recognizable, and/or respected. (var. [to] **put** [somewhere] **on the map**)
ex: "Don't forget I'm the one who put y'all on the map."

[to] **put** [something] **on the shelf** phrase (prison sl.) new school
1. to save something for another time [usually in the context of a punishment].
ex: "I'mma put this on the shelf, but if you mess up, that's your ass."

[to] **put** [someone] **on to** [something] v. (general sl.) old & new school
1. to alert someone. 2. to provide information to someone for his/her benefit.
ex: "I'm the one who put you on to the scam."

[to] **put** [someone] **on to** [someone] v. (general sl.) old & new school
1. to introduce two people of the opposite sex to each other at the behest of one of them in the attempt to start an intimate relationship with the other one; to play matchmaker.

ex: "When you gonna put me on to your cousin?" "I want you to put me on to your other friend."

[to] **put** [someone] **on to** [one's] **connect** v. (drug sl.) old & new school
1. to introduce someone to one's drug supplier.
ex: "When you gonna put me on to your connect?"

[to] **put one/two/three in** [someone] v. (criminal sl.) old & new school
1. a covert way to refer to the shooting of someone one, two, three times. (var. [to] **put a couple in** [someone])
ex: "Po-po put two in ya man."

[to] **put** [someone] **out there** phrase (general sl.) new school
1. to put someone on the spot. 2. to reveal someone's real intentions. (var. [to] **put** [something] **out there**)
ex: "I still can't believe you put me out there like that over a female." "She the one who put that out there about you."

[to] **put** [one's] **peoplez on point** v. (general sl.) old & new school
1. to alert or make one's friends/loved ones aware.
ex: "Make sure you put ya peoplez on point so there's no confusion when I get back."

[to] **put** [one's] **pimp hand down** v. (w. coast sl.) old & new school
1. to discipline someone by either smacking them or threatening to smack them.
ex: "I'm about to put my pimp hand down in two minutes, keep it up."

[to] **put salt on** [someone's] **name** phrase (e. coast sl.) new school
1. to start a rumor or lie about someone in an attempt to discredit or ruin one's reputation. (var. [to] **sh** on** [someone's] **name**) See also: [to] **throw salt**
ex: "Your ex is puttin' salt on your name all over the hood."

[to] **put sh** in the game** phrase (e. coast sl.) new school
1. to deceitfully twist around the truth. 2. to start a rumor or tell a lie in an attempt to discredit or ruin one's reputation. 3. to cheat.
ex: "It wouldn't be you, if you didn't put some sh** in the game."

[to] **put sh** on smash** v. (general sl.) nw school
1. to put things under one's control, influence, or authority [as a result of one's determination to be a leader of his/her field]. (var. [to] **put** [something] **on smash**)
ex: "I'mma show you how you put sh** on smash in a minute."

[to] **put** [one's] **smack down** phrase (w. coast sl.) old & new school
1. the act of slapping someone with an open hand.
ex: "If I hafta come in there, I'm comin' in there to put my smack down."

put some muscle in ya hustle phrase (general sl.) new school
1. a term used to encourage someone to try harder or apply more effort.

put some pep in ya step phrase (general sl.) old school
1. a way to tell someone to hurry or move faster.

[to] **put somethin'** in [someone's] **head** v. (general sl.) old & new school
1. to convince someone to think another kind of way, according to your opinion, input, or perceptions on a situation; to influence another's thought negatively.
ex: "You keep lettin' your friends put somethin' in your head, that's where the problems keep coming from."

put somethin' on it [then] phrase (southern sl.) new school
1. a term used to prod someone into wagering something against you [usually used challengingly]. See also: **bet it up**
ex: "If you so sure, put somethin' on it."

[to] **put that steel** [up] **in** [someone] v. (prison sl.) new school
1. to stab someone using a makeshift knife. (var. [to] **put that thing/thing-thing** [up] **in** [someone])
ex: "He was known for puttin' that steel in dudes."

[to] **put the bullsh** aside** phrase (general sl.) old & new school
1. to put one's differences with another aside for a common cause or in an attempt to move past those differences. (var. [to] **put the bullsh** to the side**)
ex: "Why y'all just can't put the bullsh** aside for one night at least."

[to] **put the fear of God in** [someone] phrase (general sl.) new school
1. to scare someone through intimidation.
ex: "I don't know how, but she put the fear of God in them catz."

[to] **put the full court press on** [someone] phrase (e. coast sl.) new school
1. to employ all kinds of tactics from intimidation to humbleness to pressure someone into letting you have your way.
ex: "The full court press won't work on my momz."

[to] **put the police on** [someone] phrase (southern sl.) new school
1. the act of calling the police or going to the police station to file a complaint against someone. (var. [to] **put the man/cops on** [someone])
ex: "Next time I'mma put the police on ya ass." "I think he put the police on me."

[to] **put the wood on** [a female] phrase (e. coast sl.) new school
1. a male term for having sex with a female.
ex: "Once I put that wood on Shortie she fell in love."

[to] **put them bees on** [someone] phrase (southern sl.) old & new school
1. to hit someone quickly and repeatedly while fighting. (var. [to] **drop them bees on** [someone])

ex: "Soon as I started puttin' them bees on'em he took off."

[to] **put** [one's] **thing down** phrase (e. coast sl.) new school
1. to perform outstandingly. 2. to achieve something that is testament to one's skills or talents. 3. to put forth effort; to give something a try. (var. [to] **put it down**, [to] **put** [something] **down**)
ex: "You went out there and really put ya thing down." "I'm about to put it down in here."

put those back in ya pocket phrase (general sl.) old school
1. a witty term used to dismiss someone who has put up his/her hands like he/she wants to fight you.

[to] **put** [someone] **to bed** phrase (criminal sl.) new school
1. a term used to describe the act of murder.
ex: "It was a matter of time before somebody put'em to bed."

[to] **put** [one's] **two cents in** phrase (general sl.) old & new school
1. to give one's unwanted opinion or advice about something that doesn't concern him/her; to instigate. See also: **coachin' from the sidelines**
ex: "You forever puttin' your two cents in."

put two eggs in ya shoe and beat it phrase (general sl.) old & new school
1. a witty way to tell someone to leave or get out [a term used to dismiss].

[to] **put** [someone] **under the jail** phrase (criminal sl.) new school
1. to receive an extremely long prison sentence from the judge as a result of a friend/family member's testimony. (var. [to] **put** [someone] **up under the jail**)
ex: "They about to put ya man under the jail."

[to] **put words in** [someone's] **mouth** phrase (general sl.) old & new school

1. to lie and say someone said something and he/she did not. 2. to speak for someone without authorization. 3. to misinterpret what someone said and then pass that misinterpretation to someone else. *ex: "Stop puttin' words in my mouth."*

put ya blue suede shoes on, we about to dance phrase (e. coast sl.) new school
1. a witty way to inform someone that you and him/her are about to have a physical fist fight. (var. **put ya dancin' shoes on** [we about to tango])

put ya hands on me, you gonna draw back a nub phrase (southern sl.) old & new school
1. a witty way to warn someone not to hit you or not to put his/her hands on you [usually used as a threat or as a response to a threat].

q

Q-boro n. (e. coast sl.) old & new school
1. Queensbridge housing projects in Queens N.Y. (var. **Q.B., The Bridge**)

[a] **q.t.** n. (general sl.) old & new school
1. a quarter (.25¢)

[a female who's a] **quarter piece** adj. (general sl.) new school
1. an extremely good looking female [usually with a extremely good looking body to go with her looks].
ex: "Nothin' but quarter pieces hang up in there."

quarters n. (drug sl.) old & new school
1. twenty five dollar amounts of an illegal drug.
ex: "Police caught ya man with three quarters."

quick fast in a hurry phrase (southern sl.) new school
1. a way to say, "immediately", "right now", "right away", or "as fast as you can".
ex: "All I know is, you better get here quick fast in a hurry."

[someone who's] **quiet as a church mouse** adj. (general sl.) old & new school
1. shy; timid. 2. extremely quiet around others.
ex: "I remember dude when he was quiet as a church mouse."

quiet is kept phrase (prison sl.) old & new school
1. a term used as a prelude to divulging a secret to someone. 2. a way to say, "between me and you" when discussing something with someone that is supposed to be a secret.

ex: "Quiet is kept, I did hit dude's girl over the summer." "She cheated on 'em, quiet is kept."

quiet storm adj. (general sl.) old & new school
1. discreet; to maintain a low profile. (var. [to] **play the quiet storm**)
ex: "As long as we keep it quiet storm I'm madd cool with this."

[to] **rack up** [something] v. (general sl.) old & new school
1. to accumulate a large amount of. (var. [to] **rack up on**
[something])
*ex: "They racked up all them points in the last half." "I seen ya
moms rackin' up on that free cheese."*

[someone who's] **rackin' in the dough** phrase (general sl.) new
school
1. one who is making large amounts of money.
ex: "They should be rackin' in the dough after this album."

[that] **rah rah sh**** adj. (e. coast sl.) new school
1. unruly and disruptive behavior. (var. [to be] **on some** [ol'] **rah
rah sh****)
*ex: "Don't come in here with that rah rah sh**." "He tried to
scare me with some of that rah rah sh**."*

[a] **rain closet** n. (southern sl.) new school
1. a shower.
ex: "Tell'em I said call me when he gets out the rain closet."

[a] **raincoat** n. (sexual sl.) old & new school
1. a condom.

[to] **rain on** [someone] v. (general sl.) old & new school
1. to repeatedly hit someone. (var. [to] **bring the rain down on**
[someone])
ex: "Yo, you seen Shortie try to rain on me?"

[to] **raise** v. (general sl.) old & new school
1. to leave; to depart from. (var. [to] **raise up**, [to] **raise up outta**
[somewhere]) See also: [to] **jet**, [to] **step**

ex: "Call me a cab, I'm about to raise. "

raise up phrase (w. coast sl.) old & new school
1. a playful or sarcastic way to tell someone to leave, leave you
alone, or stop doing something that is annoying you.
ex: "Raise up dawg, can't you see I'm busy."

[to] **rank on** [someone] v. (e. coast sl.) old & new school
1. the act of making someone the brunt of one's jokes and
humorous quips. See also: [to] **snap on** [someone]
ex: "He ranked on dawg all night long."

[a] **ransom** n. (criminal sl.) old & new school
1. an extremely high bail set by the judge; a bail so high one is not
likely to make. (var. [a] **ransom bail**)
*ex: "The D.A. was the one who asked for the ransom and the judge
went along with the program."*

[a] **rap** n. (criminal sl.) old school
1. a firearm.

[one's] **rap** n. (general sl.) old & new school
1. one's unique ability to strike up interesting, intelligent, and witty
conversation with someone of the opposite sex enough to draw that
person's interest. (var. [one's] **rap game**)
*ex: "Ya man rap is some trash." "Yo gotta know how to rap to
them type of females."*

[to] **rap** [to/with someone] v. (general sl.) old & new school
1. to talk to/converse with someone.
ex: "Yo dawg, I need to rap with you for a minute."

[one's] **rappy** n. (w. coast sl.) old & new school
1. a term of endearment among friends; friend. 2. a close friend;
buddy. (var. [one's] **rap partner/buddy**)
ex: "Is ya rappy comin' with us later?"

[to] **rat pack** [someone] v. (e. coast sl.) new school
1. the act of several individuals attacked and assaulting one person.
See also: [to] **mob** [someone]
ex: "Shut up before we rat pack your punk ass up in here."

[a] **rat trap** n. (general sl.) old & new school
l. any dwelling or social club that is dirty, messy, and gives the
feeling of being unsafe.
*ex: "I can't believe you brought me to this rat trap." "You won't
believe the rat trap Shortie livin' in."*

[a] **ratchet** n. (criminal sl.) new school
1. a firearm; handgun.
ex: "You can get 15 years for a ratchet in the Feds."

[something that's] **raw** adj. (general sl.) old & new school
1. outstanding; unique; the best of its kind. (var. [something that's]
raw dawg)
ex: "The flicks came out raw."

raw n. (drug sl.) old & new school
1. powder cocaine. (var. **powder**) See also: **'caine**

[to go] **raw** v. (sexual sl.) old & new school
1. to have unprotected sex; sex without a condom. (var. [to go]
raw dawg, [to] **go up in** [a female] **raw**)
*ex: "You mean to tell me you went raw with Shortie?" "Sh** too
dangerous to go up in shortie raw."*

Ray Charles can see through that phrase (general sl.) old & new
school
1. a witty way to inform someone that his/her excuse, explanation,
or attempt to deceive you is transparent. (var. **a blind man can see
through that**)

[to] **reach** [on someone] v. (criminal sl.) old & new school

1. to brandish a weapon that has been concealed on one's person [usually during a confrontation and usually a firearm].
ex: "I thought he was about to reach." "When I seen her reachin' I jetted."

[to] **reach out and touch** [someone] v. (general sl.) old & new school
1. to communicate to someone that you want to have someone assaulted or confronted and have that act carried out without your physical involvement.
ex: "He had someone reach out and touch shortie's baby father over that bullsh** he did to shortie."

ready rock n. (drug sl.) old school
1. crack cocaine. See also: **crillz, bolos**

real people do real things phrase (e. coast sl.) old school
1. a term used to say "you're welcome" when someone expresses his/her gratitude for something you have done to help [usually used as a modest way to respond to someone's expressed gratitude].

real recognize real phrase (e. coast sl.) new school
1. a term of respect among peers or strangers in recognition of one's steely character.
ex: "What can I say, real recognize real."

Realadelphia n. (e. coast sl.) new school
1. Philadelphia PA.

[the] **realizm** n. (general sl.) new school
1. the truth; the facts. (var. [the] **realz/really real/real**)
ex: "I just want to know what the realizm is."

rec n. (e. coast sl.) new school
1. something one's does for enjoyment, or entertainment [not limited to sports activity]. 2. fun activities. 3. recreation.
ex: "I like doin' this for rec." "This is how I get my rec."

recognize phrase (e. coast sl.) new school
1. a playful or sarcastic way to demand the respect, recognition, or praise you deserve or have earned from one's peers. (var. **recognize it, recognize or get penalized, don't be shy recognize, open ya eyes and recognize**) See also: [you] **better recognize**
ex: "Recognize boy, I'm the best that ever did this."

recognize it phrase (e. coast sl.) new school
1. a term used to signify one's statement or actions as being "pay back" or revenge or retaliatory.
ex: "It's my turn now, recognize it."

[a] **reggie** n. (general sl.) new school
1. a right hand turn while driving.
ex: "You shoulda made a reggie two blocks ago."

[to] **regulate** v. (w. coast sl.) old & new school
1. to give orders; to set the rules. (var. [to] **regulate** [things], [someone who's a] **regulator**)
ex: "What makes you think you can come in here and regulate?"

[to] **rep** [one's neighborhood/block/city] v. (general sl.) new school
1. to verbally claim, acknowledge, or defend the reputation of where one lives. (var. [to] **represent** [one's neighborhood/block and city])
ex: "When I was young I used to rep my hood to the fullest."

[to] **represent** v. (general sl.) old & new school
1. to perform outstandingly; to put forth maximum effort [usually used to encourage or boast]. (var. [to] **rep**, [to] **represent to the fullest**)
ex: "Watch me go out there and represent." "When its your turn I want you to represent."

[to] **respect** [one's] **gangster** phrase (e. coast sl.) new school
1. to respect one's boldness, directness, or unwavering position.
See also: [something's that's] **gangster**

ex: "I hafta respect ya gangster."

respect mines phrase (general sl.) old & new school
1. a matter of fact way to demand someone give you the respect, praise, or recognition deserved for an accomplishment, performance, or goal obtained. (var. **respect this/it** [homie/baby boy/son/kid])
ex: "You gonna learn how to respect mines boy!"

respect my/the game phrase (general sl.) old & new school
1. a matter of fact way to demand or declare that one should respect, admire, or give praise to your abilities, achievement, or talents [usually used boastfully].
ex: "You need to respect my game shortie." "That's what's wrong with you now, you don't respect the game."

respect the/my hustle phrase (e. coast sl.) new school
1. a hip way to respond to another's jealous criticism about how one is making his/her money [whether legally or illegally].

[to] re-up phrase (drug sl.) old & new school
1. to replenish one's supply of drugs with some of the profit made from previous supplies.

re-up money n. (drug sl.) old & new school
1. the money one uses to replenish his/her supply of drugs when the previous supply has all been sold.
ex: "Dawg, ya broad ran off with the re-up money."

[my] ribs are touchin' my back phrase (general sl.) old & new school
1. a witty way to declare one's hungriness. 2. a term used to describe one's skinniness. (var. **someone whose ribs are touchin'** [his/her] **back**)
ex: "We need to pull over cause my ribs are touchin' my back."

[to] **ride** [someone] v. (general sl.) old & new school
1. to persistently criticize or reprimand someone about his/her
performance, behavior, or attitude; to nag.
ex: "I'mma ride you 'til you do better."

[to] **ride dirty** v. (criminal sl.) old & new school
1. the act of driving with something illegal in one's automobile
[usually refers to weapons and/or drugs].
ex: "Let me know if y'all ridin' dirty before I get in here."

[to] **ride for** [someone] phrase (w. coast sl.) old & new school
1. to provide and show one's unwavering support for someone in
any kind of situation good or bad; to stand by someone's side when
he/she is in trouble [even if it means putting oneself in harms way].
(var. [to] **ride with** [someone)
*ex: "I'mma ride for you no matter what." "I'm ridin' with my man
who looked out."*

[to] **ride** [someone's] **jock** phrase (general sl.) old school
1. to be extremely envious and infatuated with someone's talents,
reputation, or wealth. (var. [to] **ride** [someone's] **balls/tip/love
muscle/d**k**)
ex: "They been ridin' my jock for years."

[to] **ride on** [someone] v. (w. coast sl.) old & new school
1. to travel by automobile [usually with one's friends] in search
of one's enemy/enemies for the purpose of having a violent
confrontation. (var. [to] **ride on** [one's enemies])
*ex: "When they find out who did this, you know they gonna ride
on them fools."*

[to] **ride or die** phrase (w. coast sl.) new school
1. a term used to describe someone who is willing to take chances
even if it involves putting oneself in danger to help a friend and/or
to make money. (var. [someone who's a] **ride or die** [person], [a]
ride or die chick, [to] **ride or die for/with** [someone])
ex: "You know I'mma ride or die with you, you my dawg."

[to] **ride** [something] **out** v. (general sl.) old & new school
1. to remain steadfast and diligent until a crisis is resolved. (var.
[to] **ride** [something] **out with** [someone])
ex: "I'mma ride this out dawg."

ride out phrase (general sl.) new school
1. a way to tell someone to, "get lost", "beat it", or "get away from
me" when dismissing that person and his/her boast, claim,
assertion, excuse, or explanation.
ex: "Ride out man, I don't believe that."

[something that's] **ridiculous** adj. (e. coast sl.) new school
1. outstanding; unique; the best of its kind. See also: [something
that's] **bananas**
ex: "His flow is ridiculous." "Ya man got the ridiculous handle."

[to] **rif** v. (general sl.) old & new school
1. to be argumentative; to complain; to nag; 2. to talk smartly. (var.
[to] **rif with** [someone])
*ex: "Them chicks be riffin' too much." "I heard y'all was riffin'
earlier."*

right... right phrase (e. coast sl.) new school
1. a term used to express a false sense of concern with something
someone is telling you [usually used to mock someone discreetly].
ex: "Right ..... right, I woulda ask'er that too."

rillas n. (southern sl.) new school
1. thugs; young "street" individuals. 2. an abbreviation for the word
gorilla. See also: **gorillas**
ex: "Me and a bunch of my rillas crashed the door."

[a automobile that's] **rimmed up** phrase (general sl.) new school
1. a automobile that has expensive rims for its tires. See also: [a
automobile that's] **sittin' on chrome**

[to] **rip** [something] v. (general sl.) old & new school
1. to give an outstanding performance; to perform excellently. (var.
[to] **rip** [something] **up**, [to] **rip sh** up**)
ex: "Ask them whether or not I ripped it last night."

[to] **rip** [someone] v. (prison sl.) old & new school
1. to cut or slash someone with a razor [usually across the face or
neck requiring stitches]. See also: **a buck fifty**
ex: "That's the kid that tried to rip me."

ripped adj. (general sl.) old & new school
1. drunk; intoxicated.
ex: "Them broads left the party ripped."

[someone who's] **ripped up** adj. (general sl.) old & new school
1. one who has a very defined lean muscular physique. (var.
[someone who's] **ripped**)
*ex: "You couldn't tell how ripped up she was 'til she took off her
clothes."*

[one's] **rizzie** n. (e. coast sl.) new school
1. one's automobile or "ride".
ex: "How you like the new rizzie?"

Ro n. (general sl.) new school
1. a Range Rover jeep. (var. [a] **Range**)

[one's] **road dawg** n. (general sl.) old & new school
1. a term of endearment among friends; friend. 2. a friend one
spends a great deal of time with. (var. [one's] **roady**)
*ex: "That's my road dawg." "I'm bringin' my road dawgs this
time."*

[to] **rob Peter to pay Paul** phrase (general sl.) old & new school
1. to take money that was meant for one thing and use it for
something else [usually to pay a bill or debt].
ex: "I had to rob Peter to pay Paul to get us this."

[someone who's] **robbin' the cradle** phrase (sexual sl.) old & new school
1. one who is dating or intimate with someone who is clearly too young for him/her.
ex: "I didn't think you was into robbin' the cradle."

[to] **rock** [something] v. (general sl.) old & new school
1. to wear something.
ex: "Let me show you how to rock that." "He was rockin' that last week."

[to] **rock** [something] v. (general sl.) old & new school
1. to give an outstanding or excellent performance; to give a performance that excels one's peers or competition.
ex: "They rocked the crowd all night." "Them catz be rockin'."

rock n. (drug sl.) old school
1. pieces of crack cocaine.

[to] **rock** [someone] phrase (criminal sl.) old & new school
1. a way to describe the act of murder.
ex: "I heard ya man got rocked in D.C." "Word is he had somethin' to do with dawg gettin' rocked."

[to] **rock a vest** phrase (criminal sl.) old & new school
1. to wear a bullet proof vest. See also: **vested up**
ex: "They caught ya man rockin' a vest."

[to] **rock** [one's] **ice** v. (general sl.) old & new school
1. to wear one's expensive diamond jewelry
ex: "Did you see her rockin' her ice at the award show?"

[a] **rock star** n. (drug sl.) old school
1. a person who smokes and/or is addicted to crack cocaine.
ex: "I know you didn't have that rock star in my car."

[to] **rock the house** phrase (general sl.) old & new school
1. to give an outstanding performance.
ex: "They went up there and rocked the house."

[to] **rock** [someone] **to sleep** (prison sl.) new school
1. to lull someone into a false sense of friendship or security after he/she has wronged or disrespected you while you plot your revenge against him/her.
ex: "I got duke rocked to sleep."

[to] **rock** [something] **up** phrase (general sl.) new school
1. to add diamonds to a piece of jewelry.
ex: "How much is that gonna cost to have it rocked up?"

[to] **rock** [something] **up** v. (drug sl.) old & new school
1. to turn powder cocaine into crack cocaine and then chop the crack into smaller pieces for retail sale.
ex: "The cops raided the house as they was rockin' up 2 ounces."

rocks n. (general sl.) old & new school
1. diamonds.

[a] **rodeo** n. (e. coast sl.) new school
1. a gathering where a lot of females are expected to show up.
ex: "I been waitin' for this rodeo all week."

[a] **Roley** n. (general sl.) new school
1. a Rolex watch.

[to] **roll** v. (general sl.) old & new school
1. to leave. 2. the act of travleing. (var. [to] **roll out**, [to] **ride/ride out**)
ex: "What time y'all rollin' out?" "They already rolled out."

[to] **roll** [a certain kind of way] phrase (general sl.) old & new school

1. to carry oneself in a way that exudes and magnifies one's authority, character, influence, or capabilities in a way that others might find intimidating.
ex: "Why you didn't' tell me he rolled like that?"

[to] roll deep phrase (general sl.) old & new school
1. to travel with a large entourage; to be in the company of a large group. (var. **[to] roll heavy/thick/with a mob**)
ex: "Everywhere they go they roll deep."

[to] roll on [someone] v. (general sl.) old & new school
1. to aggressively confront someone [with the possibility of the confrontation escalating into a physical fight]. (var. **[to] roll up on** [someone]) See also: **[to] step to** [someone]
ex: "I didn't like the way you rolled on me."

roll out phrase (southern sl.) new school
1. a witty way to dismiss someone's ridiculous or foolish comment.
ex: "Roll out, you heard that on the news."

[to] roll out on [someone] v. (general sl.) old & new school
1. to abandon someone. 2. to cut one's ties to another [usually without explanation or reason].
ex: "Two years later, shortie just rolled out."

[to] roll tight [with someone] phrase (general sl.) old school
1. to be a close friend of someone. (var. **[people who] roll tight**)
ex: "Me and you always gonna roll tight no matter ."

[to] roll with [someone] v. (general sl.) old & new school
1. to accompany or travel with someone. 2. to show support for someone; to back someone.
ex: "Who you rollin' with this time?" "I gotta roll with the boy Moe Deezy."

[someone who's] **rollin'** adj. (southern sl.) old & new school
1. making large amounths of cash [usually through illegal means].
ex: "I heard them dudes is rollin' now."

romance with no finance is a nuisance phrase (southern sl.) old
& new school
1. a witty term females use to declare a male has to be financially
stable in order to have a intimate relationship with her.

[to] **roof** [something] v. (general sl.) old school
1. the act of throwing an object up on a roof top purposely. (var.
[to] **roof** [someone's] **sh****)
*ex: "He roofed my cell phone cause I was kickin' it with my
friend."*

[to] **rope** [someone] **off** v. (general sl.) old & new school
1. to catch someone doing wrong. 2. to intrap or snare someone.
*ex: "Shortie roped me off comin' out the strip club." "Watch how I
rope ya man off."*

roped off v. (criminal sl.) old & new school
1. arrested.
ex: "Let me tell you how she got roped off."

R.O.R. n. (criminal sl.) old & new school
1. an acronym for "Release on One's Recognizance" when a
person is released from court without having to post bail.
ex: "This judge doesn't give R.O.R.'s very often."

[a] **roscoe** n. (criminal sl.) old & new school
1. a firearm; handgun.

[someone who's] **rotten** adj. (criminal sl.) new school
1. someone who has cooperated with law enforcement in an
investigation against a friend or love one and/or has testified in
court against a friend or love one.
ex: "I been told you that dude was rotten."

[the] **Rotten Apple** n. (e. coast sl.) new school
1. New York City.

[a] **rough neck** n. (e. coast sl.) old & new school
1. a thug; a young "street" tough.
ex: "You cool and everything but you still a rough neck."

[to] **rough** [someone] **off** v. (e. coast sl.) new school
1. to get one's way or take another's possessions through intimidation; to bully someone.
ex: "I'm tired of you comin' in here tryin' to rough me off." "They roughed off the basketball court."

[to] **round/sound on** [someone] v. (general sl.) old school
1. to sarcastically put someone in his/her place [often in a loud tone of voice].
ex: "I know this clown ain't tryin' to round on you like that."

rowdy adj. (general sl.) old & new school
1. disruptive; loud and unruly. (var. **rowdy rowdy**)
ex: "Things about to get rowdy in here." "Don't bring them rowdy ass friends of yours."

rub it on ya chest phrase (e. coast sl.) new school
1. a sarcastic way to turn down someone's offering of something tangible after he/she first told you no when you asked for that item.
ex: "I don't want it now, you can rub it on ya chest."

[a] **ruler** (pron. ru'la) n. (drug sl.) old school
1. a cigarette of marijuana joint laced with crack cocaine. (var. [a] **ruley, woola blunt**, [a] **woo**)
ex: "If you smoke rulers sooner or later you'll be hittin' the pipe."

[a] **rump shaker** n. (general sl.) new school
1. a female with an extremely large butt. 2. a female or male exotic dancer.

ex: "Shortie got the madd rump shaker." "We met a few rump shakers down in Daytona."

[to] run [something] v. (general sl.) old & new school
1. to be in control over; in command; in charge. (var. **[to] run sh****)
ex: "I run this around here." "You don't run nothin'."

[to make someone] run [something] v. (criminal sl.) old & new school
1. to rob someone of his/her possessions [usually through the use of intimidation].
ex: "Every time I see you, I'mma make you run somethin'."

[to] run across [someone's] **mind** phrase (general sl.) old & new school
1. to suddenly think of someone or something. (var. **cross** [someone's] **mind**)
ex: "You ran across my mind earlier."

[to] run game phrase (general sl.) old & new school
1. to lie, deceive, or manipulate someone or a situation for one's own gain. (var. **[to] shoot game at/on** [someone)
ex: "I can tell when you tryin' to run game."

[to] run into a brick wall phrase (southern sl.) new school
1. to make a mistake or bad decision. (var. **[to] bump** [one's] **head**)
ex: "You not going to use me to recover every time you run into a brick wall."

run it/that phrase (criminal sl.) old & new school
1. a term used to command someone to hand over his/her possessions when being robbed or bullied.
ex: "You gonna hafta run that jacket too."

[to] run [one's] **jibs** v. (southern sl.) old & new school
1. the act of talking too much; to divulge too much information. (var. **[to] run** [one's] **mouth/mouth like 95 south**)

ex: "You need to tell that dingy broad to stop runnin' her jibs."

[to] **run** [one's] **number up** v. (person sl.) new school
1. to commit an act while incarcerated that increases one's original prison sentence.
ex: "I almost ran my number up messin' with them catz."

[to] **run off with the mouth** phrase (general sl.) old & new school
1. to say something one isn't supposed to say [usually revealing some sort or information that is supposed to be secretive]. 2. to say something that is offensive or disrespectful.
ex: "That's your problem, you always runnin' off with the mouth." "You keep runnin' off with the mouth."

[to] **run** [someone] **raggity** v. (general sl.) old school
1. to take advantage of someone to the extent it causes that person emotional strain and to behave erratically.
ex: "That young girl runnin' your boy raggity."

[to] **run through** [someone] v. (general sl.) old & new school
1. to totally dominate one's opponent.
ex: "I ran through all them bums."

[to] **run through** [a female's/male's] **crew/click** phrase (sexual sl.) old & new school
1. to have had sex on different occasions with a female/male and one or more of that person's friends.
ex: "Shortie tryin' to run through the whole crew." "We ran through the whole click."

[people who] **run together** phrase (general sl.) old & new school
1. people who spend a great deal of time going places and socializing together. (var. [to] **run with** [someone])
ex: "We been runnin' together for years."

[to] **run up in** [a female] v. (sexual sl.) new school
1. a male term for casual sex with a female.

ex: "I heard you tryin' to run up in my chick." "You gonna run up in the wrong one, one day."

[to] **run up in** [someone's] **spot/crib** phrase (e. coast sl.) old & new school
1. to forcibly enter one's dwelling or place of business with the intent to rob and/or injure him/her.
ex: "They ran up in his momz crib."

[to] **run up on** [someone] v. (general sl.) old & new school
1. to aggressively confront someone [with the possibility of the confrontation escalating into a physical fight].
ex: "He ran up on'em for no reason."

[to] **run** [someone] **up on some bullsh**** v. (general sl.) new school
1. to mislead someone [often causing controversy, trouble or precarious situations].
ex: "This the second time you run me up on some bullsh**."

[to] **run with/by** [oneself] v. (general sl.) old & new school
1. to stay to oneself; to not keep the company of friends.
ex: "I been runnin' by myself for the longest." "I always run by myself."

[to] **run with lames/suckers/herbs** v. (general sl.) old & new school
1. to keep the company of people considered not cool, hip or streetwise.
ex: "You been runnin' with lames since High School."

run ya house phrase (general sl.) new school
1. a way to tell someone, "do it your way", "you're the boss", or "you're in control" [usually used as a term of encouragement].
ex: "I'm not gonna say anything, run ya house."

[a] **runner** n. (drug sl.) old school

1. one who brings customers to a street level drug dealer [often to support one's own drug habit]. See also: [a] **worker**
ex: "Look, I know you I remember when you was just a runner."

[one's] **runnin' partner** n. (general sl.) old & new school
1. one's friend; a friend one spend a great deal of time going places and/or socializing with. (var. [one's] **runnin' buddies**)
ex: "This my new runnin' partner."

[someone who's] **runnin' wild** phrase (general sl.) old & new school
1. one who exhibits reckless, rebellious, and disruptive behavior. See also: [someone who's] **O.C.**
ex: "Yeah, somebody told me shortie runnin' wild now."

[to] **rush** [someone] v. (general sl.) old & new school
1. to overpower or overwhelm someone by surging forward with the momentum of a group or crowd thus neutralizing the effort to block people from moving foward. (var. [to] **rush** [someone's] **spot/crib**)

[a] **rusty nickel** n. (e. coast sl.) new school
1. a female who was extremely good looking when she was younger, but now that she is older her looks are haggard, unkempt, and roughly aged [a female who's the opposite of a dime].
ex: "Only chicks that go there are rusty nickels."

S

[a] **sack** n. (drug sl.) old & new school
1. a small bag of an illegal drug [usually sold in five, ten, or twenty dollar amounts for one's personal use].
ex: "I threw ya sack in the toilet." "All the sacks looked like this."

salt n. (general sl.) old & new school
1. the lie, rumor, or negative innuendo people use to ruin one's reputation, credibility, or friendships with others. (var. [to] **pour/sprinkle/throw salt on** [someone]) See also: [to] **put a black eye in** [someone's] **ball game**)
ex: "I heard all kinds of salt about you." "Shortie tryin' to put salt all over ya name."

salty adj. (general sl.) new school
1. mad; angry; upset; "pissed off". See also: **heated, vex**
ex: "I think he's a lil salty with you right now."

samething make you happy, make you sad phrase (general sl.) old & new school
1. a term used to remind someone not to get too cocky, over excited, or head strung because things can go from good to bad quickly. (var. **samething make you laugh, make you cry**)

[to] **sandbag** [someone] v. (general sl.) old & new school
1. to lie in order to stall, avoid, or give someone the run around.
ex: "I got this feelin' Shortie sandbaggin'."

sandmich n. (general sl.) old & new school
1. sandwich.
ex: "Pick me up a turkey sandmich."

[a] **sap** adj. (general sl.) old school

1. someone not cool or hip. 2. someone easily fooled or made a fool of. (var [a] **sap sucker**) See also:[a] **Herb**
ex: "I don't know that sap."

sap rap adj. (general sl.) old school
1. poor pick up lines, excuses, or explanations. 2. ridiculous things one says in his/her attempt to sound cool or hip.
ex: "Look, save the sap rap." "Spare me the sap rap."

save it for David phrase (general sl.) old school
1. a sarcastic way to dismiss someone's attempt to explain, offer a excuse, or use a pick up line [also used to dismiss someone's tough talk]. (var. **save the sap rap for a handicap cause I can walk** [muhf**ka], **save the drama for your momma/for Wonder Rama**, [you can] **save that sh****, **save the rif for Heathcliff**)

[to] **say** [something] **foul** [to someone] v. (general sl.) old & new school
1. extremely distrespectful, derogatory, or mean spirited. (var. [to] **say** [something] **foul** [about someone])
ex: "I'm not even gonna say who said something foul about you."

[to] **say** [something] **foul out of** [one's] **mouth** v. (general sl.) old & new school
1. extremely disrespectful, derogatory, or mean spirited.
ex: "How you gonna say something foul out ya mouth like that?"

say it, don't spray it phrase (general sl.) old & new school
1. a witty way to inform the person one is talking to that he/she is spitting while he/she is talking [to add emphasis put a hand in front of the face while using term].
ex: "My man, say it, don't spray it."

say what you mean and mean what you say phrase (general sl.) old & new school
1. a term used to encourage someone to make sure he/she is sure about what he/she wants to say before saying it.

say word! interj. (e. coast sl.) new school
1. an enthusiastic way to express doubt, question one's claim, or put one on the spot about his/her truthfulness [used as a way to prod someone to reaffirm himself/herself]. (var. **say word to your mother/to your momma/to everything you love/ to God**) See also: **word up?**
ex: "You seen my girl with who, say word!" "Say word that wasn't you I seen last night."

[someone who's] **scandalous** phrase (e. coast sl.) new school
1. one who purposely creates controversy for others as a result of being jealous and envious. 2. deceitful; untrustworthy.
ex: "Thanks to your sister and her scandalous ass friends, my girl found out."

[to] **scandlize** [someone's] **name** phrase (e. coast sl.) new school
1. to spread rumors, lies, or negative innuendo about someone in an effort to ruin that person's reputation, credibility, or friendships with others. 2. to attribute a misdeed to someone who is innocent of wrongdoing.
ex: "When you on top, there's always gonna be people out there tryin' to scandlize your name."

[a] **scank** n. (general sl.) old school
1. one who is easy to have sex with and/or has numerous sex partners.
ex: "My momz called Shortie a scank to her face."

[a fremale who's] **scanktafied** adj. (southern sl.) new school
1. a way to describe a female who is easy to have sex with and/or has numerous sex partners.
ex: "You need to take ya lil scanktafied self home."

scared money don't get no money phrase (e. coast sl.) old & new school

1. a term used to prod someone into investing his/her money in an attempt to make more money when that person is acting hesitant [usually used while gambling or wagering].

scared? .... say you scared phrase (general sl.) old & new school
1. a way to mock or taunt someone who is displaying a sense of hesitation [usually used when trying to prod someone into doing something]. (var. [if you] **scared.... jump/ get in my pocket,** [if you] **scared.... buy a dog**)

[to] **scare the sh** outta** [someone] v. (general sl) old & new school
1. to scare someone really bad.
ex: "Watch me scare the sh** outta shortie."

[someone who's] **scared to death** phrase (e. coast sl.) new school
1. a way to emphasize someone being extremely scared. (var. [someone who's a] **scared ass**)
ex: "Get your scared to death ass outta here." "She lyin' cause she was scared to death."

[to] **scheme** v. (criminal sl.) old & new school
1. to watch and plot against someone for the purpose of taking something that person possesses; to plan to rob someone. (var. [to] **scheme on** [someone], [to] **scope** [someone] **out**, [to] **plot on** [someone])
ex: "I'm tellin' you, them catz was schemin' on us."

[to] **school** [someone] v. (general sl.) old & new school
1. to give someone knowledge or information that he/she didn't have; to teach or instruct. (var. [to] **school** [someone] **to** [something])
ex: "Let me school you, before you get in trouble around here."

school'em before I fool'em phrase (southern sl.) old school
1. a witty way to instruct someone to teach and/or give someone information that he/she doesn't have to prevent that person from being taken advantage of.

[to] **scoop** [someone] v. (general sl.) new school
1. to meet someone for the first time and acquire his/her phone number for the intention of getting to know that person intimately. (var. [to] **scoop a dime piece/hot one/cutie**)
ex: "I scooped this Shortie on the bus today." "I tried to scoop this dime piece at my momz job."

[to] **scoop** [someone] **up** v. (general sl.) old & new school
1. to meet or pick up someone for the purpose of traveling together. (var. [to] **swing by** [to/and get someone])
ex: "How about I scoop you up about six?" "I'll swing by and get you first."

scramble n. (drug sl.) old school
1. heroin.

[to] **scramble** v. (drug sl.) old & new school
1. a term used to refer to the act of selling illegal narcotics [usually in an open air drug area or on the retail market]. (var. [someone who] **scrambles**)
ex: "They been scramblin' on that block for years."

[a] **scrambler** n. (drug sl.) old & new school
1. one who sells drugs in an open air drug area or on the retail market; a low level drug dealer.

Scrams n. (e. coast sl.) old & new school
1. a name used to refer to someone whose name you do not want to use as a sign of disrespect, disdain, or as a sign his/her unimportance. (var. **Scram Jones**)
ex: "You and Scrams gettin' a lil close."

[to] **scrap** v. (southern sl.) old & new school
1. the act of fighting someone physically.
ex: "They almost got to scrappin' over shortie." "I don't wanna scrap with you dawg."

scratch n. (general sl.) old & new school
1. money.
ex: "Where's the rest of my scratch?"

[to] **scream on** [someone] v. (e. coast sl.) new school
1. to yell, shout, or talk loudly to someone when scolding, reprimanding, belittling, or berating someone. See also: [to] **bark on** [someone]
ex: "Yo, shortie screamed on ya man in front of everybody."

[the] **screw face** adj. (e. coast sl.) old & new school
1. a mean or tough stare or expression. (var. [to] **give** [someone] **the screw face** [look])
ex: "Why I gotta get the screw face?"

[to] **screw up** [one's] **face** phrase (e. coast sl.) new school
1. to frown; to look or stare at someone with a mean facial expression. (var. [to] **screw** [ones] **face up**)
ex: "You can screw up your face all day long, and the answer is still gonna be no."

[a] **scrub** adj. (southern sl.) new school
1. one who needs to use the influence, power, and/or financial success of others to get attention or respect.
ex: "Sometimes you can't tell the difference between a scrub and a baller 'til its too late."

[to] **scuffle** [with someone] v. (general sl.) old & new school
1. to fight or struggle in close quarters.
ex: "I seen you out there scufflin' with them broads."

scurred adj. (southern sl.) new school
1. a witty way to pronounce the word "scared".
ex: "Don't be scurred." "You look like you scurred to me."

[to] **see** [someone] v. (e. coast sl.) new school
1. to confront someone [with the possibility of the confrontation escalating into a physical fight]. 2. the act of competing against another; to take someone up on his/her challenge.
ex: "Tell ya cousin if he tryin' to see me, he know where I'm at." "You not ready to see me."

[if you] **see a pack of wild pit bulls lookin' for me, point them in my direction/give them my address** phrase (southern sl.) new school
1. a term used to declare one's toughness or being unafraid when someone call his/her toughness or bravery into question [also used as a response to a verbal threat or challenge]. (var. [if you] **see me an' a bear about to fight ... pour honey on me**, [if you] **see me an'a lion about to fight .... tie a pork chop around my neck**)

[if you] **see me an'a bear fightin'...help the bear** phrase (southern sl.) new school
1. a witty way to inform someone you don't want or need his/her help [often used sarcastically when turning down someone's help]. (var. **help the bear**)

see with ya eyes not with ya hands phrase (general sl.) old & new school
1. a witty way to tell someone "don't touch" [usually used as a warning].

see you and I wouldn't wanna be you phrase (general sl.) old school
1. a playful or sarcastic way to inform someone that he/she is on his/her own [often used when declining or dismissing one's request for help].

see you when I see you phrase (general sl.) old & new school
1. an unenthusiastic way to say "good bye" when seeing someone again isn't important.

[a male's] **seed** n. (e. coast sl.) old & new school
l. his child; children.
ex: "How many seeds do you have?"

[to] **sell** [someone] **a dream** phrase (general sl.) old & new school
l. to paint a false picture for someone for the purpose of conning or
taking advantage of him/her; to lie convincingly.
ex: "I knew you was sellin' my girl a dream."

[to] **sell** [someone] **death** phrase (e. coast sl.) new school
1. the act of talking tough and sounding threatening as a scare
tactic to intimidate. 2. to threaten someone with great bodily injury
without the intentions of following through with said threat. (var.
[to] **sell death to** [someone])
ex: "Every time you come in here, you sellin' death."

[to] **sell out** phrase (general sl.) old & new school
1. to compromise one's position, morals, character, or friendship
for financial or material gain, a better position, or for self
gratification. (var. [someone who's a] **sell out**)
*ex: "People sell out everyday." "When you sell out you hafta live
with that."*

[a] **semi** n. (criminal sl.) new school
1. a covert way to refer to any semi-automatic handgun.
(var. [a] **semi-auto**)
ex: "I hid the semi in the bushes."

[to] **semi-f**k with** [someone] phrase (e. coast sl.) new school
l. to have a less than cordial or mediocre relationship or friendship
with someone. 2. to deal with someone infrequently. (var. [to]
semi-mess with [someone])
*ex: "I only used to semi-f'**k with duke so I wouldn't know all
that."*

[to] send [someone] **a smoke signal** phrase (southern sl.) new school
1. to contact someone via mail, phone, two way pager, or e-mail. See also: [to] **hit** [someone] **on the hip**
ex: "I'll send you a smoke signal when I find out."

[to] serve [someone] v. (general sl.) old school
1. to beat someone miserably. 2. to out perform one's opponent overwhelmingly. (var. [to] **get served**)
ex: "She served shortie in the last set."

[to] serve [someone] v. (drug sl.) old school
1. to do a hand-to-hand drug transaction on the retail level [usually in an open air drug area].
ex: "Hold up while I go serve these people."

[one's] set n. (w. coast sl.) old & new school
1. the neighborhood and/or gang one claims to represent or belong to. (var. [to] **claim** [one's] **set**)
ex: "We not from the same set."

[someone who's] set adj. (general sl.) old & new school
1. rich; wealthy; financially secured. (var. [someone who's] **set for life**)
ex: "He's set now that he won that lawsuit."

[to] set it v. (e. coast sl.) old school
1. the act of starting a physical confrontation or violent disturbance. 2. a term used to incite others into displaying disruptive or violent behavior. (var. [to] **set it on** [someone], **set it off**)
ex: "We about to set it in here."

[to] set it off on [someone] **ass** phrase (e. coast sl.) old & new school
1. to beat someone up miserably [often used to threaten someone with a beating]. (var. [to] **set it off on** [someone's] **punk/lame/bit** ass**)
ex: "Don't you know I will set if off on ya ass in here?"

[to] **set it on** [someone] v. (e. coast sl.) old school
1. to attack someone [usually after a heated or ongoing argument]
ex: *"They was about to set it on ya man for a minute."*

[to] **set it out** [for someone] phrase (e. coast sl.) new school
1. the act of displaying one's hospitality in a very grand way; to extend one's generosity to one's guest.
ex: *"You had to see they way they set it our for us when we got there."*

[a] **set skinny** n. (w. coast sl.) old school
1. a neighborhood female who hangs around the neighborhood male gang.

[to] **set trip** v. (w. coast sl.) old & new school
1. to dislike and/or to start a problem with someone because he/she is from a different neighborhood or gang than you. 2. to show preferential treatment to someone because he/she is from the same neighborhood or gang as you. (var. [to] **set trip on** [someone])
ex: *"I know these fool not about to set trip."*

[a female who's] **settin' it out** phrase (prison sl.) new school
1. a female who is slyly giving intentional views of the private areas of her body. (var. [to] **set it out**)
ex: *"Did you see the way Trina was settin' it out in her last video?"*

[to] **sew** [something] **up** v. (general sl.) old & new school
1. to secure something; to put something under one's control or influence. (var. [to] **have** [something] **sewed up**, [to] **have** [someone] **sewed**)
ex: *"I'm about to sew this thing up." "I got that sewed up dawg."*

[someone who's] **sex** adj. (e. coast sl.) old & new school
1. cowardly. 2. afraid; scared. (var. [someone who's] **p**sy / pus**)
ex: *"When it came down to it, ya boy turned sex."*

[to] **sex** [someone] v. (sexual sl.) old & new school
1. the act of having sex. See also: [to] **knock** [a females's] **boots**
ex: *"They been in here sexin' for hours."*

sexcellent adj. (sexual sl.) new school
1. a way to describe outstanding sex. (var. **sextraordinary**)
ex: *"Last night you was sexcellent."*

shabby adj. (general sl.) old school
1. of poor quality. 2. dirty; messy.
ex: *"He came in that old shabby suit he always wears."*

[to] **shack up** [with someone] phrase (general sl.) old school
1. to live with someone without being married to him/her.
ex: *"We just shackin' up for the time being." "He shackin' up with my baby mother."*

[someone who's] **shady** adj. (general sl.) old & new school
1. untrustworthy, sneaky, or deceitful. See also: [someone who's]
cruddy
ex: *"Them Brooklyn broads too shady for me, and I'm from Brooklyn."*

[to] **shake** [someone] v. (general sl.) old & new school
1. to covertly escape from or get rid of someone.
ex: *"I tried to shake these broads all night."*

shake n. (drug sl.) old & new school
1. the crumbs left over after chopping up big pieces of crack cocaine for retail sale.

[a] **shake bag** n. (drug sl.) old & new school
1. the crumbs left over from chopping up big pieces of crack cocaine packaged for retail sale.
ex: *"All I got is shake bags left."*

[a] **shakedown** v. (prison sl.) old & new school
1. a thorough search of one's person, property, or living area.
ex: "They been in here shakin'down, I can tell."

shake them haters phrase (general sl.) new school
1. a term used to encourage someone to be vigilant when others
around him/her exhibits signs of jealousy and envy. (var. [to]
shake the haters)

shake ya money maker phrase (southern sl.) old & new school
1. a playful and fun way to encourage or cheer someone on while
he/she is dancing socially or as an exotic dancer. (var. **shake what
ya momma gave ya**)

shakers n. (southern sl.) new school
1. a female/male exotic dancer; a stripper. (var. **dancer**)

[someone who's] **shakin' like a pair of Las Vegas crap dice**
phrase (w. coast sl.) new school
1. a witty way to emphasize someone's fear; to be extremely
scared. (var. [someone who's] **shakin' like dice/ like a California
earthquake**)
*ex: "When I looked, shortie was shakin' like a pair of Las Vegas
crap dice."*

shams n. (e. coast sl.) new school
1. a name used to refer to a "secret lover" [usually used by
females].
ex: "I'm hangin' out with my shams tonight."

[a] **shank** n. (prison sl.) old & new school
1. a homemade knife or sharpened weapon. See also: [a] **blicky**
ex: "They in there lookin' for shanks."

[to] **shank** [someone] v. (prison sl.) old & new school
1. to stab someone with a homemade knife or sharpened weapon.
ex: "They found'em shanked in his cell."

Shaq diesel adj. (e. coast sl.) new school
1. to have strength; strong. 2. the abilibilty to out muscle one's
opponent. (var. [to] **get Shaq diesel on** [someone])
*ex: "That's one of them Shaq diesel moves." "Lets go in here and
get Shaq diesel on these catz."*

sharks adj. (e. coast sl.) new school
1. young street toughs; thugs. See also: **wolves, gorillas**
*ex: "I try my best to stay away from the sharks at my school and
around my way."*

[someone who's] **sharp** adj. (general sl.) old & new school
1. intelligent; street smart. 2. not naive.
ex: "Don't sleep on shortie, she's sharp."

[a] **sheep dog** n. (e. coast sl.) old school
1. a sheep skin or shearling coat.
ex: "My first sheep dog was tan."

shell adj. (southern sl.) new school
1. disruptive; loud and unruly. 2. extremely funny. 3. to cause an
unpleasant scene.
ex: "Ya boy went shell in here." "Your uncle is shell."

shell toes n. (e. coast sl.) old school
1. an old style of Adida sneakers.

sherm n. (drug sl.) old & new school
1. embalming fluid.

she's disobedient with the wrong ingredient phrase (e. coast sl.)
new school
1. a playful or sarcastic way to point out a female's bad attitude,
unpleasant disposition, or evil mannerism.

[someone who's] **shifty** adj. (general sl.) new school
1. sneaky; deceitful; untrustworthy. 2. one who is without loyalties.
(var. [someone who's] **shifty low down gritty and grimy**)

ex: "Them some shifty ass catz you hang with."

shine n. (e. coast sl.) new school
1. gold jewelry.
ex: "You can't wear your shine to school no more."

[to] **shine** v. (general sl.) new school
1. to perform outstandingly; to out perform one's opponent. 2. to receive a great deal of attention and/or praise. (var. [to] **shine on** [someone])
ex: "You definitely shined out there." "It's your time to shine dawg."

[to] **shine on** [someone] v. (e. coast sl.) new school
1. to display an arrogance or cockiness in an to attempt to show off or overshadow someone. 2. to upstage someone.
ex: "Let me tell how ya cousin tried to shine on me in front of my manz an'nim."

shines n. (e. coast sl.) new school
1. gold caps for one's teeth. See also: **fronts**
ex: "I'm thinkin' about gettin' 2 more shines."

[one's] **sh**** n. (general sl.) old & new school
1. a way to refer to one's property or possessions. (var. [one's] **stuff**)
ex: "Learn how to leave people's sh** alone." "That's my sh**." "Take your sh** and go."

[to] **sh** a brick** phrase (general sl.) old & new school
1. a way to decribe being extremely scared. 2. a term used to compare fright to a bowel movement. (var. [someone who] **sh**ted a brick**) See also: **bimmie**
ex: "I was about to sh** a brick when I heard her car pull up."

sh** ain t no joke phrase (general sl.) old & new school
1. a term used to emphasize the seriousness and/or importance of a situation or statement.

ex: "I keep tellin' y'all sh** ain't no joke."

[to] **sh** down** [someone's] **back** phrase (e. coast sl.) new school
1. to out perform someone; to display superior skill or talent than one's opponent [often used to critique one's performance or as a boast used to taunt one's opponent]. (var. [to] **sh** on** [someone], [to] **sh** all over** [someone])
ex: "I sh** down ya man's back in the third quarter." "How'd you let him, of all people, sh** down your back like that?"

[a] **sh** jack** n. (prison sl.) new school
1. a toilet bowl. (var. [a] **shitter**)

[one's] **sh** list** n. (e. coast sl.) new school
1. one's mental list of the people he/she is upset with and/or has wronged him/her. (var. [to be] **on** [one's] **sh** list**)
ex: "You on my sh** list now." "I can't ask'er cause I know I'm on her sh** list."

[to] **sh** on** [someone] v. (e. coast sl.) new school
1. to treat someone unpleasantly or mean. 2. to go back on a promise; to disappoint someone.
ex: "I know why shortie sh**tin' on me like that." "I would never sh** on you that's my word."

sh** on a shingle n. (prison sl.) new school
1. a grotesque meal consisting of an unidentifiable meat gravy poured over biscuits [usually served every Thursday throughout the Federal Prison system].
ex: "If it's sh** on a shingle I'm not goin."

sh** or get off the pot phrase (southersn sl.) new school
1. a term used to prod someone into making a decision when that person is acting hesitant [usually used to put someone on the spot].
ex: "It's your turn, sh** or get off the pot player."

shiznit n. (e. coast sl.) new school
1. a covert way to say sh**.
ex: "What kinda shiznit was that?"

Shoalin n. (e. coast sl.) new school
1. Staten Island, N.Y.
ex: "Wu-Tang put Shoalin on the map."

shoes n. (southern sl.) new school
1. new and/or expensive rims for an automobile's tires.
ex: "What kinda shoes you thinkin' about puttin' on ya whip."

[someone who's] **shook** adj. (e. coast sl.) new school
1. scared; afraid. (var. [to] **have** [someone] **shook**) See also: **noid**
ex: "You should have seen his face, dawg was shook."

shook ones n. (e. coast sl.) new school
1. people who are scared and /or act cowardly.
ex: "Shook ones don't hang out in here."

[to] **shoot** [someone something] v. (general sl.) old & new school
1. to give or send someone something.
ex: "I still you need you to shoot me that." "I was hopin' you could shoot me somethin'."

[to] **shoot** [someone] **a curve** v. (general sl.) new school
1. to lie to or mislead someone; to be deceiving. (var. [to] **shoot** [someone] **some bullsh****)
ex: "I can't believe I let shortie shoot me a curve."

[to] **shoot** [someone] **a fair one** v. (general sl.) old & new school
1. to have a fair fist fight with someone.
ex: "Ask'em if he wants to shoot a fair one."

[to] **shoot** [someone] **a foul/dirty look** v. (general sl.) old & new school
1. to give someone a mean look or glare.
ex: "He'e not the only one shootin' dirty looks at us in here, look."

[to] shoot [someone] **a kite** v. (prison sl.) old & new school
1. to write and send someone a letter or short message to or from prison.
ex: "I need to shoot my manz a kite."

[to] shoot at the drawers v. (sexual sl.) new school
1. a male term describing the act of trying to get a female to have sex through cool conversation, sweet talk, flattery, and manipulative suggestions. (var. **[to] shoot at** [a female's] **drawers**)
ex: "I wound up shootin' at the drawers all night and still nothin'."

[to] shoot by [someone's] **house/crib/cribo** v. (general sl.) old & new school
1. to travel to one's dwellings [usually for a brief time period].
ex: "We gonna shoot by ya house and then go pick them up."

[to] shoot G at [a female] v. (general sl.) new school
1. to use cool or hip talk to impress or grab a female's attention in hopes of getting to know her better. (var. **[to] spit/shoot game at** [a female])
ex: "Let's go over there and shoot some G at them chicks."

[to] shoot joints v. (general sl.) old school
1. to fist fight; to box. (var. **[to] throw joints**)
ex: "Back in the days you got your respect if you knew how to shoot joints."

[to] shoot the breeze [with someone] v. (general sl.) old school
1. to casually converse.
ex: "We was just there shootin' the breeze."

[to] shoot the gift phrase (general sl.) old & new school
1. to use one's verbal charm in an attempt to meet or get to know someone of the opposite sex more intimately.
ex: "Yo go over there and shoot the gift to them cuties."

[someone who's] **shootin' bad** phrase (general sl.) old & new school
1. without money; destitute. See also: [someone who's] **doin' dirt ball bad**
ex: "I know what you mean, I'm shootin' bad myself."

[a male who's] **shootin' blanks** phrase (sexual sl.) old & new school
1. a term used jokingly in reference to a male who is sexually active but doesn't have any children.
ex: "I rather be shootin' blanks then having kids at a young age."

[someone who's] **short** phrase (prison sl.) old & new school
1. one who doesn't have very long left on his/her original prison sentence. (var.[someone who's] **shorter than a mosquita peter**)
ex: "I'm too short for that nonsense."

[someone with] **short arms and long pockets** phrase (e. coast sl.) new school
1. a witty way to mock someone for pretending to be wealthy yet you know he/she is not.
ex: "Who you talkin' about, ya man over there with the short arms and long pockets?"

short con phrase (general sl.) old school
1. a plan, story, or deception used to con or take advantage of someone immediately.
ex: "I'm about to use the short con on Shortie."

short eyes n. (sexual sl.) old & new school
1. pornographic material [a magazine or video].
ex: "All short eyes are banned from Federal prison."

[a males] **shortie** (pron. Shawtie) n. (e. coast sl.) new school
1. one's girlfriend; intimate female friend.
ex: "Meet my new shortie." "You wanna be my shortie?"

[a] shortie n. (e. coast sl.) new school
1. a female.
ex: "Yo, check out shortie over there." "Shortie clockin' you."

shortie n. (e. coast sl.) new school
1. a term of endearment among friends; friend. 2. a name used to address someone whose name you do not know or do not want to use as a sign of discontent.
ex: "I got you shortie." "Na, you keep that shortie."

[one's] shortie n. (general sl.) old & new school
1. one's child.
ex: "I'm expecting a lil shortie in November."

shortie do-right n. (e. coast sl.) old & new school
1. a nickname for a female who is cool, hip, and popular with her male peers.
ex: "I'm hangin' with shortie do-right and her peoples tonight."

shortie boom boom n. (e. coast sl.) old school
1. a name used to refer to a female who has a big butt or a butt worthy of praise.
ex: "I seen you over there with shortie boom boom."

shortie forty n. (southern sl.) new school
1. a name used to refer a female who is overweight or who consumes alcohol excessively. (var. **shortie one forty, shortie McForty**)
ex: "I think shortie forty losing a lil weight."

shortie rock n. (e. coast sl.) new school
1. a name used to refer to a female who is hip and cool. (var. **shortie do-wop, shortie love**)
ex: "What's poppin' shortie rock?"

shortie sh** stain phrase (general sl.) old & new school
1. a nickname for a female who has poor hygiene habits or

exhibits sloppiness and untidiness.
ex: "Tell me I ain't see you with shortie sh** stain last night."

[a] **shot** n. (general sl.) old school
1. a female
ex: "I met this bad lil shot earlier."

[a] **shot of life** phrase (sexual sl) old & new school
1. a covert term males use to refer to a "orgasm".
ex: "Last time you had a shot of life?"

[a] **shotty** n. (criminal sl.) old & new school
l. a shotgun. (var. [a] **sawed off**)
ex: "Grandpa gave me a shotty for my birthday."

shoulda woulda coulda phrase (general sl.) old school
1. a way to mock someone who uses "I should of", "I would of", or "I could of" as an after thought when acknowledging a mistake or bad decision. (var. **woulda coulda shoulda**)
ex: "Shoulda woulda coulda but you didn't now its too late."

[to] **shout** [someone] **out** v. (general sl.) old & new school
l. to give someone a verbal acknowledgment. (var. [a] **shout out**)
ex: "I wanna shout my peoples out in Allenwood."

show and prove phrase (e. coast sl.) old school
l. a term used to put someone on the spot to prove himself/herself.
ex: "If you think you can, show and prove."

[to] **show boat** [on someone] v. (general sl.) old school
1. to show off in an attempt to bring attention to oneself.
ex: "Here he goes show boatin' again." "I didn't come here to show boat."

[to] **show** [someone] **love** v. (e. coast sl.) new school
l. to extend one's generosity.
ex: "When I was locked up, Heavy showed me madd love."

show me the dummy, not the money phrase (southern sl.) new school
1. a witty way to ask someone to introduce you to someone whom he/she thinks will fall for a ridiculous scheme or someone who is easy to take advantage of, or manipulate

[to] **show out** v. (general sl.) old & new school
1. to cause an unpleasant and/or embarrassing scene by acting disruptive, unruly, or zany. (var. [to] **show** [one's] **ass**)
ex: "Guess who was the one to show out last night?" "She showed her ass from the time we got there 'til the time we left."

[to] **shut** [someone] **down** v. (general sl.) new school
1. to prevent or not allow a particular action. 2. to put a stop to someone.
ex: "Ya momz gonna shut you down once she sees your report card."

[to] **shut sh** down** phrase (general sl.) old & new school
1. to put a immediate stop to an action [either temporarily or permanently].
ex: "Every time they come through they shut sh** down." "I remember when Ewing used to shut sh** down at the Garden."

shut up! interj. (general sl.) old & new school
1. an enthusiastic way to express shock or disbelief when one is told something that he/she finds hard to believe.

[someone who's] **shystee** adj. (e. coast sl.) new school
1. unscrupulous; untrustworthy.
ex: "You hafta watch them Brooklyn catz, they madd shystee."

siced adj. (e. coast sl.) new school
1. excited. 2. cocky; overly confident.
ex: "What you gettin' all siced for?"

[to be] **sick** [about/over something] adj. (e. coast sl.) new school
1. extremely disappointed or let down. 2. mad; upset.
ex: "I was sick when I read the letter." "I was sick about that sh**."

[something that's] **sick** adj. (e. coast sl.) new school
1. outstanding; unique; the best of its kind.
ex: "Dawg's new ablum is sick dawg."

[one who's] **sick** [with his/her performance/ability/skill] adj. (e. coast sl.) new school
1. one who performs outstandingly; to have a unique style of doing things. 2. the best at what one does.
ex: "Ya man sick with the rhymes dawg." "Ya man was sick on the court last night."

sick as a dog adj. (general sl.) old & new school
1. to feel extremely ill; a term used to emphasize how sick someone feels.
ex: "I woke up this mornin' and was sick as a dog."

[the] **sick d**k** adj. (sexual sl.) new school
1. a male with a sexual transmitted disease.
ex: "I think I caught the sick d**k down in Myrtle Beach bike week."

sick to [one's] **stomach** adj. (general sl.) old & new school
1. extremely sick. 2. extremely distressed.
ex: "I left outta there sick to my stomach." "If you woulda seen her, you woulda been sick to ya stomach."

[one's] **side hustle** phrase (e. coast sl.) new school
1. something one does to supplement his/her main source of income. (var. [a] **side hustle**)
ex: "I only do this as a side hustle." "I found a new side hustle."

[one's] **side joint** phrase (e. coast sl.) new school
1. a male's mistress or a female's secret lover.

ex: "I think my pops got a side joint somewhere." "She found her a side joint."

[a] **sideline baller** n. (e. coast sl.) new school
1. a male who lacks the financial means to spend large amounts of money freely and is jealous, envious, and critical of those who can [often pretending to be someone who can spend money freely].
(var. [a male] **ballin' from the sidelines**)
ex: "Man I don't pay attention to none of these sideline ballers."

[the] **silent killer** n. (sexual sl.) new school
1. H.I.V. the virus that causes A.I.D.s.
ex: "Come to find out, duke had that silent killer."

silent killers n. (e. coast sl.) new school
1. people who are infected with HIV or AIDS and knowingly have unprotected sex without informing their partner of their HIV or AIDS status.
ex: "That's the thing, you can't tell who the silent killers are these days."

silly rabbit phrase (general sl.) old school
1. a witty way to tease someone whose plot or plan to deceive you has been foiled or discovered.
ex: "You blew your only chance, silly rabbit."

[someone who's] **simple minded** adj. (general sl.) old school
1. one who demonstrates a limited thinking capacity; not too intelligent. See also: [a female who's] **dingy**
ex: "How simple minded can you be?"

[a vehicle that's] **sittin' on chrome** phrase (w. coast sl.) old & new school
1. a vehicle that has expensive chrome rims on its tires and/or has been accessorized in chrome.

[a vehicle that's] **sittin' on dubs** phrase (w. coast sl.) old & new school

1. a vehicle that is equipped with 20", 22", or 24" rims for its tires. (var. [a vehicle that's] **sittin' on them things**)

[someone who's] **sittin' on firm** phrase (general sl.) new school
1. one who earns or has access to large amounts of money; wealthy.
ex: "This move here should have me sittin' on firm."

sizzurp n. (drug sl.) new school
1. cough syrup and alcohol mixed together. (var. **syrup**)
ex: "Dudes down south like to drink that sizzurp."

skee'd up phrase (drug sl.) old & new school
1. to be high from powder cocaine. 2. the act of sniffing powder cocaine. (var. **skee'd**)
ex: "He can't tell me they weren't in there gettin' skee'd up." "She looked skee'd to me."

[to] **skeet** v. (sexual sl.) old & new school
1. a term males use to refer to "ejaculation". See also: [to] **bust a nut**
ex: "I skeeted all over the front seat."

[to] **skeez** [someone] v. (sexual sl.) old & new school
1. to have meaningless sex or a one night stand with someone knowingly.
ex: "All he tryin' to do is skeez you." "He's lookin' to get skeezed tonight."

[a] **skeezer** n. (sexual sl.) old school
1. one who knowingly engages in meaningless sex and one night stands [usually refers to females].
ex: "And take ya lil skeezer friend with you."

[a] **skid bid** n. (prison sl.) old & new school
1. a jail sentence of no more than 12 months.
ex: "The judge ain't givin' out them skid bids like she used to."

skid marks n. (general sl.) old & new school
1. doo-doo stains in one's underwear.
ex: "Would you believe this grown ass man has skid marks in his draws."

skins n. (sexual sl.) old & new school
1. a covert word males use to say "vagina" or sex.
ex: "How was the skins?" "The skins was all that." "Did you get them skins yet?"

[a female whose] **skins are phat** adj. (sexual sl.) old & new school
1. a term males use to describe the goodness of a female's vagina.
(var. [a female whose] **skins are/was all that/like that**)
ex: "I heard the skins are phat."

skinnin' and grinnin' phrase (southern sl.) new school
1. to grin or smile slyly; a elated smile.
ex: "I knew she was up too no good, with all that skinnin' and grinnin'."

skull n. (sexual sl.) new school
1. oral sex. See also: **brains**

[to] **skunk** [someone] v. (general sl.) new school
1. to keep one's opponent scoreless during the entire game which you have beaten him/her in. (var. [a] **skunk**)
ex: "I skunked ya man three times." "I'm about to skunk you with this shot here."

skunk n (drug sl.) new school
1. a type of marijuana.

slabs n. (drug sl.) old school
1. pieces of crack cocaine that retail for $50 and $100 dollar amounts.

[to] **slam** [someone] v. (general sl.) old & new school
1. to physically pick someone up off the ground and throw him/her to the ground or against something using maximum strength.
ex: "The ol' head slammed the youngster for dissin' him."

[something that's] **slammin'** adj. (general sl.) old & new school
1. outstanding; unique; the best of its kind.
ex: "A lot of the Phat Farm is slammin'."

[to] **slay** [a female] v. (sexual sl.) new school
1. a term males use for having sex.
ex: "I been tryin' to slay shortie for years."

[to] **sleep on** [someone] v. (general sl.) old & new school
1. to underestimate; take for granted. (var. [to] **sleep on** [something], [to] **sleep**)
ex: "Don't sleep on Shortie, she's not slow at all." "Them catz be sleepin' on me."

sleepy head n. (general sl.) old & new school
1. a name used to address someone who has just awakened or looks sleepy.
ex: "Wake up sleepy head." "Time for bed sleepy head."

Slice n. (general sl.) old school
1. a term of endearment among friends; friend. (var. **Home Slice**)
ex: "Whassup Slice." "Ask Slice is he goin' or not."

[somewho has a] **slick mouth** adj. (general sl.) old & new school
1. sarcastic; obnoxious; disrespectful; rude.
ex: "She can come, but I'm not tryin' to hear her slick mouth tonight."

[to] **slide** v. (general sl.) old & new school
1. to leave; depart from. (var. [to] **slide off**)
ex: "We about to slide dawg." "I think you need to slide off."

[to] **slide up in** [a female] v. (sexual sl.) new school
1. a covert way males refer to having sex.
ex: "I wanted to slide up in shortie bad as a muhf**ka."

Slim n. (general sl.) old & new school
1. a term of endearment among friends; friend. 2. a way to address someone whose name you do not know or do not want to use in front of others.
ex: "Yo, Slim just came out ya crib Dun."

[a] **slimmy** n. (general sl.) old school
1. a female. 2. a name used to address a female whose name you do not know. (var. [a] **slim goodie**)

[to] **sling** [something] v. (general sl.) new school
1. the act of selling something [usually used in reference to drugs]. (var. [to] **sling them things/rocks**)
ex: "You gonna get caught slingin' them drugs one day." "Help me sling the rest of these tapes."

[to] **sling** [someone's] **back out** phrase (sexual sl.) new school
1. to perform outstandingly during sex [usually used as a boast among males].
ex: "Ask your girlfriend how I slung her back out."

[to] **sling them thangs** phrase (criminal sl.) new school
1. to carry a firearm. (var. [to] **tote them thangs**)
ex: "They threatened to come back slingin' them thangs."

[to] **slip** v. (general sl.) old & new school
1. to make a mistake or bad decision due to one's carelessness and/or lack of paying attention. 2. to lose stature. 3. the declining of one's performance and/or talents. (var. [to] **catch** [someone] **slippin'**) See also: [to] **fall off**
ex: "I think you slippin' Son." "People startin' to say you slippin' dawg."

[I'll] **slip, dip, and bust your lip** phrase (general sl.) old school
1. a playful and witty way to threaten someone with beating him/her up.

[to] **slob** [someone] v. (general sl.) old & new school
1. to insert one's tongue in another's mouth while kissing; to French kiss. (var. [to] **slob** [someone] **down**) See also: [to] **bust slob**
ex: "I bet you didn't even slob her yet." "I was slobbin' her down on the stair case."

[to] **slob a/the knob** phrase (sexual sl.) old & new school
1. the act of performing oral sex on a male.
ex: "She said straight up, I don't slob the knob."

slot time phrase (prison sl.) old & new school
1. the allotted time certain prisoners have secured for themselves through fear and intimidation for their exclusive use of the telephone [usually a half hour or hour when other prisoners receive 5 minutes].
ex: "The only way you get slot time is if you take it or buy if from someone."

slow down low down phrase (general sl.) old school
1. a way to tell someone to, "slow down", "take it easy", or "calm down". (var. **slow ya roll**)

slow money sho' money phrase (southern sl.) old & new school
1. a term used to advise someone that earning one's money legally is better than taking the chance of making fast money illegally and the risks illegal money involves.

slow motion phrase (general sl.) new school
1. a term used to respond to someone inquiry about one's well being [signifies that one is "alright", "okay", or, "takin' it easy"]. (var. **slow mo**)
ex: "I'm all right, slow motion you know."

slow neck n. (sexual sl.) new school
1. a covert term males use to refer to "oral sex" from a female.

[to] **slow roll** [someone] v. (general sl.) old & new school
1. to take one's time with someone [usually when one is trying to take advantage of or con him/her out of something]. (var. [to] **slow roll** [something])
ex: "You need to learn how to slow roll these catz." "We not in no hurry, we gonna slow roll money."

[someone who's a] **slug** adj. (e. coast sl.) new school
1. unscrupulous; untrustworthy; petty; deceptive. (var. [to do] **slug sh****)
ex: "I found out the hard way Slim was a real slug." "You can't come around me doin' that slug sh**."

slugs n. (southern sl.) new school
1. gold teeth.

slugs n. (criminal sl.) old & new school
1. bullets.
ex: "He got hit with about three slugs."

[to] **slug** [someone] **up** v. (criminal sl.) new school
1. to shoot someone; to be shot.
ex: "Police tried to slug my man up for nothin'."

slugged up phrase (southern sl.) new school
1. diamond encrusted gold teeth.
ex: "I seen dawg in the mall, dude whole mouth is slugged up."

slum adj. (e. coast sl.) old & new school
1. fake jewelry or imitation clothing trying to be passed off as being real or authentic; anything forged.
ex: "Tryin' to be slick he bought slum." "That's that slum sh**."

[someone who's] **slum** adj. (e. coast sl.) new school
1. petty; low down; untrustworthy, unscrupulous and holds an overrated opinion of his/her character, status, or worth. See also: [someone who's] **some sh****
ex: *"You was slum in H.S. and you slum now."*

[to] **slum** [someone] v. (e. coast sl.) old & new school
1. to sell someone something that you know is fake or imitation under the guise that he/she is receiving something real or authentic.
ex: *"The easiest people to slum is tourists."*

[to] **slum** [someone] v. (e. coast sl.) new school
1. to use trickery and deception in an attempt to con someone into thinking you are being honest and trustworthy.
ex: *"I told you he was gonna slum you." "Look how ya ann tried to slum me."*

slum ass [person's name/title] phrase (e. coast sl.) new school
1. a term affixed to the name or title of someone when describing that person as being someone unscrupulous, untrustworthy, or petty. (var. [a] **slum ass** [person])
ex: *"I can't believe she came with the slum ass supervisor."*

[to do/pull/try some] **slum sh**** phrase (e. coast sl.) new school
1. the act of doing something that's unscrupulous, deceitful, or petty.
ex: *"That's was some real slum sh** you did."*

[to] **slump** [someone] v. (criminal sl.) new school
1. a term used to describe the act of murder. (var. [to] **slump and dump** [someone])
ex: *"Homes got slumped in 2000."*

[to] **smack** [someone] **silly** v. (e. coast sl.) new school
1. to smack someone as hard as one can [sometimes repeatedly].
ex: *"Don't you know I will smack you silly?" "Don't make me smack you silly."*

[to] **smack the blood out** [someone] phrase (general sl.) old & new school
1. to smack someone as hard as one possibly can. (var. [to] **smack the blood/taste outta** [someone's] **mouth,** [to] **slap fire from** [someone's] **mouth,** [to] **slap the sh***/ the natural sh***/livin' sh*** outta** [someone])
ex: "His momz smacked the blood out'is ass."

[something that's a] **small thing** phrase (general sl) old & new school
1. insignificant; trivial; not worth getting upset about.
ex: "That's a small thing dawg."

small thing to a giant phrase (general sl.) new school
1. a term used to declare something is insignificant, trivial, or not worth getting upset about [usually used to dismiss one's attempt to upset you].

[to] **smash** [a female] v. (sexual sl.) new school
1. the act of having sex.
ex: "How long did it take you to smash Shortie?"

[to] **smash** [someone] v. (e. coast sl.) new school
1. to give someone something [usually refers to giving someone drugs to sell]. (var. [to] **smash** [someone] **off**)
ex: "I'll be over there after I go smash my manz."

[to] **smash** [a male] **off** v. (sexual sl.) new school
1. a term males use to refer to receiving oral sex from a female.
ex: "I tried to get shortie to smash me off, but she wasn't haven't it."

[to] **smash** [someone] **out** v. (general sl.) new school
1. to beat someone up badly. (var. [to] **mash** [someone] **out**) See also: [to] **punish** [someone]
ex: "He came this close to gettin' smashed out."

smashed adj. (general sl.) old & new school
1. drunk; intoxicated.

smell good n. (general sl.) new school
1. cologne or perfume.
ex: "Can I use some of ya smell good?" "Check-out this smell good shortie copped for me."

smell me phrase (w. coast sl.) new school
1. a term used to say, "feel me", "listen to this", "give me a moment and hear me out", "try to understand/relate to me/this". (var. [you] **smell me?**)
ex: "Smell me on this homie." "Smell me for a minute."

smoke n. (drug sl.) old school
1. marijuana.

[to] **smoke** [someone] v. (general sl.) old & new school
1. to out run someone. (var. [to] **smoke the sh** outta** [someone])
See also: [to] **leave** [someone] **in the dust/wind**
ex: "He had boots on and he still smoked ya homeboy."

[to] **smoke** [someone] v. (criminal sl.) old & new school
1. a covert way to refer to homicide or murder [usually resulting from gunfire].
ex: "I heard you almost got smoked son."

[to] **smoke up** [one's] **money** v. (drug sl.) old & new school
1. to spend all one's money buying crack cocaine during a binge. (var. [to] **smoke up all** [one's] **money**)
ex: "I can't believe she smoked up all the rent money."

[someone who's] **smoked out** adj. (drug sl.) old & new school
1. one who is heavily addicted to smoking crack cocaine. (var. [someone who's] **smoked** [the f**k] **out**)
ex: "Somebody said she was smoked out."

[a] **smoker** n. (drug sl.) old school
1. one who smokes and is addicted to crack cocaine. (var. [a]
smoker loker [loker])
ex: "If she with them smokers, you not tellin' me she's not a smoker too."

[someone who's] **smokin'** phrase (drug sl.) old & new school
1. one who smokes crack cocaine.
ex: "Guess who's smokin' now?" "Since when you started smokin'?"

[something that's] **smokin'** adj. (general sl.) old school
1. outstanding; unique; the best of its kind. See also: [something that's] **on fire**
ex: "Them joints was smokin' back in the day."

[someone who's] **smokin' like a chimney/freight train** phrase (general sl.) old & new school
1. to smoke cigarettes or crack cocaine heavily.
ex: "They been smokin' like a chimney all weekend."

[to] **snake** [someone] v. (e. coast sl.) new school
1. to betray; to display disloyalty towards a friend/loved one.
ex: "I just heard Homes snaked me."

snake sh** v. (e. coast sl.) new school
1. acts and behaviors that are unscrupulous, deceitful, or petty.
ex: "When you do that snake sh**, you put all of us in jeopardy."

snakes n. (general sl.) old & new school
1. people who pretend to be one's friend but who covertly engage in plots to ruin one's reputation, credibility, or relationships with others. 2. people who are untrustworthy, unloyal, and unscrupulous towards friends and family members. (var. [someone who's a] **snake**)
ex: "You knew he was a snake before this happened."

[to] **snap on** [someone] v. (general sl.) old & new school
1. to make fun of or ridicule someone. 2. to respond to someone harshly, rudely, or obnoxiously.
ex: "They was snappin' on Shortie shoes." "I asked'er one question and she snapped on me for no reason."

snaps n. (general sl.) old & new school
1. jokes; humorous and witty quips.

[to] **snatch** [someone's] **mouth** v. (southern sl.) new school
1. to leave one's opponent speechless after you beat him/her in a contest that he/she bragged about winning. (var. [to] **get** [one's] **mouth**)
ex: "I'mma snatch that mouth before the game is over."

[to] **snatch** [someone's] **pocket** v. (criminal sl.) old & new school
1. to forcefully reach into and/or grab one's pants pocket in an attempt to steal his/her possessions [often causing the pocket to rip or tear open spilling the contents on the ground]. (var. [to] **snatch pockets**)
ex: "My dawg K.B. got three years for snatchin' pockets in Manhattan."

[a] **sneak thief** n. (prison sl.) old & new school
1. one who steals other people's property stealthily. (var. [to] **sneak thief** [someone])
ex: "If people find out you a sneak thief, you have madd problems on your hands."

[to] **sneak through** phrase (general sl.) new school
1. to travel through an area discreetly or with hopes of not being seen. (var. [to] **creep through**)
ex: "I'mma sneak through later to check you."

[a] **sneaker pimp** n. (general sl.) old school
1. one who only wears tennis shoes [even when not appropriate].
ex: "When she was young her and all her friends were sneaker pimps."

sneaks n. (general sl.) old school
1. tennis shoes; sneakers.

sniff n. (drug sl.) old & new school
1. powder cocaine.
ex: "I was buggin' when she pulled out the sniff."

snitches get stitches phrase (prison sl.) old & new school
1. a term used to declare that one can and/or will be cut or injured in a way that requires stitches for telling or cooperating with an authority [usually law enforcement authorities].

[one's] **snot box** n. (general sl.) old & new school
1. a person's nose.
ex: "The ball hit Slim in his snot box."

[someone who's] **snotty** adj. (general sl.) old & new school
1. obnoxious; rude; one who displays an unpleasant attitude. 2. one who has a highly overrated opinion of his/her own character and/or self worth.
ex: "I told that snotty broad about herself." "Why you hafta always be so snotty?"

[a] **snub** n. (criminal sl.) old & new school
1. any snub-nosed handgun.
ex: "Duke tried to sneak the snub in the club and got caught."

[to] **snuff** [someone] v. (e. coast sl.) old school
1. to punch someone in the face, mouth, or jaw when one isn't paying attention [usually during a confrontation or argument].
ex: "Just make sure he don't snuff me."

so and so n. (general sl.) old school
1. a term used to refer to someone whose name you don't remember or don't feel is important or relevant.
ex: "So and so told me you not goin'." "Whassup with you and so and so?"

[someone who's] **so sweet** [he/she] **gives** [you] **a cavity** phrase
(southern sl.) new school
1. someone who is extremely gullible, easily fooled, taken
advantage of, or conned. (var. [someone who's] **unbelievably
sweet**)

[someone who's] **soft** adj. (e. coast sl.) old & new school
1. cowardly; afraid; scared. (var. [someone who's] **soft as
cotton/as baby sh**/as baby sh** dipped in baby oil**) See also:
[someone who's] **ass**
ex: "I found out today that ya man is soft."

[someone who's a] **solider** (pron. solja) adj. (general sl.) old &
new school
1. a stand up individual; someone proven to endure during trying
situations. 2. a term of endearment among friends; friend. 3. a way
to address someone whose name you don't know.
ex: "I want nothin' but soliders with me."

soldier rags n. (southern sl.) new school
1. bandanas.
ex: "You can't wear solider rags in here."

[someone who's] **some sh**** adj. (e. coast sl.) new school
1. no good at his/her word; irresponsible. 2. petty.
ex: "I'mma be the first to tell you, ya man some sh**."

somebody's rotten phrase (general sl.) new school
1. a term used when one smell the odor of a fart [usually when
he/she doesn't know who did it]. (var. **somebody smell like they
wanna be alone**)
ex: "Somebody rotten up in here."

somethin's gotta give phrase (general sl.) old & new school
1. a term used to express exasperation. 2. a way to say, "something
has to change", "we have to come to some sort of conclusion".
ex: "Somethin's gotta give, we can't go on like this forever."

somethin' in the milk ain't white phrase (southern sl.) new school
1. a term used to speculate that something is amiss or express one's suspicions.

[a female who's] **somethin' special** adj. (e. coast sl.) new school
1. extremely good looking; sexy.
ex: "Word up son, shortie somethin' special."

[someone who's] **sometimin'** adj. (e. coast sl.) old & new school
1. one who is inconsistent with his/her behavior or treatment towards family and friends; unpredictable.
ex: "You the one who's always actin' sometimin'." "You can't be sometimin' with me."

[something that's] **so-so** adj. (general sl.) old & new school
1. mediocre; not that good and at the same time not that bad.
ex: "The party was so-so." "The dress she picked out was so-so."

so you wanna be a greata potata? phrase (southern sl.) new school
1. a witty way to respond to one's sudden display of boldness or toughness.

Son n. (e. coast sl.) new school
1. a term of endearment among friends; friend. 2. a way to address someone whose name you don't know or don't want to use in front of others. (var. **Son Son**)
ex: "Tell Son to meet us uptown later."

[to] **son** [someone] v. (e. coast sl.) new school
1. to manipulate or intimidate someone into being your follower because that person wants to be accepted by you and/or wants to be your friend. (var. [to be someone's] **son/son dula**)
ex: "We about to son this cat." "That's my son."

[that] **sounds good!** phrase (general sl.) old & new school
1. a sarcastic way to dismiss someone's empty threat or boastful
claim. (var. [all] **that sh** sounds good!**)

[one's] **soup coolers** n. (general sl.) new school
1. one's lips.
ex: "Your boy got some hellava soup coolers."

[to] **soup** [someone] **up** phrase (general sl.) old & new school
1. to give someone a false sense of confidence; to flatter falsely.
(var. [to] **soup** [someone's] **head up**)
ex: "I don't hafta soup you up about this."

[someone who's] **souped** adj. (general sl.) old & new school
1. one who has an overrated opinion of his/her charcater or worth;
conceited; to act cocky or over confident. (var. [someone who's]
souped up)
ex: "He's souped because he won the championship."

South Boogie n. (e. coast sl.) new school
1. the South Bronx, N.Y.

South Cack n. (southern sl.) new school
1. South Carolina. (var. **South Cacky/Cackalacka/
ckalack/Cackalacky**)

[to] **spank** [someone's] **ass** v. (e. coast sl.) old school
1. to badly beat someone in some form of competition. (var. [to]
spank [someone])
ex: "When its my turn I'mma spank that ass."

[something that's] **spankin'** adj. (general sl.) old school
1. outstanding; unique; the best of its kind.
ex: "The new shoes I picked up are spankin'."

spare me the bullsh** [aiight?] phrase (general sl.) old & new school
1. a sarcastic way to respond to someone ridiculous excuse or attempted explanation [often used dismissingly].
ex: "Come on man, spare me the bullsh**, if you don't wanna go just say you don't wanna go."

[to] **spark** [something] v. (e. coast sl.) new school
1. the act of starting a fight or physical confrontation.
ex: "As soon as he started lyin' we sparked it."

[to] **spark a conversation** v. (general sl.) old & new school
1. to start a conversation. (var. [to] **spark a convo**)
ex: "Guess who tried to spark a conversation with me?"

[to] **spark** [something] **up** v. (general s1.) new school
1. the act of lighting a cigarette or marijuana.
ex: "When you gonna spark that up?"

[to] **spaz** v. (e. coast sl.) new school
1. to become loud, disruptive, and unruly when upset causing an unpleasant scene. (var. [to] **spaz out** [on someone])
ex: "Shortie really spazzed on me at the club." "Don't make me spaz in here."

[someone who's one's] **speed** adj. (general sl.) old & new school
1. someone who is compatible, similar to, and easy to relate to as oneself. (var. [to be the same] **speed** [as someone])
ex: "I wanted to tell you, but shortie was never your speed."

[something that's one's] **speed** adj. (general sl.) old & new school
1. something that is on the same level of comprehension as one's ability to understand or handle.
ex: "Here, you take this one, this a lil more your speed."

[to] **speed-ball** v. (drug sl.) old school
1. to shoot cocaine directly into one's vein.

ex: "I busted in the room and shortie in there speed ballin' I was like you gotta leave yo."

[someone who's] **speed ballin'** v. (general sl.) old & new school
1. one who is proceeding recklessly and dangerously. (var. [someone who's] **speedin'**)
ex: "Let me holler at you dawg, cause you speed ballin'." "You can't see it, but you speedin'."

[a] **speed knot** n. (general sl.) old school
1. a sizable bump which appears on one's head or eye immediately after being hit with an object or fist. (var. [to] **give** [someone] **two speed knots runnin' concurrent/running wild**)
ex: "I see that lil speed knot ya girl put on your head."

speed on before you get pee'd on phrase (e. coast sl.) new school
1. a sarcastic way to dismiss someone [usually when that person is annoying you]. See also: **get somewhere**

[to] **spend cheese** phrase (general sl.) old & new school
1. to spend money.
ex: "He about to spend all his cheese on shortie." I spent too much cheese already."

[to] **spin** [someone] v. (e. coast sl.) new school
1. to use deception, lies,or excuses to avoid or stall someone. (var. [to] **give** [someone] **a/the spin move**, [to] **use the spin game on** [someone])
ex: "You always tryin' to spin me." "I'm tired of y'all spinnin' me."

[someone who's a] **spin master** adj. (e. coast sl.) new school
1. someone with the unique ability to use deception, lies, or excuses to avoid or stall someone.
ex: "Here comes the spin master." "You talkin' to the spin master right there."

[to] **spin on** [someone] v. (e. coast sl.) new school
1. to leave the company of another suddenly, covertly, or slyly. (var. [to] **spin off on** [someone])
ex: "I'm about to spin on this lame." "You hafta learn how to spin off on catz like that."

spinach n. (drug sl.) new school
1. marijuana.

[to] **spit** v. (e. coast sl.) new school
1. to talk; the unique style one uses to rap his/her Hip-Hop lyrics.
2. to say something charming and flattering to someone of the opposite sex. (var. [to] **spit** [something] **at** [something])
*ex: "Ya boys was spittin' some real sh** in there." "I spit my best stuff at Shortie."*

[to] **spit fire at** [someone] v. (criminal sl.) new school
1. the act of shooting one's gun at someone. (var. [to] **spit flames/them thangs/them thang thangs at** [someone])
ex: "They came through spittin' fire at ya boy."

[to] **spit game** phrase (general sl.) old & new school
1. to use charm, flattery, or verbal deception as a way to manipulate or take advantage of someone. (var [to] **spit game at** [someone])
ex: "You won't get nowhere tryin' to spit game at Shortie."

[to] **spit game in** [a female's/shorite's] **ear** phrase (general sl.) new school
1. to say things that are nice and flattering to a female in an attempt to get to know her better.
ex: "I came in here, spit a lil game in shortie's ear and when the night was over she bounced with me."

[to] **spit out on** [someone] v. (prison sl.) old & new school
1. the act of spitting the razor blade one has hidden in the mouth into his/her hand. (var. [to] **spit out/an ox**)
ex: "He wasn't expecting me to spit out, and that's how I caught 'em."

[to] **split** [someone's] **head to the white meat** phrase (southern sl.) new school
1. a term used to decsribe the injuries one will succumb to for doing something foolish or reckless [usually used as warning]. 2. to beat one's opponent mercilessly. (var. [to] **split** [someone's] **sh**/wig**)
ex: "One day somebody gonna split ya head to the white meat for that dumb sh**."

[to] **splurge** v. (general sl.) old & new school
1. to spend money freely on one's friends or on oneself [usually spending a large amount of money on a gift].
ex: "You deserve to splurge on yourself sometimes."

[to] **spread love** phrase (general sl.) new school
1. to extend one's generosity; to be charitable; to help another. (var. [to] **spread the love**)
ex: "They come back to the hood to spread love."

[someone who's] **sprung** adj. (sexual sl.) old & new school
1. one who has become emotionally attached to his/her lover because of sex. (var. [to] **have** [someone] **sprung**)
ex: "She used to have you sprung." "He's sprung over that chickenhead."

[someone who's] **square** adj. (general sl.) old & new school
1. one who is not "cool" or "hip". (var. [someone who's] **square as a cardboard box**)
ex: "I didn't realize how square you was."

square biz phrase (general sl.) old school
1. a way to affirm or reaffirm one's thought or position leaving no room for doubt [often used when trying to convince].

[to] **square up on** [someone] v. (general sl.) old & new school
1. to take a confrontational stance towards another.
ex: "I know you not tryin' to square up on me."

squares n. (general sl.) old & new school
l. cigarettes. See also: **joes, hump backs**
ex: "In N.Y. squares are $7.50 a pack."

[to] **squash** [something] v. (general sl.) old & new school
l. to resolve; put an end to a disagreement or misunderstanding.
(var. [to] **squash** [a beef])
ex: "I thought y'all squashed that already."

[to] **squeal** [on someone] v. (criminal sl.) old school
1. to inform on another [usually to law enforcement agents].
(var. [a] **squealer**)
ex: "I heard he was about to squeal." "I'm tellin' you, ya man gonna squeal."

[to] **squeeze off** v. (general sl.) new school
1. to fart (flatulate). (var. [to] **squeeze one off**)
ex: "Dam, somebdoy squeezed off in here."

[to] **squeeze off** v. (criminal sl.) new school
1. to shoot a gun. (var. [to] **squeeze triggers**)
ex: "Who squeezed off first?"

S.T. phrase (e. coast sl.) new school
1. an abbreviation for "small talk".
ex: "We was just doin' a lil S.T." "Thanks for the S. T."

[to] **stab the box** phrase (sexual sl.) new school
l. a male term for having sex. (var. [to] **stab** [a female's] **box**)
ex: "Be careful cause dudes like that only wanna stab the box."

[a] **stack** n. (general sl.) old & new school
l. large amount, of money [sometimes bundled together or in wads].
ex: "How many stacks you think they got in there?"

[to] **stack** v. (general sl.) old & new school
1. to save one's money. (var. [to] **stack** [one's] **paper**)
ex: "For now on I'm stackin' to get this whip."

[a female who's] **stacked** adj. (sexual sl.) old & new school
1. a female who has a big butt and/or breasts. (var. [a female who's] **stacked like that**)
ex: "Her cousin was definitely stacked kid, for real."

[someone who's] **stacked like that** phrase (general sl.) old & new school
1. wealthy; rich; financially secure.
ex: "You know Diddy and Jigga stacked like that."

[to] **stamp** [something] v. (e. coast sl.) new school
1. to approve of; to be in support of; to agree with. 2. to give one's guarantee. (var. [to] **put** [one's] **stamp on** [something]).
ex: "I don't believe he stamped that." "I already stamped that for you."

[to] **stand on** [one's] **word** v. (general sl.) old & new school
1. to unequivocally stand by one's claim, statement, or truthfulness.
ex: "They just wanna know do you stand on ya word?"

stand up! Interj. (e. coast sl.) new school
1. an enthusiastic shout or chant used to incite and ignite people's attention to an event or performance.

[to] **start actin' funny** v. (general sl.) old & new school
1. to go from a pleasant demeanor to an unpleasant one for no apparent reason with a friend or love one [often shifting to rude, obnoxious, or offensive behavior]. (var. [someone who's] **actin' funny**)
ex: "Just don't get up in here and start actin' funny on me."

[one's] **stash** n. (general sl.) old & new school
1. one's property which he/she chooses to hide from others. 2. the place where one hides his/her possessions. [often refers to drugs and/or one's valuables]. (var. [one's] **stash spot/crib/house**)
ex: *"I doubt if they'll be able to find my stash this time around."*

[a] **stash box** n. (criminal sl.) old & new school
1. a secret compartment in a automobile used to hide guns or drugs.
ex: *"I had the stash box by the gas tank."*

static n. (general sl.) old school
1. problems or situations that can possibly lead to a physical confrontation. 2. trouble.
ex: *"Ain't nobody lookin' for no static in here."*

stay chisel phrase (e. coast sl.) new school
1. a term used to say, "stay well" or wish one well [used when departing company, ending a conversation, or written communique]. (var. **stay real**)
ex: *"Stay chisel homie and I'll talk to you later." "Until we talk again, stay chisel."*

stay on ya grizzly phrase (e. coast sl.) new school
1. a term used to encourage someone to remain focused an dedicated to whatever means that person uses to earn his/her money. (var. **stay on ya grind**, [to] **stay on** [one's] **grizzly/grind**)
ex: *"You gonna come up but you hafta stay on ya grizzly."*

stay outta grown folks business phrase (southern sl.) new school
1. a term used to dismiss someone's attempt to intervene, interrupt, give adivce or opinion about something that does not concern him/her. (var. **didn't your mother teach/ tell you to stay out of grown folks business**)

stay sucker free phrase (e. coast sl.) new school
1. a term used to advise or instruct someone to stay away from people who mean him/her no good, are negative, or lack goals.

stay up phrase (southern sl.) old school
1. a term used to wish someone well when departing company or ending a letter or coversation.
ex: "Y'all stay up, I gotta leave now."

S.T.D. phrase (e. coast sl.) new school
1. a playful abbreviation for saying "scared to death" when discussing someone's fear [usually used as a tease].
ex: "Them catz was S.T.D when we came through."

[to] **steal** [someone] v. (southern sl.) old & new school
1. to punch someone in the face, mouth, or jaw when that person is least expecting it [usually during an argument]. (var. [to] **steal the sh** outta** [someone]) See also: [to] **jap** [someone]
ex: "His momz tried to steal the teacher for kickin'em out the graduation."

[to] **steam** v. (drug sl.) new school
1. to smoke marijuana. See also; [to] **burn**
ex: "I didn't know you steam."

steel n. (criminal sl.) new school
1. a firearm; handgun.

steel n. (prison sl.) old & new school
1. a homemade knife made of steel.

[one's] **steelo** (pron. stee-low) n. (e. coast sl.) new school
1. one's reputation, character, or style. (var. [one's] **steez**)
ex: "You know my steelo." "I heard about your steelo."

[a] **steerer** n. (drug sl.) old school
1. one whose job it is to direct drug related traffic or people in search of drugs to where the drugs can be purchased [often to feed one's own drug habit]. (var. [a] **runner**)
ex: "When the police came, they even locked up the steerer."

[a] **steering charge** n. (criminal sl.) old school
1. a criminal charge for soliciting people and steering drug traffic to a drug location.
ex: "He got a twenty dollar bail for a steering charge and he can't make bail.

[a] **stem** n. (drug sl.) old & new school
1. a glass instrument used to smoke crack cocaine out of. (var. [a] **straight shooter**)
ex: "You could see the stem in her pocket."

[to] **step** v. (general sl.) old & new school
1. to leave. 2. a term used to tell someone to leave. (var. [to] **step off**)
ex: "I had to step for a lil while." "Didn't she tell you to step?"

[to] **step** [one's] **game up** phrase (e. coast sl.) new school
1. to exert more effort in an attempt to enhance one's performance or excel one's position. (var. [to] **step up** [one's] **game**)
ex: "I see right now I need to step my game up." "I had to step up the game to get shortie."

[to] **step to** [someone] v. (general sl.) old & new school
1. to approach or confront someone.
ex: "You wanna step to me?" "You can get stepped to."

[to] **step to** [one's] **business** phrase (e.coast sl.) old & new school
1. to confront one's problems [even if that problem is with someone else and it may lead to a physical confrontation]. (var. [to] **step to that mans business,** [to] **step to** [someone's] **business**)
ex: "I don't even hafta tell you, but you know you need to step to your business."

[to] **step to the left on** [someone] phrase (general sl.) old & new school
1. to slyly or discreetly leave the company of someone without informing that person of your intentions; to desert someone.

ex: "Go around the back, we about to step to the left on these chickenheads."

[to] **step up** phrase (general sl.) old & new school
l. to assume responsibility; to take control. (var. [to] **step up to the plate**)
ex: "Your the oldest, so you need to step up."

[to] **step up in** [somewhere] phrase (general sl.) old & new school
1. to arrive; to make one's presence known when arriving. (var. [to] **step up in the spot/house**)
ex: "I felt the vibes as soon as we stepped up in here."

[to] **stick** [someone] v. (criminal sl.) old & new school
1. to rob someone. (var. [to get] **stuck**)
ex: "They got 10 years for stickin' the mailman."

[to] **stick a battery in** [someone's] **back** phrase (e. coast sl.) new school
l. to wrongly or falsely encourage someone to do something wrong or illegal. 2. to give a false sense of confidence. See also: [to] **geese** [someone] **up**
ex: "You don't hafta stick no battery in my back, I'll do it if I want to."

[to] **stick** [someone] **in a house/crib** phrase (general sl.) old & new school
1. to buy or rent a house or apartment for someone.(var. [to] **stick** [someone] **up in a house/crib**)
ex: "I'm about to stick Shortie up in a house soon."

[one's] **stick man** n. (w. coast sl.) old school
l. one's best friend; the friend one can depend on in times of trouble.
ex: "All I gotta do is call my stick man."

[a] **stickup kid** n. (criminal sl.) old & new school
1. a male who has a well known reputation for robbing drug dealers or other criminally associated persons.
ex: "The original 50 cents was a notorious stickup kid from Brooklyn."

stick yaself Tony phrase (e. coast sl.) new school
1. a term used to tease, taunt or mock one's opponent when he/she makes a error and/or after you score a point against him/her. (var. **stick yaself**)

sticks and stones might break my bones, but these rights and lefts will kill you phrase (southern sl.) new school
1. a witty way to respond to someone who is calling you names in attempt to provoke you.

sticky icky n. (drug sl.) new school
1. a type of marjuana. (var. **sticky**)
ex: "Shortie brought back a bag of that sticky icky."

still an' all... phrase (general sl.) old & new school
1. a term used as a prelude to elaborating on one's thought/opinion during a conversation. (var. **yet an' still**)
ex: "Still an' all I think we should do it my way."

stimo adj. (drug sl.) old school
1. marijuana; any illegal narcotic. 2. the state of being high from an illegal narcotic. 3. drunk; intoxicated. (var. **stimuli, stimulated**)
See also: **lifted, zooted**
ex: "They had to throw the stimo out the window." "When they came back they was stimo."

[someone who's] **stingie** adj. (general sl.) old & new school
1. one who doesn't share with others; extremely frugal with spending expenditures.
ex: "Your Boy was too stingie for me."

[to look] **stink/stank** adj. (general sl.) old & new school
1. to have an outwardly appearance of being someone who is easy
to have sex with because one is scantly dresses and very flirtatious
[usually used in reference to females].
*ex: "Don't bring them stink broads to my party." "Don't she look
stank?"*

[a] **Stinkin' Lincoln** n. (e. coast sl.) old school
1. a Lincoln Town Car or Lincoln Continental.
ex: "Yeah, I'm still drivin' my Stinkin' Lincoln."

stinky n. (southern sl.) new school
1. marijuana. (var. **stinky stink/stank/stinky**)
*ex: "The cops kept the bag of stinky." "We threw the stinky out the
window."*

[to] **stir sh** up** phrase (general sl.) old & new school
1. to start a controversy.
*ex: "When y'all two get together, y'all always stir some sh** up."
"You forever stirrin' sh** up around here."*

[a] **stoggie** n. (general sl.) old school
1. a cigarette. (var. [a] **stog**)
ex: "That was my last stoggie."

[to get] **stole on** v. (southern sl.) old & new school
1. the act of being punched in the face, mouth, or jaw unexpectedly
catching one by surprise. (var. [to get] **stole**, [to get] **stole by**
[someone])
ex: "This old lady stole ya man for jumpin' the line."

[to] **stomp a mud hole in** [someone's] **ass** phrase (general sl.) old
& new school
1. to beat someone up badly. 2. to beat one's opponent mercilessly
during competition; to lose miserably.
*ex: "We about to stomp a mud hole in y'all ass." "I got a mud hole
stomped in my ass."*

[to] **stomp** [someone] **out** v. (general sl.) old & new school
1. to use one's fcct to physically assault someone when that person is laying on the ground defenseless.
ex: "If I wouldn't have ran, they woulda stomped me out." "I had to stop 'em from stompin' you out."

[to] **stomp with the big dawgs** phrase (general sl.) new school
1. to socialize with, compete against, or do business with people who are just as or more successful than you.
ex: "After this deal I'll be stompin' with the big dawgs."

[one's] **stompin' grounds** n. (general sl.) old & new school
1. one's neighborhood and/or the places one likes to frequent.
ex: "The whole Brooklyn was my stompin' grounds."

stones n. (general sl.) old & new school
1. dimaonds.

stones n. (drug sl.) old & new school
1. pieces of crack cocaine sold for $5-$50 amounts.

stop frontin'! interj. (general sl.) old & new school
1. an enthusiastic way to tell someone to "stop pretending" or "stop lying" [usually when one is boasting or making outrageous claims].
ex: "You need to stop frontin' cause she won't even talk to you." "I was there so stop frontin'!"

stop playin'! phrase (general sl.) old & new school
1. an enthusiastic way to express skepticism about something someone has said [usually used to prod someone for more details or affirming himself/herself].
ex: "Stop playin', she ain't say that about me." "She showed up with who, stop playin'"

stop the grinnin' and drop the linen phrase (sexual sl.) new school

1. a witty way to tell a female or male to get undressed so the two of you can have sex.

straight adj. (general sl.) old & new school
1. rich; wealthy. (var. **straighter then straight**)
ex: *"After this lick here, we gonna be straight!"*

[someone who's] **straight** adj. (general sl.) old & new school
1. satisfied; fine; okay; not in need.
ex: *"I'm straight with this." "Y'all straight?" "We straight after this."*

[someone who's] **straight** adj. (e. coast sl.) new school
1. a stand up individual; a good person; someone who can be trusted. See also: [someone who's] **good people**
ex: *"How do you know he's straight?" "My man here is straight."*

[someone who's] **straight** adj. (drug sl.) old & new school
1. someone who is in possessions of drugs that are for sale.
ex: *"We'll be straight in a hour." "Which one of y'all straight?"*

[to] **straight** [do/say something] v. (general sl.) old & new school
1. to do or say something without hesitation or remorse; to boldly do or say something. (var. [to] **cold** [do/say something])
ex: *"I straight told'er what I feel." "She straight slapped the mess outta dude."*

straight lace with no chase phrase (southern sl.) new school
1. a term used to affirm or reaffirm one's thought or position leaving no room for doubt or debate. 2. a way express being in agreement. (var. **straight up/up and down/up with no chaser**)

straight like that! phrase (w. coast sl.) old & new school
1. a term used as an exclamation point after one's boast, threat or challenge to add emphasis.
ex: *"I won three times in a row, straight like that!"*

[to] **straighten** [someone] v. (southern sl.) new school
1. to correct or to set one straight in a matter of fact way; to reprimand someone. (var. [to] **put a straightenin' on** [someone])
ex: "I'm about to go straighten this dude right now."

[to] **straighten** [one's] **face** v. (southern sl.) new school
1. to correct or set straight a mishap one created. 2. to redeem oneself. 3. to pay one's debt.
ex: "Its time for you to straighten your face." "I want to come straighten my face this week."

[someone who's] **straighty straight** adj. (general sl.) new school
1. financially secure; rich. 2. in a nice position.
ex: "When I get home, I plan to be straighty straight." "They straighty straight now."

[to be] **straight-up** [with someone] v. (general sl.) old & new school
1. to be honest and up-front with someone [even if it means you have hurt that person's feelings]. (var. [someone who's] **straight-up**)
ex: "I'm only being straight-up with you homie." "You know I'mma always be straight-up with you."

[a] **strap** n. (criminal sl.) old & new school
1. a firearm; handgun.

[to] **strap up** v. (sexual sl.) new school
1. to don a condom.
ex: "All I'm sayin' is, you better strap up."

strap up phrase (general sl.) old & new school
1. a term used to tell someone to "prepare to fight" as a confrontation, argument, or misunderstanding escalates.
ex: "Strap up sucker we about to do this."

strap up or get slapped up phrase (e. coast sl.) new school
1. a witty way to tell someone to "prepare to fight" as a
confrontation, argument, or misunderstanding escalates.

strapped v. (criminal sl.) old & new school
1. to be in possession of a concealed firearm. (var. [someone
who's] **strapped up**)
ex: *"Nobody gettin' in here strapped."*

[a male who's] **strapped** adj. (sexual sl.) new school
1. a male who has a well endowed penis.
ex: *"Ask your girl if I'm strapped or not."*

[someone who's] **strapped like the Feds** adj. (general sl.) new
school
1. wealthy; to make or have access to large amounts of money.
ex: *"Them catz strapped like the Feds now."*

straps n. (sexual sl.) new school
1. condoms.
ex: *"That was my last strap." "I don't go nowhere without the
straps son."*

[a] **street pharmacist** n. (drug sl.) new school
1. an illegal drug dealer.

[a] **street sweeper** n. (criminal sl.) old & new school
1. an automatic shotgun with a 12-18 round clip.

[to] **stress** v. (general sl.) old & new school
1. to worry. (var. [to] **stress** [about/over something])
ex: *"There's no need to stress yet." "I can see you stressin'."*

[to] **stress** [someone] v. (general sl.) old & new school
1. to pressure someone. 2. to cause someone mental and/or
emotional anguish.
ex: *"Shortie keep stressin' me about some bullsh**."*

[to] **stretch** [someone] **out** v. (criminal sl.) new school
1. a way to refer to the act of murder. 2. to have someone laid out on the ground at gun point during a robbery.
ex: "Them catz was about to stretch ya man out back there and he don't even realize it."

[to] **stretch out on** [someone] v. (e. coast sl.) new school
1. to test or go beyond the limits of one's patience with behavior that is disrespectful and/or rebellious. (var [to] **stretch on** [someone])
ex: "She's being punished for tryin' to stretch out on me, comin' in here at two in the mornin'."

stretched out phrase (prison sl.) old & new school
1. to receive an extremely long prison sentence.
ex: "The judge definitely stretched me out this time."

[a female who's] **strictly d**kly** phrase (sexual sl.) old & new school
1. a female who is heterosexual [often used when a female is reaffirming her sexual preference].
*ex: "No hon don't get that twisted I'm strictly d**kly."*

[to] **string-up** v. (prison sl.) old & new school
1. to commit suicide by hanging oneself.
ex: "They said he tried to string-up twice in one week."

[a] **strip** n. (drug sl.) old & new school
1. an open area where people congregate openly dealing drugs.
ex: "Police raided the strip right as we was leaving."

stripes n. (general sl.) old & new school
1. the respect, recognition, or praise one receives for his/her achievement and/or solid character. See also: **props**
ex: "I gotta give you stripes for that."

Strong Island n. (e. coast sl.) old & new school
1. Long Island, N.Y.

[someone who's] **stuck in the system** phrase (criminal sl.) new school
1. someone who's in jail waiting to appear in court or in prison serving a prison sentence.
ex: "How long ya man gonna be stuck in the system?"

[someone who's] **stuck like Chuck** phrase (e. coast sl.) new school
1. in trouble; in a very bad situation. 2. unable to go anywhere; stuck in one position.
ex: "If we get caught, we stuck like Chuck." "Looks like we stuck like Chuck for a while."

[someone who's] **stuck on stupid** phrase (e. coast sl.) new school
1. one who makes the same mistakes. 2. one who asks ridiculous questions or says ridiculous things. 3. one who cannot understand the importance of his/her actions.
ex: "What are you stuck on stupid?" "Man them chickens must be stuck on stupid."

[one's] **student** n. (e. coast sl.) new school
1. a mocking way to refer to one's opponent or adversary.
ex: "Who him, that's my student." "Who said you can use my student?"

study long study wrong phrase (general sl.) old & new school
1. a term used to taunt someone about taking too long to think/make a decision [often used as a prodding tool].

[to] **stunt** [someone] v. (general sl.) new school
1. to make a fool out of someone.
ex: "Shortie tried to stunt me in front of my peoples."

[a] **stunt** n. (e. coast sl.) old & new school
1. a female who is easily influenced and/or manipulated by a male because of his perceived wealth and/or reputation [usually because of the females naivety or low self esteem].
ex: "I can't bring these stunts to my house."

[to] **stunt** v. (general sl.) new school
1. to show off in an attempt to bring attention to oneself [usually flaunting one's material wealth or possessions as attention grabbers]. (var. [someone who's] **stuntin'**)
ex: "You don't hafta stunt for me Shortie, be yourself."

[a] **stunt dummy** adj. (e. coast sl.) new school
1. a male who knowingly does things that are dangerous, reckless, and/or careless [often for the purpose of getting attention]. (var. [a] **stunt man**)
ex: "How can you take advise from this stunt dummy."

stupid?! interj. (general sl.) old & new school
1. a term used to enthusiastically question someone's claim, boast, or truthfulness. 2. a term used to affirm or reaffirm one's position or thought leaving no room for doubt. (var. **you stupid?!**)
ex: "Stupid?!, she's not leavin' with you." "I coulda did that stupid?!"

[to] **stut** [something] v. (southern sl.) new school
1. to express concern; to worry or think about. (var. [to] **stut** [someone])
*ex: "I ain't stuttin' that sh** 'til tomorrow." "Why you stuttin' that boy?" "I wouldn't stut that."*

[to] **style** [on someone] v. (general sl.) old school
1. to exhibit behavior that exudes an overrated air of one's self worth or importance; to act conceited. (var. [to] **style and profile** [on someone])
ex: "You should have seen the way she tried to style on me in front of her friends."

[to] **sucker punch** [someone] v. (southern sl.) old & new school
1. to punch someone in the face, mouth, or jaw when he/she is least expecting you to [usually during an argument or misunderstanding].
ex: "Next thing I know Shortie sucker punched the dude."

[to] **sucker stroke** [someone] v. (e. coast sl.) new school
1. to offer fake flattery or praise for the purpose of getting someone to do something you want. 2. to employ tact when attempting to con someone. 3. to "stroke" someone's ego.
ex: "Why does it feel like you tryin' to sucker stroke me about this."

[to] **sugar coat** [something] v. (general sl.) old & new school
1. to cover up the seriousness of a situation or problem changing certain details to make the situation or problem sound not as serious [usually for the sake of sparing someone's feelings].
ex: "You just tryin' to sugar coat this sh**." "The truth is the truth, so don't try and sugar coat it."

[a] **sugar daddy** n. (general sl.) old school
1. a male who spends large amounts of money on a female to start or maintain an intimate relationship with her.
ex: "I need to find me a new sugar daddy tonight."

suicide jewels n. (e. coast sl.) new school
1. expensive and/or gaudy jewelry which can get a person killed during a robbery attempt.

suicide missions phrase (sexual sl.) new school
1. unprotected sex. 2. unprotected sex with a known drug addict or prostitute.

[to] **suitcase** [something] v. (prison sl.) old & new school
1. to secrete something in between the fold of one's buttocks or up one's rectum [usually as a way to smuggle and conceal illegal contraband in prison].
ex: "The only way you can get it in, is you gonna hafta suitcase it."

suited adj. (general sl.) new school
1. ready; prepared. (var. **suited and booted**)
ex: "I'll be suited in about a hour."

[a] **Super Bubble** n. (e. coast sl.) new school
1. a Lexus 400GS/LS.

sure as sh** stink phrase (general sl.) old & new school
1. a term used to affirm or reaffirm one's position or thought
leaving no room for doubt or question.
*ex: "Sure as sh** stink I woulda told'em he had to leave." "I'll be
there, sure as sh** stink."*

sure you right phrase (general sl.) old & new school
1. a sarcastic way to mock someone who you know is wrong and is
steadily trying to convince you that he/she is right; to agree with
someone falsely for the sake of argument [used to dimiss].

[a] **survival kit** n.(prison sl.) old & new school
1. a jar of peanut butter and a jar of jelly.

[someone who's] **suspect** adj. (e. coast sl.) new school
1. one's whose behavior or actions are questionable. (var.
[something that's] **suspect**)
ex: "Ya mans an'nim suspect dawg."

swayzee v. (e. coast sl.) new school
1. to leave; depart from.
ex: "I'm swayzaee after this part."

[to] **swear up and down** phrase (general sl.) old & new school
1. to repeatedly claim one's innocence and/or truthfulness.
*ex: "He swore up and down it wasn't him." "Yo Shortie, I swear
up and down, I'll never do that to you again."*

[to] **sweat** [someone] v. (general sl.) old & new school
1. to give someone too much attention because one is overly
infatuated or envious [with hopes that he/she will reciprocate the
same amount of attention to you].
*ex: "Catz like me don't sweat nobody." "She just want you to
sweat her."*

[to] **sweat** [something] v. (general sl.) old & new school
l. to worry or fret over something.
ex: "I wouldn't even sweat that if I was you."

[a] **sweat box** n. (general sl.) old & new school
l. a dance club that becomes extremely hot inside due to poor ventilation and/or lack of a central air system.
ex: "Don't you ever bring me to this sweat box again."

[to] **sweat bullets** phrase (general sl.) old school
l. to be extremely worried and/or sacred.
ex: "You had me in this muthaf**ka sweatin' bullets."

[someone who's] **sweet** adj. (e. coast sl.) new school
l. easily fooled, taken advantage of, manipulated, gullible, or conned.
ex: "When he first started working here, he was sweet." "I got a sweet boss."

[something that's] **sweet** adj. (e. coast sl.) new school
l. easy; not difficult; not challenging.
ex: "I had a sweet job for a long time."

[to be] **sweet on** [someone] v. (general sl.) new school
l. to be infatuated with someone of the opposite sex; to have a "crush".
ex: "You can tell he's sweet on your cousin." "I was really sweet on shortie 'til' she tried to play me."

[to] **swell up on** [someone] v. (general sl.) new school
l. to take an aggressive stance or posture towards someone during a confrontation, argument, or misunderstanding. (var. [to] **swell up** [one's] **chest**)
ex: "Next time you swell up on me, I'mma knock the sh** out you."

[to] **swerve** v. (w. coast sl.) new school

1. to turn and/or switch lanes suddenly while driving; to dodge in and out of traffic.
ex: "They was swervin' the whole trip down here."

swine n. (general sl.) old & new school
1. pork and any product which contains pork as an ingredient. See also: **wully**
ex: "Put that back, that got swine in it."

swine is divine, its boss with hot sauce phrase (general sl.) old & new school
1. a witty way to respond to someone who is criticizing you for eating pork or a product which contains pork.

[to] **swing an epp with** [someone] phrase (sexual sl.) old & new school
1. to have a one night stand with someone. (var. [to] **swing an epp**)
ex: "My friend don't wanna swing no epps with you." "All we did was swing an epp."

[to] **swing on** [someone] v. (general sl.) old & new school
1. to throw a series of punches at someone. (var. [to get] **swung on**)
ex: "I'm tellin' you right now, swing on me, expect to get swung back on."

[to] **switch gears on** [someone] v. (general sl.) new school
1. to change the subject or direction of a conversation hastily in an attempt to confuse, avoid, or deceive.
ex: "As soon as she asked me where you were I switched gears on 'er real quick."

[to] **switch up** [on someone] v. (general sl.) old & new school
1. to change one's attitude and demeanor towards his/her friends or love ones because one has accomplished or acquired something that others have not.

ex: "That's one thing about you cuz, you never switched up once you got on."

switches n. (w. coast sl.) old & new school
1. the switches which control the hydraulic system in one's automobile allowing the car to bounce up and down when the switches are used.

[a] **sword** n. (sexual sl.) old & new school
1. a covert term males use to refer to a "penis".

[a] **system** n. (general sl.) old & new school
1. an audio system for an automobile [usually a customized one].
ex: "What kind of systems you have in there?" "I heard your system from two blocks away."

[someone who's] **7:30** adj. (e. coast sl.) old & new school
1. crazy; unstable; insane. (var. [someone who's] **seven thirty**) See also: [someone who's] **bugged**
ex: "Why all your friends act 7:30?"

[a] **6** n. (general sl.) new school
1. a Mercedes Benz 600 series. (var. [a] **600**)
ex: "I picked up Shortie in the 6."

_**t**_

tackhead [females] adj. (general sl.) old & new school
1. females who display no class or stlye. 2. unladylike.
ex: "I hope you not thinkin' about takin' these tackheads."

[someone who's] **tacky** adj. (general sl.) old & new school
1. one who lacks good taste and manners.
ex: "I still can't believe how tacky you are."

[something that's] **tacky** adj. (general sl.) old & new school
1. something that lacks style; run down; shabby. 2. of poor quality.
ex: "They all wore the same tacky outfits."

[the] **tail end of** [something] phrase (general sl.) old & new school
1. right before or very close to the end. (var. [the] **front end of**
[something])
*ex: "All you heard was what was said at the tail end of the
conversation."*

[to] **take a charge** [for someone] v. (criminal sl.) old & new
school
1. to confess to a criminal act in order to get one's accomplices off
the hook without being charge or prosecuted for the same criminal
act. (var. [to] **take the weight** [for someone])
ex: "I took the charge cause he couldn't stand another felony."

take a chill pill phrase (general sl.) old school
1. a way to tell someone to calm down, relax, or take it easy. See
also: **chill out**
ex: "We all need to take a chill pill for a second."

[to] **take a hit** [on something] v. (general sl.) new school

1. to take a lost financially [usually as a result of taking a gamble].
2. to accept and shoulder the blame of a action [that one may not necessarily be the cause of].
ex: "I took another hit on that Knicks game." "I might hafta take the hit this time." "I can't afford to take this hit."

[to] **take a "L"** phrase (general sl.) new school
1. to lose. 2. to accept one's lost or defeat without seeking revenge or recovery of what was lost. (var. [to] **take a loss** [on something])
ex: "This time I think takin' a "L" ain't that bad." "Everybody takes a "L" one time or another."

[to] **take a plea** phrase (general sl.) old & new school
1. to give up, quit, or submit. See also: [to] **cop out**, [to] **lay down**
ex: "I'mma give you a chance to take a plea before I take this last shot."

[to] **take** [a lie/rumor/innuendo] **and run with it** v. (general sl.) new school
1. to take something one hears and spread it around to others without knowing or caring if it is factual and true [usually because that person likes to gossip about others].

[to] **take** [something] **back to the essence** phrase (e. coast sl.) old school
1. to go back to the beginning or basics.
ex: "For this to work, we have to go back to the essence." "I'mma take y'all back to the essence."

[to] **take** [something] **back to the old school** phrase (general sl.) new school
1. to demonstrate how to do something that was done a long time ago. 2. to make one reminisce. (var. [to] **take** [someone] **back to the old school**, [to] **take it back on** [someone])
ex: "Watch this, I'mma take y'all back to the old school."

[to] **take flight** v. (general sl.) old school

1. to leave in a hurry; to run away from.
ex: "As soon as he seen you comin' he took fight."

[to] **take** [someone] **for a joke** phrase (general sl.) new school
1. to not take one seriously.
ex: "She been takin' you for a joke all this time."

[to] **take** [something] **for what it is** phrase (general sl.) old & new school
1. to accept or reject something on the basis of first impression or under assumption.
ex: "All I can do is take it for what it is."

[to] **take** [someone's] **head off** phrase (general sl.) old & new school
1. to respond to someone rudely, harshly, and/or sarcastically.
ex: "I asked'er one thing and she tried to take my head off."

[to] **take** [someone's] **head off** v. (general sl.) old & new school
1. to land a mighty blow to one's head or face [often knocking the person to the ground].
ex: "She dam near took ya head off."

[to] **take** [someone's] **heart** phrase (general sl.) old & new school
1. to intimidate someone into submission and/or into cowardliness.
ex: "I can take ya heart anytime I'm ready."

take it easy greazy phrase (general sl.) old school
1. a witty way to tell some to calm down, relax, or take it easy. See also: **chill**

[to] **take it how you wanna** [take it] phrase (general sl.) old & new school
1. a way to tell someone you "could care less" how they perceive your comment or threat. (var. **take it any way you wanna** [take it])

[to] **take one for** [someone] phrase (criminal sl.) old & new school
1. to take a gunshot that was intended for someone else.
ex: "Them broads talkin' about they want a man who would take one for them, ain't near one of them gonna take one for a player."

[to] **take one to the head** phrase (drug sl.) new school
1. to smoke a stick or "blunt" of marijuana.
ex: "We took one to the head, on the ride over here."

[to] **take** [someone] **out his/her character** phrase (e. coast sl.) new school
1. to make someone lose his/her composure [usually as a result of being taunted or angered].
ex: "As soon as she said that, she took dude out his character."
"Try not to let him take you out your character."

[to] **take/steal** [someone's] **shine** phrase (general sl.) new school
1. to take the focus or attention from someone who is being praised and have it shifted to you.
ex: "She's over there tryin' to take your shine."

[to] **take shorts** phrase (general sl.) old & new school
1. to allow oneself to be pushed around, disrespected, belittled, or taken advantage of. (var. [to] **take a short**)
ex: "Ya man an'nim down south takin' madd shorts." "I'm tellin' you now, I'm not takin' no shorts."

[to] **take shorts** phrase (drug sl.) old & new school
1. to allow someone to purchase a small quantity of drugs without having the exact amount of money. (var. [to] **come short**)
ex: "We not takin' any shorts today." "Can you take a short from me 'til friday?"

take the base out ya voice phrase (e. coast sl.) old school
1. something you tell someone who's talking to you in a loud tone.

[to] **take the buck outta** [someone] v. (southern sl.) new school

1. to quell one into cowardice or submission. 2. to squash one's rebellious behavior or attitude.

ex: "I see how the Feds take the buck outta a lot of dudes."

[to] **take** [something] **to another level** v. (general sl.) new school
1. the act of advancing or elevating a situation, relationship, or one's performance.

ex: "I think she tryin' to take this to another level." "Why you tryin' to take this to another level?"

[to] **take** [something] **to heart** phrase (general sl.) new school
1. to take one's action or statement personal, offensive, or serious when it wasn't intened to be taken like that.

ex: "You take too much to heart these days."

[to] **take** [someone] **to school** phrase (general sl.) old & new school
1. to teach or show someone how to do something [often used to taunt one's opponent].

ex: "I'm about to take you to school young boy."

[to] **take** [something] **to the house** phrase (general sl.) new school
1. to win [usually an award or trophy]. (var. [to] **bring** [something] **to the house**)

ex: "We about to take this to the house." "If y'all win this game, y'all take the trophy to the house."

[to] **take** [one's goal/plan] **to the moon** phrase (general sl.) new school
1. to exert maximum effort while pursuing the success and advancement of one's goal or plan.

ex: "Yo son, we about to take this to the moon."

[to] **take** [something] **to the streetz** phrase (general sl.) old & new school

1. to handle a situation or exact revenge without involving the police [even if it leads to a violent confrontation]. (var. [to] **handle** [something] **on the streetz**)
ex: "As long as they know, if they start somethin' we takin' it to the streetz."

[to] **take work from** [someone] v. (drug sl.) old & new school
1. to receive drugs from someone to sell. 2. to rob someone of his/her drugs he/she was selling.

[a female who] **takes it to the throat** v. (sexual sl.) new school
1. a female who performs oral sex on a male.
ex: "I can look at her and tell she takes it to the throat."

[someone who's] **takin' a dirt nap** phrase (criminal sl.) new school
1. a way to refer to someone who has died [usually as a result of foul play].
ex: "I thought you knew, Homes been takin' a dirt nap for years."

talk ain't never killed nobody phrase (southern sl.) new school
1. a term used to respond to someone's tough talk and/ or threats. 2. a term used to explain why you chose to ignore or walk away from a verbal confrontation. (var. **talk ain't never made a nose bleed**)

[to] **talk big sh**** phrase (general sl.) old & new school
1. to talk extremely belligerent or offensive in an attempt to taunt someone into a challenge or make oneself appear tough [usually used to prod one into a confrontation]. (var. [to] **talk madd sh****)
ex: "For a lil guy, you talk big sh**." "Yo kid, they was in here talkin' madd sh** about you."

[to] **talk cash sh**** [to/about someone] v. (general sl.) old & new school
1. to say things that are totally disrespectful, offensive, or derogatory to or about someone [usually in an attempt to discredit or destroy his/her relationship with others].

ex: "You stood there and let shortie talk cash sh** to you and your people."

[to] **talk crazy** phrase (general sl.) old & new school
1. the act of bringing up things that have nothing to do with an arugment, debate, or heated discussion. 2. to say things that offend or disrespect someone when upset or angry. (var. [to] **talk crazy to/stupid to** [someone])
ex: "Lets go, she in there talkin' crazy again."

[to] **talk** [someone's] **ear off** v. (general sl.) old & new school
1. the act of talking to someone repeatedly going over the same subject [often without allowing that person to contribute his/her thoughts fully to the conversation]. (var. [someone who] **can talk his/her ass off**)
ex: "I had to sit there while she talked my ear off."

[one's] **talk game** phrase (southern sl.) new school
1. one's unique ability to persuade or sound convincing. 2. one's ability to verbally intimidate or scare others. (var. [to] **have a mean talk game**)
ex: "You got a nice lil talk game." "I'm hip to your talk game."

[to] **talk greazy about** [someone] phrase (e. coast sl.) new school
1. to say extremely negative and/or disrespectful things about someone.
ex: "I hate to be the one to tell you, but he was in here talkin' real greazy about you yesterday."

[to] **talk greazy to** [someone] phrase (e. coast sl.) new school
1. to talk to someone disrespectfully; to say things purposely to offend or belittle someone.
ex: "Being that I was wrong, I ain't say nothin' when she talked greazy to me."

talk is cheap phrase (general sl.) old & new school

1. a way to say, "words alone don't amount to anything its the actions behind the words that arc priceless".
ex: "I don't get involved with that, cause talk is cheap."

[to] **talk junk** v. (general sl.) old & new school
1. to talk offensive, disrespectful, or belligerent to or about someone. (var. [to] **talk sh**/smack/yang**) See also: [to] **pop sh****
ex: "I caught them talkin' junk about you." "She was talkin' madd junk about you."

[to] **talk on** [someone] v. (criminal sl.) new school
1. to give law enforcement information about a friend or loved one's illegal activity.
ex: "I knew that lame was gonna talk on me."

[to] **talk out the side of** [one's] **neck** phrase (general sl.) old school
1. to talk tough and issue threats no one is taking seriously. 2. to speak negatively about a situation before knowing all the details or facts. 3. to say things that don't make sense. (var. [to] **talk outta** [one's] **ass**)
ex: "He's always talkin' out the side of his neck."

talk show sh** phrase (southern sl.) new school
1. controversial situations [usually involving rumors, innuendo, love triangles].
*ex: "Don't put me in any of that talk show sh**."*

[to] **talk stupid** [to someone] v. (e.coast sl.) new school
1. to talk extremely disrespectful or offensive to someone [usually someone one used to be friends with].
ex: "You not gonna talk stupid to me in my own house."

[to] **talk that/some backwards ass sh**** phrase (general sl.) new school

1. a term used to dismiss someone's statements, empty threats, tough talk or nagging as ridiculous, fr ivolous, meaningless, or dumb.
ex: "You always talkin' that backwards ass sh** about people."

[to] **talk that big willie talk** v. (general sl.) old & new school
1. to make boastful claims and exaggerations of one's wealth and ability to live luxurious ly.
ex: "You can tell the fake ones, they the ones always talkin' that big willie talk."

[to] **talk that gangster sh**** phrase (e. coast sl.) new school
l. to talk tough in an attempt to scare and intimidate others. (var.
[to] **talk that murder one sh**/that killer sh****)
ex: "You don't hafta talk that gangster sh** to me." "You the only one always talkin' that gangster sh**."

[to] **talk that lovey-dovey talk/sh**** v. (general sl.) old & new school
1. to express oneself lovingly and affectionately to someone of the opposite sex [often in attempt to convince that person that one is sincere about the way he/she feels].
ex: "Oh now you wanna talk that lovey-dovey talk cause you locked down."

[to] **talk to** [someone] **any kinda way** v. (e. coast sl.) old & new school
1. to talk to someone disrespectfully or without regard to his/her feelings. (var. [to] **talk to** [someone] **any which way**)
ex: "You ain't gonna be comin' in here talkin' to me any kinda way."

talk to me, I'll talk back phrase (southern sl.) new school
l. a witty way to inform someone that you are open for conversation upon answering the telephone instead of saying hello.

[to] **talk** [up] **under** [one's] **breath** v. (general sl.) old & new school
1. to mumble something inaudible [usually when disgruntled or angry].
ex: "Say what you gonna say don't talk under ya breath."

[to] **talk** [someone] **up** phrase (general sl.) old & new school
1. the coincidence of talking about someone and have that person suddenly appear.
ex: "We musta talked you up." "I hope we don't talk 'em up this time."

[you can] **talk ya ass off** phrase (southern sl.) old & new school
1. a way to tell someone he/she can talk as long as he/she wants to or say what he/she wants and you still won't be convinced or change your mind.
ex: "You can talk ya ass off, you still ain't goin'."

[you] **talkin' just to hear yaself talk** phrase (general sl.) old school
1. a term used to inform someone that he/she is wasting his/her time talking to you or that he/she isn't saying anything worth while or meaningful [usually used as a way to dismiss someone's tough talk or rhetoric]. (var. [you] **talkin' loud but ain't sayin' nothin'**)

talkin' quick ain't always talkin' slick phrase (general sl.) new school
1. a way to inform someone that he/she can't fast talk you.

[someone who's] **talkin' that b-b-b-bullsh**** phrase (e.coast sl.) new school
1. a sarcastic way to refer to someone who is making empty threats, talking belligerently, or being offensive in an attempt to taunt you into a challenge or in an attempt to intimidate.
*ex: "You the one always talkin' that b-b-b-bullsh**."*

[someone who's] **talkin' that whooptie-woo** v. (e. coast sl.) old school
1. someone who is talking tough and making empty threats about beating someone up.
ex: "You the one always talkin' that whooptie-woo." "Don't talk that whooptie-woo to me."

[someone who] **talks a mean one** phrase (southern sl.) new school
1. someone who is masterful at intimidating people through tough talk and empty threats yet lacks enough will and courage to back his/her words up with action. (var. [someone who] **talks a real good one**)
ex: "One thing for sure, ya man talks a mean one." "I already know she talks a real good one."

[to] **tap** [a female] v. (sexual sl.) new school
1. a male term for having sex with a female.
ex: "Shortie let you tap that yet?"

[to] **tap dance** [for someone] v. (southern sl.) old & new school
1. to act subservient to get one's way or with hopes of receiving preferential treatment.
ex: "I don't tap dance for nobody."

[to] **tap** [someone's] **jaw** phrase (general sl.) old & new school
1. to punch someone in the jaw. See also: [to] **chin check** [someone]
ex: "Don't think I won't tap that jaw."

[to] **tap** [a female's] **spine** v. (sexual sl.) new school
1. a male term for having sex. (var. [to] **twist** [a female's] **spine sideways**)
ex: "After dinner we went back to her crib and I tapped her spine for two hours straight."

tapped-out phrase (general sl.) old school
1. moneyless; destitute. (var. **tapped**)

ex: "I wish I could right now, but I'm tapped out."

tar n. (drug sl.) old & new school
1. brown colored heroin. See also: **boy, p-funk**

tat-ow! interj. (southern sl.) new school
1. an enthusiastic expression of confidence or excitement upon accomplishing or achieving one's goal [also used to signal completion of a task]. See also: **boo-yow!**

tattoos n. (criminal sl.) new school
1. scars left from gunshot wounds.
ex: "Was it worth the two tattoos?"

[to] **tax** [someone] v. (e. coast sl.) old & new school
1. to take something from someone through force, trickery, or intimidation. (var. [to] **tax** [someone] **for his/her sh****)
ex: "I tax them every time they come in here."

[to] **tear ass** v. (general sl.) old & new school
1. to run extremely fast [usually to avoid capture].
ex: "You can tell he about to tear ass, look at 'em."

[to] **tear** [a female's] **back out** phrase (sexual sl.) new school
1. to exhibit stamina and the dominant role during sex. (var. [to] **tear** [a female] **out the frame**)
ex: "I tore your girlfriend's back out, but I haven't heard from her since."

[to] **tear** [someone] **out the frame** phrase (c. coast sl.) new school
1. to beat one's opponent mercilessly during competition or physical confrontation.
ex: "For two games straight, I tore the fool out the frame."

[to] **tear sh** up** v. (general sl.) old & new school
1. to perform outstandingly. 2. to demonstrate destructive or disruptive behavior.

ex: "We about to go in there and tear sh** up." "He tore sh** up by hisself."

[a] **tech** n. (criminal sl.) old & new school
1. a nine millimeter machine pistol.

tee'd off adj. (general sl.) old school
1. extremely mad; furious. (var. [to] **tee** [someone] **off**)
ex: "You could tell I was tee'd off right?" "You always doin' something to tee me off."

teenage rims n. (southern sl.) new school
1. automobile tire rims with measurements between 13 and 19 inches.

tell'em so [I/we] **don't hafta smell'em** phrase (general sl.) new school
1. a witty way to tell someone to tell someone else to take a bath.

tell him/her what time it is phrase (general sl.) old & new school
1. a way to tell someone to explain something to someone else.
ex: "You need to tell'er what time it is tonight."

tell it to the judge phrase (general sl.) old school
1. a sarcastic way to dismiss someone's attempt to explain himself/herself.
ex: "Best thing you can do is tell it to the judge."

tell ya story walkin' phrase (e. coast sl.) old school
1. a sarcastic way to dismiss someone you particularly don't want to listen to complain, give an excuse or explanation.
ex: "Come on man tell ya story walkin'."

[a] **tender rony** adj. (general sl.) old school
1. an attractive female. (var. [a] **tender vittle**, [a] **tender thang**)
ex: "That was my lil tender rony back in the days."

tennises n. (southern sl.) old school
1. sneakers. (var. **sneaks**)
ex: "I can't afford to buy you $100 dollar tennises."

[someone who's] **terrible** adj. (general sl.) new school
1. petty; unmoral; unscrupulous; deceiving; not trustworthy. 2. a way to refer to someone's unbelievable or unorthodox behavior. (var. [behavior that's] **terrible**)
ex: "You know, that's terrible, I never shoulda brought you with me."

[to] **test** [someone] v. (general sl.) old & new school
1. to push, provoke, or challenge someone's patience or tolerance level. (var. [to] **test** [one's] **nerve/last nerve**)
ex: "The last thing you want to do is test me." "You about to test my last nerve."

[to] **test** [someone's] **knuckle-game** v. (e. coast sl.) new school
1. to provoke someone into a physical confrontation because one feels he/she can beat that person in a fight.
ex: "What, you tryin' to test my knuckle-game?" "My man wanna test ya man knuckle-game."

that ain't about nothin' phrase (southern sl.) new school
1. a term used to dismiss someone's attempt to intimidate and/or taunt you. 2. a way to signify that something is not worth getting upset about. (var. **that sh** ain't about nothin'**)

that ain't for me and you phrase (e. coast sl.) new school
1. a term used in response to a friend or love one's offensive, sarcastic, and/or disrespectful remark or action in an effort to point out friends and family don't act like that towards each other.
ex: "That ain't for me and you Dawg, we too cool for that."

that ain't my style phrase (general sl.) old & new school
1. a term used to deny a action one is being accused of.
ex: "I don't care what you say, that ain't my style."

that ain't nothin' but that bullsh** phrase (southern sl.) new school
1. a term used to point out someone's unfairness, wrongful treatment, and/or deceptive ways. (var. **that ain't nothin' but that bullsh** in your life**)

that ain't nothin' but the truth phrase (southern sl.) new school
1. an enthusiastic way to express being in agreement or signal that someone is absolutely right. 2. a way to say, "I couldn't have said it better myself." (var. **you know that's right**)

that all phrase (general sl.) old & new school
1. a term used to say, "that's all you have to do" [usually used when trying to prod someone in proving himself/ herself].
ex: "Go home and get the money, that all." "Just tell her you can't make it, thats all."

that don't even sound right phrase (general sl.) old & new school
1. a term used to express suspicion or doubt about one's statement, explanation, or claim.
ex: "I'm sorry, but that don't even sound right."

[a male who's] **that dude** adj. (e. coast sl.) new school
1. a term used to praise an extraordinary male who excels past the heights of his peers.
ex: "You that dude for real cuz."

that's good money phrase (general sl.) new school
1. a correct description, assessment, or prediction. 2. a guarantee.
See also: [to] **call good money**

that goes without sayin' phrase (e. coast sl.) new school
1. a term used to express that something is obvious and/or is a well known fact. (var. **that's plain as day, that's obvious to a duck**)
ex: "I'd do anything for my Shortie, that goes without sayin'."

559

[a firearm] **that has a body on it** phrase (criminal sl.) old & new school
1. a firearm that has been involved in a homicide.
ex: "He sold him a biscuit with a body on it."

[someone who has] **that sh**** phrase (general sl.) new school
1. H.I.V. [the virus that causes AIDS].
ex: "I heard shortie might have that sh**."

that sh** don't move me phrase (general sl.) new school
1. a term used to inform someone that you are not intimidated by his/her tough talk and/or threats. (var. **that sh** don't phase me**)
ex: "Look here Slim, that sh** don't move me."

that sh** is see through [all day long] phrase (general sl.) new school
1. a term used to express one's ability to see pass someone's lie, deception, or con. (var. **that sh** is weak/ transparent** [all day long])
ex: "Between you and me, that sh** is see through."

that speaks for itself phrase (e. coast sl.) new school
1. a term used when an answer to a question is obvious or unquestionably clear. (var. **that's self explanatory**)
ex: "We know we all can't go in there at one time, that speaks for itself."

that thing n. (general sl.) old & new school
1. a covert way to refer to an object. (var. **that**)
ex. "Did you pick up that thing for me?" "He still got that for you if you want it."

that thing/thang n. (sexual sl.) new school
1. the H.I.V. or AIDS virus. (var. **that monster/blicky/thou yow**)
ex: "Madd people got that thing and they don't even know it."

that thing-thing n. (criminal sl.) new school

1. a firearm; handgun. (var. [a] **thing-thing**, [a] **thang-thang,
them thang-thangs, that thing**)
*ex: "They tried to sneak that thing thing in here." "I heard he
carries a thing-thing everywhere he goes."*

that was a hellava demonstration [you put down] phrase (e. coast
sl.) new school
1. a hip and enthusiastic way to praise someone for his/her
excellent and outstanding performance or achievement.

that white stuff phrase (drug sl.) new school
1. powder cocaine.
*ex: "They busted a truckload of that white stuff on the N.J.
Turnpike."*

that'll get ya head split phrase (general sl.) new school
1. a way to warn someone that consequences of his/her actions will
be severe. (var. **that'll get you ten to tewnty**)

that'll work phrase (general sl.) old & new school
1. a hip way to agree.
ex: "Pick you up at six, that'll work."

that's a done deal phrase (e. coast sl.) new school
1. a term used to announce "the end" or "ending" of something
[also used to finalize or signal finality]. (var. **that's a done deally**)
See also: **it's a wrap**
ex: "That's a done deal son, when can I pick that up from you?"

that's a terrible thing phrase (general sl.) new school
1. a term used as a fake expression of sympathy.

that's all she wrote phrase (general sl.) old & new school
1. a term used to signify the end or finish. 2. a way to say, "it's
over". See also: **it's a wrap**
ex: "Sorry dawg, that's all she wrote."

[now] **that's bad** phrase (general sl.) old & new school
1. a playful or sarcastic way to criticize someone's actions, behavior, and/or character upon observing that person doing something shameful, petty, or not classy.
ex: "That's bad dawg, Shortie took the waitresses tip off the table."

that's between a and b, [you need to/I'mma] **see** [ya/my] **way outta this/it** phrase (general sl.) old & new school
1. a witty way to tell someone to mind his/her business or for one to signal he/she doesn't want to get involved in someone's else's business.

[now] **that's deep** phrase (general sl.) new school
1. a term used to signify a action or thought as being very significant in meaning.
ex: "Dawg, if she said that, that's deep."

[now] **that's game** phrase (general sl.) old & new school
1. a term used to say that something someone is saying is a lie, a deception, and/or con. (var. [now] **that's bullsh**, that sh** is game**)
ex: "That's game, if he had it he'd show you."

[now] **that's gangster** phrase (e. coast sl.) new school
1. an enthusiastic way to acknowledge an action or thought as being daring, bold, and/or courageous.
ex: "Invitin' all your girlfriends to your party, that's gangster."

that's how we do it around here phrase (e. coast sl.) new school
1. a term used as a way to boast and/or give oneself praise for doing something outstanding. (var. **that's how we do it, that's how we get down around here**)

that's how you get down? phrase (e. coast sl.) new school
1. a term used to question one's actions, behavior, and/or character when that person does something one finds surprising, confusing, or unbelievable.

ex: "That's how you get down now dawg?"

that's like dot on dice phrase (e. coast sl.) new school
1. a term used to signal that something is 100% guaranteed;
something is a sure thing.
ex: "I already told you we gettin' in, that's like dot on dice."

that's like tryin' to squeeze blood from a turnip phrase (general
sl.) old & new school
1. impossible; undoable.

[now] **that's love** phrase (e. coast sl.) new school
1. a term used to express gratitude for someone's generosity. 2. a
way to say, "that's fine", "that's agreeable", or "that's satisfactory"
with me.
*ex: "That's love dawg, I couldn't have done it by myself." "Seven
o'clock, that's love with me."*

that's mandatory phrase (general sl.) old & new school
1. a term used to say that something is a must.
*ex: "That's mandatory, we goin' back." "We watchin' that at six
o'clock, that's mandatory."*

that's me phrase (general sl.) old & new school
1. a term used to declare ownership of something. (var. **that's me**
[all day])
ex: "That's me now dawg."

that's money phrase (general sl.) old & new school
1. guaranteed; a sure thing. (var. **that's** [like] **money in the bank**)
ex: "Don't worry about it, that's money."

that's my manz an'nim phrase (e. coast sl.) new school
1. a hip way to acknowledge a group of males one considers
to be his friends. (var. **that's my man an'nim**)
ex: "Yeah yeah yeah, that's my manz an'nim from B.K."

that's [just] **my regular** phrase (general sl.) new school
1. a term used to boast or praise oneself for doing something
outstanding [also used when accepting a compliment].
ex: "That wasn't luck, that's my regular."

that's my [good] **word!** phrase (general sl.) old & new school
1. a term used to affirm or reaffirm one's position or thought
leaving no room for doubt [usually used when trying to convince
someone you are telling the truth].
*ex: "I won't say nothin', that's my word." "That's my word, if you
believe her I'm outta here."*

that's my work phrase (e. coast sl.) new school
1. a boisterous way to take credit and give praise to oneself at the
same time. (var. **you see my work**)

that's not/ain't you phrase (general sl.) old & new school
1. a term used when telling someone that his/her behavior or
actions aren't consistent with his/her normal behavior or actions.
(var. **that ain't you**)
*ex: "You be tryin' to act like them, but that's not you." "I know
that ain't you."*

that's on everything phrase (e. coast sl.) new school
1. a term used to affirm or reaffirm one's position or thoughts
leaving no room for doubt [usually used when attempting to
convince]. (var. **that's on everthing I love**)
ex: "That's on everthing, I'll be here when you get back."

that's on you phrase (general sl.) old & new school
1. a way to inform someone that a decision is his/her choice to
make. 2. a way to say, "that's your choice/ decision", "if that's
what you want to do", "I don't care what you do", or "so what".
*ex: "That's on you Slim, I'm goin'." "If you can't wait,
that's on you."*

that's payback from way back phrase (southern sl.) new school
1. a term used to inform someone that a specific action was
retaliation for a previous wrong he/she inflected on you.

[something] **that's** [someone's] **sh**** phrase (general sl.) old &
new school
1. something one finds entertaining [usually used in reference to
music, dance, or tevelvision].
*ex: "Good Times used to be my sh**." "Let me hear that, that's
my sh**."*

that's that [person's name/title of authority] **I know** phrase (e.
coast sl.) new school
1. a term used to mock or taunt one's opponent when he/she makes
a mistake or misses an opportunity to score a point against you in
competition.
ex: "That's the Jay Boogie I know."

that's that bullsh** [in ya life] phrase (e. coast sl.) new school
1. a way to reprimand someone for doing something petty,
extremely disappointing or shameful. 2. a term used to express
one's discontent or exasperation with an unfair situation or
treatment. (var. **that's that sucker sh**/bit** sh****)

that's that sh** phrase (e. coast sl.) old & new school
1. an enthusiastic way to emphasize something that one finds
enjoayable, entertaining, or pleasurable.
ex: "That's that sh** right there Dawg."

that's the dumbest thing since leather baseball caps phrase
(southern sl.) new school
1. a way to express how stupid, ridiculous, or outrageous
something is.
(var. **that's the dumbest thing since paper condoms**)

that's the sh** that kills me phrase (general sl.) old & new school
1. a term used to indenify something that is specifically triggering
your anger. (var. **that's the sh** that pisses me off**)

ex: "He didn't even call to thank me, that's the sh** that kills me."
"That's the sh** that kills me, I never asked you for nothin'."

that's what ya mouth say phrase (southern sl.) new school
1. a term used to dismiss one's claims or threats [usually used challengingly and/or sarcastically].

that's what's up phrase (general sl.) new school
1. a term used to express one's approval, praise, or support of another's assessment or thought [also used in recognition of one's performance or achievement]. (var. [now] **that's whassup**)
ex: "Shortie in them tight ass jeans, that's what's up for real."

that's what's wrong with people now phrase (general sl.) new school
1. a sarcastic way to respond to someone's unwanted and unsolicited advice or opinion and/or when one is inquiring about affairs which don't concern him/her. (var. **that's what's wrong with people now they don't mind** [know how to mind] **their business**)

that's why the graveyard full/filled/packed now phrase (general sl.) old & new school
1. a playful or sarcastic way to reprimand someone for being nosy.
2. a witty way to tell someone to "mind your business" [when that person is asking questions about something that doesn't concerns him/her].

that's ya work? phrase (e. coast sl.) new school
1. a way to ask someone does he/she deserve credit for something.
ex: "That's ya work Dawg?"

the average Joe n. (general sl.) old & new school
1. a modest male whose character, behavior, or actions are similar to a group of males who are not very exciting, outgoing, ambitious, spontaneous, or who doesn't exhibit leadership qualities. (var. **the average Joe Blow**)
ex: "She said she don't wanna deal with the average Joe."

the beast coast n. (e. coast sl.) new school
1. a way to refer to the East coast of the United States.

the bing n. (prison sl.) old & new school
1. the punitive section of a prison or jail; solitary confinement.
ex: "I spent my last three months in the bing."

the Board n. (prison sl.) old & new school
1. the Parole Board.
ex: "I been to the Board twice and got shot down twice."

[something that's] **the bomb** adj. (general sl.) new school
1. outstanding; unique; the best of its kind. (var. [something that's]
the bomb diggy/diggity/ditty)
ex: "That card you sent me was the bomb."

The Boogie Burnt Down n. (e. coast sl.) old school
1. the Bronx, N.Y. (var. **the B.X.**)

The Boogie Down n. (e. coast sl.) old & new school
1. the Bronx, N.Y. (var. **The Boogie Down Bronx**)
ex: "Hip-Hop started in The Boogie Down."

The Bottom n. (southern sl.) new school
1. Miami, Florida. See also: **M.I.A.**
ex: "I know some good people from The Bottom."

the butt n. (sexual sl.) old & new school
1. a covert way to refer to sex.
ex: "You think I just want the butt." "Now that you got the butt are you still going to call me?"

the County n. (criminal sl.) old & new school
1. a way to refer to the County Jail, City jail, or local lockup.
ex: "She left his ass in the County to rot."

the deuce n. (e. coast sl.) old school
1. 42nd Street in Manhattan. (var. **forty doo-wop, forty deuce**)
ex: "I posed to take her to the deuce tonight."

the dirty dirty n. (southern sl.) new school
1. a hip way to refer to any southern state.
ex: "We met while she was going to college in the dirty dirty."

The East n. (e. coast sl.) old & new school
1. the East New York section of Brooklyn N.Y.
ex: "My first crib was in The East."

the fall-back section phrase (e. coast sl.) new school
1. a fictitious place or area to send someone who has said
something ridiculous, negative, or un-encouraging. (var. [to]
put/send [someone] **to the fall-back section**)
*ex: "I'm about to drop ya man off in the fall-back section for
talkin' like that."*

the fort n. (general sl.) old school
1. one's dwellings or place of business.
*ex: "Meet me back at the fort." "Keep the fort in order while I'm
gone."*

The Fort n. (e. coast sl.) old & new school
1. the Fort Greene public housing complex in Brooklyn NY.

the game n. (criminal sl.) old & new school
1. a term used to refer to drug dealing. (var. **the drug game**)
ex: "There's only two ways out the game, death or prison."

[someone with] **the gift to gab** phrase (general sl.) old & new
school
1. one who has the unique ability to convince and/or persuade
others with words. 2. one who talks eloquently.
ex: "You was born with the gift to gab." "Use your gift to gab."

the gift that keeps on giving phrase (sexual sl.) new school
1. the herpes virus.

the God n. (e. coast sl.) old & new school
1. a term of endearment and respect used in reference to a male friend; friend [also used when referring to oneself]. (var. **the God** [one's name])
ex: "When the last time you heard from the God?" "Is the God Unique there?"

the grown-up phrase (sexual sl.) new school
1. a covert way to refer to sexual intercourse.

[something that's] **the hottest sh** out** adj. (general sl.) new school
1. something that is better than anything that is similar to it.
ex: "Nas ether was the hottest sh** out for a minute."

The Island n. (prison sl.) old & new school
1. Rikers Island Detention Facility. (var. **The Rock**)
ex: "I hafta go pick up my man from The Island."

[something that's] **the joint** adj. (general sl.) old school
1. outstanding; unique; the best of its kind.
ex: "That's the joint now." "That was the joint back in the days."

the jump-off phrase (e. coast sl.) new school
1. the start of an event or gathering. 2. an event or gathering.
ex: "What time is the jump-off?" "Are there gonna be chicks at this jump-off?"

the kid n. (general sl.) new school
1. a way to refer to oneself.
ex: "You know the kid wasn't goin' for that." "She said she's diggin' the kid."

[something that's] **the lick** adj. (general sl.) old & new school
1. a good idea or plan.

ex: "Gettin' there about two in the mornin' is the lick." "Stayin' to watch the fight with you was the lick."

the loose booty phrase (e. coast sl.) new school
1. diarrhea.
ex: "He been in the crib all day, with the loose booty." "That burrito gave me the loose booty."

[someone who's] **the man** adj. (general sl.) old & new school
1. a male whose character and/or performance excels and/or stands out amongst his peers. 2. the male in charge, with the connections or influence [used as a compliment or praise].
ex: "You know you the man right?" "Go in there and show them who the man is."

the man n. (criminal sl.) old school
1. a term used to refer to the police. See also: **five-o, jake**
ex: "We got stopped by the man for nothin'."

The Most High n. (general sl.) old & new school
1. a term used when making reference to God or a higher deity.
ex: "You always have to give praise to The Most High."

The Nation n. (general sl.) old & new school
1. The Nation of Islam.
ex: "I think she joined The Nation."

the next man phrase (general sl.) new school
1. a way to refer to a male in the third sense.
ex: "I'm not spendin' money on you so you can look good for the next man."

the okeydoke phrase (general sl.) old & new school
1. the lie, con, or deception used to trick, sucker, or take advantage of someone. (var. **the ol' okeydoke**)
ex: "You almost fell for the okeydoke." "Ya man tried the ol' okeydoke."

the older you get the dumber you get phrase (general sl.) old school
1. a term used when scolding someone for making a stupid mistake, comment, or decision.

the only thing bad about you is your breath phrase (southern sl.) new school
1. a witty way to dismiss someone's tough talk or empty threats.

the package n. (sexual sl.) new school
1. the H.I.V. or AIDS virus. (var. **that package**)
ex: "He don't know who gave'em the package."

the pen n. (w. coast sl.) old & new school
1. prison. 2. the penitentiary. See also: **up-north**
ex: "I took care of the lil homie in the pen."

the p-now n. (prison sl.) old & new school
1. prison or jail. 2. a way to say, "the penal system". (var. **the p-nile**)
ex: "He been to the p-now three times."

the price of tea just went up in China phrase (southern sl.) old school
1. a witty way to inform someone that the price for your help or doing a favor has just been increased [usually as a result of that person doing something which offended you].

the real phrase (general sl.) old & new school
1. the truth; the facts. (var. **the really real/realz**)
ex: "Is this the real?" "Somebody already gave me the really real."

[something that's] **the real deal Holyfield** adj. (southern sl.) old school
1. outstanding; unique; the best of its kind. 2. authentic. (var. [something that's] **the real**)
ex "When it comes to Hip-Hop, KRS is the real deal Holyfield."

the rest n. (general sl.) old & new school
1. one's apartment or house. 2. where one lives. (var. [where someone] **rests at**)
ex: "Lets go back to the rest." "I invited her and her friends to the rest."

the runnin's phrase (general sl.) old school
1. the whole story; the facts; the details. 2. the truth.
ex: "Did Shortie tell you the runnin's?" "I need to know what the runnin's are."

[someone who's] **the sh**** adj. (general sl.) old & new school
1. one whose talents and performance stands out amongst his/her peers; to be the best at what one does. (var. [someone who's] **the shiznit**)
ex: "You think you the sh**." "I am the sh**."

[something that's] **the sh**** adj. (general sl.) old & new school
1. outstanding; unique; the best of its kind. (var. [something that's] **the sh**s/shiznit**)
ex: "I like that, that's the sh**."

the side pocket n. (prison sl.) new school
1. the punitive or segregated part of a prison where prisoners spend time in solitary confinement [usually for disciplinary reasons]. See also: [the] **bing**
ex: "They took'em to the side pocket for fightin'."

the store-man n. (prison sl.) old & new school
1. the inmate who inmates can go to borrow or purchase items that are normally sold through the prison commissary [at an inflated price because inmates are receiving such items on credit].
ex: "Every jail got a store-man."

the sure shot adj. (general sl.) old school
1. outstanding; unique; the best of its kind.
ex: "This gots to be the sure shot."

the wild thing n. (sexual sl.) old school
1. a way to refer to sex.
ex: "She hasn't done the wild thing in awhile." "Sound like your parents in there doin' the wild thing."

them boys phrase (southern sl.) new school
1. a term used to refer a tough group of guys [who are not necessarily one's friends].
ex: "You know them boys from Brooklyn don't play."

them my peoples phrase (general sl.) new school
1. a term used to acknowledge a group of people who are one's friends. See also: **my manz an'nim**
ex: "They wouldn't violate, them my peoples."

them peoples n. (criminal sl.) new school
1. a term used to refer to law enforcement agents or agencies connected to law enforcement.
ex: "Them peoples been by here looking for you again."

them thangs/things phrase (drug sl.) new school
1. kilograms of cocaine.
ex: "I got them things for twenty a pop." "How many of them thangs you want?"

there's a fungus among us phrase (general sl.) old school
1. a witty way to declare that a foul order or stench is coming from someone in the general area yet who remains unidentified.

they bangin' in Little Rock phrase (w. coast sl.) new school
1. a covert way to announce there's an illegal dice game going on.

they say Neports not su-ports phrase (e. coast sl.) new school
1. a term used to complain when someone asks for a cigarette [often turning the person down or making it clear that he/she has to buy his/her cigarettes]. (var. **this ain't no/a party pack, you grown buy ya own**)

[a female who's] **thick** adj. (general sl.) old & new school
1. a female who has a big butt, thighs, and/or breasts. (var. [a female who's] **thick as a govermint mule/as all out doors/ as a muhf**ka**)
ex: "She used to be thick, 'til she started usin' drugs."

[a female who's] **thick as grandma's gravy** phrase (southern sl.) new school
1. a female who has a big butt, large thighs, and large breasts; a body worthy of praise.
ex: "I seen shortie in a bathin' suit, yo kid I'm tellin' you, she's thick as grandma's gravy."

think it ain't phrase (southern sl.) new school
1. a term used to affirm or reaffirm one's position or thought leaving no room for doubt [usually used when being questioned about a fact or the truthfulness of a claim]. (var. **think it ain't when it is**)
ex: "Think it ain't, this game is about to be over."

[you] **think my head screw on backwards?** phrase (general sl.) old & new school
1. a term used in response to someone's foolish attempt to tell you something unbelievable or outrageously ridiculous in an effort to deceive or con you. (var. [you] **think my head screws off and on?**)

[someone who] **thinks he/she is jive slick** phrase (general sl.) new school
1. one who thinks he/she possesses an unique ability to con, manipulate, or deceive people.
ex: "This chick be thinkin' she jive slick, but I'm hip to all her bullsh**."

[someone who] **thinks he/she is the sh**/sh**s** phrase (general sl.) old & new school
1. one who has an overrated opinion of his/her self worth, importance, status; conceited.

ex: "You just think you the sh**."

[someone who] **thinks his/her sh** don't stink** phrase (general sl.) old & new school
1. someone who is quick to criticize others and who doesn't think or like to admit that he/she does wrong.
ex: "You one of those same people who don't think that their sh** stinks."

[a male's] **third leg** n. (e. coast sl.) old & new school
1. a covert way to refer to a penis.
ex: "She tried to kick my third leg."

[someone who's] **thirsty** adj. (e. coast sl.) new school
1. desperate; in urgent need.
ex: "When you thirsty, ain't no tellin' what you'd do to get a couple dollars." "Some catz come home from prison madd thirsty."

this is some bullsh** phrase (general sl.) new school
1. a matter of fact way to express one's discontent, dissatisfaction, annoyance, disbelief, frustration, surprise or unfair treatment. (var. **this is some real/straight/straight-up bullsh**, this is that real/straight/straight-up bullsh****)
ex: "I don't believe this, this is some bullsh**."

this that and the 3rd phrase (general sl.) old & new school
1. a way to refer to all the different things someone has said during a single conversation.
ex: "I dunno, she came in here talkin' about this that and the 3rd and I was like, yo you hafta talk to him about that."

this that boy [one's name] phrase (southern sl.) new school
1. a term used to announce oneself to a group of people. 2. a term used to give oneself a verbal acknowledgement. (var. **that's that boy** [the person's name])
ex: "This that boy Moe Deezy, I'm back believe me."

[someone who's] **thorough** adj. (e. coast s1.) old & new school
1. a stand up individual who possess a character that is unwavering during pressure or dangerous situations. (var. [a female who's a] **thorough bred)**
ex: "Shortie thorough as they come." "The time can make thorough catz lay down sometimes."

three piece catz n. (general sl.) old school
1. males who are legally employed.
ex: "She datin' this three piece cat now."

[someone who's] **through** adj. (criminal sl.) old & new school
1. someone who has received or facing an extremely long prison sentence. 2. someone no longer able to perform to his/her past excellence. (var. [someone who's] **through dealin')**
ex: "They got busted in N.C., they through."

[to] **throw a block for** [someone] v. (general sl.) old & new school
1. to purposely obscure the view for a friend or love one to avoid others from observing what he/she is doing [usually done by positioning one's body in a way that puts one out of view of others]. (var. [to] **throw a block)**
ex: "You think you can throw me a block?"

[to] **throw a brick** phrase (criminal sl.) old & new school
1. the act of committing a crime for money.
ex: "There's been times I came this close to throwin' a brick." "I'm not throwin' no more bricks."

throw a dog a bone phrase (general sl.) old & new school
1. a witty way to ask someone to help you financially [usually by lending you money]. (var. **throw a bum a crumb)**

[to] **throw a fit** phrase (general sl.) old & new school
1. to become outraged and disruptive [usually as a result of being upset]. (var. [to] **throw a natural fit)**
ex: "When she found out I was lyin', Shortie threw a fit."

[to] **throw** [them] '**bows** phrase (southern sl.) new school
1. the act of throwing or flinging one's elbows in a fight or basketball game.
ex: "We started throwin' them 'bows to get through the crowd."

[to] **throw** [some] **bullsh** in the game** phrase (general sl.) new school
1. to lie or do something deceptive in an attempt to derail one's plan, effort, or goal [while attempting to ruin one's reputation or credibility].
ex: "Then here she comes tryin' to throw some bullsh** in the game."

throw'd adj (southern sl.) new school
1. drunk; intoxicated.
ex: "Man I was so throw'd I couldn't even drive home last night, I had to take a cab." "Shortie an'nim got throw'd at the club last night."

[to] **throw down** phrase (e. coast sl.) old school
1. to fist fight; to box. (var. [a] throwdown
ex: "They outside about to throw down."

[to] **throw joints** phrase (e. coast sl.) old school
1. to fist fight; to box. See also: [to] **shoot joints**
ex: "I left when I seen Shortie and her momz about to throw joints."

[to] **throw** [one's] **set up** v. (w. coast sl.) old & new school
1. to make some sort of hand gesture or signal in one's representation of one's gang or organization. (var. [to] **throw up** [one's] **set**)

[to] **throw shade** phrase (general sl.) old & new school
1. to act stuck up and/or snobbish. 2. to purposely ignore and/or act like one is better than people he/she one used to socialize with [usually when one acquires material or financial wealth and/or a position of stature]. See also: **highside**

[to] **throw them thangs** phrase (southern sl.) new school
1. to have the ability and skill to fist fight or box. See also: [to]
shoot joints
*ex: "I know one thing you better know how to throw them thangs
talkin' like that."*

[to] **throw them things up** [for one's neighborhood/click] phrase
(general sl.) new school
1. the act of making some sort of hand gesture to signal one's
representation and respect towards his/her neighborhood, city,
state, or friends, or organization.
*ex: "I know I have to throw them things up for my manz an'nim
locked down."*

[someone who's] **throwin' bricks at the penitentiary** phrase
(criminal sl.) old & new school
1. someone who is doing things that can and will eventually send
him/her to jail or prison.
ex: "I'm tired of throwin' bricks at the penitentiary."

[to] **trust** [someone] **like that** phrase (general sl.) old & new
school
1. to trust someone unconditionally/100 percent.
ex: "No offense, but I don't trust nobody like that."

thug love n. (general sl.) new school
1. the unconditional love between friends or mates who consider
themselves "thugs" or "thugged out".
*ex: "The reason you can't understand it, cause this is thug love
Shortie."*

thug passion n. (e. coast sl.) new school
1. an alcoholic beverage named Alize'.

[someone who's] **thugged out** adj. (general sl.) new school
1. a young individual who projects an image of being a tough guy
and/or criminal through his/her actions, behavior, and personality.
(var. [someone who's] **thuggin' it**)

ex: "You haven't seen ya man in awhile, yo Dawg thugged out for real."

thugs adj. (general sl.) new school
1. young individuals who have a tough guy and/or criminal persona. (var. [someone who's] **thuggish)**
ex: "There's more to life than being a thug."

[to] **thump** phrase (general sl.) old & new school
1. to fist fight. (var. [to] **thump with** [someone])
ex: "Shortie said she wants to thump with your new girl."

[something that's] **thumpin'** adj. (general sl.) old & new school
1. outstanding; unique; the best of its kind.
ex: "Tell me these new G-Unit joints ain't thumpin'."

[a female who's] **tight** adj. (e. coast sl.) new school
1. extremely good looking and always has a stunning appearance.
ex: "What happened to shortie she used to be tight."

[a male who keeps himself] **tight** adj. (e. coast sl.) new school
1. well groomed and dresses nicely.
ex: "Homes been tight since High School."

[people who are] **tight** adj. (general sl.) old & new school
1. extremely close friends.
ex: "I'm tight with all my peoples."

[something that's] **tight** adj. (general sl.) new school
1. outstanding; unique; the best of its kind. (var. [something that's] **tight to death)**
*ex: "Tina Turner new sh** is tight."*

[to be] **tight** [about/over something] v. (e. coast sl.) new school
l. angry; upset; seething. (var. [to be] **tight** [with someone])
ex: "I wouldn't say anything right now, she kinda tight over what you said."

[to] **tighten** [someone] **up** v. (general sl.) old & new school
1. to give or loan someone something as a favor or a sign of one's generosity. 2. to show someone preferential treatment. See also: [to] **hook** [someone] **up**
ex: "You think you can tighten us up the next time you come to town?"

tighten up phrase (general sl.) old & new school
1. a term used to advise and/or encourage someone to concentrate or put more effort into what he/she is doing.
ex: "Tighten up Dawg, we can win this."

[to] **tighten up on** [someone] v. (general sl.) old & new school
1. to be more strict with someone than you have been in the past.
ex: "I'mma hafta tighten up on you 'til I see better grades."

tigobitties n. (southern sl.) new school
1. a covert term males use to say, "big ol' titties", or "titties".

[to get] **Timberland'd up** v. (e. coast sl.) new school
1. a term used to describe a person being kicked while on the ground by an individual or group of individuals who happen to have on boots made by Timberland.
ex: "We catch ya man on the A train we gonna Timberland his ass up."

timbos n. (e. coast sl.) old & new school
1. Timberland brand boots. (var. **tims**) See also: **40 belows**
ex: "Slim came to school the first day rockin' some timbos and shorts."

[to] **tip in** [somewhere] v. (general sl.) old & new school
1. to arrive at one's destination.
ex: "Don't come tippin' in here past twelve." "Guess what time she tipped her ass in here?"

tipsy adj. (general sl.) old & new school
1. slightly or almost drunk.
ex: "You was a lil more than tipsy."

[someone who's] **tired** adj. (general sl.) old school
1. one who is not cool or hip. 2. one who follows outdated or corny styles, trends, or fashions.
ex: "Here comes your tired friends." "You are so tired its unbelievable."

[something that's] **tired** adj. (general sl.) old school
1. something made or put together in poor taste and/or poor quality [usually used as a negative way to critique].
ex: "And she had the nerve to come to the dance in these tired blue suede shoes."

tired [excuses, explanations, pick up lines, raps, jokes] adj. (general sl.) old school
1. of poor quality or in poor taste.
ex: "I'm through with all ya tired excuses."

[a] **titty shot** phrase (sexual sl.) new school
1. the intentional or unintended exposure of a female's breasts.
ex: "I heard she did a titty shot in this new movie." "There's a titty shot of her in the new Source issue."

to the utmost phrase (general sl.) old & new school
1. to the best of one's ability. 2. with all sincerity.
ex: "I loved Shortie to the utmost."

to this day... phrase (general sl.) old & new school
1. a way to say, "up until to this very day" when referring to the present [often used as a prelude].
ex: "To this day I still say she stole my ring and bracelet."

toast n. (criminal sl.) old & new school
1. a firearm; handgun. (var. [a] **toaster**)
ex: "They looked everywhere for the toast."

[a] **toe hold** phrase (southern sl.) new school
1. an advantage, slight edge, or small opportunity used for future progress.
ex: "All I need is a toe hold, and I'll be back in business."

[to] **toe-tag** [someone] v. (criminal sl.) new school
1. a covert way to refer to a homicide.
ex: "Somebody finally toe-tagged ya man."

[to] **toke** v. (drug sl.) old school
1. the act of smoking marijuana.
ex: "I seen you back there tokin'."

toke 'til you choke phrase (drug sl.) new school
1. a hip way to encourage someone to continue smoking the marijuana that he/she is smoking until he/she has had enough.

[to] **tongue** [someone] v. (sexual sl.) old & new school
1. to stick one's tongue in another's mouth while kissing; to French kiss. (var. [to] **tongue** [someone] **down**, [to] **have/put tongue all down** [someone's] **throat**, [to] **tongue kiss**)
ex: "I don't tongue on the first date."

[a female's] **tongue skills** adj. (sexual sl.) new school
1. a covert way to praise a female's ability to perform oral sex [usually a male's term].
ex: "Yo son, shortie tongue skills ain't nooo joke."

[someone who's] **too light in the ass** phrase (general sl.) old new school
1. a witty way to dismiss someone as being physically unable to compete or pose any serious threat [often used to taunt one's opponent].
ex: "Dawg, you too light in the ass to mess with me."

[you] **too light to fight, too thin to win** phrase (general sl.) old & new school

1. a witty way to taunt someone about not having what it takes to beat you and/or compete against you [also used to dismiss someone's tough talk and/or threats].

too many Chiefs and not enough Indians phrase (general sl.) new school
1. a term used to point out a group's difficulty to accomplish anything because everyone wants to be the person giving the orders.

[someone who's] **too short for a long conversation** phrase (prison sl.) old & new school
1. someone who's extremely close to finishing his/her prison sentence.

[a] **tool** n. (criminal sl.) old & new school
1. a firearm; handgun. (var. [a] **tooly**)
ex: "Police found the tools they used."

[to] **toot** [caine] v. (drug sl.) old school
1. to sniff cocaine.
ex: "They caught 'em tootin' in the bathroom at work and fired his ass."

tootbrush up'd phrase (prison sl.) new school
1. to be in possession of a toothbrush that has been made into a weapon [usually by sharping the end or affixing a razor to the end part].

[someone who's] **tore up** adj. (general sl.) old & new school
1. unattractive; not appealing. 2. haggard and unkempt. 3. to look much older than one's real age. (var. [someone who's] **tore up from the floor up**) See also: [someone who's] **beat up from the feet up**
ex: "I seen a picture of shortie and she tore up."

tore up adj. (general sl.) old & new school
1. drunk; intoxicated.
ex: "They came back from the party tore up."

[to] **toss** [someone] v. (sexual sl.) new school
1. the act of having sex. (var. [to] **toss** [someone] **up**)
ex: "I heard you was tryin' to toss my friend."

[to] **toss** [something] **at** [someone] v. (general sl.) old & new school
1. to share an idea or thought with someone in hopes of soliciting an opinion or advice. (var. [to] **toss** [something] **up in the air**)
ex: "I want to toss this at you and see what you think."

[to] **tote them burners** phrase (criminal sl.) new school
1. the act of carrying guns.
ex: "When I get out this time, I'm done totin' them burners."

[to] **touch** [someone] v. (e. coast sl.) new school
1. the act of bringing great bodily harm to someone [possibly resulting in death]. (var. [to] **touch** [someone] **up**, [to] **touch** [someone's] **wig**)
ex: "You can get touched boy, don't get that twisted."

[to] **touch paper** phrase (e. coast sl.) new school
1. to make or have access to large amounts of money [usually acquired through shady or illegal means].
ex: "Them catz frontin' they ain't never touch no paper." "We was out there touchin' real paper."

[to] **touchdown** phrase (prison sl.) old & new school
1. to return home after completing one's prison sentence. 2. to arrive. (var. [to] **touch the town**)
ex: "I'm about to touchdown real soon."

[something that's] **tough** adj. (general sl.) old school
1. outstanding; unique; the best of its kind.
ex: "Wait 'til you see this tough outfit I got for the party."

tough titty phrase (general sl.) old & new school
1. a playful or sarcastic way to say, "too bad" or "that's your problem" when someone is complaining about your treatment towards him/her.
ex: "That's tough titty but you're not goin'."

[someone who's a] **toy** adj. (e. coast sl.) old school
1. one who is not cool, hip, or in the know. (var. [someone who's a] **toy ass** [person])
ex: "I seen'er with this toy earlier."

toy cops n. (general sl.) old & new school
1. security guards.
ex: "Its the toy cops that give you the most hassle at the mall."

[a female's] **track record** phrase (e. coast sl.) new school
1. a female's sexual past, background, and/or reputation.
ex: "You hafta find out what her track record look like first Dawg."

[to] **transform on** [someone] v. (e. coast sl.) old school
1. to gather one's friends or family members in a group for the purpose of showing strength, support, and unity when one is confronted with a situation where one feels threatened by more than one person.
ex: "Don't start no sh** up in here, that whole family will transform on you in a heartbeat."

trap n. (general sl.) old & new school
1. money.
ex: "How much trap you bring with you?"

[a] **trap off** adj. (general sl.) old & new school
1. a situation or action designed or destined to get one in trouble or in a very precarious situation.
ex: "That's a trap off son, I would chill." "And the thing about it, I already knew it was a trap off."

[to] **trap** [oneself] **off** v. (general sl.) old & new school
1. to do or say something that gets one in trouble and/or caught.
ex: "I bet you any amount of money, he goes in there and traps himself off." "He let the police trap 'em off."

trapped off phrase (criminal sl.) old & new school
1. arrested; caught in the act. See also: **hemmed up**
ex: "All five of them got trapped off in N.C."

[something that's] **trash** adj. (general sl.) new school
1. poor in quality; unsatisfactory. (var. something that's] **straight trash**) See also: [something that's] **garbage**
*ex: "I bought his new album and that sh** is trash."*

traum n. (drug sl.) new school
1. marijuana. (var. **trauma**)

[a] **tre deuce** n. (criminal sl.) old & new school
1. a 32. caliber handgun.

[a] **tre eight** n. (criminal sl.) old & new school
1. a 38. caliber handgun.

[to] **treat** [someone] **like a stepchild** phrase (general sl.) old & new school
1. to treat someone mean, with neglect, and/or unfair. (var. [to] **treat** [someone] **like a nappy headed stepchild/a wet food stamp/sh** on a stick**)
ex: "I'm tired of you treatin' me like a step child."

[to] **treat** [someone] **like dirt/sh**** v. (general sl.) old & new school
1. to treat a friend or loved one in a mean and disrespectful way.
*ex: "I couldn't let her keep treatin' me like sh** so I left."*

treat yaself, don't cheat yaself phrase (southern sl.) old & new school

1. a term used to encourage someone to treat himself/herself to something nice or to an extra expenditure.

trees n. (drug sl.) new school
1. marijuana.
ex: "The cops found madd trees in the truck."

[to] **trick** [one's] **money** v. (w. coast sl.) old & new school
1. to spend one's money foolishly or recklessly in an attempt to impress others or when pursuing friendship/ intimacy with someone of the opposite sex. (var. [to] **trick on** [someone], [to] **trick** [something] **on** [someone]) See also: **a trick**
ex: "This fool tricked all his money on a stripper, and he doesn't have the money to pay his rent."

[a] **tricked out** [automobile] adj. (w. coast sl.) old & new school
1. a vehicle that has been accessorized.
ex: "You see that tricked out truck over there?"

tricknowledgy phrase (e. coast sl.) new school
1. lies; half truths; deceptions.
ex: "He definitely knows how to use tricknowledgy when he wants to get his way."

[someone who's] **tried and true** phrase (general sl.) new school
1. someone who has proven to be a real friend showing unwavering support through the good times and bad.
ex: "I gotta make Shortie wifey, she's tried and true."

[someone] **tried by twelve and/but hung by one** phrase (criminal sl.) new school
1. someone who has been convicted in a jury trial because of the testimony given by a friend of love one.

[someone who's] **trife** adj. (e. coast sl.) new school
1. petty; lowdown; without morals. 2. irresponsible and undependable. (var. [someone who's] **triflin'**, [someone who's] **livin' the trife life**)

ex: "Shortie madd trife Dawg." "You too trife for me."

[one's] **triflin' mental** n. (e. coast sl.) new school
1. irresponsible and often deadbeat dad.
ex: "If you think that's bad, then I need to tell you about my triflin' mental."

[to] **trim** [someone] v. (general sl.) old &new school
1. to sucker, fool, or con someone out of something [usually money]. 2. to win all of one's money gambling against him/her.
(var. [to] **trim** [someone] **for his/her sh****)
ex: "I'm about to go in here and trim these catz."

trim n. (sexual sl.) old & new school
1. a covert term males use for sex and/or the vagina.
ex: "Shortie ain't given up no trim."

[to] **trip** v. (general sl.) new school
1. to make a big deal out of something trival [usually resulting in an unpleasant scene]. 2. to act unruly and disruptive when upset or angered. (var. [to] **trip on** [someone], [to] **trip out on** [someone])
ex: "Before you start trippin' let me tell you what happened."

[a] **triple beam** n. (drug sl.) old & new school
1. a special scale to weigh drugs with.

triple beams dreams n. (drug sl.) old & new school
1. dreams people have about getting rich in the drug trade.

[someone who's] **triple "F"** adj. (e.coast sl.) new school
1. a "fake", a "fraud", and a "phony".
ex. "I knew you was triple "F" when I first met you."

[someone who's a] **troll** adj. (general sl.) old & new school
1. unattractive; ugly.
ex: "I coulda died when he showed up with that troll."

troop n. (general sl.) old school
1. a term of endearment among friends; friend. 2. a way to address someone whose name you do not know or don't want to use in front of others. (var. **trooper**)
ex: What time you got troop?"

[to] **troop for** [someone] v. (general sl.) old & new school
1. to show unwavering support for someone through the good times and bad [even if it means putting oneself in jeopardy].
ex: "I never thought he'd troop for me like this."

[to] **troop** [something] **out** phrase (general sl.) old & new school
1. to remain steadfast and resilient during times of troubles [even if it means putting oneself in jeopardy for a friend or love one]. (var. [to] **troop** [something] **out with** [someone])
ex: "You sure you wanna troop this out with me?"

troop [it] **outta state** v. (drug sl.) old & new school
1. to travel to another state to sell drugs. (var. [to] **troop in and outta state**)
ex: "My manz want me to troop with him outta state."

[someone who's a] **trooper** adj. (general sl.) old & new school
1. a stand up individual who won't bow to pressure and shows unwavering support for a friend during the good times and bad [even if it means putting oneself in jeopardy].
ex: "You found yaself a real trooper."

tropical n. (drug sl.) new school
1. marijuana.

truck jewels phrase (e. coast sl.) old school
1. big gaudy gold chains.
ex: "Slick Rick still rockin' truck jewels."

true phrase (e. coast sl.) new school
1. a term used to express being in agreement with and/or being able to relate to someone. (var. **true that/ indeed**) See also: **word**

ex: "True, I think its best we leave up outta here."

[someone who's] **true to the game** adj. (general sl.) old & new school
1. one who is dedicated to his/her profession, trade, or means of acquiring money [whether legal or illegal]. (var. [someone who's] **true to** [what he/she is doing])
ex: "Catz like me is true to the game."

trust me phrase (general sl.) new school
1. a term used to affirm or reaffirm one's position, claim, or thought leaving no room for doubt. (var. **trust me on that**)
ex: "Trust me, if they said they comin' they comin'." "You gonna pay me my money, trust me."

truth be told... phrase (general sl.) old & new school
1. a way to say, "truthfully" or "between you and me" [often used in prelude to expressing a honest or secretive thoughts].
ex: "Truth be told, you could have been left."

[to] **try** [someone] v. (general sl.) old & new school
1. to test the boundaries and limitations of one's tolerance, patience, and/or relationship with you. 2. the attempt to con, deceive, or take advantage of someone [usually for financial gain]. (var. [to] **try** [one's] **hand**)
ex: "I can't believe you tried me like that." "Keep tryin' me like that."

[to] **try** [someone's] **chin** phrase (general sl.) old & new school
1. a term used to threaten someone with testing his/her fighting or boxing skills.
ex: "You gonna make me try that chin."

[to] **try** [one's] **hand** phrase (general sl.) old & new school
1. to take a chance; the attempt to seize an opportunity.
ex: "The only way you gonna know is if you try ya hand." "I can't blame you for tryin' ya hand."

[to] **try some** [ol'] **bullsh**** v. (general sl.) old & new school
1. to attempt something that is deceptive, cunning, or disrespectful
with a friend or love one. (var. [to] **pull some** [ol'] **bullsh****)
ex: "There you go tryin' some bullsh** again."

[someone who's] **tryin' to catch** phrase (general sl.) old & new
school
1. one who is attempting to meet someone of the opposite sex.
ex: "Leave me alone, don't you see I'm tryin' to catch?"

tryin' to make a dollar outta fifteen cents phrase (general sl.)
old & new school
1. a term used to declare one's attempt to make money to
supplement his/her income.
ex: "I'm just out here tryin' to make a dollar outta fifteen cents."

[to] **tuck** [one's] **jewels** phrase (e. coast sl.) old school
1. to hide or secrete one's jewelry out of view when one is scared
of being robbed.
*ex: "A lot of these supposedly killer rappers have to tuck their
jewels when they go back around their way."*

[to] **tussle with** [someone] v. (general sl.) old & new school
1. to scuffle or struggle. 2. to engage in a minor physical
altercation.
*ex: "It was just a small tussle, its over now." "I don't want to
tussle with you over this."*

[an automobile that's] **tv'd up** phrase (general sl.) new school
1. an automobile that has tv's in the headrests and/or flip down
television monitors.
ex: "It wouldn't be right if I didn't get the whip tv'd up."

twankies n. (southern sl.) new school
1. a brand of expensive rims for automobile tires.

tweed n. (drug sl.) new school
1. marijuana.

tweeded adj. (drug sl.) new school
1. the state of being high from marijuana.
ex: "They police found them gettin' tweeded in the back of the bus."

[to] **twerk** [one's body] v. (southern sl.) new school
1. to work one's body on the dance floor or in the bed during sex. 2. to gyrate one's hips.
ex: "Shortie really knows who to twerk it."

[to] **twist** [a female] v. (sexual sl.) new school
1. a covert way to refer to sexual intercourse. (var. [to] **twist** [a female] **out**)
ex: "I was just about to twist shortie before you called."

[to] **twist** [someone's] **cap** phrase (criminal sl.) new school
1. a term used to describe being shot in the head. (var. [to] **twist** [someone's] **cap back**) See also: [to] **peel** [someone's] **head back**
ex: " That's the second time they tried to twist ya mans cap."

twisted adj. (general sl.) new school
1. drunk; intoxicated.
ex: "And she had the nerve to show up twisted"

twisted adj. (e. coast sl.) new school
1. confused; mistaken. 2. angry; upset; mad.
ex: "You have that twisted." "Don't get that twisted." "That's who got me twisted." "Yeah, I was kinda twisted about that."

two bullets runnin' wild phrase (prison sl.) old & new school
1. two 1 year prison sentences to be served consecutively.

[someone who's] **two faceded** adj. (general sl.) old & new school
1. someone you talk to in confidence who goes behind your back and talks about you and your secrets to others; a friend who talks negatively about you to people he/she knows you do not like and/or socialize with.

ex: "Your problem is, you too two faceded."

[to be] two minutes off [someone's] ass phrase (general sl.)
old & new school
1. very close to beating that person up [often used as an empty threat].
ex. "You need to stop playin' cause I'm already two minutes off your ass."

[to] two piece [someone] v. (e. coast sl.) new school
1. to punch someone in the face, mouth, or jaw two times in rapid succession [usually when one isn't expecting to be hit]. (var. **[to] give [someone] a two piece**)
ex: "Next thing you know she hit'em with a two piece."

two tears in a bucket, muhf**k it phrase (general sl.) old school
1. a matter of fact to say "I don't care", "whatever", or "so what" [usually used in an argument to signal that one is not afraid or unintimidated].

type hot adj. (e. coast sl.) new school
1. extremely mad, angry, or upset.
ex: "I seen it in her face, she was type hot about that there."

2 triple 0 n. (e. coast sl.) new school
1. the year 2000. (var. **2G**)
ex: "How'd you bring in the 2 triple 0?"

[a] 10¢ grit adj. (e. coast sl.) new school
1. a witty way to describe one's attempt to scare or intimidate people with a mean or tough glare or facial expression. (var. **[a] fake ass grit**)
ex: "Homes, you ain't scarin' nobody with ya lil 10¢ grit."

24-7 adj. (general sl.) old & new school
1. all the time; constantly. (var. **24-7-365**)
ex: "You can call me here 24-7."

[a] **3 pound 7** n. (criminal sl.) old & new school
1. a .357 caliber handgun. (var. [a] **3 five 7**)
ex: "He got shot with a 3 pound 7."

[the] **3rd coast** n. (southern sl.) new school
1. a hip way to refer to the combination of southern states.
ex. "3rd coast Hip-Hop is killin' the radio right now."

u

udeen (pron. uh'deen) phrase (e. coast sl.) old school
1. a very long period of time. (var. **ud**)
ex: "He ain't been around here in udeen." "I haven't seen your cousin in udeen."

[an] **ug-mug** adj. (e. coast sl.) new school
1. someone extremely unattractive; ugly. See also: **mugly**
ex: "She found herself a real ug-mug this time."

[the] **ultimate lick** phrase (general sl.) old & new school
1. a full proof or foil proof plan to acquire something [usually involves doing something wrong or against the law].
ex: "Yo Dun, I came up with the ultimate lick."

umpteen times phrase (southern sl.) old & new school
1. many times; repeatedly.
ex: "She called me umpteen times over the weekend."

[someone who's] **under pressure** adj. (general sl.) new school
1. intimidated and/or scared of someone.
ex: "I had that whole block under pressure for years."

[you] **underdig?!** phrase (w. coast sl.) new school
1. a matter of fact way to ask someone "do you/can you understand?" 2. a term used to assure or reassure one's thought, boast, or claim is undoubtedly true.
ex: "Six o'clock or I'm leavin' ya underdig?!" "Can you underdig what I'm tellin' you?"

[someone whose] **understanding is zero** phrase (e. coast sl.) new school

1. someone who won't listen to reason or rationale because he/she is upset or angered. 2. someone who refuses to consider the consequence of his/her behavior. (var. [someone with] **zero understanding**)
ex: "Her understanding is zero right now after what you did."

[a] **universal beatdown** adj. (e. coast sl.) old school
1. a beating that involves a group attacking and beating one individual.
ex: "Her and her sisters gave her ex a universal beatdown."

[to be] **up in** [a female] v. (sexual sl.) new school
1. a term males use for having sex. (var. **[to] go up in** [a female])
ex: "You mean to tell me, you was up in Shortie without wearing a condom?"

[to be] **up in** [someone's] **business** phrase (general sl.) old & new school
1. to be in someone's personal affairs for the sole purpose of being nosy. (var. **[to be] all up in** [someone's] **business**)
ex: "Every time I turn around, you up in my business."

[to be] **up in** [someone's] **spot** phrase (general sl.) new school
1. the act of visiting someone's dwellings or place of business.
ex: "We was up in my manz spot shootin' dice last night." "Guess who I ran into up in Moe's spot the other day?"

up in this piece phrase (general sl.) old & new school0
1. a hip way to say "in here" when referring to one's immediate location. (var. **up in this bit****)
ex: "Why nobody dancin' up in this piece?"

up-north n. (prison sl.) old & new school
1. the New York State prison system. (var. **up-state, up in the mountains**)
ex: "I never been up-north." "I'm goin' up-north to see my man."

[to be] up on [things] phrase (general sl.) old & new school
1. to be informed; aware; in step with current events, trends, and styles.
ex: *"You hafta stay up on things in this business."*

up sh** creek phrase (general sl.) old & new school
1. in extremely bad trouble; in a hopeless situation.
ex: *"I hate to say it, but ya man an'nim up sh** creek this time."*

Up-Top n. (e. coast sl.) new school
1. New York City.
ex: *"When the last time you been Up-Top?"*

ups adj. (general sl.) new school
1. a way to describe one's ability to jump high. (var. [someone with/who has] **ups**)
ex: *"Cause he so short, you wouldn't think he had ups like that."*

uptowns n. (e. coast sl.) old & new school
1. Air force one Nike tennis shoe.
ex: *"We was sportin' uptowns for years."*

use ya noodle phrase (general sl.) old school
1. a hip way to tell someone to think.
ex: *"All you hafta do is use ya noodle to get the answer."*

used d**k phrase (sexual sl.) old school
1. a term females use to refer to an ex-boyfriend or someone she has had the experience of having sex with.
ex: *"She can have'em, that used d**k." "Why would I want your used d**k?"*

used ta was a roosta, 'til I choked that chicken phrase (southern sl.) new school
1. a term used to mock someone who is talking about or making claims about what he/she "used to do" or is using the words "used to" in his/her conversation.

v

[a] **V.** n (general sl.) new school
1. an automobile; vehicle.
ex: "Where you park the V kid?"

V.A. n. (e. coast sl.) old & new school
1. Virginia.
ex: "Dawg an'nim had V.A. locked down for years."

[to] **vamp** [someone] v. (e. coast sl.) old school
1. the act of one individual being beaten up by a group. (var. [to] **vamp** [someone] **out**)
ex: "They tried to vamp ya friend on the train comin' home from school."

vested up phrase (criminal sl.) old & new school
1. the wearing of a bullet proof vest. (var. [to] **vest up**)
ex: "You can't come in here vested up."

vex adj. (general sl.) old & new school
1. upset; angry; mad; frustrated; annoyed.
ex: "She might be vexed when she sees us together."

[a] **V.I.** n. (prison sl.) old & new school
1. a social visit or visitor received by someone incarcerated.
ex: "Who came to see you on ya V.I.?" "I seen 'is girl on the V.I. and she looks all right."

[a] **vic** n. (criminal sl.) old & new school
1. a victim. 2. a way to refer to someone who is the target of a con, scheme, or plot aimed at taking advantage of him/her.
ex: "Here comes my vic now." "Ya man's a vic."

[to] **vic** [someone] v. (criminal sl.) old & new school
1. to take one's possessions by force, intimidation, or through deception. 2. to make someone a victim.
ex: "They vic'd ya man for his sneakers."

vice n. (southern sl.) old school
1. narcotic detectives.
ex: "You know the vice lookin' for you right?"

[something that's] **vicious** adj. (general sl.) old & new school
1. outstanding; unique; the best of its kind.
ex: "That outfit she had on was vicious."

[someone who's] **vicious** adj. (e. coast sl.) new school
1. the best at what he/she does; performs excellently. (var. [someone who's] **vicious at/with** [something])
ex: "Them boys vicious on the mike." "When they did their show, them catz was vicious."

[someone who's] **vicious** adj. (e. coast sl.) new school
1. a way to describe someone who is incredibly petty, untrustworthy, or dubious as well as an incredible liar.
ex: "Yo son, ya shortie is vicious, guess what she told my girl?" "You better watch shortie, she's vicious."

[to] **violate** v. (e. coast sl.) new school
1. to wrong or disrespect someone through words or acts. (var. [to] **violate the program**) See also: [to be] **in violation**
ex: "You didn't hafta violate like that." "Next time you violate Dawg, its on."

W

[to] **wail** v. (prison sl.) new school
1. to guess. 2. the act of pretending to be informed and/or knowledgeable about something one knows little about. 3. to make outrageous claims [usually about one's ability, past experiences, or sexual conquests]. (var. [someone who's] **wailin'**)
ex: "Why you always wailin'?" "You need to stop all that wailin'."

[to] **wail on** [someone] v. (general sl.) old & new school
1. to strike someone repeatedly and uncontrollably.
ex: "She just walked up on'em and started wailin' on his ass." "She wailed on'em for ten minutes."

[to] **wail up on** [the correct answer] phrase (prison sl.) new school
1. to guess and get a correct answer; to get lucky. (var. [to] **wail up on** [something])
ex: "Ain't no way you not gonna tell me, you didn't wail up on that answer."

[to] **wait in the cut** phrase (general sl.) old & new school
1. to wait discreetly or patiently. (var. [to] **wait in the cut for** [someone])
ex: "She told me to wait in the cut 'til she knows somethin'."

wake ups phrase (prison sl.) old & new school
1. the amount of days until one completes his/her prison sentence and can go home. (var. [to] **have** [a specific number] **of days/months on the wake up**)
ex: "I got like 16 days on the wake up."

Walies n. (e. coast sl.) old & new school
1. Clark Walabies shoes. (var. **WB's, Walos**)

ex: "I just copped a pair of purple Walies."

[to] walk around with [one's] **ass hangin' out** phrase (general sl.)
old & new school
1. to wear clothes that reveal too much of a female's private
anatomy.
*ex: "She always walkin' in here with her ass hangin' out, like
that's cute."*

[to] walk around with [one's] **mouth/lip poked out** phrase
(general sl.) old & new school
1. to pout.
ex: "She been walkin' around with her mouth poked out all day."

[to] walk around with [one's] **tongue hangin' out** phrase
(general sl.) old & new school
1. to have a look of desperation.
ex: "I hate when you walk around with ya tongue hangin' out."

[to] walk [one's prison sentence] **down** phrase (prison sl.) new
school
1. to have more than 75% of one's prison sentence completed.
ex: "Yo Dawg, I almost walked this bid down."

[a] walkin' dead man adj. (prison sl.) old & new school
1. an individual with an extremely long prison sentence [usually a
life sentence with no chance of parole].
ex: "Ya manz a walkin' dead man now."

[one's] walkin' papers phrase (general sl.) old school
1. the notification one receives from his/her mate which informs
him/her that the person is ending the relationship [usually
notification is verbal].
ex: "Its about time shortie got her walkin' papers."

[a] wanksta adj. (e. coast sl.) new school

l. one who is not cool, hip, or in the know; a nerdy individual.
See also: [a] **lame**
ex: "I haven't seen so many wankstas in my life."

[a] **wanna be** phrase (general sl.) old & new school
l. one who attempts to imitate the character and behavior of a
"street" tough individual.
ex: "You're nothin' but a wanna be."

[a] **wanna be super hero** phrase (general sl.) old school
l. a person who has decided to take on the role of a good samaritan
or mediator during a tense or violent situation.
*ex: "What's up with this wanna be super hero?" "Nobody asked
this wanna be super hero."*

[to] **want for nothin'** phrase (general sl.) new school
l. to have everything one needs and wants; to be financially secure
and independent. (var. [someone who's] **not wantin' for nothin'**)
ex: "Didn't I make sure you never wanted for nothin'?"

war stories phrase (prison sl.) old & new school
l. tales of one's experiences in the "street" and/or in prison
[usually entailing action and drama].
*ex: "That's him over there tellin' his war stories again." "Tell me
a couple war stories."*

water n. (drug sl.) old & new school
l. embalming fluid; PCP.

[to] **wax** [someone's] **ass** v. (e. coast sl.) old school
l. to beat someone up. (var. [to] **get** [one's] **ass
waxed**)
ex: "You almost got your ass waxed in there."

[something that's] **way...** adj. (e. coast sl.) new school
l. a term used to put emphasis on one's description of something
outstanding, unique, or the best of its kind.

ex: "They doin' it way big out there in L.A." "That hat looks way cool on you."

way back when phrase (general sl.) old & new school
1. a long time ago; in the past. (var. **way back**)
ex: "I know them from way back when."

we can do this phrase (general sl.) old & new school
1. a term used to affirm one's willingness to have a physical confrontation with someone who is challenging him/her. (var. **we can do this like Brutus**)
ex: "I don't care, we can do this."

we don't kick it like that [anymore/no more] phrase (general sl.) old & new school
1. a way to inform someone that you and another person aren't friends and/or involved intimately anymore.
ex: "Since I found out, we don't kick it like that."

we go back like Caddilacs phrase (southern sl.) new school
1. a term used to profess a friendship that has lasted a long number of years. (var. **we go back like 8 track**)

we tighter than a fat lady's girdle phrase (southern sl.) new school
1. a witty term used to profess a very close friend or friendship. (var. **we tighter than big booty girls in spandex**)

[something that's] **weak** adj. (general sl.) old & new school
1. poor in quality or performance. (var. **weak** [excuses, explanations, pick up lines, raps])
ex: "You know what, that was the weakest sh** I ever heard in my life."

[to] **wear** [something] v. (southern sl.) new school
1. to have the blame, responsibility, or guilt placed upon you unjustly without recourse to prove one's innocence.

ex: "I hate to tell you, but you gonna hafta wear this one."
"I'mma make sure you wear this."

[to] **wear an ass whippin'/kickin'** phrase (southern sl.) new school
1. to begrudgingly accept being beaten up or defeated [usually in a physical altercation].
ex: "Let's see how well you can wear this ass whippin' I'm about to put on you."

[to] **wear** [someone's] **ass out** phrase (southern sl.) old & new school
1. to beat someone up. 2. to beat someone into submission.

[to] **wear** [someone's] **ass out** phrase (sexual sl.) old & new school
1. the act of having sex for an extended length of time; to demonstrate endurance during sex. (var. [to] **wear** [someone] **out**)
ex: "Girl ... let me tell you, he tried to wear my ass out last night."

[to] **wear** [someone] **like a new pair of shoes** phrase (general sl.) old & new school
1. to beat someone up [usually used as a threat].
ex: "Boy, I'll wear you like new pair of shoes."

weed n. (drug sl.) old & new school
1. marijuana.

[someone who's] **weeded** adj. (drug sl.) old & new school
1. one who is high from smoking marijuana. (var. [to get] **weeded**)
ex: "They all showed up weeded." "They went outside to get weeded."

[one's] **weedman** n. (drug sl.) old & new school
1. the person one gets his/her marijuana from on a regular basis.
2. a marijuana dealer. (var. [one's] **weed-connect**)
ex. "They just busted ya weedman."

[a] **weekend thug** phrase (general sl.) new school
1. someone who pretends to be a "street" individual with a "tough guy" and/or criminal persona but who is really someone who tries to stay out of trouble.

[a] **weekend warrior** phrase (prison sl.) old & new school
1. someone sentenced to spend a specific number of weekends in jail.

[a] **weekend wife** n (e. coast sl.) new school
1. a female a male is intimately involve with outside of his committed relationship/marriage; a male's mistress/secret lover.
ex: "I plan on chillin' with my weekend wife for the next two days."

West Bubble F**K n. (general sl.) old & new school
1. a term used to describe anyplace far. 2. an imaginary place that is far away.
ex: "She lived all the way out in West Bubble F**k."

wet n. (drug sl.) old & new school
1. embalming fluid; a covert name for "PCP". See also: **dust**

[to] **wet** [someone] v. (criminal sl.) new school
1. the act of shooting someone [often causing one's death]. (var. [to] **wet** [someone] **up**)
ex: "Duke tried to wet my man over his baby mother."

[to] **wet throat** [someone] v. (e. coast sl.) old school
1. to deny or reject one's request. See also: [to] **dead** [someone]
ex: "When he comes back tell 'em he's wet throat."

[something that's] **whack** adj. (general sl.) old & new school
1. poor in quality and performance. 2. not "cool" or "hip". (var. [something that's] **wiggie wiggie whack**)
ex: "That was the whackest movie I ever seen." "Those clothes are whack now."

whassup? phrase (general sl.) old & new school
1. an enthusiastic way to greet someone. 2. a term used as a
prelude to questioning one's actions, behavior, and/or one's well
being. (var. **whassup with...?**)
*ex: "Whassup Dawg?" "Whassup with you?" "Whassup with that
hair style?"*

what I look like? [to you?] phrase (general sl.) old & new school
1. a sarcastic way to question someone who is trying to convince
you of something that is clearly outrageous, unbelievable, or
ridiculous.
ex: "You can't expect me to believe that, what I look like to you?"

what kind/type of sh** you on?! phrase (general sl.) old & new
school
1. a matter of fact way to question one's actions, thoughts, or
behavior that you find shocking or unbelievable.
ex: "All I wanna know is what kind of sh** you on?!"

what part of "no" you don't/can't/ain't understand? phrase
(e. coast sl.) new school
1. a witty way to respond to someone who you have already told
"no" to but is still trying to get what he/she wants from you. (var.
**what part of "no" you don't/can't/ain't understand the "n" or
the "o"** [part ?])

what part of the game is this? phrase (e. coast sl.) new school
1. a playful or sarcastic way to express surprise, shock, or disbelief
of one's actions, behavior, or thoughts. (var. **what part of the
game is that?**)
ex: "What part of the game is this, you posed to be with me."

what part you ain't understand? phrase (e. coast sl.) new school
1. a term used to emphasize your position, claim, or instructions
when someone acts like he/she is confused, in doubt, or
challenging you. 2. a term used to reaffirm one's answer as being

"no". (var. **what part of** [the statement] **don't/didn't/can't you understand?**)
ex: "I said you can't go, what part you ain't understand?"

what they hit/hittin' for? phrase (southern sl.) new school
1. a term used as a way to inquire about the cost of something. (var. **what** [something] **hit/is hittin' for**)
ex: "Call me when you know what they hittin' for."

what you gonna do, barbecue or mildew? phrase (southern sl.) old & new school
1. a witty way to prod someone into making a decision [usually when one is acting very hesitent or unable to decide].
ex: "Its gettin' late, what you gonna do, barbecue or mildew?"

what you want to be up?! Phrase (general sl.) old & new school
1. a matter of fact way to respond to someone who uses the term "what's up" or "whassup" in a confrontational, challenging, or taunting way [used to exude one's willingness to standup for himself].
ex: "You tell me, what you want to be up?"

what you workin' with? phrase (e. coast sl.) new school
1. a term used to ask someone how much money he/she has to spend or at his/her disposal.
ex: "I got twenty, now how much you workin' with?"

what the hell? phrase (general sl.) old & new school
1. a playful or sarcastic way to express surprise, shock, or disbelief of one's actions, behavior, or thoughts. (var. **what the?**)

whatever! interj. (general sl.) old & new school
1. a sarcastic way to say, "so what", "I don't care", "it doesn't matter/make a difference" [usually used to dismiss or discount something someone is telling you].
ex: "Whatever Dawg, that's up to you." "Whatever, just don't come back cryin' when you lose."

whatever, whatever! phrase (general sl.) new school
1. a term used to declare one's willingness and courage to stand up for himself/herself [when challenged or threatened]. (var. **whatever's clever**)
ex: "Whatever, whatever Slim, its your call."

what's crackulatin'? phrase (w. coast sl.) new school
1. a witty way to greet someone. 2. a term used as a way to inquire about one's well being. (var. **what's percolatin'?/crackin'?/ crackalackin'?**)
ex: "What's crackulatin' with you Dawg?"

what's hap'nin captin? phrase (southern sl.) new school
1. a witty way to greet someone. 2. a term used as a way to inquire about one's well being.
ex: "What's hap'nin captin, I haven't seen you around here in awhile."

what's his/her face phrase (general sl.) old & new school
1. a way to refer to someone whose name you forgot or don't want to use as a sign of disrespect. (var. **what's his/her name**)
ex: "What you and what's her face doin' together?"

what's really good? phrase (general sl.) new school
1. a hip way to greet someone while at the same time inquiring about that person's well being. (var. **what's good?, what's the word?, what's poppin'?, what's goin' on?**)
ex: "What's really good homie, I haven't seen you in a couple days."

what's the deal? phrase (general sl.) old & new school
1. a term used to greet someone. 2. a term used as a way to inquire about one's well being [sometimes when one appears to be in trouble]. 3. a term used to inquire about information.(var. **what's the dilly/dilly-o/dealy/deal yo/ diddeal/dizzeal?**)
ex: "What's the deal Cuz?" "First I wanna know what the dealy is."

what's wrong, ya straightener broke? phrase (southern sl.) new school
1. a way to taunt and show contempt for someone who has threatened to "straighten" you for offending or disrespecting him/her.

[to] wheel [something] v. (general sl.) old & new school
1. the act of driving.
ex: "I had to wheel a rental 'til I got my whip fixed."

when in doubt go without phrase (southern sl.) new school
1. a way to advise someone not to do something that he/she isn't sure about. (var. **when in doubt do without**)

when [one's] ship comes in phrase (general sl.) old school
1. a way to refer to one's acquiring of a substantial amount of money.
ex: "I'mma take care of you when my ship comes in." "My ship finally about to come in."

when you play, you gotta pay phrase (general sl.) old school
1. a way to advise or warn someone when you do wrong eventually you will have to pay the consequences.

wherever you might be, let ya gas run free phrase (general sl.) old school
1. a witty way to respond to someone accusation that you farted.

where my Dawgs at? phrase (c. coast sl.) new school
1. a enthusiastic way to solicit and/or rally support among one's male friends.

where [one] rest at phrase (general sl.) old & new school
1. where one lives.
ex: "That's where we used to rest at." "Where you rest at Dawg?"

where you get heart from? phrase (general sl.) old & new school
1. a term used to question one's sudden display of courage, bravery, or boldness. (var. **where he/she get heart from?**)

where's ya heart at? phrase (general sl.) old school
1. a term used to question one's courage or bravery [usually used as a way to prod someone into doing something he/she shows hesitancy or reservations about doing].
ex: "You can do that, where ya heart at?"

whichumacallit (pron. which-um-ma-call-it) phrase (general sl.) old & new school
1. a term used to refer to something or someone you have forgotten the name of. (var. **whatchumacallit**)
ex: "You remember whichummacallit from 224." "I left the whichummacallit on the bus."

[one's] whip n. (general sl.) new school
1. the car one owns; an automobile. (var. **whips**)
ex: "I'm about to get me a new whip." "That's the second whip you crashed."

[to] whip [an automobile] v. (e. coast sl.) new school
1. the act of driving.
ex: "What you whippin' around in now?" "I was whippin' down the Ave., and ran into your old girl."

[someone who's] whipped adj. (sexual sl.) old & new school
1. someone who is blindly in love with someone because the sex between them is outstanding or the best he/she has ever experienced [even if feeling this way causes one to be manipulated and/or taken advantage of]. (var. **[to] whip** [someone])
ex: "You can't see it, she's tryin' to whip you." "Looks to me like you already whipped."

[one's] whizzy n. (e. coast sl.) new school
1. the car one owns; an automobile.

ex: "I need to go get my whizzy washed."

whoa! interj. (general sl.) new school
1. an enthusiastic way to express shock, surprise, or disbelief. 2. a term used to get someone's attention [usually by interrupting that person].
ex: "Whoa, she didn't tell me y'all were going steady."

[something that's] **whoa!** adj. (e. coast sl.) new school
1. outstanding; unique; the best of its kind. (var. **like whoa!**)
ex: "Shortie's sister is whoa!"

whoadie n. (southern sl.) new school
1. a term of endearment among friends; friend. 2. a way to address someone whose name you do not know or don't want to use in front of others.
ex: "Call me later tonight whoadie."

who I look like, Sam Sausage Head?/Eddie Spaghetti soup me up when you ready? phrase (general sl.) old & new school
1. a witty way to question something someone is trying to convince you of that sounds unbelievably ridiculous.

who want it? phrase (e. coast sl.) new school
1. a matter of fact way to ask "who wants a confrontation with me?" (var. **who want it with me?, who wanna see me?, who want it with the kid?**)
ex: "I'm right here, who want it?" "Who want it with M. Deezy?"

whoop there it is phrase (southern sl.) new school
1. an enthusiastic way to express excitement [usually when one accomplishes a goal or task]. 2. a term used to taunt and tease one's opponent when you score a point against him/her.

who's the man? phrase (general sl.) old & new school
1. a way to ask, "who's the best?" [usually used when taunting one's opponent].

why you always hafta take it to the body? phrase (southern sl.)
new school
1. a way to ask someone, "why every time I say something you
think I'm speaking in sexual overtones or making sexual
references." (var. **why you always hafta take it there?**)

[something that's] **wicked** adj. (e. coast sl.) old & new school
1. outstanding; unique; the best of its kind. 2. something that is
"cool" or "hip".
ex: "Jermaine's house is wicked."

[a female who's] **wide as all outside** phrase (southern sl.) new
school
1. a way to describe a female who is fat and/or has a bigg butt.
ex: "She's wide as all outside now."

[someone who's] **wide open** adj. (general sl.) new school
1. infatuated. (var. [to] **have** [someone] **wide open**)
ex: "Your cousin wide open over Shortie sister."

[to] **wife** [a female] v. (general sl.) new school
1. to make a female your one and only girlfriend. (var. [to] **make**
[a female] **wifey**)
ex: "I'm about to wife Shortie."

[a] **wife beater** n. (southern sl.) new school
1. a white cotton tank top undershirt.

wifey n. (e. coast sl.) new school
1. a male's one and only girlfriend. 2. a pet name males use for
their girlfriend.
ex: "Wifey invited y'all over for dinner." "Who that, wifey?"

[a female who's] **wifey material** adj. (e. coast sl.) new school
1. a female who has all the qualities that a male envisions his wife
should have [intelligent, responsible, grounded, classy, loyal,
independent, stylish, spiritual, hip, down to earth].

ex: "I'm startin' to feel Shortie might be wifey material."
"She's definitely wifey material."

[one's] **wig** n. (general sl.) new school
1. a person's head. 2. a way to refer to the hair on a female's head.
(var. [one's] **wig piece**)
ex: "He cut his wig shavin'." "Give ya girl some money so she can
get her wig done."

[to] **wig out** v. (w. coast sl.) old & new school
1. to explode in anger causing an unpleasant scene. (var. [to] **wig**
out on [someone])
ex: "I'm out, shortie about to wig out in here."

[to] **wild out** v. (e. coast sl.) old & new school
1. to demonstrate disruptive, unruly, or destructive behavior. 2. to
act zany or outrageous. (var. **wildin'**)
ex: "We wild out down in Myrtle Beach." "You know they be
wildin' everywhere they go."

Willadelphia n. (e. coast sl.) new school
1. Philadelphia PA.

[a] **willie** n. (e. coast sl.) old school
1. one who makes and spends large amounts of money freely and
frequently; one who is wealthy. (var. [someone who's] **the**
williest) See also: [a] **big willie**
ex: "Brooklyn was full of willies back in the mid-eighties."

[someone who's] **wired** adj. (drug sl.) old & new school
1. one who is high from powder or crack cocaine. (var. [someone
who's] **wired up/for sound**)
ex: "She looks wired to me."

[someone who's] **wishy washy** adj. (general sl.) old school
1. emotionally unpredicatable. 2. moody.
ex: "With her ain't no tellin', she's too wishy washy."

[to be] **with** [something] phrase (general sl.) old & new school
1. to be in support of and willing to partake in an action [even if it means putting oneself in jeopardy]. See also: [to be] **down for** [something]
ex: *"You with this?" "I can get with that."*

[one's] **wiz** n. (e. coast sl.) new school
1. one's girlfriend.
ex: *"I can't stay, I gotta go pick up my wiz."*

[a] **wolf** n. (e. coast sl.) new school
1. a young "street" tough with a criminal persona. (var. **wolves**)
ex: *"You don't want me to send them wolves to come see you."*

[a] **wolf pack** phrase (e. coast sl.) old & new school
1. a marauding group of young "street" thoughs.
ex: *"He wasn't fast enough and got caught by a wolf pack comin' out the club."*

[a male who's] **wolfin'** adj. (prison sl.) new school
1. one male whose beard is full grown and not groomed and in need of grooming. (var. [someone who's] **wolfin' it**)
ex: *"I been wolfin' for three month."*

[someone who's] **wolfin'** v. (general sl.) old school
1. talking tough and/or making verbal threats. (var. [to] **sell wolf tickets**)
ex: *"Dawg be wolfin' like he a real gangster."*

[a recording artist whose CD goes] **wood** adj. (e. coast sl.) new school
1. performs poorly on the sales chart.
ex: *"His first CD was phat, the next one went wood."*

[a male's] **wood** n. (sexual sl.) new school
1. a covert word for penis.

word! phrase (general sl.) old & new school
1. a term used to affirm or reaffirm one's position or thought leaving no room for doubt or debate [usually used when trying to convince]. 2. a term used to express being in agreement or being able to relate with someone. (var. **word up, word to miz/big bird/Herb/momma, word is bond, word life**)
ex: "Word Dawg, I couldn't believe it was her."

word? phrase (general sl.) old & new school
1. a term used to question the truthfulness or accurateness of what someone is telling you. See also: **say word**
ex: "Word, that's what you heard?" "You think we have a chance, word?"

word to grannies panties phrase (e. coast sl.) new school
1. a witty way to affirm or reaffirm one's position, claim, or thought leaving no room for doubt or debate [usually used when trying to convince]. (va r. **word to Herb bust'is head on the curb** [drinking thunder bird].
ex: "Word to grannies panties, I seen it for myself."

[to] **word wrestle** v. (southern sl.) new school
1. to argue.
ex: "I see all you wanna do is word wrestle."

[to] **work** [someone] v. (criminal sl.) new school
1. to badly injure someone through an act of violence [usually a beating or stabbing].
ex: "I felt sorry for scrams, the way Dawg worked'em."

[to] **work** [someone] v. (e. coast sl.) new school
1. to employ deception or trickery in one's attempt to manipulate and/or take advantage of someone.
ex: "How much money you work'em for?" "I feel like you tryin' to work me."

work n. (drug sl.) old & new school

1. a covert way to refer to powder or crack cocaine [on the retail or wholesale level].
ex: *"They got caught bringin' work outta town."*

[to] **work** [something] **off** v. (drug sl.) old & new school
1. to settle one's debt by selling drugs for the person who is owed for free until one debt is paid.
ex: *"That's all right, you gonna hafta work that off."*

[something that's] **workin'** adj. (general sl.) old school
1. outstanding; unique; the best of its kind.
ex: *"That new dress is definitely workin'."*

[someone who's] **workin'** v. (drug sl.) old & new school
1. one who has drugs in his/her possession for sale.
ex: *"I think he's workin' up the block." "Are y'all workin' yet?"*

[someone who's] **workin' with them peoples** phrase (criminal sl.) new school
1. one who is a confidential informer for a law enforcement agency or is cooperating with the D.A.'s office in the prosecution of a friend or love one.
ex: *"All this time you ain't know he was workin' with them peoples?"*

works n. (criminal sl.) old & new school
1. a covert way to refer to an armed robbery or home invasion. See also: [a] **jooks**
ex: *"They was doin' works from here to V.A."*

[someone who's] **worsesome** adj. (southern sl.) new school
1. annoying; a pest. (var. [someone who's] **worrisome**)
ex: *"That's one worsesome child."*

[to] **wrap up** v. (prison sl.) new scool
1. to prepare to fist fight. 2. a way to tell someone to prepare to fight. (var. **wrap up or get slapped up, wrap up like a mummy get knocked out like a dummy**)

[to] **wreck** [something] v. (general sl.) old & new school
1. to give an outstanding performance. (var. [to] **wreck shop/sh****)
ex: "They just came in here and wrecked it."

wully n. (southern sl.) new school
1. pork; anything that contains pork by-products.

$\underline{\boldsymbol{x}}$

X n. (drug sl.) new school
1. ecstasy; a dangerous mind altering drug.
ex: "You can get 20 years for sellin' X."

y

ya ass is grass phrase (general sl.) old school
1. a witty way to tell someone he/she is in trouble [also used to taunt or intimidate one's opponent].
ex: "When you get over here, ya ass is grass."

ya dam skippy phrase (general sl.) old & new school
1. a matter of fact way to agree or affirm one's position or thought leaving no room for doubt or debate as to what one means. (var. **you dam skippy**)

ya dig? phrase (general sl.) new school
1. an enthusiastic way to ask someone does he/she understand or relate to what you are saying. 2. a term used to affirm or reaffirm one's position or thought leaving no room for doubt or debate. (var. **ya na'mean?, ya heard?, ya heard me?, ya un'stand?**)
ex: "As long as you bring it back I'm cool, ya dig?"

ya heart may belong to Jesus, but ya ass belongs to me phrase (southern sl.) new school
1. a witty way to taunt or intimidate one's opponent. 2. a term used to inform someone he/she is in or about to get in trouble with you [also used when you have one at a disadvantage].

Yack n. (w. coast sl.) new school
1. Cognac brand alcohol.

[to] yap v. (e. coast sl.) new school
1. to talk [usually about things one is not supposed to talk about]. See also: **[to] run [one's] mouth**
ex: "Them catz be yappin' like broads." "Stop yappin' and listen."

[to] yap [someone] v. (criminal sl.) new school

1. to take someone's possessions through the use of force; to rob someone.
ex: "They tried to yap my man at the club."

[a] **yardy** n. (general sl.) old & new school
1. someone of Jamaican decent. (var. [a] **yard mon**)
ex: "One of my best friends was a yardy." "Do you know the yard mon, Frenchy?"

yay n. (w. coast sl.) old & new school
1. a covert way to refer to cocaine. (var. **yay-o, yay-yo**) See also: **blow, candy**
ex: "You hafta get out my house with that yay."

[the] **Yay area** n. (w. coast sl.) old & new school
1. the San Francisco Bay area. (var. [the] **Bay area**)
ex: "Most catz from the Yay area, on that player sh**."

yeah high/tall/big adj. (general sl.) old school
1. a term used to describe the approximate height or weight of something or someone.
ex: "Last time I seen you, you was only yeah tall."

yeah right phrase (general sl.) old & new school
1. a playful or sarcastic way to express doubt and/or suspicion about something one is trying to convince you of.
ex: "You lost your keys, yeah right."

yeast n. (drug sl.) old school
1. baking soda [the main ingredient added to powder cocaine to produce crack cocaine].

[to] **yeast** [someone] **up** v. (general sl.) old school
1. to give someone a false sense of confidence; to flatter falsely; to stroke one's ego.
ex: "I remember you tried to yeast me up when I first met you."

[to] **yell like a** [lil] **bit**** phrase (general sl.) old & new school
1. to yell, scream, or holler extremely loud [for a male sometimes at a high pitch]. (var. [to] **scream/holla like a** [lil] **bit****)
ex: "Shut up, cause we heard you yellin' like a bit**."

[a] **yes man** adj. (prison sl.) new school
1. one who will agree with anything someone says even when he/she knows that person is lying or doesn't know what he/she is talking about.
ex: "It seems to me all you lookin' for is a yes man."

Y. 0. n. (e. coast sl.) old & new school
1. Yonkers, N.Y.

Yo n. (e. coast sl.) new school
l. a term of endearment among friends; friend.
ex: "Whassup Yo?" "I'm not tellin' you again Yo." "Did you bring that Yo?"

Yo phrase (general sl.) old & new school
l. an cnthusiastic way to get someone's attention [often in an attempt to alert them].
ex: "Yo, watch where you goin'." "Yo yo yo, don't bring that in here."

Yo what up son? phrase (general sl.) old & new school
1. a hip way to greet a male friend or family member. 2. a hip way to inquire about a male's well being/welfare [usually when he looks bothered or feeling down].

you a bad man phrase (general sl.) old & new school
1. a playful or sarcastic way to tell someone he/she is courageous and/or daring. 2. a term used to mock someone making an outrageous claim. (var. **youse a bad man**)
ex: "You a bad man, if you told'er that."

you a goffer, cause you'll go for anything phrase (general sl.) old & new school

1. a term used to reprimand someone for being so gullible, foolish, and easily taken advantage of.

you a payer I'm a playa phrase (southern sl.) new school
1. a witty way to dismiss a male's boast of being a ladies man meaning to suggest that he pays women to be intimate with him.

you ain't gonna kill nothin', let nothin' die phrase (general sl.) new school
1. a term used to dismiss someone's tough talk and/or verbal threats. 2. a way to tell someone he/she is not as tough as he/she thinks or want people to think.

you ain't know? phrase (southern sl.) new school
1. a term used to affirm or reaffirm one's position or thought leaving no room for doubt or debate [also used to exude confidence]. (var. **you don't know?, you don't know you better ask somebody**)

you ain't never lie phrase (southern sl.) new school
1. a term used to express being in agreement with someone's point or assessment. 2. a way to say, "you're right", or "I agree with you".
ex: "You ain't never lie, cause Shortie do have a bad attitude."

you all that? [now?] phrase (general sl.) old & new school
1. a term used to question someone's overrated opinion of his/her self-worth or his/her conceitedness. (var. **you think you all that?** [now?])
ex: "Oh, you think you all that cause you got a new whip?"

you beat phrase (general sl.) new school
1. a playful or sarcastic way to inform someone that he/she has been suckered, tricked, or conned out of something and there's nothing that he/she can do about it.
ex: "All I can tell you is you beat Dawg."

you best believe... phrase (general sl.) old & new school
1. a term used in prelude to making a matter of fact statement or empty threat [usually when wanting to convey seriousness].
ex: "You best believe she ain't coming back in here." "You best believe I'mma get my money."

you better say I did phrase (southern sl.) new school
1. a matter fact way to respond to someone who asks you did you do something that you already done. 2. a way to say "do you [even] have to ask?".

you [musta/done] **bumped ya head** phrase (southern sl.) new school
1. a term used to express shock, surprise, and/or disbelief with one's actions or thoughts. (var. **you** [musta/done] **fell down and bumped ya head**)
ex: "Come on man, you musta bumped ya head thinkin' I'mma pay that much for that."

you can talk ya ass off phrase (southern sl.) new school
1. a playful or sarcastic way to say, "I don't care what you say", "you can say what you want", or "you can talk all you want" [when one is steadfast in his/her belief that he/she is right or not convinced]. (var. **you can talk all you want, you can talk 'til ya mouth catch on fire**)
ex: "You can talk ya ass off, I know who I saw."

you can't eat/talk with dirt/rocks in ya mouth phrase (e. coast sl.) new school
1. a term used to warn someone that something he/she is doing can get him/her killed when that person is trying to convince you that the danger is worth the risk.
ex: "You can say all you want to, but you can't eat with dirt in ya mouth."

you can't get with this phrase (general sl.) old & new school
1. a playful or sarcastic way to tease or taunt someone about not having the ability to compete against you or not having what it takes to convince you to have an intimate relationship.
ex: "Stop playin' cause you know you can't get with this."

you can't play dead phrase (general sl.) new school
1. a playful or sarcastic way to mock one's claim of being able to play something extremely well.
ex: "I seen you play, and you can't play dead."

you can't see me phrase (general sl.) new school
1. a playful or sarcastic way to tease or taunt someone about not having the ability to compete against you. (var. **you couldn't see me with x-ray vision**)
ex: "I'm not gonna waste my time, cause you can't see me."

you could sell sand at the beach phrase (general sl.) new school
1. a term used to praise someone for having a unique gift for convincing others of things that aren't true. (var. **you could sell cows milk/Eskimos ice**)

you couldn't shake me in a earthquake phrase (general sl.) new school
1. a way to tease or taunt someone for not having the ability to get away from you.

you crazy? phrase (general sl.) old & new school
1. a enthusiastic way to express surprise, shock, or disbelief with one's claims or statements. 2. a term used to disagree adamantly. (var. **you gots to be crazy!**)
ex: "You crazy, why you bring her here?" "Go back and get them, you crazy?"

you dead right phrase (general sl.) old & new school
1. a sarcastic way to agree with someone [even if you don't agree] for the sake of an arguement.

ex: "You dead right, I shouldn't even had said nothin' to him."

you dead wrong phrase (general sl.) old & new school
1. a playful or sarcastic way to reprimand someone for being spiteful.

you don't hafta lie to kick it phrase (general sl.) new school
1. a term used to inform someone that he/she doesn't have to make up things in an attempt to fit in or to be friends with you.

you don't have it in you phrase (general sl.) old & new school
1. a playful or sarcastic way to tease or taunt someone for not having the courage and/or the ability to back up his/her claims or tough talk.

you don't hear me though (pron. dough) phrase (southern sl.) new school
1. a term used to affirm or reaffirm one's claim, boast, or position leaving no room for doubt or debate [used in an attempt to get someone to take you serious].

you don't know me like that phrase (general sl.) new school
1. a sarcastic way to respond to someone's misplaced assessment, statement, or prediction pertaining to one's personal business and affairs [usually used dismissively and when offended].
ex: "You don't know what I'm gonna do cause you don't know me like that." "Hold up, first of all you don't know me like that."

you don't wanna put nothin' on that phrase (southern sl.) new school
1. a term used to prod or challenge someone to a bet or wager. (var. **you don't wanna bet nothin'**)

you ain't/not ready for this phrase (general sl.) old school
1. a nonchalant way to dismiss someone's challenge, empty threats or tough talk he/she is using to prod you into a confrontation. (var. [stop fakin'] **you don't want none**)

you feelin' froggy? phrase (southern sl.) old & new school
1. a witty way to challenge someone to make the first move when he/she is acting like he/she wants to fight you. (var. [if] **you feel like a frog … leap/a glass … break**)

you got all the sense phrase (southern sl.) new school
1. a playful or sarcastic way to reprimand and/or chastise someone for thinking he/she is smarter than you or "slicker" than you [usually used after catching someone trying to out "slick" you]. (var. **you think you got all the sense**)
ex: "Boy, you got all the sense, now you really not going with us."

you got game [with you] phrase (general sl.) old & new school
1. a term used to acknowledge someone's attempt to con, deceive, or sucker you after you catch him/her in the act or after you figured out the plot.
ex: "One thing I can say about you is, you got game."

you got life f**ked up phrase (e. coast sl.) new school
1. a matter of fact way to tell someone he/she has the wrong idea or concept of how things should go [usually used when reprimanding someone for having a negative or self-destructive attitude or behavior].
ex: "You got life f**ked up if you think I'm payin' for this." "I'm not goin' nowhere, you got life f**ked up."

you got me? phrase (general sl.) old & new school
1. a way to ask someone if he/she will cover for you, grant you your request, or assume responsibility for something on your behalf.
ex: "Let me know Dawg, you got me?"

you got me f**ked up [with somebody else] phrase (e. coast sl.) new school
1. a matter of fact way to say "you have me mixed up/confused with someone else" when someone has mistaken your character to be soft, easily fooled, taken advantage of, manipulated, or conned.

(var. **you got me f**kd up/confused with somebody else/the
next man/one of your females**)

you got more balls than a blind gunfighter phrase (southern sl.)
new school
1. a witty way to praise someone for being daring, courageous, or
brave.

you got more game than Parker Bros. phrase (general sl.) old
school
1. a term used to acknowledge one's unique ability to lie
convincingly [also used when one feels he/she has been conned or
lied to]. (var. **you got more game than the NBA**)

you got that beat phrase (general sl.) new school
1. a term used to boost one's confidence about being better than
his/her opponent.
*ex: "Don't worry about that, you got that beat." "I seen it too, but
you got that beat."*

you got that comin' phrase (general sl.) new school
1. a way to assure or reassure someone that he/she is going to get
what he/she has coming without hassle or delay.
ex: "Don't even worry about that you got that comin'."

you gots to be in it, to win it phrase (general sl.) old & new
school
1. a term used to encourage someone to give something a try and/or
to participate in something.

you gotta have a rabbits foot stuck up your ass phrase (southern
sl.) new school
1. a witty way to tell someone he/she is very lucky. (var. **you
musta been born with a rabbit's foot stuck up your ass**)

you grown get ya own phrase (e. coast sl.) new school
1. a witty way to respond to someone who asking you to give
him/her some of something [usually cigarettes].

you have your whole life to be stupid, why you wanna start today? phrase (southern sl.) new school
1. a witty way to reprimand someone for doing or saying something stupid, ridiculous, or outrageous.

you [the one] **illin', I'm chillin'** phrase (general sl.) old school
1. a term used in response to someone who is accusing you of "illin'" [causing an unpleasant scene or being disruptive].

you in everything but a hearse/casket phrase (southern sl.) new school
1. a witty way to reprimand someone for being nosy and/or giving his/her unwanted advise or opinion about a matter that doesn't concern him/her.

you jigglin' baby phrase (e. coast sl.) old school
1. a term used to compliment and/or give praise to a female for looking good or accomplishing something. (var. **you got it goin' on**)

you just bumpin' ya gums phrase (southern sl.) new school
1. a term used to dismiss someone's tough talk and/or threats. (var. **you just runnin' ya mouth/ talkin' to hear yaself talk**)

you just talkin' cause you got a mouth phrase (southern sl.) new school
1. a sarcastic way to dismiss someone who is making no sense at all in his/her attempt to get his/her point across.

[if] **you keep cryin' what the baby gonna do?** phrase (southern sl.) new school
1. a playful or sarcastic way to taunt someone who's complaining to you [usually about you being unfair].

you know how it goes phrase (general sl.) old & new school
1. a term used to point out that one is already familiar with the procedure or situation. (var. **you know how it go/it is, you know the deal/the dealy/the dealy-o/the dealin's**)

ex: "This the second time, so you know how it goes."

you know how we do phrase (general sl.) old & new school
1. a term used to affirm or reaffirm one's commitment and trust to a friend/friendship. (var. **you know how we do it/get down/kick it**)
ex: "Here take the car, you know how we do it."

you know it phrase (general sl.) old & new school
1. a term used to affirm or reaffirm one's position, claim, or thought leaving no room for doubt or debate. 2. a term used to express being in agreement or able to relate with someone's position, claim, or thought. (var. **you know that's right, you know this/that, you know it like a poet**)

you know my style phrase (general sl.) new school
1. a term used to boast about having a outstanding reputation or unique way of doing things.
ex: "You know my style Dawg." "Shortie can't front cause she know my style."

you know what it is phrase (general sl.) new school
1. a term used to tease or taunt one's opponent when your winning is inevitable. (var. **you know what this is**)

you know what this is phrase (criminal sl.) new school
1. a term used to inform someone that he/she is about to robbed [used in holdup situations]. (var. **you know what this is you seen it on t.v. and you heard it on the radio**)
ex: "Don't look surprised, you know what this is."

you move any slower, you'll be standin' still phrase (southern sl.) new school
1. a witty way to reprimand someone for moving too slow.

you more confused than three blind mice in a cheese factory phrase (southern sl.) new school

l. a witty way to reprimand someone for not being able to make up his/her mind.

you must be out your rabbit ass mind phrase (general sl.) old & new school
1. a playful or sarcastic way to respond to someone who says something that is stupid, ridiculous, or outrageous [often used to respond to one's off handed suggestion]. 2. a term used to say "no" or express being in disagreement. (var. **you must be smokin'/stupid/on dope or dog food**)

you only sayin'/said it cause it's true phrase (e. coast sl.) new school
1. a boastful and conceited way to accept a compliment, praise, or recognition.

you pretty, [yeah] **pretty ugly** phrase (general sl.) old & new school
1. a witty way to insult someone's looks.

you rather run through hell with gasoline draws on [than mess/f**k with me] phrase (southern sl.) new school
1. a witty way to respond to someone's tough talk/threats or taunts [also used to show one isn't intimidated]. (var. **you rather slide down a razor blade butt** [ass] **naked into a pool of alcohol/smack the judge on sentencin' day/wrestle a bear in your mutha's underwear/ smack the preacher on Easter Sunday in front of a packed church**)

you short phrase (southern sl.) new school
1. a playful or sarcastic way to tell someone he/she has been cheated, taken advantage of, or deceived. 2. a term used to inform someone that he/she is too late or missed out on an opportunuty.

you slicker than goose grease phrase (southersn sl.) new school
1. a witty way to praise someone for having the unique ability to out wit someone or lie convincingly. (var. **you slicker than an oil spill**)

you slower than a car wash on a rainy day phrase (southern sl.)
new school
1. a witty way to criticize someone for moving too slow. (var. **you
slower than a one arm painter/a turtle on crutches**)

you smokin'?! phrase (general sl.) old & new school
1. a witty way to question someone's actions, thoughts, or behavior
when that person does or says something questionable. (var. **you
smokin'**)
ex: "You smokin', I never said that."

you so petty, you'd steal the butter off a blind man's biscuit
phrase (southern sl.) new school
1. a witty way to reprimand or criticize someone for being
extremely petty, unscrupulous, or deceiving.

you sound stupid phrase (general sl.) old & new school
1. a playful or sarcastic way to reprimand someone for saying
something stupid, ridiculous, or unbelievable. (var. **you sound like
a fool/like you look ...** [stupid])
ex: "I'm not goin' in there, you sound stupid."

you still got milk on your breath phrase (general sl.) new school
1. a term used to dismiss someone as being too young. (var. **you
still suckin' on a titty**)

you sweeter than bear meat phrase (southern sl.) new school
1. a witty way to tease or taunt someone for being gullible, easy to
beat, or manipulate. (var. **you sweet like a marshmallow treat**)
See also: [someone who's] **sweet**

you the man phrase (general sl.) old & new school
1. a term used to praise or congratulate a male. 2. a sarcastic way
to mock someone's authority [usually when that person is trying to
exert his/her authority].

you the man, I'm just a fan phrase (general sl.) new school
1. a modest way to reflect the praise, recognition, or congratulations back to the person who is giving them to you.

you think I got stupid stamped on my forehead? phrase (general sl.) old & new school
1. a witty way to express suspicion or doubt as to one's truthfulness.

you think you the sh** phrase (general sl.) old & new school
1. a term used to reprimand someone for acting conceited or extremely self-centered. (var. **you think you the sh**s/all that/got it goin' on/like that**)
ex: "You think you the sh** cause you got a new car?"

you trippin' harder than a one legged girl in a double-dutch contest phrase (southern sl.) new school
1. a witty way to inform someone that he/she is causing an extremely unpleasant scene [usually that person is being disruptive].

you wanna box or kick rocks? phrase (e. coast sl.) new school
1. a witty way to ask someone if he/she wants to fight or leave.

you wasn't arrested, you was rescued phrase (prison sl.) old school
1. a term prisoners use to tease other prisoners about their physical condition when they first arrived in the prison as being haggard and unkempt compared to their present physical condition groomed and rested.

[now] **you worryin' about the wrong thing** phrase (southern sl.) new school
1. a playful or sarcastic way to reprimand someone for giving his/her unwanted and unsolicited advise or opinion about your personal affairs. 2. a term used to say, "mind your business", "keep your opinion/advice to yourself".

you wouldn't beat a egg for breakfast phrase (general sl.) old & new school
1. a witty way to dismiss someone's tough talk and/or verbal threats. 2. a way to tell someone he/she isn't as as tough as he/she thinks or wants people to think. (var. **you wouldn't throw rice in a wedding/water at a pool party/play dead in a murder movie**)

you wrong as all out doors phrase (general sl.) old & new school
1. a term used to reprimand someone for being spiteful, mean, and/or cruel. (var. **you wronger than two left shoes**)
ex: "You hurt her feelin's Dawg, you wrong as all out doors."

you'd tell somethin' phrase (southern sl.) new school
1. a sarcastic way to tell someone he/she would cooperate with the police if caught doing something wrong [usually because that person is always acting scared or hesitant]. (var. **you'll tell somethin'**)
ex: "I have a strong feelin' you'd tell somethin' in a minute."

[something that's] **young** adj. (e. coast sl.) new school
1. a piece of clothing that is too small for the person wearing it. (var. [something that looks] **young on** [someone])
ex: "Take that young ass jacket off." "That sweater is madd young on you."

[one's] **young boy** n. (southern sl.) new school
1. a way to refer to one's younger friend.
ex: "My young boy posed to meet us here later."

youngin' n. (southern sl.) new school
1. a way to address someone who is clearly younger than you. (var. **youngster, young buck**) See also: **jit**
ex: "Watch the way you talk to me youngin'."

your breath [smell] **so bad, you can smell it when ya mouth closed** phrase (e. coast sl.) new school

1. a witty way to insult someone about having bad breath. (var.
**your breath [smell] so bad, it smell like you got two midgets in
ya mouth with sh** on their shoes**)

your eyes may shine, your teeth may grit, but none of this
[name of item] **you may get** phrase (general sl.) old school
1. a witty way to tease someone about not giving him/her
something he/she wants.

your mouth ain't no prayer book/bible phrase (southern sl.) new
school
1. a term used to express suspicion and/or doubt that someone is
telling you the truth no matter how hard he/she tries to convince
you.

your mouth movin' but you ain't sayin' nothin' phrase (general
sl.) old & new school
1. a term used to dismiss one's tough talk and/or verbal threats
[also used to show one isn't intimidated].

your name must be doo-doo cause you play like some sh**
phrase (e. coast sl.) new school
1. a witty way to negatively criticize one's performance during
some form of competition. (var. **you some cut/sh**/stir fried
sh****)

your name must be Keith, cause you always sweatin' somebody
phrase (general sl.) old school
1. a witty way to tease someone for being annoying and pestering
in his/her attempt to pursue an intimate relationship with someone.

yuck mouth adj. (general sl.) old & new school
1. extremely bad breath.
*ex: "Before you talk to me, you need to get rid of that yuck
mouth."*

z

[to] **zeek** [someone] v. (e. coast sl.) old & new school
1. to make a noticeable mistake while giving someone a haircut [usually causing a crooked hair line].

[a] **zeekbilican** adj. (e. coast sl.) old school
1. one who is not "cool" or "hip", nerdy.

[a] **zombie** n. (drug sl.) old school
1. a way to refer to someone addicted to crack cocaine.
ex: "The zombies don't start comin' out 'til twelve."

zoom zooms and wham whams n. (prison sl.) old & new school
1. candy threats; junk food.
ex: "He spent all his allowance on zoom zooms and wham whams."

zoned out adj. (general sl.) new school
1. the inability to comprehend or relate to what's going on around you or in a situation.
ex: "I just zoned out while I was there."

[someone who's] **zooted** adj. (e. coast sl.) old school
1. drunk and/or high from marijuana.
ex: "They came home from Roxy's zooted like a mug."

Talking Hip-Hop & Urban slang using the "izz" sound

A very intricate part of using and talking Hip-Hop and Urban "street" slang is the ability to alter the pronunciation of words by adding additional sounds or syllables. This system of word change allows users the opportunity to converse covertly around people who are unfamiliar with this tongue twisting kind of speech.

As you will learn, by adding the "izz" sound you can change the pronunciation of a word, while retaining the meaning or context in which you are using the word. This unique system of altering the sound of a word can be used whether using Hip-Hop and Urban slang or using proper English words, the meaning of the word always stays the same.

I have chosen the "izz" sound for this book because it is the most commonly used and heard variation spoken among young people who speak Hip-Hop and Urabn "street" slang.

Because there is no absolute structural standard that can explain this word altering system, the attempt to explain this system in terms of consonants, compound words, double consonants, or when and whether something is proper or not proper would only confuse you. So by following the examples set forth in this section you will learn how to use this system fluently and with ease. Going from single word usage to conversing in whole sentences.

On the following pages you will find a list of words in their original form then followed by the altered hybrid form of the word and a contextual demonstration using the altered word.

Example:
back (bizz-ack)........I hope you got my bizzack on this.
time (tizz-ime)........There's not enough tizzime.

This simple, easy-to-read, easy-to-follow beginners guide and list of words will familiarize you with and help you develop a large vocabulary of other words using this system in a short period of time. Allowing you to covertly converse or eaves-drop on those who are using this type of coded jargon.

Note: Keep in mind, some words don't work with this system of altering words so if the word you are trying to alter doesn't have that certain pronounceability that comes so easy with other altered words, then don't use this system for that particular word.

Appendix (from A to Z)

a

able (iz-zable).......................I won't be izzable to.
above (a-bizz-ove)................I'm abizzove all that.
about (a-bizz-out)................We abizzout to do this.
apple (iz-zapple) ....I got me a izzapple computer.
act (iz-zact)...........................Izzact like you want it.
amp (iz-zamp)................. She tried to izzamp my man.
account (a-kizz-zount)...........On whose akizzount?
attach (a-tizz-atch)...............She became atizzatched to me.
address (ad-driz-zess)...........I gave her your addrizzess.
attack (a-tizz-ack)................He's the one who atizzacked me.
adopted (a-dizz-opted).........They adizzopted me.
alone (a-liz-zone)................You can't leave me alizzone.
almost (all-mizz-ost)...........Almizzost, but no cigar.
alert (a-lizz-ert)....................Stay alizzert.
amount (a-miz-zount)...........It amizzounts to this.
atone (a-tiz-zone)................You need to atizzone your ways.
apart (a-pizz-art)..................Its tearin' me apizzart.
allow (a-liz-zow)..................Don't alizzow him to do that.
around (a-riz-zound).............I'll see you arizzound.
angry (iz-zangry).................She looked izzangry to me.

b

bad (bizz-ad)..........................How bizzad is it?
broad (briz-zoad)...................Leave them brizzoads alone.
ball (bizz-all)........................They down south bizzallin'.
broke (brizz-oke)..................Them cats brizzoke now dawg.
bamma (bizz-ama)................For a bizzama, you all right.
bread (briz-zead)................Have my brizzead dawg.
beast (bizz-east)...................I'm a bizzeast at this.
borrow (bizz-orrow).............Can I bizzorrow your car?
bomb (biz-zomb)..................That's the bizzomb dawg.
bound (biz-zound)................We N.Y. bizzound whoadie.
bricks (brizz-icks) ....They found three brizzicks.

busted (bizz-usted) ....They all got bizzusted.
beef (bizz-eef).....................You tryin' to start bizzeef?
bus (bizz-us)........................This my bizzus.
butt (bizz-ut)........................Ya manz is bizzut.
bum (bizz-um).....................He used to be a bizzum.
blaze (blizz-aze)..................You wanna blizzaze this?
blame (blizz-ame)................I'm not taking the blizzame.
bring (briz-zing)..................Brizzing that with you.
black (bliz-zack).................. I like the blizzack better.

c

car (kizz-ar)..........................She crashed the kizzar.
cut (kizz-ut)..........................How bad is the kizzut?
came (kizz-ame)....................You shoulda kizzame.
curse (kizz-urse)..................This place is kizzursed.
cipher (cizz-ipher) ....Pass that around the cizzipher.
crowded (criz-zowded) ....That place stay crizzowded.
cake (kizz-ake)....................So what you got kizzake
camp (kizz-amp)..................We part of the same kizzamp.
change (chiz-zange)..............Something has to chizzange.
connect (k'nizz-ect)..............They busted my k'nizzect.
class (cliz-zass) ....New clizzasses start tomorrow.
crash (crizz-ash)..................We crizzashed the party.
clap (cliz-zap)......................Police clizzap'd ya man.
crime (crizz-ime)..................Crizzime don't pay.
cramp (criz-zamp)................You crizzampin' my style
cold (kizz-old)....................Its madd kizzold outside.
champ (chiz-zamp)..............How's it goin' chizzamp?
crazy (crizz-azy)..................Man that chick was crizzazy.
chump (chiz-zump)................You always been a chizzump.
climb (clizz-imb)..................We might have to clizzimb out.

d

dawg (dizz-awg)	That's on me dizzawg.
drink (drizz-ink)..................	You've had enough to drizzink.
dam (dizz-am)......................	I don't give a dizzam.
drown (driz-zown)..............	They almost drizzowned.
date (diz-zate)......................	What's todays dizzate?
damage (diz-zamage)...........	If its dizzamaged take it back.
dark (diz-zark).....................	It's too dizzark in here.
draw (drizz-aw)..................	Here comes big drizzaws.
dime (dizz-ime)...................	He dropped a dizzime.
dollars (dizz-ollars).............	Time to get off them dizzollars.
dig (dizz-ig)........................	Dizzig Shortie over there.
drill (driz-zill).....................	Yo she tried to drizzill me.
deaf (dizz-ef)......................	Are you dizzef or what?
doubt (dizz-out)	I have my dizzouts.
deal (diz-zeal).....................	Dizzeal the cards.
don't (diz-zon't)...................	Dizzon't even try it.
dome (diz-zome).................	The dizzome cracked in half.
do (diz-zoo)........................	What you wanna dizzoo?
down (diz-zown)..................	How can I be dizzown?
dial (dizz-ile)......................	What number did you dizzile?

e

eat (iz-zeat)..........................We about to izzeat.

escape (e-scizz-ape)..............Tell me how you escizzaped.

edge (izz-edge)....................You livin' on the izzedge.

effect (e-fizz-ect)..................This efizzects all of us.

east (iz-zeast)........................We really from the izzeast.

emerge (e-mizz-erge)............When did this emizzerge?

elected (e-liz-zected).............Who elizzected you for this?

effort (izz-effort).................That took a lot of izzeffort.

endorsed (en-dizz-orsed)......I could have endizzorsed you.

enclosed (en-clizz-osed).......I enclizzosed two pictures.

entered (iz-zentered)............As soon as we izzentered it began.

erratic (e-rizz-atic)...............Stop acting erizzatic.

end (iz-zend)........................That was the izzend.

erase (e-rizz-ace).................We can't just erizzace it.

elastic (e-lizz-astic).............You tore the elizzastic.

ear (iz-zear)..........................I think its an izzear ache.

entwined (en-twizz-ined).....How'd you get entwizzined in this?

earth (izz-irth) ....That's my izzirth.

exam (ex-iz-zam).................She givin' a quicky exizzam.

<u>f</u>

fact (fiz-zact).......................I want to know the fizzacts.

fool (fizz-ool)....................Whassup fizzool?

family (fizz-amily)...............We all fizzamily.

fun (fizz-un).......................Let's have some fizzun.

famous (fizz-amous)............I'll make you fizzamous.

freak (friz-zeek)...................Let's get our frizzeek on.

feel (fiz-zeel)......................I fizzeel you on that.

fly (flizz-i)..........................Shortie too flizzi.

friend (frizz-end)................We just frizzends.

free (friz-zee)......................I'll be frizzee soon.

floss (flizz-oss)...................The chicks was flizzossin'.

fan (fizz-an)........................I got love for my fizzans.

fiend (fizz-ean)...................Ya manz a fizzean now.

flame (flizz-ame)................I seen the flizzames.

first (fizz-irst).....................Fizzirst come, fizzirst serve.

five (fizz-ive).....................I need fizzive more.

fry (frizz-i).........................I want a small frizzi.

far (fizz-ar)........................How fizzar is it from here?

feet (fiz-zeet).....................She got some big fizzeets.

fruits (frizz-oots)................Pick up some frizzoots for me.

g

game (gizz-ame)..................You got madd gizzame.
great (grit-zate)....................What so grizzate about that?
gain (giz-zain)....................What is there to gizzain?
greedy (grizz-eedy)..............You too grizzeedy.
giant (jiz-ziant)....................That's a jizziant step.
gum (gizz-um)....................Give me a piece of gizzum.
ghost (gizz-ost)....................I was about to be gizzost.
green (grizz-ean)..................You was grizzean when we met.
gram (grizz-am)....................That's about 62 grizzams.
gold (gizz-old)....................Do you have that in gizzold?
grimy (griz-zimy)................Why you so grizzimy?
grown (grizz-own)...............You not grizzown yet.
gone (gizz-on)....................That been gizzon.
guess (gizz-ess)....................Take a wild gizzess.
gun (gizz-un)........................I hate gizzuns.
guard (gizz-ard)...................Put your gizzards up.
going (gizz-owing)...............Where y'all gizzowing?
grind (grizz-ind)..................I'm about to get grizzind on.
grape (grizz-ape)..................I'll take grizzape.
glad (glizz-ad)....................Be glizzad for small things.

h

ham (hizz-am).........................I don't eat no hizzam.
holla (hizz-olla)....................Hizzolla at me later.
half (hizz-af).........................Save me hizzaf.
home (hiz-zome)...................I'm going hizzome for awhile.
hide (hizz-ide)......................Don't hizzide from me.
Herb (Hizz-erb)....................She Hizzerb'd you.
hint (hiz-zint)........................You had enough hizzints.
happy (hiz-zappy)................She looks hizzappy to me.
hear (hiz-zear)......................I hizzearr you.
house (hizz-ouse).................We in the hizzouse.
hook (hizz-ook)....................They hizzooked me up.
hit (hiz-zit)...........................Take a hizzit and pass.
hot (hizz-ot).........................That was hizzot to death.
help (hizz-elp)......................Hizzelp me with this.
hole (hizz-ole)......................I'm still in the hizzole.
hurry (hiz-zury)....................You need to hizzury.
hurt (hizz-irt).......................I was hizzirt about that.
hops (hizz-ops)....................Slim got madd hizzops.
heart (hizz-art).....................Where's your hizzart?
hand (hizz-and)....................I need a hizzand.

i

ice (izz-ice)............................How much the izzice run you?

island (izz-island)................I was on the izzisland in 89.

in (izz-in)............................You izzin there now.

illin' (iz-zillin')...................Ya was izzillin' last night.

if (iz-zif)............................Only izzif you knew.

iron (izz-iron).......................Can I borrow your izziron?

itch (iz-zitch)........................She izzitchin' to try.

irk (iz-zirk)...........................He's been izzirkin' me all day.

ink (iz-zink)..........................That's a izzink stain.

incline (in-clizz-ine)............We're inclizzined to know.

invest (in-viz-zest)...............I got a lot invizzested.

idol (izz-idol).......................That's my izzidol.

insight (in-sizz-ight).............We need some insizzight.

intake (in-tizz-ake)...............What's your intizzake?

impulse (im-pizz-ulse)........We moved on impizzulse.

indeed (in-diz-zeed).............That's right indizzeed.

it (iz-zit)..............................That's izzit right there.

inside (in-sizz-ide)...............We got the insizzide scoop.

implant (im-plizz-ant).........Those are implizzants.

icon (i-kizz-awn).................You a ikizzawn now.

j

jack (jizz-ack)......................No way jizzack.

joint (jizz-oint)......................I likes her new jizzoint.

jam (jizz-am)......................I'm in a real jizzam.

jerk (jiz-zerk) ....They about to jizzerk us.

jap (jiz -zap)......................She jizzapped ya man.

just (jizz-us) ....I jizzus called.

jewels (jiz-zools)................That was a nice jizzool.

jury {jizz-ury)......................The jizzury reached its verdict.

joke (jizz-oke)......................The jizzoke is on you.

job (jizz-ob) ....You need to find a jizzob.

jail (jizz-ail)........................When you get out of jizzail?

jealous (jiz-zealous) ....You just jizzealous.

jelly (jiz-zelly)......................Pass the jizzelly please.

jump (jizz-ump)...................I don't jizzump for nobody.

Joe (jiz-zoe).........................Call Jizzoe for me.

jeep (jizz-eep)......................What kind of jizzeep is that?

jean (jiz-zeans)...................These jizzeans don't fit.

jot (jizz-ot)..........................Jizzot this down for me.

janky (jizz-anky)................Move ya jizzanky ass back.

jar (jizz-ar).........................Open this jizzar for me.

k

king (kiz-zing)......................He's the former kizzing.

knock (nizz-ock)...................Nizzock before you come in.

keep (kizz-eep)....................Kizzeep that to yourself.

kick (kiz-zick)....................She tried to kizzick in my door.

knife (nizz-ife)....................Cut this with ya nizzife.

killed (kizz-illed).................He coulda been kizzilled.

kind (kizz-ind)....................That was kizzind of you.

kite (kizz-ite)......................Did you get my kizzite?

know (niz-zoe)....................You nizzoe something.

key (kiz-zee).......................I can't find the kiz-zee.

knuckle (nizz-uckle).............I'm on my nizzuckles dawg.

knot (nizz-ot)......................He pulled out a nizzot.

kiss (kizz-iss).....................Kizziss my ass.

kin (kizz-in).........................They ain't no kizzin to me.

karat (kizz-air-it).................I bought her 24 kizzairits.

kingpin (king-pizz-in)..........He's the former kingpizzin.

kept (kizz-ept)....................I shoulda kizzept it.

kosher (kizz-osher).............Its kizzosher with me.

known (nizz-own)................I shoulda nizzown.

keel (kizz-eel)......................It just kizzeeled over and died.

!

lame (lizz-ame).....................That was real lizzame.
lost (lizz-ost)........................You lizzost and that's that.
lack (lizz-ack).......................You lizzackin' something.
love (lizz-ove).....................You really lizzove this guy?
liar (lizz-ire)........................You always been a lizzire.
late (lizz-ate).......................Its too too lizzate.
left (lizz-eft).......................He lizzeft two hours ago.
long (liz-zong).....................That's too lizzong for me.
line (lizz-ine)......................I'm drawin' the lizzine.
lounge (lizz-ounge)..............We can lizzounge over here.
lazy (lizz-azy)......................You too lizzazy for me.
lie (lizz-i)...........................Don't lizzi for him.
lonely (lizz-only)..................I get lizzonly too.
laugh (lizz-af).....................I need a good lizzaf.
loot (liz-zoot)......................We about to get this lizzoot.
lump (lizz-ump)...................Take ya lizzumps like a man.
like (lizz-ike)......................I never lizziked that.
loose (1iz-zoose)..................I turned him lizzoose.
look (lizz-ook)....................You lizzookin' good.
level (liz-zevil)...................We going to another lizzevil.

m

mad (mizz-ad)......................I'm not mizz-ad at you.
might (mizz-ight) ....I mizzight try this.
mack (miz-zack)..................Let's get our mizzack on.
master (miz-zaster).............He has the mizzaster key.
man (miz-zan)......................Them my mizzans.
more (mizz-ore)...................You want some mizzore?
mean (miz-zean)..................Don't be so mizzean.
money (mizz-oney).............You better get my mizzoney.
miss (mizz-iss)....................Mizziss me with that.
mail (mizz-ail).....................Did I get any mizzail?
mom (mizz-om)...................He came with his mizzoms.
munch (mizz-unch).............We about to mizzunch.
mall (mizz-all)....................Meet us at the mizzall.
match (mizz-at-ch).............Who won the mizzatch?
mouth (mizz-outh).............Your mizzouth too big.
mike (mizz-ike)...................He rocked the mizzike.
mold (mizz-old)..................It's all mizzoldy now.
monkey (mizz-un-key).........Mizzunkey see, mizzunkey do.
meat (mizz-eat)...................I stop eating mizzeat.
murder (mizz-er-der)...........They said it was mizzerder.

n

name (nizz-ame)...................What's her nizzame?
now (nizz-ow).......................I'm in trouble nizzow.
nasty (nizz-asty)..................You nizzasty.
next (nizz-ex)......................Who's nizzex?
nice (nizz-ice)......................Don't try to act nizzice now.
nerve (niz-serve).................You have some nizzerve.
night (nizz-ight)...................It happened last nizzight.
need (nizz-eed)...................You nizzeed me now.
not (nizz-ot).........................I'm nizzot going.
near (niz-zear)....................You dam nizzear killed me.
note (nizz-ote).....................I got your nizzote.
nickel (niz-zickel) ....The judge gave'em a nizzickel.
nail (nizz-ail)......................She gettin' her nizzails done.
north (nizz-or-th).................Are you from up nizzorth?
needle (niz-zee-dle).............Nizzeedles don't scare me.
numb (nizz-umb).................That sh** left me nizzumb.
nine (nizz-ine)....................That's the whole nizzine.
nosy (nizz-osey).................You being too nizzosey now.
noway (no-wizz-ay)............Nowizzay I can believe that.
number (nizz-um-ber).........She hit the nizzumber for $100.

o

object (ob-jizz-ect)...............That's the objizzect.

one (wizz-un) ....I got wizzun of those too.

off (izz-off)...........................My shot is izzoff.

on (izz-on)............................We about to get izzon now.

out (izz-out).........................Put'em izzout this time.

okay (o-kiz-zay)...................That sound okizzay to me.

own (iz-zone)........................You don't izzone me.

owe (iz-zoe).........................I don't izzoe you nothin'.

old (izz-old).........................You too izzold for this.

odor (izz-odor).....................What's that izzodor?

oil (izz-oil)...........................You have some baby izzoil?

open (izz-open)....................Leave it izzopen.

ox (izz-ox)...........................She's strong as a izzox.

outcry (out-crizz-i)..............That lead to an outcrizzi.

only (izz-only).....................Izzonly if you knew.

onion (izz-onion).................I picked up three izzonions.

organic (or-gizz-an-ic).........I eat strictly orgizzanic.

over (izz-over)....................Its izzover dawg.

order (izz-order)..................Who izzordered this?

once (wizz-unce).................Wizzunce upon a time.

P

pass (pizz-ass).....................Let that pizzass.
pork (pizz-ork).....................That got pizzork in it.
partner (pizz-art-na) ....Look here pizzartna.
props (priz-zops)...................I hafta give you your prizzops.
paper (pizz-aper)...................Get ya pizzaper dawg.
pump (pizz-ump)...................We don't pizzump like that.
player (pliz-zay-er)...............Talk to me plizzayer.
proud (prizz-oud)..................You've made me prizzoud.
punk (pizz-unk)....................He really pizzunked you.
post (pizz-ost)......................He plays the low pizzost.
pal (pizz-al)..........................Are we still pizzals?
plain (pliz-zain)...................That was plizzain to see.
point (pizz-oint)...................What's the pizzoint?
plea (pliz-zee)......................He took a 5 year plizzee.
plenty (plizz-enty)...............There's plizzenty left.
pray (priz-zay).....................You better prizzay I don't win.
peace (piz-zease)..................Pizzease dawg.
pull (piz-zull)......................That's what you call pizzull.
petro (pizz-et-tro)................We had them pizzettro.
paid (pizz-aid)....................We all got pizzaid.

q

quart (quizz-ort).....................I only need a quizzort.

quiz (quiz-izz).......................We havin' a pop quizizz.

quote (quizz-ote)..................Quizzote me on that.

quick (quiz-zick)..................That was quizzick.

quam (quizz-alm)..................I don't have any quizzalms.

queens (quiz-zeens)...............We picked up quizzeens.

question (quizz-estion).........That's not the quizzestion.

quite (quizz-ite)...................You are quizzite right.

quiet (quizz-i-et)..................Please be quizziet.

quarter (quizz-or-ter)...........This is the first quizzorter.

quantity (quiz-zaunity).......We need more quizzauntity.

quaint (quizz-aint).................Isn't this quizzaint?

queer (quiz-zear)..................That was quizzear.

quilt (quizz-ilt).....................How much for the quizzilt?

quench (quizz-ench).............That quizzenched my thirst.

quarrel (quiz-zar-el) ....I don't want to quizzarel.

quip (quiz-zip)....................Enough with the quizzips.

quake (quizz-ake)................It wasn't a major quizzace.

quack (quizz-ack)..................I don't need a quizzack.

quest (quiz-zest)..................We are on a quizzest.

r

raw (riz-zaw)..........................She gave it to you rizzaw.
rule (riz-zule)........................You knew the rizzules.
ran (rizz-an).........................He rizzan for no reason.
right (rizz-ight)...................Rizzight or wrong.
real (riz-zeal)......................I'm keepin' it rizzeal.
run (rizz-un)........................All you gonna do is rizzun.
red (riz-zed)........................I like the rizzed one.
round (rizz-ound)................I'm makin' my rizzounds.
reach (rizz-each).................I been tryin' to rizzeach you.
roach (rizz-oach).................Kill that rizzoach.
rap (riz-zap).......................Stop with the corny rizzaps.
roll (rizz-oll).......................Let's rizzoll.
ring (riz-zing).....................Let it rizzing.
rock (rizz-ock)...................Time to rizzock and rizzoll.
rape (rizz-ape)...................He caught a rizzape charge.
remorse (re-mizz-orse)........He showed remizzorse.
rain (rizz-ain).....................I smell rizzain.
rambo (riz-zam-bo).............He did a rizzambo.
role (rizz-ole)....................She's playin' a rizzole.
ride (rizz-ide)....................Which one is your rizzide?

s

salt (sizz-alt)	Why you throwin' sizzalt?
sun (sizz-un)	After the sizzun go down.
same (sizz-ame)	We not the sizzame.
safe (siz-zafe)	I need to feel sizzafe.
snake (sniz-zake)	That was some snizzake sh**.
size (sizz-ize)	What sizzize you need?
shortie (shizz-orty)	This my new shizzorty.
shame (shizz-ame)	That's a shizzame.
shit (shizz-it)	That's that shizzit.
sleep (sliz-zeep)	I'll never slizzeep on her.
slim (sliz-zim)	She was always slizzim.
slick (sliz-zick)	You not slizzick enough.
smart (smizz-art)	Why you gettin' smizzart?
smack (smizz-ack)	I aughta smizzack you.
sack (siz-zack)	I got five on that sizzack.
smoke (smizz-oke)	I been quit smizzokin'.
shot (shizz-ot)	I got shizzot twice.
sick (siz-zick)	She got the sizzickest flow out.
shystee (shizz-ice-tee)	Brooklyn cats are shizzicetee.
scare (scizz-air)	Don't tell me you scizzaired

t

talk (tizz-alk)........................You tizzalk too much.
turn (tizz-urn)........................Its my tizzurn.
tap (tizz-ap)...........................You tizzap that yet?
top (tiz-zop)..........................Tizzop that.
team (tiz-zeam)....................We all on the same tizzeam.
truck (triz-zuck)...................That's a nice trizzuck.
throop (trizz-oop)................Pass that trizzoop.
that (thiz-zat)......................Whassup with thizzat?
train (trizz-ain)...................Catch the trizzain.
tell (tizz-el)..........................Tizzel you what.
trip (triz-zip)........................Why you trizzipin'?
track (triz-zack)...................Do you know her trizzack record?
thought (thizz-aught)............I thizzaught about it.
thin (thizz-in).......................Shortie madd thizzin.
tax (tiz-zax)..........................You can get tizzaxed too.
teeth (tiz-zee-th)...................Brush ya tizzeeth.
try (trizz-i)...........................Don't even trizzi it.
thug (thizz-ug)....................They say you a thizzug.
trick (triz-zick)...................Youse a cold trizzick.
toss (tizz-oss)......................I'm tryin' to tizzoss your girl.

u

under (izz-under)................Look izzunder there.
ugly (iz-zugly)....................That's an izzugly attitude.
unique (u-niz-zeek)..............I find that unizzeek.
up (izz-ups).........................Slim got madd izzups.
urban (izz-urban)................This is izzurban for real.
united (u-nizz-ited)..............We hafta stay unizzited.
untold (un-tizz-old)..............That's the untizzold story.
upset (up-sizz-et)................He looked upsizzet to me.
unfold (un-fizz-old).............Lets watch it unfizzold.
untrue (un-triz-zoo).............All of that is untrizzoo.

v

van (vizz-an)........................Lets wait for the vizzan.
vex (vizz-ex).......................They left here vizzexed.
virus (vizz-irus)..................The vizzirus is serious.
veal (viz-zeal).....................She cookin' vizzeal.
Viking (Vizz-i-kin').............You livin' with a Vizzikin'.
vice (vizz-ice).....................He looks like vizzice.
voice (vizz-oice).................You have a vizzoice now.
vocal (vizz-ocal).................You are very vizzocal.
volley (vizz-olley)..............I heard a vizzolley of shots.
vest (viz-zest)....................You have on your vizzest?

w

wail (wiz-zail)......................That's a wizzail.
won't (wiz-zon't)..................I bet you she wizzon't.
way (wiz-zay)......................No wizzay!
word (wizz-erd)...................Wizzerd to the mutha.
wait (wizz-ate)......................At least you can wizzate.
wild (wizz-ild)......................That was wizzild.
whack (wiz-zack)..................That sounds wizzack to me.
wife (wizz-ife)......................Where's your wizzife?
warrant (wizz-ar-ent)............I might have a wizzarent.
watch (wiz-zot-ch)...............Wizzotch my back.
work (wizz-irk)....................Who's wizzirk is this?
wrong (rizz-ong)..................I was rizzong for that.
write (rizz-ite)......................Rizzite me sometimes.
weed (wiz-zeed)...................I don't smoke wizzeed.
wine (wiz-zine)....................I've had too much wizzine.
worth (wizz-earth)...............What's it wizzearth to you?
wully (wizz-ully)..................That got that wizzully in it.
warm (wizz-or-m).................It feels wizzorm to me.
white (wizz-ite)....................Got that in whizzite?
walk (wizz-alk)....................Try and wizzalk it off.

X

x-ray (x-riz-zay)...................I need to get an x-rizzay.
x-rated (x-rizz-ated).............This posed to be x-rizzated.
x (izz- ex-ed)......................They got izzexed out.

Y

yard (yiz-zard).....................I spent about a yizzard.
you (yiz-zoo)......................That's all on yizzoo.
yang (yiz-zang)..................She talk too much yizzang.
yell (yizz-el).......................You can't yizzel in here.
yap (yiz-zap)......................Quit all the yizzappin'.
young (yiz-zung).................She's definitely too yizzung.
yank (yiz-zank)...................I'll yizzank that weave out.
York (Yizz-ork)...................We bounced to Yizzork PA.
yoke (yizz-oke)...................She put'em in a yizzolk.
year (yiz-zear)....................This is my yizzear.

Z

zone (zidd-own)..................I was in a ziddown.
zoo (zid-doo)......................I took'em to the ziddoo.
zees (zid-dees)....................I about to clock some ziddees.
zero (zid-dero) ....It's below ziddero out there.

AKA'S (Hip-Hop & Urban Nicknames)

Whether you call them aka's, aliases, nicknames, or "street" names, individuals who are a part of the Hip-Hop and Urban culture often adopt names which differ from the names that were given to them at birth. Most adopted names are somehow a reflection of that individual's character, personality, past or present behavior, or used as a comparison to an action. For example, a individual named "eat'em up" is someone who is known to be greedy or fat.

On the following pages you will find the most original and unique aka's, aliases, nicknames, or "street" names of people known to me either personally of through others.

A.D..Silk
Big Boston...................................Champ
Slaughter..Bull
Rocky Mel..Fu
Lite...Righteous
Fu Quan...Sham
Tragic...Supreme
Buddah...Preme
Prime...................................Rock Head
Bounty...................................Charlie-O
Dirt Bike Mike.............................Free
Tank...Jelly
Boon..Nuke
Dank...Mookie
Greengo....................................Ju-Bone
Jaz...Pop
Stumbles.....................................Blinky
Blinky Pop....................................Big B
Parlay...Skeet
Skeeter....................................Broadway
Truck.....................................Knock out
Lucky....................................Hollywood
Trinny...Toutter
Noodles.......................................Foolish
Bad News................................Preme-O
Fifty Cent....................................Rome
Map..Big Ive
Ivan the Terrible...............Short Stop
Half...Drac
Life..Natural
Mark the Spark..............Fleetwood Mac
Shortie Do-Wop............................o-Wop

L.B...L. Bar
El...Moe Dawg
Headache..Speed
Shoe.................................Shoe Shine
D Wiz...Bossy
Binky...............................50 Joints
Lo...Los
Head Mo..Fats
Moet...Blacky
Doobie.............................Shitty Will
Cash...Money
Quack..Webb
Stretch..Just
Justice...............................Tony Rome
2 Gun..6 Guns
Homocide......................................Craze
Pie...Pie Face
Remy...Unique
U-Nee...............................Killer Ben
Jackpot...............................Joe Black
Cat..T Nice
Sun God................................Squiddly
Man...Lil Man
Pope...Popcorn
Darkside.................................T Black
Breeze..Briggy
Rock...Twizz
GG...Rock
Heav...Heavy
Ice...Butter
Ice Cold.....................................Gator
Madd...Disco
Brain...Cola
Wip wop.......................................Juice
Spooky.......................................Apples

Pinky......................................Scoop
Scope....................................Time Out
Half Time.............................Scooby
Tick..Vegas
Bean......................................Beans
Ninja....................................Goldie
Smurf...................................Overtime
Tre.......................................Jay Money
Face......................................Bigs
Polite...................................C Low
Gold Teeth..........................Dice
Bully..E
Bullet......................................Ill
Everlastin'............................Tye
Tye Stick...............................Fly Tye
Video....................................Ev
Ever...................................Wee Known
Blu.......................................Big Lou
Lil Larry...............................Six Nine
Twelve..................................R.B.
John John.............................Scientific
Sleepy..................................Mingo
Bingo....................................True
True God..............................Fleet
Easy......................................Batty
Fame....................................Foundation
G Wiz...................................Nut
Masterful.............................Born
Cowboy...............................Uzi
Wonderful........................Shrimp Lover
Chin......................................China
June......................................Bob Cat
G Money.............................Fierce

Previews Of Future Books

Street Talk
da
GRIMY version

SUMMER 2005
Streettalk101.com

Getting Pass Prison:
A Road Map For Success!

Coming Soon

Streettalk101.com
Streettalk101.net

By: Randy "Moe Deezy" Kearse and Donald Brooks

Once Upon A Time In Brooklyn...

In his first novel, Randy "Moe Deezy" Kearse tells a gripping tale of friendship, greed, and the ultimate betrayal. A story that at times reads like a memoir, the reader is left to ponder whether this vivid tale is a figment of his imagination or a true story based on real characters and real events. For all its grittiness, *Once Upon A Time In Brooklyn* is also a story about survival. After reading this book, you'll never see the so-called "game" the same again.

Coming Winter 2005
Visit www.STREETTALK101.com
Visit www.STREETTALK101.net

Game 101
Play At Ya Own Risk

Visit www. STREETTALK101.com
www. STREETTALK101.net

Shout-Outz!

Shake aka Terrance Jeffries outta Brownsville ballin' from BK to GA (I'mma make them a believer son don't call it a comeback!!), **Wells** aka Joel aka Kevin Bellegarde reppin' da Bush East Flatbush **BK** (you one of the last few THOROUGH young catz stay sucker free), **K.T.** aka Kevin Taylor Midwood Ave. **BK** (I'm about to take this to the moon kid), **Son** aka Robert Keys outta Brownsville BK (real people do real things), **Coach** aka Colin Shakespeare outta Hartford CT. and **Cali** (you the man I'm just a fan), **Jerry** aka Jerry Lynch reppin' Sweets Bar in N. Trenton originally from Bristol, **PA** (an old school playa with new school moves), **G. Whiz** aka Frederick Hollingshed originally from Strong Island layin' it down in Schenectady NY (I still got love you son HOLLA!), **Big Lou** aka Louis Ramos outta Queens NY (a go hard Borica), **Big White** aka Edgar White carryin' SC on his back (I'mma be comin' through), **Todd Spears** outta Harrisburg PA (you make the paper the paper don't make you they better act like they know), **E.D.** aka Eric Downs reppin' that O.H.10 (let me find out!!!), **Flaco** aka Carlos Idrovo off of Cortelyou Rd. in Flatbush BK. (I recognize ya steez kid you madd smooth), **Money** aka Reginald Rice from outta Brownsville BK, (you Brooklyn to the core shun, aiight?!), **Johnny Getz** aka Troy Nolan Bazilio off of Pacific & Nostrand in Crown Heights Brooklyn (your fight game is on one million you ain't layin' down for nothin' or nobody), my manz **Lite** aka Dana Couchman reppin' tha Harlemworld (you move smooth kid), **Pretty Thug** aka Santos Almodovar off of Eastwood St. Bethlehem, PA (ya graffiti and art skills are on one million good lookin'), **Dap** aka Jeffery Johnson off Gates Ave BK & Nassau Rd Strong Island NY (you keeps it real gangsta son a real Brooklyn cat from way back), **Amir** aka Deondra King off of 20 Norris North Realadelphia (you move smoother than average Philly catz I recognize ya steez kid), **True** aka Travis Bullock outta Roosevelt Projects in Brooklyn (ya gettin' money game is in a class by itself I respect ya hustle), **Nephew** aka Naquan Settle outta Staten Island NY (I still got love for you ain't nothin' change holla! Don't ever think different), **K.B.** aka Kevin Blackwell from St Mary's county Maryland (one of the realest catz outta B.More I've run into I peeped ya steez son), **Renee Kearse** from Peekskill NY (I got love for you you peoplez fa-real). **"The Scrapper"** aka Shihee Fowler reppin' Dickerson St. in East Trenton, New Jeruez (you been ballin' since I first met you ten blickies ago so I know what it is when you touch-down), **Big Shakez** aka Mustafa off of 187 in the BX (you one of them official gorillas from the "Boogie Down" I peep'd ya steez), another one of my manz from the BX **Big "E"** aka Edgar A. Sanchez holdin' it down for T.D.O. family 162 Da Hill (one of those silent heavy hitters from the "Boogie Down" reppin' T.D.O. to the fullest), the young boy **Boo** aka Gary Wiggins outta DC author of the next Urban/Street head-banger, *Live by the Streetz – Die by the Streetz* (you got the gift kid), **Gee Scott** aka Greg Scott one of the original ballers who made and make "**Harlem World**" what it is today (Harlem ain't been the same). **Mike** aka Roal Phillips reppin' 161st St. out in South Jamaica Queens (one of the realest catz from South Jamaica and you still built like that), a shout out to the original Article Don **Fox** aka Merrick Falesbork from Rockford down in Kingston Jamaica (all bonafide bad mon salute you hear?), **Danny** aka Daniel Gonzalez off of Audubon Ave. in Money Makin' Manhattan (stay focused man and get at ya boy for this paper), **Big E** aka Eric Spencer originally from Fort Greene now hold in' it down in the G-Boro (I ain't forget about you kid, it's all love ain't nothin' change), **Wall St. E** aka Ed Lawrence outta Uniondale in Strong Island currently down in Jamaica W.I. doin' it big (yo son what up I'm about to get my weight back up holla!), to the Undisputed Heavyweight Don of Brooklyn that boy **Calvin Klien** aka Calvin Bacote (I doubt if they ready for part II son fake catz wait for things to happen REAL catz make things happen), **Worm** aka Dwight Collins reppin' Centerville Project in Camden New Jeruez (yah help was instrumental in making this happen love is love son), **Big B** aka Richard B. Graves outta Burlington North Cackalacky (you're one

of the few good dudes from N.C. that I've run into), **Frenchy** aka
Howard French outta Jamaica by way of Jamaica W.I. (I don't talk
just to be talkin' French), Shout out to my **Harlemworld** mob-
Ed aka **Jig** aka **Jigga** aka Edward Barton from 112 St. (Harlem
make money- Brooklyn take money – you real homie), **Wu'** aka
Tau' McBean (the epitome of a young Harlem money getter), **Sal**
aka Soloman Wright (you rep Harlem but BK is in your blood),
Pup aka Benjamin Collier (one of Harlem early elite that made it
what it is today), **The Bruiser** aka Ronald Paul (rated "street"
N.B.A. eligible), **Jabar** aka David Swift off of Saratoga Ave. in
BK and **Pop** aka David Williams off of Hutchinson St. in
Realadelphia PA (y'all two of the realest dudes I've run into in a
long time), **Dana Hines** reppin' Smashachusetts (and bringin' that
poetic fire to the streetz), I hafta shout my man **Hunts Brizzard**
over there at the Cenegal Manor Nightclub and Restaurant on
Farragut & Glenwood in East Flatbush Brooklyn (son, all I'm
sayin is have the V.I.P. ready when I come through), my man
Gene aka Eugene Smith outta East NY Brooklyn (definitely a
smooth criminal), a hun'ned shout outz to that boy **Sharky** aka C.
Bates off of Burke Ave in the B.X. (you headed for the Balla's
Hall of Fame cause ya ballin' game is on one million), **Salim** aka
Anthony Parker from 28th Street Camden New Jereuz (the last of a
dyin' bred of real dudes stay rizzeal), **Silver Dollar** aka Reginal
McNair outta Douglas projects on Amsterdam Ave. reppin'
Harlemworld (you one of them smooth Harlem dudes), **Ra-Ra**
aka Robert Cole from East Orange New Jeruez Orange Project's
craziest (youse a wild dude but you real), **Gee Money** aka Jentzen
Grimes off West North and Monroe in Baltimore (you got the
official come up get that paper), **Big D** aka Darnell Cooper one of
those Brick City Ballers (I know you had 16th Ave. in Newark
SHOOK!), gots to shout out to my man **Robert Kirby** from
Vineland aka Crimeland New Jeruez (you the man fa real- fa real),
Rajah Miller reppin' Pleasantville NJ (the realest cat outta
Pleasantville dudes can't see you), **J.K.** aka John Kierce (you
from New Haven but you thug like Brooklyn you thorough son),
World aka Eric Capers (even though you one of those funny-style
Harlem cats your input was appreciated now fall-back

and let me show you how it's done), Yo **Life** aka Robert O'Conner from East N.Y. Brooklyn that muhf**kin Gunsmoke (What up Kemosabbie? Holla at ya boy ain't nothing change), **Jesse King** outta B-More (dudes be talking but I know you a "go-rilla" for real). Shout out to my lil my from Red Hook Projects **Strategic** aka Samuel Covington reppin' Brooklawn to the fullest (you in there), Yo **Supreme** aka Alfred Shuler off of E. Barringer St. Illadephia PA. (you know I had to shout you out as much as you looked out for the kid you the realest now make bail), **Howie** aka Howard Jones from Richmond VA. (I know you somewhere drivin' somebody crazy you a nut), **Ace** aka Marshall Hughes (stink pink gators for my Detroit playa HOLLA AT YA BOY! It's all love from this hooligan from Brooklyn), **Big C** aka Adam Clayton Sider outta Queens N.Y. (it's a small world we definitely gonna bump again), My compadre **Q-King** aka Rudy Emsoto off of 165th & Gerald Ave. in the B.X. (you definitely one of the coolest and realist Dominicans I know you looked out on the strength Viva Villa Duarte son), **Littles** aka John Little off of Valentine Ave in the B.X. (yo son it's gonna down like I told it would it's all love still holla at ya boy), **Jurgen Blaaker** a thugged out young buck from Holland (let them catz know you repped your country when you was here), the homie **Big Lou** aka Ronnel Carter a real West Coast G throwin' up that West Siiide (you get mad love from the east), my lil muf**kin' man **Tatu'** aka Alfonso Ortiz carryin' San Juan La Perla Puerto Rico on his back (you gangsta shortie and that's all to it), **Mac** aka **Money Mac** aka Frankie Mac from Money Makin' Manhattan (it's your world son and everything it), the original rude boy gun-mon pun street **Tony** aka Anthony Miller from Jamaica W.I. and Canada (you run things, things no run you), the one **Scotty Dred** aka Scott Bass from St. Croix U.S. V.I. (nuff respect to the Dred), **Jay Boogie** aka Mark Verhasselt down in Fayetteville North Cackalacky (everything is still love shun holla at ya boy), **Bird** aka Redd Bird outta Birmingham AL (I've been tryin' to get up witchou you see it's poppin' off holla), **Donnie** aka Donald Sellman reppin' that Sacramento hard in Alexandria VA (by the way you thug I know you got VA on lock), a crazy shout out to my main man **Keith**

Bullock and what not from Serenity Funeral Home down in Portsmouth VA (yeah yeah youse a good good dude and that's rare these days), **Mr. Cox** a cool ass ol' head off of Garnet St. in North Realadelphia (an ol' school playa from way back), another one of them real dudes outta B. More my man **Boopie** aka Eugene Thomas off of Pulaski St. West Ballamore (I recognize and respect ya gangsta homie), The big homie **Druid** aka D aka Dawit Shiferaw reppin' Duke street Alexandria Va (they can't see you you too cool for that stay real), Bridgeport Ct. thuggin' my mizzan **Big Saro** aka Rosario Cotto reppin' P.T. Projects madd crazy (14 blickies and you still gangsta that's how real you is) **Craig G** aka Michael Patterson off Florida St. Southside G'boro NC (G's up kid you a cool dude stay up), Chamaquito aka Hector Hernandez my marketing/promotion guru off south 2nd St Brooklawn New Yiddy Southside ya heard!? (you real kid thanks and good lookin'), Gots to shout out my man **Tim Fleming** reppin' Highland Park in SeatPleasant MD. (you about as cool as they come Tim lookout for the cookout them stories was off da hizzook), the young boy **Disco Mike** aka Michael Berry from B.F.P. East B-More (a lot of these young catz could take a lesson from you baby boy Holla!), Big up one time to the one **Lil Dread** aka Deon C. Higgins holdin' the whole Concord Ave. down in Wilmington, D-Ware (youse an original rude boy nuff respect), that boy **Larceny Larry** aka Larry Palmer outta Virginia Beach (don't hurt 'em Larry save some game for later), definitely gotta shout out my main **Ali Hall** one of the realest dudes to come outta B.T. aka Baxter Terrace on James St. in Newark New Jeruez (you came through like Ragu baby boy you played a part in this), crazy shout outs to the big homie **Big Mark** aka Big Mizzark aka Mark Thompson off of Edmonson Ave. E.A. in Baltimore MD. (it don't get not realer than you big homie the first rule is always gonna be "stay sucker free" we definitely gonna continue to build we don't talk about it we be about it), another one of my Harlemworld homies **Dana Couchman** (you know you gotta be up in here with realest you real good peoples kid even though we met through that slum ass

dude [ha-ha-ha] keep it real son). a big boy shout out to my manz
E-Z Wayne aka E-Zekiel "The Poet" aka Wayne Alexander from
Stamford C.T. Westsiide F.S. Crew definitely representin' (Them
Def Joke poets ain't got nothin' on you kid you spits that lyrical
fire ya heard!). Have to Shout – Out my lil man **Randy** aka **Baby
Boy** and his homies **Marcus** & **B.J**. all of them reppin' that C.S.C.
(I got madd love for you family), my main **Spitty E** aka Alexus
McBride off of Catherine St. in Baltimore City (you the real deal
pimp the only thing that can stop you is you), them girls **Tiffany
Evans** & **Sye Spence** aka Drama Central (y'all kill'd me with the
drama but I'm not trippin' Holla!), the homie from Crooklyn **Big
Dre** aka Andre Tucker off of Monroe St. (hold ya head up son it
gets greater later later), my girl-homie **Kendra Ollison** from
Raleigh NC and ATL (let them figure it out na' mean?), my girl
Dominique Penny aka **Dime Piece** aka DP (stay focused aiight?),
my manz **Him** aka Gary Yeung from Causeway Bay in Hong
Kong China (they got China twisted if they think y'all not gansta
over there), can't forget about my lil man from Spencer NC
Keenan Graves aka **KB** (it's all love son-son holla back), a special
shout-out to that girl **Sharae Lee** (talk to me I'll talk back holla!),
and to close things out a MADD CRAZY SHOUT-OUT to my
brother Lonnie aka **L Dawg** aka **L Boog** aka **Big L** (keep ya head
up kid you know I got you cause that's how fam do!).

Author's note

Keepin' it gangsta, gully, and real, there are parts of the Hip-Hop and Urban slang vernacular that is extremely offensive, disrespectful, and explicit to say the least. Failing to acknowledge this, STREET TALK would fall a little short in its claim to be the "OFFICIAL" dictionary and guide for the Hip-Hop and Urban slang language. This grimy part of the language which many people disapprove of, is spoken just as frequently and fluently as the verbiage found in this book. The publisher felt it necessary to omit the grimiest of the grimiest context in an attempt to balance the book's authenticity against content that directly offends anyone's gender, race, sexual preference, or ethnicity. On the "streets" we know "it is what is" and the griminess is also a intricate part of how we communicate and interact with each other. So in order to guarantee that **STREET TALK: Da Official Guide to Hip-Hop & Urban slanguage** is recognized as the one and only "OFFICIAL" slang language guidebook, I have put together a supplemental version of STREET TALK, titled, **STREET TALK: Da Grimy Version** This version is a compilation of all the slang too obscene to print. **STREET TALK : Da Grimy Version** is the icing on the cake for Hip-Hop & Urban slang language. It will be available exclusively through the streettalk101.com web site in the summer of 2005. For a sneak peek of exerts from **STREET TALK: Da Grimy Version** visit Streettalk101.com. Holla Back! Randy "Moe Deezy/Moe Diesel/Moe Betta/Moe Chedda" Kearse

About the Author

Randy "Moe Deezy" Kearse demonstrates that he has his finger on the pulse of Hip-Hop and Urban culture in many ways. With **STREET TALK** he brings life and legitimacy to a language many people find hard to understand.

Born and raised in Brooklyn, N.Y., he uses his intimate knowledge and many experiences with the elements which contribute to Hip-Hop & Urban "street" language as a means to decipher it.

From an early age his verbal aptitude has always allowed him to standout amongst his peers which often led him to take on the role of a urban "slanguist" when explaining the intricacies of using Hip-Hop and Urban slang language.

Moe Deezy provides Hip-Hop with its 5th element, along with Dj'ing, Break-dancing, Graffiti and Ryming, now there's the use of Slanguage.